8⁵⁰

JUSTICE AT WAR

Justice At War

Peter Irons

New York Oxford
OXFORD UNIVERSITY PRESS
1983

Library of Congress Cataloging in Publication Data

Irons, Peter H., 1940–
Justice at war.

Bibliography: p.
Includes index.
1. Japanese Americans—Legal status, laws, etc.
2. Japanese Americans—Evacuation and relocation, 1942–1945. I. Title.
KF7224.5.I76 1983 342.73′088 83-8190
ISBN 0-19-503273-X 347.30288

Printing: 9 8 7 6 5 4 3

Printed in the United States of America

For

Priscilla

Preface

This book tells the story of the Japanese American wartime cases—the historic cases in which the United States Supreme Court upheld in 1943 and 1944 the military orders that forced more than 110,000 Americans of Japanese ancestry from their West Coast homes into ten internment camps scattered from the California desert to the swamps of Arkansas.

These cases arose in 1942 when four young American citizens—Gordon Hirabayashi, Minoru Yasui, Fred Korematsu, and Mitsuye Endo—raised constitutional challenges to the internment orders. In June 1943 the Supreme Court unanimously upheld the criminal convictions of Hirabayashi and Yasui for violations of the order that imposed a nighttime curfew on "all persons of Japanese ancestry." Eighteen months later, in December 1944, the Court divided 6-to-3 in affirming Korematsu's conviction for "remaining in" a prohibited area—his hometown—in violation of a military exclusion order. The Court held without dissent on the same day, in deciding the habeas corpus case brought by Endo, that Congress had not authorized the continuing detention of concededly "loyal" citizens; however, the justices avoided ruling on her constitutional objections to the internment program.

I began work on this book in 1981 as a legal historian, intending simply to write an account of these cases from their inception through their final decision. My focus was less on the four test case challengers or the nine Supreme Court justices than on the forty lawyers who participated on both sides of the Japanese American cases. My interest was in examining the differing legal strategies and tactics these lawyers employed in wrestling with important and unsettled issues of constitutional law, viewed against a backdrop of wartime pressures and passions. A study of these cases, I thought, might help to illuminate the process of justice at war.

When my research began, I had no idea that its results would take me in January 1983 to the federal courthouse in San Francisco. Joined by several other lawyers—most of them third-generation Japanese Americans whose parents had been interned by military order—I filed in the district court clerk's office a lawsuit that sought the reversal of Fred Korematsu's criminal conviction. Two weeks later, I added my name as attorney of record to identical suits filed in Seattle and Portland on behalf of Gordon Hirabayashi and Minoru Yasui. All three suits were brought under an obscure and little-used provision of federal law that permits criminal defendants who have exhausted all their appeals and who have served their sentences to reopen their cases. The only grounds for such proceedings, known in legal jargon as "petition for a writ of error coram nobis," are that the original trial was tainted by "fundamental error" or that the conviction resulted in "manifest injustice" to the defendant.

At a crowded press conference in the San Francisco Press Club, held just after the filing of the initial petition, the three original defendants—now in their mid-sixties—described their feelings about this joint effort to clear their records. A college senior in 1942 and now a sociology professor in Canada, Gordon Hirabayashi predicted that a reversal of the convictions would give the Japanese American community "a new sense of perspective" on the internment, and provide "a new surge of confidence to those who felt they were under a cloud" because of their race. Min Yasui, a young Portland lawyer when he defied the curfew order and now director of community relations for the city of Denver, recalled his anger at "rotting in a stinking jail cell in Oregon" for more than nine months of solitary confinement. "It will all be justified if we can rectify the injustice that was done," he added. Fred Korematsu, a shipyard welder in 1942 and now an industrial draftsman, still lives in the California town in which he was arrested. "I was sent to jail as a criminal," he said, "even though I knew I wasn't. I love this country and I belong here."

What led to the effort to reverse these three criminal convictions after forty years was the evidence uncovered during the research for this book. This documentary record reveals a legal scandal without precedent in the history of American law. Never before has evidence emerged that shows a deliberate campaign to present tainted records to the Supreme Court.

The Justice Department files in these cases—released in response to my Freedom of Information Act request—include documents in which the government's own lawyers charged their superiors with the "suppression of evidence" and with presenting to the Supreme Court a key military report that contained "lies" and "intentional falsehoods." My research also uncovered military files that disclose the alteration and destruction by War Department officials of crucial evidence in these cases. Rather than expose to the Court the contradictions between this evidence and claims made by Justice Department lawyers, military officials literally consigned the offending documents to a bonfire.

The responsibility for this legal scandal extends beyond the ranks of the government's lawyers. Leaders of the American Civil Liberties Union bear much of the blame for the outcome of the Japanese American cases. The lawyers who represented Hirabayashi and Korematsu—whose cases resulted in the most significant of the Supreme Court opinions—were recruited by local ACLU branches. In challenging the legal basis of the criminal charges filed in these cases, the ACLU lawyers initially attacked the constitutionality of the presidential order that authorized the internment program. My research in the files of the ACLU and its West Coast branches disclosed that personal and partisan loyalty to Franklin D. Roosevelt, who signed this order, led the ACLU's national board to bar such a constitutional challenge in subsequent appeals. This policy decision, which triggered a fierce internal battle within the ACLU, crippled the effective presentation of these appeals to the Supreme Court.

The actions of both groups of lawyers raise profound questions of legal ethics and professional responsibility. Lawyers are subject to a code of ethics that requires them to "zealously" represent the interests of their clients. In their examination of witnesses at trial, their presentation of oral testimony and documentary evidence, their framing of legal briefs, and their arguments to appellate courts, lawyers are bound by the dictates of the adversary system to present the strongest case possible; it is the task of opposing lawyers to probe the weaknesses in these cases and to offer countering evidence and arguments.

But there are limits to the adversary system. Lawyers not only represent their clients but also function as officers of the courts, sworn to canons of fairness and justice. The same code of ethics—supported by judicial decisions—requires that lawyers present to the courts only that evidence they know to be truthful, and that they contain their briefs and arguments within the bounds of the trial records. In addition, lawyers are commanded to avoid any appeal to racial prejudice. Violation of this injunction constitutes a serious breach of legal ethics.

The wartime setting of the Japanese American cases put this code to the test. These trials and appeals took place against the historic background of West Coast hostility to those of Japanese ancestry, and with the Japanese attack on Pearl Harbor and brutality in the Philippines fresh in the public's minds. Forced to defend wartime orders that restricted the liberties of "all persons of Japanese ancestry," government lawyers devised a two-pronged strategy: they first argued that "military necessity" had prompted the issuance of the internment orders; and they justified their application to all Japanese Americans on the ground that the "racial characteristics" of the members of this minority predisposed them to the commission of acts of espionage and sabotage.

In searching for evidence to support these claims, Justice Department lawyers relied upon the War Department for supporting records. The resulting debates over the veracity of these records, which centered on the *Final Report* of General John L. DeWitt—the West Coast military commander who both recommended and supervised the internment program—are recounted in detail in this book. Briefly summarized, these debates centered around the suspicions of two Justice Department lawyers, Edward J. Ennis and John L. Burling, that DeWitt's claims that Japanese Americans had committed acts of espionage were untrue. The corroboration of their suspicions by the FBI and the Federal Communications Commission led to a dramatic showdown with Assistant Secretary of War John J. McCloy. Determined to alert the Supreme Court to the falsity of DeWitt's charges, Ennis and Burling had inserted a crucial footnote in the government's Supreme Court brief in the Korematsu case, informing the Court of the "contrariety of evidence" on the espionage allegations. Justice Department records of this last-ditch battle charge that McCloy intervened with Solicitor General Charles Fahy and prevailed on him to remove this explicit confession from the brief.

This episode, perhaps the most significant of the many conflicts over the Japanese American cases, highlights the ethical dilemmas faced by the lawyers who participated in them. Those like McCloy, who remained unbending in their defense of the internment and unrepentent about their roles in the wartime cases, felt no sense of conflict between conscience and duty. Ennis represents the larger group who felt this conflict keenly during the war and who later confessed their complicity in depriving Japanese Americans of their constitutional rights. But even Edward Ennis, forced to choose in 1944 between the dictates of his professional role and the demands of his conscience, swallowed his doubts and signed the government's brief in the Korematsu case.

My brief account of this episode here is not intended as an indictment of either McCloy or Ennis. They share the responsibility for their wartime actions with other government lawyers and officials, with the ACLU lawyers and board members, and with the lower-court judges and Supreme Court justices who ruled on the Japanese American cases.

In writing this book, I have allowed these lawyers, officials, and judges to speak for themselves, not only in recounting their actions but in discussing their responses to the ethical questions they faced some four decades ago. The record of what they said and wrote, both at that time and since, seems to me an adequate basis on which the readers of this book can individually reach their own conclusions about the adequacy of these responses.

I have incurred a great many debts in the process of writing this book, which I am glad to acknowledge here. The American Philosophical Society provided funding for the initial stages of my research, for which I am most grateful. In looking for the documentary record of the Japanese American cases, I received invaluable assistance from librarians and archivists at the following institutions: the National Archives and Records Service in Washington, D.C. and Suitland, Maryland; the Department of Justice; the Library of Congress Manuscript Division; the Franklin D. Roosevelt Library in Hyde Park, New York; the Harvard Law School Library; the University of Michigan Library; the Columbia University Oral History Collection; the University of Washington Library; the California Historical Society in San Francisco; the Bancroft Library of the University of California, Berkeley; and the Manuscript Division of the Princeton University Library.

Many of those who played key roles in the Japanese American cases are no longer alive. Among this group are President Roosevelt, Secretary of War Henry L. Stimson, Attorney General Francis Biddle, Solicitor General Charles Fahy, General John L. DeWitt, ACLU director Roger Baldwin, and all of the Supreme Court justices who decided the cases. Most of these persons, however, left a record of official and personal papers, and I have consulted all those that are available. Librarians and archivists at the institutions listed above helped me greatly in finding these records and in suggesting additional sources. I am also grateful to Hugo L. Black, Jr., who gave me permission to examine the papers of his father in the Library of Congress.

In an effort to supplement the documentary record with personal recollections, I conducted interviews with as many of those who participated in these cases as I could locate. Of those who worked in the Justice Department, I interviewed Edward J. Ennis, James H. Rowe, Jr., Arnold Raum, Nanette Dembitz, and Alfonso J. Zirpoli. Although John J. McCloy declined my request for an interview, I spoke with both Adrian S. Fisher and John M. Hall, who served as McCloy's deputies in the War Department. Philip Glick discussed with me his work as Solicitor of the War Relocation Authority. I conducted a telephone interview with George E. Sterling, who headed the Radio Intelligence Division of the Federal Communications Commission.

Several of those who served as law clerks to members of the Supreme Court during this time provided me with valuable insights and information about the Court's deliberations on the wartime cases. The former clerks I interviewed were Bennett Boskey, Victor Brudney, Vern Countryman, Philip Elman, Harry Mansfield, and John Pickering.

The lawyers who represented the three criminal defendants at their trials—Wayne M. Collins for Korematsu, Frank L. Walters for Hirabayashi, and Earl F. Bernard for Yasui—have since died. Among those who participated in the defense ranks in other capacities, I interviewed Arthur Barnett and Mary Farquharson of the Gordon Hirabayashi Defense Committee; Ernest Besig, director of the Northern California branch of the American Civil Liberties Union; Clifford Forster, ACLU staff counsel in New York; Osmond Fraenkel, ACLU general counsel; Charles Horsky, who represented Korematsu before the Supreme Court; and James Purcell, counsel for Mitsuye Endo.

I also interviewed for this book—and now represent—Gordon Hirabayashi, Min Yasui, and Fred Korematsu. Lest there be any question, I should make clear that I conducted these interviews and began writing this book before my involvement in the legal effort to reverse their convictions. This book is not intended as a brief on their behalf; the petitions filed with the courts reflect my separate participation in these cases as a lawyer.

The staff of the Commission on Wartime Relocation and Internment of Civilians, before which I testified in December 1981 as a member of a legal panel at a hearing in Cambridge, Massachusetts, provided me with considerable assistance in answering questions and helping me to locate records. Charles Smith, Donna Komure, Angus Macbeth, and Aiko Herzig-Yoshinaga made my research task much lighter with their cooperation. Jack Herzig, whose fund of knowledge about the internment program is inexhaustible, was particularly helpful to me.

None of those who provided me with research assistance, or whom I interviewed, bears any responsibility for what I have written. That responsibility is mine alone.

Although I have tried to keep separate my dual roles as historian and lawyer in writing this book, I do want to express my gratitude to the lawyers who have joined me as counsel for Gordon Hirabayashi, Min Yasui, and Fred Korematsu. They include Dale Minami, Lori Bannai, Don Tamaki, Dennis Hayashi, Mike Wong, Russell Matsumoto,

Bob Rusky, Karen Kai, Hoyt Zia, Kathryn Bannai, Art Barnett, Peggy Nagae, and Frank Chuman. These lawyers, who have worked with me on a volunteer basis, have donated enormous amounts of time, legal skill, and dedication to this effort. Dale Minami in particular has done an amazing job of coordinating the legal research and logistical support of this remarkable team, and Don Tamaki has effectively handled our relations with the press and the public. Over the past year, these people have become not only my colleagues but my close friends.

This book owes a great deal to the editorial skill, persistence, and encouragement of Susan Rabiner of Oxford University Press. Susan has combined her functions as critic and morale-booster in guiding me through the editorial process. Kathy Antrim of the Oxford staff used up several blue pencils and packages of yellow tabs in subjecting my manuscript to the scrutiny of an excellent copy editor. Michele Wenzel, Monica Paskvan, and Bobbie Sutera put huge chunks of this manuscript into the word processor that I have yet to master and produced (almost) perfect copy. My colleagues in the political science department of the University of California, San Diego, have been supportive and critical in just the right proportions. Steven Erie, who has listened to me think aloud for hours at a stretch, helped me in turning my unstructured thoughts into a more structured book.

At this writing, the petitions that seek to vacate the criminal convictions of Gordon Hirabayashi, Min Yasui, and Fred Korematsu are pending in the federal courts in which they were tried in 1942. The government has not yet filed its responses to their petitions. I am unable to predict what position the government will take, when the petitions will be decided, or what rulings will be made on them. But regardless of their outcome, I agree with the conclusion of the Commission on Wartime Relocation that the Supreme Court opinions in the cases of these three men have been "overruled in the court of history." It is gratifying to me—both as historian and lawyer—that the research for this book has made it possible to argue that the convictions in these cases should be overruled in the courts of law.

San Diego, California P.I.
April 1983

Contents

JUSTICE AT WAR

I

"Let's Not Get Rattled"

THE FEDERAL BUILDINGS stretched along Constitution Avenue in Washington stood virtually deserted on December 7, 1941. Depending on their cultural bents, government workers relaxing at home that Sunday afternoon tuned their radios to the "National Symphony Hour" or the football game between the hometown Redskins and the Philadelphia Eagles. Pressing duties, however, placed two lawyers among the corporal's guard of officials at their desks that quiet day. As general counsel of the Immigration and Naturalization Service, Edward J. Ennis worked in the annex to the block-square headquarters of the Department of Justice at Tenth Street. The office of Assistant Secretary of War John J. McCloy was located in the cavernous Munitions Building, a mile away at Twentieth Street.

The duties that required Sunday service of Ennis and McCloy stemmed from fears of an imminent breakdown of the strained diplomatic negotiations between Secretary of State Cordell Hull and Admiral Kichisaburo Nomura, the Japanese ambassador in Washington. Should the two countries sever relations, or even go to war, the Justice Department would become responsible for internal security measures, while the War Department would shoulder the tasks of national defense. Contingency plans for American involvement in the war that already engulfed Europe, and its potential expansion to the Pacific, had existed for more than two years. With relations between Japan and the United States at the breaking point, Ennis and McCloy were working under pressure to update the wartime plans of their respective departments.

Long-standing commitments had taken both Attorney General Francis Biddle and Solicitor General Charles Fahy away from Washington on December 7. Secretary of War Henry L. Stimson had spent that morning in his office but had left around noon for lunch at Woodley, his imposing urban estate. In the absence of their superiors, Edward Ennis and John McCloy were the ranking officials of their departments that afternoon.

While these two lawyers reviewed documents and conferred with aides, Secretary of State Hull waited patiently in his office close by the White House for the arrival of Ambassador Nomura and special envoy Saburo Kurusu. A courtly Tennessean, Hull respected Nomura as an experienced diplomat. Close in age—Hull at seventy was Nomura's elder by only six years—the two men knew each other well and shared a plain-spoken yet reserved temperament. The Japanese diplomats had promised to present Hull at this meeting with their government's reply to the latest American proposal for resolving the growing rift between the two Pacific powers. Hull was fully aware, however, that Nomura had been increasingly shunted aside by the Japanese militarists whose conquest of Manchuria and dreams of an "East Asian Co-Prosperity Sphere" had led to alliance with Hitler and Mussolini.

Hull consequently harbored no illusions that his meeting with Nomura and Kurusu would lead to diplomatic resolution of conflicts rooted in power politics. The most that Hull expected from this meeting, scheduled at Nomura's request for one o'clock, was additional time to prepare for the inevitable outbreak of war in the Pacific. Accustomed to Japanese punctuality, the Secretary of State became understandably concerned when an hour passed without the arrival of his expected visitors. Hull was also concerned that President Franklin D. Roosevelt, who was expecting a report on the outcome of the diplomatic meeting, might conclude that the Secretary of State had neglected to inform the Chief Executive.

Hull's concerns gave way to shock when he received a call from Roosevelt shortly after two o'clock, reporting that Japanese planes had bombed the American naval fleet berthed at Pearl Harbor in Hawaii. The President had learned of the sudden attack only minutes before from Secretary of the Navy Frank Knox. The smoke from bombed ships and planes still billowed over Pearl Harbor when Nomura and Kurusu arrived at Hull's office. Roosevelt had instructed Hull to "receive their reply formally and coolly and bow them out." Without a mention of the Japanese attack, the Secretary of State accepted from his visitors their government's message that "it is impossible to reach agreement through further negotiations" and dismissed them. Hull later learned that Ambassador Nomura had been given no forewarning by his superiors of their plans to bomb Pearl Harbor.[1]

Throughout the afternoon of December 7, millions of Americans remained glued to their radios as fragmentary reports of the surprise attack grew into accounts of disaster. Secretary Hull and his State Department staff were as helpless as these stunned citizens to respond to the outbreak of war. Responsibility for the defense of the United States, both internal and external, abruptly shifted to the Department of Justice and the War Department.

Edward Ennis was in his Justice Department office on December 7 "because," he later recalled, "I was very concerned about the breakoff of relationships with the Japanese ambassador in Washington. I was very scared about it, apparently more scared than they were at Pearl Harbor. While I was working I got a call from the immigration office in Honolulu, saying that Pearl Harbor was under attack." Ennis realized immediately the need to inform his superiors and to mobilize the departmental staff. "I called the Attorney General, who was in Detroit making a speech to a Polish organization; then I called the Solicitor General, who was in Philadelphia making a speech. Then I told the telephone operator to call all the assistant attorneys general and bring them into the office."[2]

Ennis next moved to implement the wartime contingency plans of the Immigration and Naturalization Service, that branch of the Justice Department with jurisdiction over the legal status of more than four million aliens resident in the United States. Over a million of these people were citizens of Japan, Germany, and Italy. Attorney General Biddle had earlier delegated to him, Ennis later explained, the task of "planning facilities to house enemies of aliens nationality if we got into the war." Ennis had been working on these internment plans when he received word of the Pearl Harbor attack. Quickly drafting an emergency proclamation that authorized the "summary apprehension" of any Japanese alien by the Justice Department, Ennis rushed this document to the White House. President Roosevelt signed the proclamation that evening.[3]

The immediate moves of War Department officials in Washington were limited. Military commanders around the world, linked by a radio communications network, learned within minutes of the Pearl Harbor attack and unsealed the wartime plans locked in safes. John J. McCloy first acted to protect key installations in Washington against possible sabotage. "When news of the attack arrived," he recalled, "I immediately began doing what I could to implement plans for the security of the nation's capital which this startling event demanded.'' Within hours, armed troops ringed the White House, the Capitol building, and other important government offices at McCloy's orders.[4]

As the afternoon of December 7 wore on, McCloy received ''urgent reports'' from military officials on the West Coast who sought instructions on measures to defend against a follow-up Japanese attack. He quickly authorized the imposition of civil defense plans that included black-outs and restrictions on vehicular traffic. Four days later, on December 11, Secretary of War Stimson designated the eight western states within the Western Defense Command as a ''theater of operations'' under military control. This Army organization had been commanded since December 1939 by Lieutenant General John L. DeWitt, who also commanded the troops of the Fourth Army from his headquarters at the Presidio in San Francisco.

At the time Ennis and McCloy first reacted to the Pearl Harbor attack, no group seemed a more likely target of retribution than the 117,000 Japanese aliens and American citizens of Japanese descent who lived in the West Coast states. Linked by color and culture to an enemy nation accused of military ''treachery'' and diplomatic deceit, Japanese Americans might well have expected a repetition of the vigilante terror experienced by German Americans during World War I. This latter group shared the racial heritage of most Americans, had largely become ''assimilated'' into the English-speaking society, and numbered more than five million. Nonetheless, hysterical press accounts of the ''rape of Belgium'' and a drumbeat of official propaganda designed to promote hatred of ''Huns'' led to retaliation against German Americans that ranged from verbal harassment to lynchings.[5]

The suddenness of the ''sneak attack'' on Pearl Harbor boded ill for the much smaller and more isolated Japanese American population. Surprisingly, the initial reaction in the area most stricken with ''Pearl Harbor panic'' was one of tolerance and understanding. Most of the ''thousands of Japanese here and in other coast cities,'' the Los Angeles *Times* editorialized on December 8, were ''good Americans, born and educated as such.'' This prestigious paper, published in the city with the country's largest concentration of Japanese Americans, urged its readers that ''there be no precipitation, no riots, no mob law.''[6]

In the first days after Pearl Harbor, the West Coast press gave prominent display to statements by Americans of Japanese descent proclaiming their loyalty. Beneath its editorial of December 8, the *Times* quoted the offer of the Japanese American Citizens League of its ''fullest cooperation and its facilities'' to the government. The press also did its best to calm the fears of a jittery public. ''Let's Not Get Rattled,'' the

Times cautioned in a December 10 editorial. It would take several Japanese aircraft carriers "together with a good-sized fleet of covering war vessels and fuel supply ships, to carry on a sustained campaign" against the West Coast, the paper noted. "Could such an aggregation of surface craft sneak up on this Coast undetected by our now aroused sky scouting forces?" Echoed by other prominent West Coast papers, such assurances helped to calm public fears and to protect the Japanese American minority from retaliation. Scattered incidents of window breaking and assaults on Japanese Americans failed to mar the general record of restraint.[7]

Some six weeks after Pearl Harbor, however, the tide of public opinion abruptly shifted. Both in the press and in statements by public officials, demands for the removal of Japanese Americans from the West Coast replaced calls for tolerance. On January 16, 1942, Los Angeles congressman Leland Ford urged in identical letters to Navy Secretary Frank Knox and FBI director J. Edgar Hoover that "all Japanese, whether citizens or not, be placed in inland concentration camps." Two weeks later the Los Angeles *Times* reversed its editorial stance and argued that "the rigors of war demand proper detention of Japanese and their immediate removal from the most acute danger spots" among the West Coast. Flowing toward the White House through the tributaries of public opinion, these currents of concern about the Japanese Americans began as a trickle and ended as a torrent.[8]

The force of these and similar demands produced their intended impact. On February 19, 1942, seventy-four days after Pearl Harbor, President Roosevelt signed Executive Order 9066. Through his directive, Roosevelt conferred on Secretary of War Stimson and his subordinates authority to designate military zones "from which any or all persons may be excluded."[9]

By the end of 1942, prodded both by "exclusion orders" signed by General DeWitt and the threat of criminal prosecution under Public Law 503, passed by Congress to enforce DeWitt's orders, all but a handful of the Japanese Americans on the West Coast had been herded behind the barbed wire of ten "relocation centers" scattered from California to Arkansas. Not until the middle of 1946—almost a year after the surrender of Japan in the wake of the Hiroshima and Nagasaki bombings that ushered in the atomic age—did the last residents of these dusty, barren camps return to their West Coast homes.

The tidal-wave shift in attitudes toward the Japanese Americans over the ten weeks between Pearl Harbor and Executive Order 9066 raises a crucial question: What factors led to the replacement of pleas for tolerance with demands for the evacuation and internment of this entire racial minority? The complex answer to this question involves forces of both historic and immediate origin. The historical background of hostility directed at Orientals—first the Chinese and then the Japanese—rode on powerful currents of nativism and prejudice. Decades of exposure to the "Yellow Peril" fever had infected the West Coast population. Calls for restraint by the press in the weeks after Pearl Harbor could not have cured the virulent disease of racism.

More recently, two years of war in Europe—despite official American neutrality and widespread isolationist sentiment—had provoked fears that fascism might prevail in its drive for world domination. Hitler had overrun all of Europe; the French had been humiliated and Germans were at the gates of Moscow. England, the sole survivor of the Nazi blitzkreig, was barely holding out. While its Axis partners terrorized Europe, for a decade Japan had been engaged in its own aggression in Asia. And in the weeks that followed Pearl Harbor, graphic reports of brutality by Japanese troops as they overran the Philippines shocked the American public. Against this backdrop of historic hostility and recent horror, the dikes of tolerance that initially protected the Japanese Americans from retribution were soon eroded and swept away.

However significant these background pressures were to Roosevelt's order, they fail to explain fully why more than six weeks elapsed after Pearl Harbor before demands for evacuation and internment gained any official support. They fail as well to explain why those government officials, both military and civilian, who initially opposed or doubted the necessity for Executive Order 9066 eventually set aside their constitutional objections and pragmatic qualms. It is an element of great importance to these questions that all but one of the federal officials most directly involved in the internal debate that preceded the President's order were lawyers. Only General DeWitt, among this group of War Department and Justice Department officials, lacked legal training. These men presumably brought to their wartime positions an awareness of the constitutional restraints on governmental action directed against racial and national minorities, and of the rights and protections of citizenship. Each of these officials acknowledged during this debate, with varying degrees of conviction, the constitutional barriers to the evacuation and internment of Japanese Americans.

In the end, however, these lawyers abandoned their doubts and objections—some quickly and others with much anguish—and turned their legal talents to the defense of Executive Order 9066 and Public Law 503. They continued to debate, both among themselves and with the lawyers who defended the handful of Japanese Americans who challenged DeWitt's orders, the balance between the government's "war powers" and the constitutional demands of due process and equal protection. The initial rounds in this debate, those that began with Pearl Harbor and ended with the internment decision, are the subjects of this and the next two chapters. The institutional politics that influenced this dispute, however, can be understood only in the context of the racial politics that affected the status of Japanese Americans.

It is ironic that, almost without exception, every argument made to justify the internment of Japanese Americans had its origin in earlier campaigns to rid the West Coast of the Chinese. The irony stems not only from the status of the Chinese during World War II as "honorary Caucasians"—a reflection of sympathy toward a country invaded by the Japanese—but also from the fact that the first immigrants from Japan were welcomed as superior to the despised Chinese. In 1869, when Chinese immigrants constituted 10 percent of California's population and anti-Chinese agitation dominated the state's politics, the San Francisco *Chronicle* noted that "the objections raised against the Chinese . . . cannot be alleged against the Japanese." Japanese immigrants included "gentlemen of refinement and culture" who, reported the press approvingly, "have brought their wives, children, and . . . new industries among us." Roger Daniels, a leading historian of the Japanese in America, concludes: "If there was a single word of protest raised against these early immigrants, I have failed to find record of it."[10]

With the long-sought passage by Congress of the Chinese Exclusion Act in 1882, the California nativist movement led by Denis Kearney (himself a recent immigrant from Ireland) turned its demagoguery against the Japanese. For another decade, however, the small number of Japanese offered a less visible target than had the Chinese. As late as 1890, the federal census recorded only 2,039 Japanese, both immigrants and native-born, in the continental states, although some 30,000 worked as contract laborers on Hawaiian sugar plantations. Over the next two decades, lured by higher wages on California farms and as replacements for the excluded Chinese, many of these Hawaiian workers and others from rural areas in Japan arrived on the mainland. Made up largely of young, uneducated single men, this group of immigrants was given none of the welcome accorded their predecessors. After a decade of relative silence, Kearney surfaced in 1892 to revive his anti-Oriental crusade. The Japanese, he declared, were "another breed of Asiatic slaves" recruited by unscrupulous "Shylocks . . . to fill up the gap made vacant by the Chinese who are shut out by our laws."[11]

Kearney's new crusade made little headway at the time—the scattering of Japanese in California had not yet aroused fears of another yellow peril—but the twin themes of his anti-Japanese oratory set the tone for later and more influential evangelists of exclusion. Kearney aimed one theme at working-class whites afraid of job competition: the Japanese, he charged, would "demoralize and discourage our domestic labor market" by working at subsistence wages. His second theme was directed at the middle class and its concern for moral purity: the Japanese attending public school were "fully developed men who know no morals but vice" and who would "debauch" their younger female classmates. Kearney cleverly turned against the Japanese their desire to escape from poverty and their eagerness to learn English even by attending grade school as teenagers or adults. Similar charges were, of course, the staples of other nativist and racist crusades: they had been used on the East Coast to great effect against Kearney's own Irish compatriots, and against Italians and Jews. But with farm labor at a premium in California's booming agricultural economy, Kearney and other anti-Japanese agitators found little support within the state's political leadership at the time.[12]

During the first decade of the twentieth century, the trickle of Japanese immigration became what the San Francisco *Chronicle* termed a "raging torrent." Compared to the total West Coast population, though, the number of Japanese arrivals was small, never exceeding 2 percent of the California population, the state where most Japanese settled. Two factors, however, led in 1905 to a revival of Kearney's quiescent crusade under the leadership of powerful politicians and California's economic elite. The first was that Japanese farm laborers, who saved most of their small wages, bought parcels of barren land and turned them into thriving truck farms. Although farms owned by Japanese occupied only 1 percent of the cultivated land in California, by 1919 they produced more than 10 percent of the total value of California produce. Japan's stunning victory in its war with Russia in 1905 and recognition of its emergence as a Pacific power also stirred fears about the potential disloyalty of Japanese immigrants.[13]

Spurred by such fears and by a press campaign with headlines such as THE YELLOW PERIL—HOW JAPANESE CROWD OUT THE WHITE RACE, calls for immigration restriction picked up political support. Organization of the Oriental Exclusion League in May 1905, a group made up largely of trade unions, and its alliance with the business-dominated Native Sons of the Golden West, combined normally antagonistic elements into a potent anti-Japanese coalition. The first target of the League's lobbying was the San Francisco school board. On October 11,

1906, the board bowed to pressure and ordered the transfer of all Japanese students to the segregated school for the Chinese. Word of this action soon reached Japan, whose government lodged a protest with the State Department. Most of the ninety-three Japanese students were aliens protected by a "most favored nation" clause in the 1894 treaty between the two nations. The ensuing diplomatic protest embarrassed President Theodore Roosevelt, who apologized to Japan and authorized Secretary of State Elihu Root to cooperate with the Justice Department in challenging the school board's action in federal court.[14]

The flap over school segregation alerted Roosevelt to the growing strength and determination of the anti-Japanese movement in California. Eager to cement good relations with Japan, Roosevelt had proposed in his annual message to Congress in November 1905 that it enact legislation "specifically providing for the naturalization of Japanese who come here intending to become American citizens." Federal law at the time limited naturalization to aliens who were either "free white persons" or "persons of African descent." Roosevelt's proposal fell victim, however, to the surge of exclusionist sentiment. As part of his deal with California officials to settle the school segregation issue, Roosevelt agreed to seek from Japan an agreement to limit further emigration to the United States. Diplomatic negotiations that extended until 1908 finally resulted in the so-called "Gentlemen's Agreement" under which Japan withheld passports to the United States from all but "laborers who have already been in America and to the parents, wives and children of laborers already resident there."[15]

The Gentlemen's Agreement effectively shut off the flow of male Japanese workers, but under its exceptions some 118,000 additional immigrants (many of them "picture brides" selected in Japan through arranged marriages) arrived in the United States between 1908 and 1924. West Coast nativists loudly protested this "loophole" and renewed their efforts for a complete halt to further Japanese immigration. While they conducted this campaign in Washington through the West Coast congressional delegation, a parallel effort in California succeeded in 1913 with passage by the state legislature of the Alien Land Law. In barring further land purchases by Japanese aliens and limiting leases on agricultural land to three years, nativists and farm-bloc legislators thought they had ended competition from productive Japanese farmers. Like the Gentlemen's Agreement, however, this law contained a loophole since it did not apply to land ownership or purchases by citizens. Japanese farmers promptly transferred land titles to their native-born children or other citizens willing to act as proxy owners. An attempt to close this loophole through a 1920 law prohibiting Japanese aliens from acting as guardians of their native-born children, passed overwhelmingly by referendum vote, similarly failed to evict Japanese farmers when the California courts struck the new law down as a violation of the Fourteenth Amendment to the U.S. Constitution.[16]

Frustrated by the state courts, the anti-Japanese movement found allies in the Supreme Court and Congress. The Alien Land Law of 1913 was directed, not at Japanese by name, but at "aliens ineligible for citizenship." Despite the limitation of federal naturalization to members of the white and black races, some federal courts had granted citizenship to applicants born in Japan. In 1922, in the *Ozawa* case, the Supreme Court put an end to this practice. Takao Ozawa, although born in Japan, had lived in the United States for twenty years, was a graduate of a Berkeley, California, high school, and had studied at the University of California. Ozawa and his family "had attended American churches and he had maintained the use of the English language in his home," the Court noted approvingly. "That he was well qualified by character and his education for citizenship is conceded," added Justice George Sutherland in his unaminous opinion. The Court admitted that distinctions of race had "no sharp line of demarcation" but nonetheless rested on "numerous scientific authorities, which we do not deem it necessary to review," for its holding that Ozawa "is clearly of a race which is not Caucasian" and which Congress had power to exclude from citizenship.[17]

Two years after the *Ozawa* decision, the campaign against the Japanese scored its culminating victory in congressional passage of the Immigration Restriction Act of 1924. Two decades of lobbying finally paid off in the provision that completely barred further Japanese immigration. This "national origins" act, which restricted immigration from other countries to quotas based on ethnic representation in the population reported in the 1890 census—and thus favored immigrants from Great Britain and the "Nordic" countries of northern Europe—was an outgrowth of the nativist and eugenics movements directed primarily against immigrants such as Italians and Polish and Russian Jews, whose introduction into American society might change the national character. Arguments for immigration restriction had been based on claims that such people were "unassimilable" into the dominant Anglo-Saxon society; differences in language and complexion, and the persistence of Old World cultures, buttressed such allegations. Only the Japanese, however, were singled out in the 1924 law for total exclusion. Japan's annual immigration quota would have been only one hundred persons in any event.[18]

Arguments for the restriction of immigration from eastern and southern Europe, rooted in alleged "national" differences, took on an overtly racist cast against the Japanese. "We cannot make a homogeneous population out of a people who do not blend with the Caucasian race," Woodrow Wilson stated during his 1912 presidential campaign. Similarly, California governor William D. Stephens urged Japanese exclusion in 1920 "entirely on the principle of race self-preservation and the ethnological impossibility of successfully assimilating this . . . flow of Oriental blood." The cruel irony of such a position, adopted by the Supreme Court in 1943 in the Hirabayashi case with a more tactful phrasing, was that Japanese Americans had struggled with particular success between 1924 and 1941 to achieve their goal of assimilation. Barred from citizenship by the Supreme Court, Japanese parents sent their native-born children to public schools where they mingled freely with their Caucasian classmates and adopted American customs of speech and dress. Many Japanese joined Christian churches, with Methodists and Presbyterians predominating, or worshipped in Americanized Buddhist churches; only a small minority of the older generation adhered to the emperor-worshipping Japanese cult of Shinto.[19]

Nonetheless, differences in age and citizenship between the two Japanese generations separated many families and created cultural tensions. The immigrant generation (known as Issei) was significantly older than the native-born group (known as Nisei)* when World War II began; in 1940, almost two-thirds of the Issei were forty-five or older, while a similar proportion of the Nisei were under twenty-one. An age gap of forty years separated many fathers from their children, and older parents often lacked facility in English and clung to Japanese customs and traditions. To the extent that Japanese aliens had failed to assimilate themselves into the dominant Caucasian culture, this phenomenon can only be considered a classic case of "blaming the victim." Kept from citizenship by Congress and the courts, and proud of their cultural heritage, Japanese aliens became visible targets after Pearl Harbor for those who found in their "lack of assimilation" evidence of potential disloyalty. Those who leveled such charges, and extended them to native-born citizens of Japanese ancestry as well, included the government lawyers who defended in court the evacuation and internment programs authorized by Franklin D. Roosevelt.[20]

This turbulent history of anti-Japanese agitation forms an essential background for understanding the debates within the government that preceded the signing of Executive Order 9066. The often acrimonious dis-

*Issei (pronounced ee-say) is the Japanese term for first generation; Nisei (pronounced nee-say) is the term for second generation.

putes among those men—the military and civilian officials most responsible for the framing of Roosevelt's order—during the ten weeks that followed Pearl Harbor and after, stemmed perhaps more from practical considerations than from purely constitutional concerns. Each of them was pressured by wartime duties, and each felt the ties of institutional loyalty. But legal questions loomed over the conflicts about the treatment of Japanese Americans at every stage of this internal debate. Positions on these questions differed from one official to the next, and few had the time or desire during this hectic period to record at length a thought-out analysis. Two of these men, however, personify the conflicts within this group of lawyers.

Chance alone had made Edward J. Ennis and John J. McCloy the first high officials in their respective departments to learn of the Pearl Harbor attack. This fortuity is worth notice, for the responses of Ennis and McCloy to this dramatic event do more than illustrate the professional dilemmas that confront government lawyers during wartime. They exemplify as well opposing approaches to the inherent conflict between emergency powers and individual rights. The policy disputes between these two men arose during the seventy-four days that followed Pearl Harbor, continued until the war ended, and surfaced forty years later in their differing reflections on the internment program that Ennis denounced and McCloy defended. In addition, each man played a primary role in the litigation that arose from challenges to Executive Order 9066. In these respects, Ennis and McCloy offer contrasting and continuing examples of the pervasive conflict between personal conscience and professional obligation.

Like many of his Depression-era colleagues, Edward Ennis looked to federal employment for both security and challenge after his graduation from Columbia Law School in 1932. An Irish Catholic and native New Yorker, Ennis joined the staff of the United States attorney in Manhattan after a year's experience as clerk to a federal circuit court judge. Seasoned by two years in the U.S. attorney's office, he shifted to Justice Department headquarters in Washington in 1937, where he worked in the small and clubby office of the Solicitor General, preparing briefs and arguing cases before the Supreme Court. After another two years, Ennis returned to New York to head the civil division of his former office.

With war on the horizon, Attorney General Francis Biddle brought Ennis back to Washington in July 1941 as general counsel of the Immigration and Naturalization Service. At Biddle's request, Ennis worked with Lawrence M. C. Smith, the career Justice Department lawyer who headed the Special Defense Unit, set up two years earlier to prepare plans for the screening and possible detention of "enemy aliens" in case of war. From reports submitted by FBI and military intelligence agents, Smith collected lists of Japanese, German, and Italian aliens subject to internment as disloyal or dangerous, and Ennis undertook to organize the facilities for their possible internment.[21]

Like many other young government lawyers, Ennis brought political liberalism and a long-standing concern for civil liberties to his New Deal service. It was these sympathies that had persuaded Biddle to recruit Ennis for the touchy task of dealing with aliens whose legal rights were minimal. The infamous Alien Act of 1798, still on the statute books, gave to the executive branch the power to deport aliens, a power the courts had rarely circumscribed with due process protections. As one scholar has noted, aliens were subject to deportation "without accusation, without public trial, without confrontation of witnesses, without defense, and without counsel." The most recent example of "deportation delirium" had been the forcible return to Russia in 1919 of anarchist Emma Goldman and two hundred other radicals on the "Red Ark." At the outset of World War II, Francis Biddle was, as he later wrote, "determined to avoid mass internment and the persecution of aliens that had characterized the First World War." In Biddle's opinion, Ennis was "ideally suited" to direct the alien enemy program—"imaginative yet practical, able to stand up to the 'brass hat,' and fully sharing my views . . . that everyone in our country, what ever his racial or national origin, should be treated with fairness."[22]

John J. McCloy, the War Department official most responsible for decisions about the treatment of Japanese Americans, was ahead of Ennis by a decade in legal practice and thirteen years in age. Born in Philadelphia in 1895, McCloy was a birthright Republican who moved from preparatory school to Amherst College to Harvard Law School, which he entered in 1916. With American entry into World War I, McCloy interrupted his law studies to join the Army and rose from lieutenant to captain during service at the front in France. After the armistice, McCloy returned to Harvard and was graduated in 1921. Wall Street practice attracted him, and for the next nineteen years he worked on corporate cases in both New York and Europe; he joined the prestigious firm of Cravath, deGersdorff, Swaine, and Wood in 1924, became a full partner in 1929, and remained with the firm until 1940.[23]

McCloy's lengthy involvement in the celebrated "Black Tom" sabotage case brought him to the attention of Secretary of War Stimson in 1940 and helps to explain his later fixation on possible sabotage on the West Coast. This cloak-and-dagger case began on the night of July 29, 1916, when scores of railroad cars filled with munitions exploded on the piers of Black Tom Island near Jersey City, killing several people and shattering the glass of many office buildings across the river in Manhattan. Suspicion that German saboteurs had engineered the explosion led to several arrests, and a rash of lawsuits seeking compensation for damages were quickly filed by railroads and insurance companies. McCloy entered the case for the Cravath firm in 1930, after the Mixed Claims Commission set up after the war to settle damage claims against Germany ruled the explosion an industrial accident. Unsatisfied claimants then retained McCloy's firm to challenge this finding. "Thus began McCloy's participation in the case," a Cravath partner later wrote, "to which he was to devote major attention for the next ten years." McCloy's sleuthing and legal research in both Europe and America finally produced proof of German sabotage. A quarter-century after the explosion, the Supreme Court finally confirmed in 1941 (after McCloy had joined the War Department) the claims of the Cravath clients.[24]

According to McGeorge Bundy, Stimson's official biographer, McCloy's work on the "Black Tom" case and the "wide knowledge of German subversive methods" he gained from it made him a "great find" as a consultant and special assistant to the Secretary of War on counterintelligence work. McCloy joined the War Department in this role in October 1940, and six months later he became Assistant Secretary of War with responsibility for political affairs. For the next five years, Bundy wrote, McCloy "was the man who handled everything that no one else happened to be handling" in the War Department. Bundy characterized McCloy as "so knowing in the ways of Washington that Stimson sometimes wondered whether anyone in the administration ever acted without 'having a word with McCloy.' "[25]

Among those with whom McCloy had frequent words about politics and policy during the war was Felix Frankfurter, the irrepressible Supreme Court justice under whom McCloy had studied at Harvard. The two men, McCloy later recalled, kept in touch daily by phone and visited each other's homes regularly. Frankfurter, who had served under Stimson as assistant U.S. attorney in New York before World War I, maintained an insatiable appetite for news of War Department policies and cultivated during World War II his contacts with both Stimson and McCloy. In turn, Frankfurter capitalized on his intimate and long-standing friendship with President Roosevelt to provide his War Department friends with easy access to the White House. Frankfurter's role in this ménage à trois provided the two Republicans in the War Department a pipeline to the President that their Democratic Justice Department counterparts, Ennis and Biddle, lacked.[26]

The outcome of the debate between Ennis and McCloy over Executive Order 9066 reflected the contrasts between the respective cabinet members under whom they served. Francis Biddle, a prototypical "Philadelphia lawyer" wedded by his Main Line heritage to the Pennsylvania Railroad and the Republican party (the two were synonymous in the state's politics for a century), prepped at Groton and was graduated *cum laude* both from Harvard College and Harvard Law School. A coveted Supreme Court clerkship with Oliver Wendell Holmes in 1911 preceded twenty-three years of corporate law practice in Philadelphia. Unlike most of his peers, however, Biddle experienced a mid-life conversion to the Democratic party and entered Roosevelt's New Deal administration in 1934 as chairman of the first National Labor Relations Board. Frankfurter quipped that he had a "la de da" personality, but Biddle displayed a core of toughness in dealing with union and industry leaders alike in this post. After he retreated to corporate practice in 1935, Biddle returned to public service four years later, first in a brief stint as a federal circuit court judge and then in an equally brief appointment as Solicitor General in the Justice Department.[27]

With the elevation of Attorney General Robert Jackson to the Supreme Court in June 1941, Biddle became his acting successor; in early September the Senate confirmed Roosevelt's nomination of Biddle to head the Justice Department. Biddle exhibited in this post a concern for civil liberties that belied his conservative past. He beefed up the Civil Liberties Unit established in 1939 and employed dusty statutes that dated to the Reconstruction Era to bring federal prosecutions of state officials in cases of police brutality, lynchings, election discrimination, and peonage. Biddle's efforts on behalf of blacks brought to the Supreme Court the *Screws* and *Classic* cases, precursors of later civil rights enforcement by the Justice Department. Against this record, Biddle also showed a sensitivity to "national security" claims. He authorized the prosecution of the Trotskyite leaders of the Socialist Workers Party under the 1940 Smith Act sedition statute, a move he later regretted.[28]

Conscious of his role as a "new boy" in Roosevelt's wartime cabinet, Biddle deferred to his senior colleagues and to the President. "I tried never to bother the President with anything that was not essential," he later wrote. Biddle struck many people as "casual" in manner and appearance, his deputy James Rowe recalled, and this aspect of his personal style placed Biddle at a disadvantage in conflicts with his fellow cabinet members. He particularly found it hard to differ with Secretary of War Stimson, whom he described later as a "heroic figure of sincerity and strength." Biddle found it hard to "talk shop" with Stimson, a reticence that took on importance during their face-to-face meetings over the evacuation issue.[29]

It is easy to understand Biddle's deference to Stimson. Although he had only a year's seniority over Biddle in Roosevelt's wartime cabinet, Stimson outranked him by twenty years in age and two terms of previous cabinet service. Born in New York City in 1867, Stimson attended Phillips Andover Academy, Yale College, and Harvard Law School. After sixteen years of Wall Street practice in the law firm founded by Elihu Root, Stimson began four decades of episodic government service in 1906 as United States attorney in New York. Responding to the importunings of Republican presidents, Stimson served as Secretary of War under William Howard Taft from 1911 to 1913 and as Herbert Hoover's Secretary of State from 1929 to 1933. A genuine elder statesman by 1940, but still at seventy-three an articulate and aggressive interventionist, Stimson was a perfect candidate for the bipartisan "war cabinet" Franklin Roosevelt hoped to fashion as an answer to the fulminations of Republican isolationists.[30]

Stimson's recruitment to the cabinet was arranged by his former protégé and long-time admirer, Felix Frankfurter. According to Bruce Allen Murphy, the justice's campaign to place Stimson in the cabinet began in May 1939 after a White House conversation at which Roosevelt expressed a lack of confidence in Secretary of War Henry Woodring. Over the next year, Frankfurter canvassed possible replacements with his friend Grenville Clark. Confident that he could pick Woodring's successor, Frankfurter quickly settled on Stimson and deputized Clark to approach him about the post. Citing his advanced age, Stimson at first demurred but then agreed that Frankfurter could convey his willingness to serve. Stimson attached several conditions, however: that he have carte blanche to choose an assistant; that Roosevelt support an immediate conscription program; and that Stimson be permitted to advocate publicly that the United States provide aid to its European allies. Frankfurter's suggestion of Stimson "struck fire" with the President. On July 9, 1940, the Senate voted without dissent to confirm Stimson in his third cabinet post in three decades.[31]

At the time of the Pearl Harbor attack, Stimson and McCloy clearly outmatched their Justice Department counterparts in influence and access to the White House. The responsibilities of his position, however, gave Edward Ennis the first move in the governmental chess game that made pawns of the Japanese Americans. Ennis had planned his opening move carefully and chose to make it against a group of Japanese aliens previously singled out for detention. This limited program created conflicts with military leaders who considered it inadequate; their heated demands for sweeping powers to control aliens raised the first specter of the issues soon to be joined.

The presidential proclamation that Ennis drafted on the afternoon of December 7, 1941, subjected to "summary apprehension" any Japanese alien "deemed dangerous to the public peace or safety of the United States" by the Attorney General or the Secretary of War. Even before Roosevelt signed the proclamation, the Justice Department began to arrest and intern several thousand aliens—including Germans and Italians as well as Japanese—already targeted by the FBI and military intelligence agencies. "A great man hunt was underway last night in Southern California," the Los Angeles *Times* reported on December 8, as federal agents "sought 300 alien Japanese suspected of subversive activities." During the night that followed Pearl Harbor, FBI and military agents assisted by local police picked up 736 Japanese aliens on the West Coast and a smaller number of Germans and Italians. Within four days, the number of Japanese arrested swelled to 1,370. By the end of the alien roundup in mid-February 1942, some 2,192 Japanese on the mainland and 879 in Hawaii had been detained. The magnitude of this initial dragnet is best measured in relative terms: it included close to 10 percent of the adult males among the Japanese aliens on the West Coast.[32]

Although plans for the arrest and internment program took concrete shape in the months before Pearl Harbor, government intelligence agencies had begun surveillance of Japanese Americans considered "subversive" a decade earlier, after Japanese armed forces occupied Manchuria and ultranationalists in Japan proclaimed the inevitability of war with the United States. According to a study by Bob Kumamoto, four separate cabinet departments had joined by 1932 "in providing a cooperative and clandestine surveillance of the entire Japanese community." As part of a general counterespionage effort, this intelligence gathering included "detailed documentation on daily activities and personal affiliations" of Japanese American leaders and infiltration of organizations with ties to Japan. A State Department report of August 1934 warned that the Japanese government "has agents in every large city in this country and on the West Coast. These people, who pass as civilians and laborers, are being drilled in military maneuvers . . . when war breaks out, the entire Japanese population on the West Coast will rise and commit sabotage."[33]

In the period before 1939, military intelligence agents conducted most of this surveillance, since the FBI lacked any mandate to engage in counterintelligence work. The Office of Naval Intelligence (ONI) in the Navy Department displayed more interest in the Japanese than the

Army's Military Intelligence Division, known as G-2, largely because the Navy had more concern with Japan as a Pacific naval power. ONI agents kept the West Coast port cities under particularly close scrutiny. In October 1935, ONI headquarters received a report of a Japanese espionage ring in Seattle and Portland: "Naval operatives determined that resident members of this ring and naval officers attached to the Japanese Embassy were secretly compiling information on strategic areas along the West Coast . . . through the subversion and exploitation of American navy personnel with the inducement of prostitutes and drugs."[34]

Japanese Americans in Hawaii became particular targets for surveillance during the prewar period. Not only did they make up more than a third of the Territory's population but their proximity to the Pearl Harbor naval base also stirred military suspicion. Contacts between members of this group and visiting Japanese merchant ships were reported to the White House in 1936 and led, in fact, to the first intimation that Japanese Americans might face internment in the event of conflict between the two countries. Responding to ONI reports of these contacts, Roosevelt sent a significant one-page memo to the Chief of Naval Operations on August 10, 1936: "One obvious thought occurs to me—that every Japanese citizen or non-citizen on the island of Oahu who meets these Japanese ships or has any connection with their officers or men should be secretly but definitely identified and his or her name placed on a special list of those who would be the first to be placed in a concentration camp in the event of trouble." Coming as it did more than five years before the outbreak of war, this expression of presidential sentiment was a chilling forecast of Roosevelt's later approval of internment on the mainland.[35]

The almost certain prospect of war in Europe, along with Japanese saber rattling in the Pacific, persuaded Roosevelt in mid-1939 to authorize an expansion of intelligence and to give the FBI a formal role in this undercover effort. On June 26, the President directed that "the investigation of all espionage, counter-espionage and sabotage matters be controlled and handled" jointly by the FBI, the ONI, and the Army's G-2 branch. "The directors of these three agencies are to function as a committee to coordinate their activities," Roosevelt ordered. A year later, the President's directive took concrete form in a "Delimitation Agreement" that gave the FBI leadership in the intelligence fraternity, with control over cases of "actual or strongly presumptive espionage or sabotage, including the names of individuals definitely known to be connected with subversive activities." G-2 was delegated responsibility over military bases and over civilians in the Canal Zone, Panama, and the

Philippines, and ONI became responsible for intelligence on naval bases and in Guam and American Samoa.[36]

The two military intelligence agencies resented their subordination to the FBI and battled with J. Edgar Hoover, the power-hungry Bureau director, for expanded roles in this unequal troika. Both ONI and G-2 claimed that surveillance of so-called "fifth-column" activities should be a military responsibility.* Civilian "fifth-column" preparations, G-2 argued in July 1940, were "essentially a part of military operation, as much as any military column. Its activities, based on previous, secret and intelligent planning, are coordinated in time and space with those of the uniformed forces of the enemy." When Hoover balked at the suggestion that the FBI relinquish its leading role in intelligence collection, his military counterparts secretly drafted a plan for a "Department X" as a super-intelligence agency headed by an independent coordinator. Before the plan reached the President, Hoover stepped in and quashed the incipient challenge to his power with threats to end FBI cooperation with ONI and G-2. Nonetheless, the military agencies expanded their surveillance of civilians to areas outside the confines of military bases.[37]

The expansion by ONI and G-2 of their intelligence efforts had one consequence of significance to Japanese Americans, not only before the Pearl Harbor dragnet but also during the litigation that challenged Executive Order 9066. Although the War Department and the Army controlled the evacuation and internment programs, ONI agents assumed control of intelligence on the Japanese population on the West Coast. John McCloy acknowledged and approved the ONI role in November 1940, in a letter to G-2 director General Sherman Miles about the secret "Department X" proposal. The ONI, McCloy wrote, "has made a particular study of the Japanese undercover system in this country and in certain other areas where the Fleet has interest. . . . Since the study of the Japanese situation has already been the subject of considerable thought and work on the part of Naval Intelligence, it would represent an economy of effort if the Navy undertake the job of presenting and maintaining an estimate of that situation."[38]

Despite their internal squabbles, agents in all three intelligence agencies collaborated in compiling lists of "subversive" and "dangerous" aliens. These lists were funneled to L. M. C. Smith in the Special Defense Unit of the Justice Department, who prepared a master list

*The term "fifth column" had only recently been coined during the Spanish Civil War by an observer who remarked that General Franco had four military columns marching on Madrid and a "fifth column" of civilian sympathizers already within the Capital.

(known as the "ABC" list) of aliens targeted for arrest in the event of war. By mid-1941, the names of over 2,000 Japanese aliens appeared on the "ABC" list. This list received its informal name from the three categories into which it divided suspect aliens. Those in Group A were identified as "known dangerous" aliens and had been the subjects of individual investigation. Many of those in this group achieved this designation because they occupied positions within the Japanese American community considered to be influential, or because their work made them likely "fifth-column" agents. According to Kumamoto, "those deemed sinister enough to warrant top billing included fishermen, produce distributors, Shinto and Buddhist priests, farmers, influential businessmen, and members of the Japanese Consulate." Those in Group B were considered "potentially dangerous" but had not been thoroughly investigated, while those in Group C "were watched because of their pro-Japanese inclinations and propagandist activities." These latter groups included Japanese-language teachers, martial acts instructors, travel agents, and newspaper editors.[39]

One source of names for the "ABC" list required only scissors and scrapbook; like its counterparts serving other ethnic groups the Japanese-language press exhaustively published the names of participants in community activities, and FBI and ONI agents assiduously read and clipped periodicals and newspapers such as the *Rafu Shimpo,* the Japanese-language paper in Los Angeles. Many whose names appeared in these periodicals openly supported the Japanese "New Order" in Asia before the war, and intelligence agents were able to compile a ready list of contributors to Japanese military and veterans organizations and those who donated tinfoil and scrap metal to the Japanese government.

A more important source of names was a list of Japanese sympathizers and espionage agents seized in March 1941, nine months before the Pearl Harbor roundup, during a break-in at the Japanese consulate in Los Angeles. Planned and executed by Lt. Commander Kenneth D. Ringle of the ONI, and conducted with the aid of the FBI and a safecracker borrowed from a local jail, this surreptitious entry turned up a "truckload of documents" that effectively dismantled a Japanese espionage network. The Ringle raid led in June to the arrest of Itaru Tachibana, a Japanese naval officer masquerading as an English-language student. Among the records photographed during the raid and those seized when Tachibana was arrested were lists of agents who had gathered intelligence in the form of maps, lists of Army and Navy installations, data on defense factories and harbors, and the locations of power stations and dams.[40]

Tachibana was charged after his arrest with "conspiracy to obtain national defense information for a foreign power." After the intercession of Ambassador Nomura on his behalf, Secretary of State Hull urged that the Justice Department drop the charge against Tachibana because "conversations with the Japanese were at a crucial stage." Tachibana was then deported to Japan, where he was assigned to coordinate Japanese espionage in Hawaii. There was no question that Tachibana headed an espionage ring on the West Coast that enlisted a number of Japanese Americans, both aliens and citizens, nor that the government knew the identities of its members. The FBI has refused to release its Tachibana file, and the names of the espionage agents remain unknown.[41]

The Ringle raid and Tachibana's subsequent arrest became significant in later disputes over the evacuation and internment of Japanese Americans. Commander Ringle himself, as the ONI agent directly responsible for intelligence on this group, believed that his prewar undercover work had identified the members of the Japanese espionage network, and he defended in subsequent reports the loyalty of Japanese Americans in general. The FBI also concluded, on the basis of Tachibana's files and its own investigations, that it had adequately identified those who deserved inclusion on the "ABC" list. A month before Pearl Harbor, Nat Pieper, the FBI Special Agent in Charge in San Francisco, reported to J. Edger Hoover that "a thorough and logical investigation of individuals reported to be engaged in espionage has been conducted [and] no evidence has been obtained indicating that any [Japanese aliens or citizens not previously investigated] have been guilty of violating any federal statutes for which prosecution would lie." Two months after Pearl Harbor, the Army's G-2 chief on the West Coast stated that Japanese intelligence came from "information learned during peace by the activities of accredited diplomatic, military and naval attaches and their agents." In short, all three intelligence agencies agreed that the Japanese espionage ring had been broken before Roosevelt signed Executive Order 9066.[42]

The task of dealing with those picked up in the "ABC" raids fell on Edward Ennis in the Justice Department. On December 22, 1941, Attorney General Biddle created the Alien Enemy Control Unit as a new departmental division and placed Ennis in charge as director. Although neither existing federal law nor the presidential proclamations drafted by Ennis provided for hearings or any form of due process for those arrested, Biddle and Ennis were determined not to repeat the worst excesses of summary detention of "alien enemies" that stemmed back to the time of John Adams and reached their climax in the "Red Raid" deportations after World War I. Biddle had assured the alien population in a public statement on December 10 that "every effort will be made to protect them from any discrimination or abuse.'' To carry out this promise, Biddle established early in 1942 a national network of Alien Enemy Hearing Boards. With three to six civilian members, most of them lawyers serving without pay, these boards were run informally, dispensing with formal rules of procedure and evidence.[43]

In announcing the boards, Biddle stressed that an informal hearing for aliens ''has been provided, not as a matter of right, but in order to permit them to present facts in their behalf'' about loyalty. In dealing with arrested German and Italian aliens, the boards displayed remarkable lenience. Of the 12,071 alien enemies arrested during the first year of the war, almost ten thousand were either Germans who belonged to pro-Nazi groups such as the German-American Bund or the militaristic Kyffhauserbund, or Italians who were members of fascist organizations. Fewer than half of the Germans and Italians were interned after their hearings. In contrast, more than two-thirds of the Japanese aliens remained in internment camps during the war. An unknown number of this group had been identified as espionage agents from the records seized in the Ringle raid and from Tachibana. It seems likely, however, that hostility toward Japanese as a race did affect decisions of the hearing boards.[44]

During the first three weeks of the war, Edward Ennis limited the Justice Department program to the arrest of Japanese aliens on the ''ABC'' list and to the imposition of fairly relaxed restraints on the activities of those who remained at liberty. Had the problem been left to Ennis, these steps would most likely have constituted the entirety of the government's wartime regulation of the Japanese American population. The presidential proclamation that Ennis had drafted, however, required that the Justice Department share its responsibility for this program with the War Department. By the end of 1941, as war news from the Pacific turned increasingly sour and reports of Japanese atrocities in the Philippines reached the public, demands for more sweeping measures came from West Coast military leaders. General DeWitt in particular urged his War Department superiors to approve moves that would affect not only aliens but also citizens of Japanese descent, moves that raised basic constitutional questions. The ensuing debate over DeWitt's demands placed the two departments on a legal collision course.

2

"An American Citizen Is an American Citizen"

LIEUTENANT GENERAL John L. DeWitt had assumed command of the Fourth Army on the West Coast on December 5, 1939, nearly two years to the day before Pearl Harbor. For this sixty-one-year-old career officer, nearing the end of four decades of military service, the assignment to the Presidio fortress overlooking the Pacific in San Francisco was intended to be his last before retirement. As it turned out, none of those who participated in the debates over evacuation and internment would play a more central role than he.

It is ironic that the wartime fate of the Japanese Americans rested largely in the hands of this bureaucrat in uniform. Caught, as he would be, in the crossfire of Justice Department lawyers and their War Department counterparts, DeWitt chose the classic response of a man in the middle—for as long as he could he vacillated between decision and indecision. In the end, however, despite his initial reservations, he adopted the hard-line policies urged on him by lawyers in uniform and thereby became the apostle of internment.

John DeWitt had spent his entire life in uniform. Born at Fort Sidney, Nebraska, in 1880 and raised on Army posts, he left Princeton University at the end of his sophomore year in 1898 to taste the excitement of the Spanish-American War. After this brief exposure to combat, he decided to remain in the Regular Army and carved out a niche for himself as a supply officer. During the years before American entry into World War I, DeWitt alternated desk duty with three tours of service in the Philippines. He spent the years from 1914 to 1917 in Washington, in the office of the quartermaster general, and served in France during World War I as director of supply and transportation for the First Army

Corps. His slow rise through the ranks of the peacetime army led to his appointment as quartermaster general in 1930. After a fourth tour of duty in the Philippines, from 1935 to 1937, and a subsequent administrative post as commandant of the Army War College, DeWitt was posted to the Presidio as the culmination of his military career.[1]

DeWitt's long career in a segregated army and in particular his service in the Philippines, service that could hardly have shielded him from the virulent anti-Asian racism that pervaded the occupying American Army, had infected him (along with many of his military colleagues) with the virus of prejudice toward blacks and Asians. Nine months before Pearl Harbor, DeWitt arranged to "just have it happen naturally that Japs are sent to Infantry units" in his command rather than to headquarters or coastal defense posts. He similarly complained, several weeks after Pearl Harbor, that the Army has assigned "too many colored troops" to the West Coast in view of the "public reaction out here due to the Jap situation." "I'd rather have a white regiment," DeWitt told the Army's chief of classification and assignment, than one that included either Black or Japanese American troops.[2]

But it was not bald prejudice that clouded DeWitt's military judgment in the days after Peral Harbor as much as fear. Along with the civilian residents of the West Coast, John DeWitt, despite his military background, shared a severe case of Pearl Harbor panic. Fears of an imminent Japanese attack on the West Coast swept through nearly all segments of the public in the weeks that followed Pearl Harbor. "The entire Pacific Coast from British Columbia to San Diego prepared for possible raids," reported the Los Angeles *Times* on December 9, 1941.[3]

Just one day earlier, DeWitt's own staff had sounded the alarm. On December 8, an Army spokesman precipitated a massive blackout with a report that thirty Japanese planes had "reconnoitered the San Francisco Bay area and other sections of California." As did all later reports of Japanese air attacks, this aerial incursion turned out to be false and at least one experienced officer under DeWitt's command, Major General Joseph W. Stilwell—who later achieved combat fame as "Vinegar Joe" during the Burma campaigns—registered concern about DeWitt's panic response. Stilwell labeled the Presidio reaction to this false alarm as "kind of jittery." Reports that circulated during the following week of a Japanese fleet steaming toward the West Coast and of further air attacks convinced Stilwell that DeWitt's intelligence units were "amateur" and that the public warnings of an impending Japanese attack authorized by DeWitt had been irresponsible.[4]

Still, it is hard to fault DeWitt for exhibiting an excess of caution in reacting to such reports, however erroneous they turned out to be; in the weeks that followed Pearl Harbor the prospect of a Japanese attack on the mainland simply could not be dismissed out of hand. And the fact that the Army and Navy commanders in Hawaii, General Walter Short and Admiral Husband Kimmel, had been cashiered from their posts in disgrace on December 16 likely increased DeWitt's resolve not to be caught napping in the Presidio.

Further, the very real presence of Japanese submarines off the West Coast—from December 17 to December 23, four Japanese submarines made eight or nine attacks on American shipping vessels, sank two tankers, and damaged one freighter—caused great apprehension in DeWitt's headquarters. Fueled by leaks of the submarines' presence were widespread reports, most from nervous civilians, of "signaling" from the coastline. Although investigation disclosed that car headlights or blackout violations were the culprits in most cases, DeWitt would later cite "hundreds of reports nightly of signal lights visible from the coast" and "intercepts of unidentified radio transmissions" as a justification for evacuation. And until February 1942, the Army's G-2 staff reported to DeWitt that "the activities of fifth columnists" were indeed a source of Japanese intelligence. On the other hand, the FBI dismissed such reports of espionage as unfounded; in the month after Pearl Harbor, DeWitt had no consistent evidence either to allay or confirm his fears that Japanese Americans were aiding the offshore submarine attacks.[5]

Yet despite the lack of a sound basis for these fears, DeWitt's first recommendation about the treatment of civilians was extreme. In a December 19 message to the War Department, he urged that "action be initiated at the earliest practicable date to collect all alien subjects fourteen years of age and over, of enemy nations and remove them to the Zone of the Interior." DeWitt did not distinguish in this request between Japanese aliens and those of German and Italian origin. His War Department superiors, however, no doubt aware that the West Coast "alien enemy" poulation of these three groups included almost a half-million members, chose simply to disregard DeWitt's proposal. Even before December 19, however, DeWitt had hinted that he had grand designs for purging the area.[6]

During a telephone talk with San Francisco FBI agent Nat Pieper on December 17, J. Edgar Hoover learned that DeWitt's staff had designated a hundred-mile-wide strip along the coast as a "combat zone" and "wanted to move all people out of this 'invasion' area who were considered undesirable." Hoover was sympathetic, but reminded Pieper that "there is no law at the present permitting us to pick up citizens" without proof of legal violations. "I do not believe that they can put over any plan to clean people out of that area unless there is some very imminent prospect of attack,'' Hoover said, adding that ''I thought the army was getting a bit hysterical'' in running to the press with sabotage reports that turned out to be unfounded. As examples of ''the Army losing their heads,'' Hoover cited such false alarms as ''the Bonneville Dam affair, where the power lines were sabotaged by cattle scratching their backs on the wires, or the 'arrows of fire' near Seattle, which was only a farmer burning brush as he had done for years.''[7]

Hoover raised no objection to Pieper's proposal that the FBI furnish DeWitt's staff with copies of the Bureau's ''Detention Index,'' which listed suspected ''subversive'' citizens targeted for arrest. The FBI chief displayed his characteristic cover-your-back caution, however, in warning Pieper ''to be very careful to have specific recommendations on every person on any of our lists so that if there is any howl afterwards, we will not be left holding the bag.'' The FBI was ''up against the Civil Liberties crowd'' and Hoover wanted to put the onus for any possible protest on the Army.[8]

Four days later, on December 22, perhaps somewhat restrained by Pieper's less than enthusiastic response, DeWitt again wired Washington, this time with a more limited and reasonable request. Against a background of bad news from the Philippines, DeWitt requested that the War Department ''urge the Attorney General to issue the necessary regulations to make proclamations of the President referring to Japanese aliens effective.'' FBI and military agents, DeWitt reported, were poised to seize contraband that might be used for espionage and sabotage but ''were powerless to act until the Attorney General issues his instructions.'' DeWitt put his request bluntly: ''This is urgent. Prompt action is required.''[9]

Roosevelt's alien-enemy proclamations had authorized restrictions on movement and had subjected to confiscation shortwave radios, cameras, firearms, and other articles that might facilitate espionage or sabotage. Caught up in the processing of arrested aliens, Edward Ennis and his small staff had in fact delayed the drafting of regulations to implement the proclamations. This delay left the Army without power to require that aliens turn in such articles, or to conduct searches for them. On December 26, Chief of Staff George Marshall wired DeWitt that Attorney General Biddle had given assurances that ''necessary regulations [were] now before him in draft form and being considered with view to early promulgation.'' DeWitt's return wire reflected his frustration: ''Cannot overemphasize urgency for immediate promulgation these regulations. Confiscation of arms, radios, cameras, etc., must not be delayed longer.''[10]

On the same day, in a second talk with Nat Pieper, DeWitt sounded out the FBI on its attitude toward a more limited project—a War Department takeover of the alien-enemy program. Pieper reported to J. Edgar Hoover over the telephone that DeWitt "is pretty much burned up" with Biddle and wanted to know "whether or not the Attorney General is ever going to do anything in this situation." What DeWitt wanted, Pieper said, were "raids on all alien homes to see that the articles are picked up." Hoover's response was once again skeptical. When Pieper told him that there were some 200,000 homes occupied by alien enemies, Hoover replied that mass raids "would not only be most difficult but would also have a very bad effect on the law-abiding people who were raided." Pieper then let Hoover know that DeWitt had informed him that if the Justice Department continued to resist DeWitt's demands for search-and-seizure powers and a compulsory registration of alien enemies, the Army would "request of the President that the powers regarding alien enemies be taken away from the Attorney General . . . and be transferred to the War Department." Since Hoover opposed FBI involvement in either raids or registration, he refrained from endorsing DeWitt's alien-enemy takeover proposal and agreed merely to bring "General DeWitt's attitude to the attention of the Attorney General."[11]

Yet clearly, DeWitt was of a different mind regarding just what could and ought to be done with regard to the West Coast Japanese American citizens, for also on that day, December 26, DeWitt had yet a third communication, this last with General Allen W. Gullion, the Army's chief law enforcement officer as Provost Marshal General.

DeWitt left no misunderstanding in responding to Gullion's report that the Washington lobbyist of the Los Angeles Chamber of Commerce had urged evacuation of all Japanese residents of that city, alien and citizen alike. DeWitt resisted. He had "thought the thing out to my satisfaction," DeWitt told Gullion, and had concluded that "if we go ahead and arrest the 93,000 Japanese [in California], native born and foreign born, we are going to have an awful job on our hands and are very liable to alienate the loyal Japanese. . . ."[12]

Nonetheless, DeWitt's conversation with Gullion on December 26 contained a number of significant arguments that would go unnoticed both at the time they were made and later on, when the government would make certain claims in defending itself in litigation that challenged DeWitt's later evacuation and internment orders. "I'm very doubtful that it would be common sense procedure" to intern the entire Japanese American population on the West Coast, DeWitt stressed to Gullion in this December 26 conversation. State and local authorities, aided by the FBI and military intelligence agents, he argued, could adequately handle the problems of espionage and sabotage. Rather than attempt the "wholesale internment" that had been urged on Gullion by others, DeWitt said that he was confident that the Army could "weed the disloyal out of the loyal and lock them up if necessary." Government lawyers, it should be noted, would later deny to the Supreme court that any loyalty-screening procedure was possible. DeWitt's final argument to Gullion during this phone conversation paid clear if unintended homage to a legal principle whose supporter he would not long remain: "An American citizen, after all, is an American citizen."[13]

DeWitt's seemingly firm rejection of the massive evacuation proposal that Gullion floated on December 26 blocked any military moves against Japanese American citizens for another month. Simultaneously alerted by Hoover to the consequences of further delay, Attorney General Biddle moved promptly in issuing DeWitt's requested regulations regarding the alien population. On December 29, all alien enemies in the Western Defense Command area were ordered to surrender radio transmitters, shortwave receivers, and certain types of cameras to local police by January 5; and on January 1, Biddle authorized the issuance of warrants to search the premises of any alien enemy on FBI representation that there was "reasonable cause" to believe contraband could be found, and also authorized arrests for contraband possession. Biddle carefully kept enforcement of these regulations out of Army hands, and he ignored DeWitt's demand for a compulsory registration program. In a further attempt to avoid friction between the War Department and the Justice Department, Biddle also agreed to a round of high-level conferences between Edward Ennis, his own lieutenant, and John McCloy of the Department of War, to deal with DeWitt's concerns and to forge a common alien-control program.[14]

The first of these conferences were conducted over the last week of 1941. Accompanying John McCloy on the War Department side were General Allen Gullion and Gullion's assistant, Major Karl Bendetsen. Accompanying Ennis was James H. Rowe, Jr., who served as deputy to the Attorney General. On the surface these conferences had an air of cordiality. But it was surface only. Joined in this seemingly common cause were men whose cordiality barely hid their underlying commitments to very different values.

Although Gullion had failed in his December 26th attempt to persuade DeWitt to support a campaign for the mass evacuation of Japanese Americans, he was far from giving up on the fight for an internment type of program. In pushing ahead, Gullion would not only become a dogmatic, diehard advocate, but would show a mastery of military politics. One weapon that would serve Gullion well, particularly in his self-assumed assault on the reticence of DeWitt, his longtime friend and colleague, was his years of legal training, training that DeWitt lacked.

John DeWitt and Allen Gullion had been friends since 1912, when both men were posted to Fort Douglas, Utah. Born in the same year as DeWitt and like him a veteran of the Philippines campaigns, Gullion was a West Point graduate who earned a law degree at the University of Kentucky in 1914 while he served at that institution as professor of military science. His career as a military lawyer began with World War I duty in France. In 1937, after two decades of service in the Army's legal corps, Gullion was appointed Judge Advocate General with the rank of major general. In August 1941, the War Department revived the law-enforcement position of Provost Marshal General, which Gullion assumed shortly after Pearl Harbor, bringing to this post a reputation as a strict disciplinarian and no-nonsense administrator.[15]

In terms of the fate of Japanese Americans, the most significant move that Gullion made as Judge Advocate General was to recruit to his staff an ambitious, industrious, young lawyer, Karl R. Bendetsen. Born in Aberdeen, Washington, in 1907, Bendetsen began his precocious military career at the age of fourteen as a member of the Washington State Guard in a high school unit. As an undergraduate at Stanford University, he joined the Officers Reserve Corps and was commissioned as an Army lieutenant when he graduated from Stanford Law School in 1932. Returning to his hometown, Bendetsen began a commercial practice and served as counsel to the business-dominated Washington State Taxpayer's Association. He left private practice in 1940 to join Gullion's office in the War Department with the rank of captain, and moved with Gullion the next year to the Provost Marshal General's office.

Bendetsen's single-minded and efficient dedication to Gullion's evacuation and internment campaign, in which he served first as liaison with DeWitt and later as director of the resulting Army program, fueled a three-step rise through the ranks from captain to colonel in less than two years. Gullion's equal as a master of the military bureaucracy, Bendetsen quickly became the decisive link between Washington and San Francisco in the campaign to overcome DeWitt's doubts about the evacuation and internment of Japanese Americans.

In his self-described role as "the Attorney General's alter ego," James Rowe brought to his relations with the War Department the political savvy and outspoken assertiveness that Biddle conspicuously lacked. He would remain at the center of the evacuation and internment controversy for the next six months, until he left Justice to join the Navy. Only thirty-two at the time, Rowe was a Montana native and Harvard Law School graduate who, like Biddle, had served a prized clerkship with Oliver Wendell Holmes at the Supreme Court. Unlike Biddle, Rowe was on close and easy terms with Roosevelt. He combined legal work in five New Deal agencies between 1934 and 1939 with his passion for politics. After plunging into Roosevelt's re-election campaign in 1936, Rowe joined the White House staff in 1939 as one of the "anonymous assistants" who linked the President to the New Deal bureaucracy. Shortly after Pearl Harbor, Roosevelt sent Rowe to the Justice Department as Assistant to the Attorney General, one of the eyes-and-ears posts that Roosevelt created in cabinet agencies.[16]

In Rowe and Ennis, the Justice Department was represented in these initial negotiations by lawyers who matched Gullion and Bendetsen in legal skill, force of personality, and institutional loyalty. Three factors, however, combined to put them on the defensive in the first round of face-to-face meetings. Biddle's deference to Secretary of War Stimson, obvious to both Ennis and Rowe, precluded any objections to War Department requests that might complicate amicable relations between the two departments. In addition, Ennis in particular felt apologetic about the delay in implementing Roosevelt's alien-enemy proclamations. Finally, Ennis and Rowe entered these conferences in the dark about the full nature and scope of the program DeWitt had in mind.

The first regulations that Ennis drafted, and Biddle announced, imposed reasonable wartime restrictions on persons who were citizens of enemy states, and raised no difficult legal questions. But these only whetted DeWitt's appetite for sweeping and stringent controls. The Justice Department lawyers did not learn in their meetings with McCloy, Gullion, and Bendetsen that DeWitt wanted explicit power to exclude aliens from areas that surrounded military installations and defense facilities. The conferees reached no specific agreements, but adopted DeWitt's request for further "on the ground" meetings in San Francisco. Their respective departments accordingly delegated Rowe and Bendetsen to meet with DeWitt at his Presidio headquarters, beginning on January 4, 1942.

The Presidio meetings went badly from the beginning. Arriving in San Francisco without an agenda of his own, Rowe discovered that DeWitt had a detailed, three-point plan that considerably exceeded the scope of the regulations issued the week before by Biddle. DeWitt's demands had in fact been drafted by Bendetsen prior to the first session and reflected Gullion's determination to push the Justice Department to its limits. As his earlier memoranda and conversations with DeWitt made clear, Gullion hoped to impose on the West Coast a martial law regime similar to that declared in Hawaii on the day of the Pearl Harbor attack. Should political considerations rule out martial law on the mainland, Gullion was willing to accept a program that put the Army in charge and that authorized the evacuation of citizens. As a first step toward this goal, Gullion had ordered Bendetsen (before the Presidio meetings) to draft an Executive Order transferring authority over the alien-control program to the War Department. Gullion admitted, however, that it "wasn't quite fair" to attempt an Army takeover without giving the Justice Department a chance to accept his minimum program, put on DeWitt's desk by Bendetsen. Pending the outcome of the meetings with Rowe, Bendetsen kept the proposed Executive Order in his briefcase.[17]

Rowe sat down with DeWitt and Bendetsen on January 4 with no idea of the Army's hidden agenda. He got no further into this meeting than the statement that he "thought he could just talk about the general problems" concerning alien-enemy control when DeWitt impatiently interrupted. His first brass-tacks demand was for "blanket authority" to enter alien premises and to "search and seize immediately without waiting for normal processes of law" or Justice Department approval. Taken aback by this proposal to ignore the Fourth Amendment's warrant requirements, Rowe begged off with the response that it was "beyond my power" to agree. "That is a legal problem that would have to be a matter of policy with the Attorney General," he replied. DeWitt answered that his concern was the apprehension of Japanese Americans with radio transmitters and shortwave sets. He wanted the power, DeWitt added, to "go in and search the house or residence and premises of every alien beginning with the Japanese right now" and to "stop every car on the highway for a time and search it—every portable, moving thing there is." The problem with "spot raids" conducted with warrants, DeWitt argued, was that "if we go to court you have to show your reason. We don't want to go to court." After his initial startled response, Rowe sat through this assault on the Constitution in silence.[18]

DeWitt went on to his second demand, that the Justice Department carry out a compulsory alien-registration program. Less than two years earlier, as part of the 1940 census, all aliens had registered their names, addresses, and occupations, and the Commerce Department (of which the Census Bureau was a part) had turned these lists over to the Justice Department. DeWitt wanted a new registration, he told Rowe, to simplify the job of FBI and military agents in conducting "mass raids" in the search for contraband. His proposal was that all aliens be required to carry an identity card with "a picture of the man" and thumb prints as a way "to keep track of him at all times." His final demand—for authority to exclude aliens from "restricted zones" on the West Coast—DeWitt explained, rested on the drain on his troops in guarding "the large number of very important defense installations and factories on the coast." As a "counter-espionage" program, DeWitt concluded, his package of demands sought from the Justice Department "a rapid, direct, legal way that I could get at this problem" without delay.[19]

The unexpected scope and specificity of DeWitt's demands left Rowe virtually speechless. He raised no objection to the second and third proposals, those dealing with the registration and exclusion proposals, neither of which went far beyond the authority implied in Roosevelt's proclamations. In addition, neither raised difficult legal problems, although the extent of the proposed "restricted zones" might subject their boundaries to a "reasonableness" test if challenged in court, as would their possible application only to Japanese Americans. But the demand for "mass raids" without warrant left Rowe aghast. His on-the-spot concession that the Justice Department was "prepared to do all the spot-raiding you want" failed to placate DeWitt and Bendetsen. Without approval from Biddle, Rowe could only temporize and promise to "come back tomorrow" after consultation with the Attorney General.[20]

After a long telephone talk with Biddle that evening, Rowe presented DeWitt the next morning with a memorandum that detailed Biddle's response to the War Department proposals. In this document, Biddle gave the first hint that he was willing to relinquish control of the alien-enemy control program. His strategy had two prongs: first, the maximum protection of the Justice Department's prerogatives; and second, casting on the War Department the onus for those actions that stretched the law. Biddle gave and took with an eye to bureaucratic and legal politics. He first promised to begin a new alien registration "within a week or ten days" but rejected DeWitt's proposal that the Army "go ahead with the registration as a military measure" with the retort that the Justice Department "feels it can conduct such a registration, through the local police authorities, much faster than the Army itself." Biddle left unstated his rebuff to DeWitt's identity card proposal.[21]

Biddle's response to the "restricted zones" plan suggests that he understood both its legal and political implications. His suggested procedure was that the Army funnel proposals for such areas through local U.S. attorneys, who would "automatically accept" Army recommendations "pending confirmation by the Attorney General. As soon as possible, a press release ordering all enemy aliens to evacuate restricted areas by a certain date and hour will be issued. Any release by the Department of Justice will specifically state that the Attorney General has designated these restricted areas at the specific and urgent request of the Commanding General." DeWitt could hardly have missed Biddle's attempt to evade any political uproar that the "Civil Liberties crowd" might precipitate in the aftermath of an exclusion program.[22]

DeWitt's demand for authority to conduct warrantless searches produced Biddle's most significant constitutional concession. The Attorney General's counterproposal seriously undercut Fourth Amendment protections: "The question of probable cause will be met only by the statement that an alien enemy is resident in such premises." While prepared to wink at the probable cause requirement for warrants, however, Biddle warned DeWitt that "under no circumstances will the Department of Justice conduct mass raids on alien enemies." Biddle underscored his objection to mass raids with a threat. Should the Army conduct such indiscriminate raids (which would necessarily involve warrantless searches of premises occupied by citizens as well as aliens), Biddle promised an appeal to Roosevelt. If he was "overruled by the President," Biddle added, he would "request the Army to supersede the Department of Justice" in the alien program. This was in fact precisely the end Gullion and DeWitt desired. Biddle's concessions on the registration and "restricted zone" issues, however, and the promise that the probable cause requirement for warrants would be reduced to a *pro forma* technicality, made a dispute with the Justice Department over the "mass raids" issues a slender pretext for a takeover attempt. Nonetheless, in probing Biddle through the meetings with Rowe, the Army officers had discovered a willingness to yield if pushed.[23]

DeWitt raised one topic in the January meeting that Rowe let pass without comment. Widespread espionage on the part of Japanese Americans, DeWitt alleged, was responsible for Japanese submarine attacks on American shipping. "Every single ship that sails from the Columbia River since the outbreak of the war has been subjected to submarine attack, every one of them," he told Rowe. "I have reason to believe that there isn't a ship leaving that they don't know about." DeWitt attributed the attacks to shore-to-ship radio communication: "I personally am convinced that there is a portable sending set operating in the Monterey Bay area. I am pretty convinced that there is one operating in the Columbia River area." Perhaps intimidated by the certitude of DeWitt's assertions, Rowe failed to question either DeWitt or Colonel

D. A. Stroh, the G-2 chief of staff who attended the conference, about the sources and reliability of these reports.[24]

Rowe's meetings with DeWitt ended in an atmosphere of mutual suspicion. Over the final two days of Rowe's visit as an emissary, he and Bendetsen labored to fashion a written agreement satisfactory to their respective superiors. This difficult task was achieved only with the addition of a codicil in which DeWitt vented for the record his displeasure with the Justice Department. His meetings with Rowe, DeWitt stated, "have been occasioned by the almost complete absence of action on the part of the Department of Justice over a period of nearly four weeks" in implementing Roosevelt's alien-enemy proclamations. On the point of greatest conflict between the two sides, DeWitt repeated his demand that the Justice Department "provide for simultaneous 'mass raids' without warning to determine the presence of prohibited articles" in alien premises. Despite Biddle's clear refusal to sanction such raids, DeWitt again requested that he "be advised by the Department of Justice of its position in this matter."[25]

DeWitt further claimed that Biddle's resistance to warrantless searches "will not solve a number of pressing problems." Constructing a half-dozen hypothetical situations—such as a home occupied by an alien husband and citizen wife, and cases of "hot pursuit" of contraband—DeWitt argued for authority to "contravene normal processes to take necessary action in an emergency" in such cases. This aide-mémoire left no doubt of DeWitt's suspicions in questioning "the extent to which the Department of Justice is prepared to assume and to discharge the responsibility of taking whatever steps are necessary for the prevention of sabotage, espionage, and other fifth column activities" by disloyal aliens. Matching this stick of doubt with a carrot of diplomacy, DeWitt professed "no wish" to assume army control of the alien program. "Impressions to the contrary notwithstanding," he stated, "the Army would accept such transfer of responsibility and authority with the greatest reluctance." Under prodding by Gullion and Bendetsen, however, this reluctance gave way within three weeks to an army takeover campaign.[26]

After Rowe's return from San Francisco, Attorney General Biddle moved expeditiously to implement the agreements reached with DeWitt. Approving a regulation drafted by Edward Ennis, President Roosevelt ordered on January 14 that a registration of all alien enemies begin the week of February 2. February also became the month of widespread search-and-seizure raids up and down the West Coast. Beginning with a mass roundup of 400 Japanese American fishermen on Terminal Island, near Los Angeles, held for questioning while their boats were searched for radio transmitters and secret codes, FBI agents and local police hunted for contraband. In conducting these raids, Hoover's agents bent the rules against "mass raids" out of shape. None of these searches turned up evidence of plans for sabotage or espionage, but overblown press accounts of the raids helped to fuel the political campaign for mass evacuation of Japanese Americans already underway.[27]

Despite his expressed impatience with Justice Department tardiness in drafting the regulations necessary to implement the President's December alien-enemy proclamations, DeWitt took longer to carry out his part of the January 5 protocol. He finally forwarded to Washington on January 21, for approval by the Attorney General, the first list of proposed "restricted zones." This list specified eighty-six "Category A" zones from which all alien enemies would be excluded, and eight "Category B" zones, to which access would be given through a "pass and permit" system. Although most "Category A" zones were small and located in sparsely populated areas, some 7,000 alien enemies (only 40 percent of them Japanese Americans) lived within their boundaries and were thus subject to exclusion.[28]

Complicating the situation were demands on DeWitt from Navy commanders that exclusion from zones under Navy control include not only aliens but all Japanese Americans who could not prove "actual severance of all allegiance to the Japanese government." Since the residential areas that surrounded naval bases along the coast, from Bainbridge Island in Washington state to San Diego, contained many Japanese American families of mixed citizenship, exclusion of aliens alone would only partly clear these areas of the group suspected of "subversive" designs and promised social disruption as well. Nat Pieper had reported to J. Edgar Hoover a month earlier that "there is a fight in progress between the Army and Navy" over the exclusion issue. The second round of this fight, when DeWitt prepared his list of "restricted zones," increased the pressures to include the Nisei citizens in the exclusion edicts.[29]

Taking DeWitt at his word, Rowe had returned from his Presidio meetings convinced that DeWitt "thinks mass evacuation is damn nonsense!" Their negotiations had dealt only with aliens, and even the agreement permitting DeWitt to propose "restricted zones" contemplated the exclusion from these areas of aliens alone. Rowe may have missed, however, the siginficance of a comment DeWitt made at the outset of their January 4 conference. In a reference to Japanese Americans in general, DeWitt confessed "no confidence in their loyalty whatsoever." He made clear the scope of his statement: "I am speaking now of the native born Japanese . . . 42,000 in California alone."[30]

Over the six weeks that ended on February 19, 1942, with presidential approval of Executive Order 9066, DeWitt's seemingly offhand comment to Rowe overshadowed his eventual capitulation to calls that Japanese American citizens and aliens alike be uprooted from their West Coast homes and moved to internment camps. Two sources of pressure, one internal and the other external, combined to erode DeWitt's initial confidence that he could "weed the disloyal out of the loyal" and his doubts that it would be "common sense procedure" to intern the entire Japanese American population on the West Coast. Internal pressure came largely from Gullion and his aide, Karl Bendetsen, who shuttled between Washington and San Francisco during this period as Gullion's emissary to DeWitt. The external source of pressure was a campaign for mass evacuation conducted jointly by West Coast politicians and the press. Bendetsen's dual role in this campaign, as Gullion's liaison both to Capitol Hill in Washington and the Presidio in San Francisco, became a crucial factor in convincing the politically inexperienced DeWitt to abandon his initial resistance to mass evacuation.

As the December 26 meeting between Gullion and Los Angeles Chamber of Commence lobbyist illustrated, calls for the mass evacuation of Japanese Americans began soon after Pearl Harbor. Scattered demands for evacuation popped up in the West Coast press as well, but they elicited no response from the War Department. This sporadic and unofficial campaign took a dramatic turn on January 16, 1942, when Congressman Leland M. Ford, a California Republican, sent identical letters to Secretary of War Stimson and Attorney General Biddle urging that "all Japanese, whether citizens or not, be placed in inland concentration camps." Ford's astounding rationalization of this proposal was that any truly loyal Japanese American could, "by permitting himself to be placed in a concentration camp," thereby prove that "he is patriotic and is working for us."[31]

Ford's blunt proposal marked the third phase of the simmering evacuation debate. Between the Pearl Harbor attack and Rowe's trip to the Presidio, lawyers dominated the debate. Rowe's negotiations with DeWitt signaled a second stage, that of military involvement. The letters sent by Ford to Stimson and Biddle added to the debate a political dimension. In taking the floor of Congress on January 20 to assert that "a patriotic native-born Japanese, if he wants to make his contribution, will submit himself to a concentration camp," Ford placed an indelible political stamp on the ensuing debate. From that point on, discussion both within the government and outside shifted from a focus on how to deal with aliens to one that included American citizens as well.[32]

The differing responses to Ford's letters gave evidence of conflict between the War and Justice departments. Biddle's reply, sent on January 24, indicated an uncompromising attitude. He informed Ford that "unless the writ of habeas corpus is suspended, I do not know any way in which Japanese born in this country, and therefore American citizens, could be interned." Biddle's reference to habeas corpus, that "Great Writ," was a direct challenge to proposals that martial law be imposed on the West Coast, as it had been in Hawaii, since a declaration of martial law carried with it a suspension of habeas corpus as an avenue of judicial relief from illegal detention.[33]

Stimson's reply to Ford, however, gave an implicit encouragement to the congressional campaign. "The internment of over a hundred thousand people," Stimson first cautioned, "involves many complex considerations." Nevertheless, he added, "the Army is prepared to provide internment facilities in the interior to the extent necessary." Stimson would later express doubts about the constitutionality of evacuation and internment. But in suggesting to Ford that he direct his lobbying efforts at the Justice Department, Stimson made inevitable further conflict between his staff and Biddle's.[34]

Karl Bendetsen, in his role as director of the Alien Division in Gullion's office, had drafted the letter sent to Ford over Stimson's signature. The eager junior officer, assigned by Gullion to maintain contact with the West Coast congressional delegation, thus became a central figure in the political assault on Biddle. The Attorney General did not welcome the lobbying campaign unleashed by Stimson's statements to Ford, but considered it his duty as a cabinet officer to listen politely to members of Congress. Ford quickly turned to Clarence Lea, a Democrat and dean of the California delegation in the House of Representatives, for aid in forging a bipartisan coalition to press for evacuation. Lea in turn deputized Alfred J. Elliott, a fellow Democrat, and Republican Jack Z. Anderson to approach the Justice Department directly. On January 27, Elliott and Anderson met with Edward Ennis to argue the case for evacuation.[35]

Ennis's congressional lobbyists had themselves been pressured by influential constituents, many of them Caucasian farmers who made no secret of the fact that they had axes to grind that had little to do with national security. Anderson in particular had been urged to seek evacuation by leaders of the Grower-Shipper Vegetable Association, a powerful force in his rural district. "We're charged with wanting to get rid of the Japs for selfish reasons,'' the group's manager told a journalist. ''We might as will be honest. We do. It's a question of whether the white man lives on the Pacific Coast or the brown man.'' Although Elliott and Anderson avoided such blatant expressions of racism, Ennis gave them no encouragement. Reporting back to Clarence Lea the negative result of their talk with Ennis, the two congressmen suggested a shift in tactics. A greater show of political force and War Department involvement might impress the Justice Department, they argued. Lea agreed, and invited the entire West Coast congressional delegation to a January 30 meeting. Ennis and Rowe accepted Lea's invitation to attend, and General Gullion delegated Bendetsen to represent the War Department.[36]

While Attorney General Biddle had to deal with congressional pressure applied against his lieutenants, Rowe and Ennis, General DeWitt was subjected to face-to-face lobbying by California state officials. DeWitt had scheduled a meeting with Governor Culbert Olson for January 27. Headlines in the Sunday newspapers on January 25 charged the atmosphere of this meeting with political tension and revived DeWitt's fears about espionage and sabotage. COMPLETE BLAME FOR HAWAIIAN DISASTER LAID TO KIMMEL, SHORT, trumpeted the Los Angeles *Times* in headlining the release of the report of the presidential commission headed by Supreme Court Justice Owen J. Roberts and charged by Roosevelt with investgation of the Pearl Harbor attack. As the headlines made clear, the Roberts Commission placed the blame for lack of preparedness before the attack on the Army and Navy commanders in Hawaii. More important to the fate of Japanese Americans on the West Coast was the commission's finding that prior to the attack a Japanese espionage network in Hawaii had sent ''information to the Japanese Empire respecting the military and naval establishments and [military] dispositions on the island.'' Along with Japanese consular officials, the report stated, the espionage ring included ''persons having no open relations with the Japanese foreign service.'' This imputation of disloyal acts to Japanese Hawaiians, flatly asserted but never documented, inflamed the mainland press and spurred the incipient campaign for the mass evacuation of Japanese Americans from the West Coast.[37]

A discernible shift in public opinion from relative tolerance to active hostility toward Japanese Americans followed release of the Roberts Commission report. On January 27, Los Angeles county manager Wayne R. Allen announced the dismissal of all county workers of Japanese descent. He based his action on the report's finding that the Pearl Harbor ''debacle had been facilitated by wide-spread espionage and fifth column work'' by Japanese in Hawaii. ''It is difficult if not impossible to distinguish between loyal and disloyal Japanese," Allen told the press in a statement later echoed by DeWitt and other defenders of evacuation and internment. A January 29 column in the San Francisco *Examiner* turned hostility to hatred. "I am for the immediate removal of every Japanese on the West Coast to a point deep in the interior," Henry McLemore wrote. "I don't mean a nice part of the interior either. Herd 'em up, pack 'em off and give 'em the inside room in the badlands. . . . Personally, I hate the Japanese. And that goes for all of them."[38]

The first gust of the Roberts Commission hurricane hit DeWitt in his January 27 meeting with Governor Olson. A liberal Democrat who had earlier urged tolerance toward Japanese Americans but who faced a tight re-election race in November, Olson now advocated a least a limited evacuation from coastal cities. In a telephone talk with Bendetsen following this meeting, DeWitt reported "a tremendous volume of public opinion now developing against the Japanese of all classes, that is aliens and non-aliens." Pressure on state officials now came from "the best people of California," DeWitt added. "Since the publication of the Roberts Report they feel that they are living in the midst of a lot of enemies. They don't trust the Japanese, none of them." A meeting two days later with Earl Warren, California's Republican attorney general and Olson's eventual gubernatorial opponent, confirmed for DeWitt that there was bipartisan support for evacuation.[39]

DeWitt's meetings with Olson and Warren eradicated his last doubts about the necessity for evacuation; the Roberts Commission blast at his counterparts in Hawaii could only have increased DeWitt's resolve to avoid their inglorious fate. When Bendetsen called from Washington on January 29, where he was preparing for the congressional meeting the next day, Gullion's aide checked to confirm that DeWitt was "of the opinion that there will have to be an evacuation on the west coast, not only of Japanese aliens but also of Japanese citizens." DeWitt expressed none of his earlier reluctance to evacuate citizens: "I think it's got to come sooner or later."[40]

DeWitt repeated his endorsement of evacuation in a telephone conversation with Gullion the next day. Reporting that state officials differed on the scope of evacuation, with some in favor of removing all Japanese Americans from the state and others advocating their relocation within California, DeWitt assured Gullion that "there's no difference of opinion about wanting them to go, and it can be done." He had scheduled a second conference with Governor Olson on February 2 to discuss the logistics of evacuation, DeWitt reported. "Then the only thing is to determine where they are going to be put," Gullion replied. "I guess you can help provide the guards to get them there." The two generals were in fact jumping the gun, since as yet they had no legal authority to move Japanese American citizens anywhere.[41]

Bendetsen approached the congressional meeting on January 30 with the full support of his military superiors, both for evacuation and for an Army takeover of the resulting program. He faced two possible sources of resistance to these plans, however. Neither Secretary of War Stimson nor his assistant, John J. McCloy, had yet expressed a firm opinion on the proposals of the two uniformed officers. As experienced lawyers and political figures, Stimson and McCloy understood that the existence of supportive political pressure would not be an acceptable defense should a course of action decided upon turn out to have been in error. Justice Department lawyers posed an even greater threat to Bendetsen's efforts.

The day before the Capitol Hill conference, Bendetsen sounded out James Rowe on the evacuation issue, in raising with him the Navy's insistent demand that Japanese American citizens be excluded from the restricted area on Bainbridge Island in Puget Sound. "I don't know how they can just kick a lot of citizens out in a prohibited area," Rowe demurred, "because if you do that then [in] every area you've already requested, you'll want citizens kicked out too, American citizens of Japanese extraction." Rowe promised to discuss this issue with Ennis before the congressional meeting but floated with Bendetsen a possible escape hatch for the Justice Department, suggesting the evacuation of citizens "if you can do it as a military problem." Rowe's intimation that Biddle might welcome a War Department takeover and thus relieve the Justice Department of this troubling problem encouraged Bendetsen and proved an accurate forecast of Biddle's eventual capitulation to political pressure.[42]

The Washington meeting called by the West Coast congressional delegation on January 30 effectively ended the evacuation debate. Within the three weeks that followed, the congressional campaign for internment overwhelmed the constitutional qualms of both Secretary of War Stimson and Attorney General Biddle and gained the support of that consummate politician, Franklin Roosevelt. Backed by the demands of powerful constitutent groups long hostile to the Japanese Americans, this campaign illustrates the dominance of politics over law in a setting of wartime concerns and divisions among beleaguered government officials.

Bendetsen, Rowe, and Ennis arrived at the meeting to find that the congressional group had drawn up a detailed program designed to remove Japanese Americans from the coastal cities. The heart of the six-point proposal asked that the War Department designate "critical areas" along the coast from which the Army would evacuate "all enemy aliens and their families, including children under 21 whether aliens or not." The evacuation process would employ a carrot-and-stick approach. Those who agreed to "voluntary resettlement and evacuation as a patriotic contribution" would receive assistance from federal agencies in finding housing and employment outside the prohibited zones. The prospect of "internment" in abandoned Civilian Conservation Corps camps faced those who failed to relocate on a voluntary basis. A key element of the plan, the three lawyers learned from the politicians, was the recommendation that the President strip the Justice Department of jurisdiction over the evacuation program and transfer control to the War Department.[43]

Bendetsen and his Justice Department counterparts left the congressional meeting with diametrically opposed reactions to the evacuation proposal. Bendetsen's response was predictably enthusiastic. He recognized, however, that approval and implementation of the plan first required the consent of Stimson and McCloy. Neither of these civilian officials had yet expressed a firm opinion on the issue of evacuating citizens, and they were unlikely to endorse the congressional program without assurance that considerations of "military necessity" overrode the constitutional questions raised by a plan that singled out Japanese Americans for removal. Bendetsen acknowledged this obstacle in reporting to DeWitt on the Capitol Hill conference. The congressmen "asked me to state what the position of the War Department was," he told DeWitt over the telephone. "I stated that I could not speak for the War Department," Bendetsen said, adding that he had voiced his own view that the Army "would be entirely willing . . . to accept the responsibility" for evacuation if the secretary of war and his military subordinates were given control along with "full authority to require the services of any other federal agency" in carrying out the task.[44]

DeWitt's position as the West Coast military commander made him an essential figure in the campaign to enlist Stimson and McCloy in the evacuation crusade. Bendetsen accordingly suggested in his January 30 conversation with DeWitt that "anything you recommend would certainly be backed up" by public opinion, and stressed that the congressmen at the meeting "were quite emphatic in their views" and "seemed to be pretty well stirred up." Prompt action in drafting a formal recommendation to the War Department was necessary, Bendetsen urged, since "public sentiment is beginning to become irresistible" and congressional demands for action required an official response. DeWitt promised to act quickly in framing a reply to the evacuation proposal.[45]

On their part, Rowe and Ennis left the congressional meeting incensed at Bendetsen's encouragement of evacuation. They promptly reported to Attorney General Biddle and urged that he intervene with Secretary of War Stimson. Biddle immediately called Stimson and secured his agreement to send McCloy to a high-level conference at the Justice Department on Sunday, February 1. In preparation for this meeting, Rowe and Ennis plotted a strategy designed to place Stimson's imprimatur on a public rebuff to the congressional proposal. The meeting in Biddle's office set the stage for a showdown over the tensions that had built up between the two departments since Rowe and Bendetsen had sparred in DeWitt's office a month earlier.

McCloy arrived for the Sunday meeting with Gullion and Bendetsen in tow, while Biddle was backed by Rowe, Ennis, and J. Edgar Hoover. According to Gullion's account of the confrontation, Rowe began with a blast at Bendetsen for overstepping his authority at the Capitol Hill meeting. Rowe added that "there is too much hysteria about this thing" and that "there is no evidence whatsoever of any reason for disturbing citizens" on the West Coast. Biddle then stepped in with a firm declaration that the Justice Department "will have nothing whatsoever to do with any interference with citizens, whether they are Japanese or not."[46]

Angered by the attack on his assistant, Gullion shot back with a challenge to the Attorney General: "Mr. Biddle, do you mean to tell me that if the Army, the men on the ground, determine it is a military necessity to move citizens, Jap citizens, that you won't help us." Biddle responded by handing to the War Department representatives the draft of a press release that he proposed to issue that evening, over his signature and that of Stimson. This nine-paragraph statement represented the tactic devised by Rowe and Ennis as retaliation for Bendetsen's performance at the congressional meeting.[47]

The document that McCloy and his colleagues quickly read began with a recital of the alien-control steps already agreed to by the two departments. It then stated that an FBI investigation of "subversive activities" had uncovered "no substantial evidence of planned sabotage by any alien," and concluded with this significant sentence: "The Department of War and the Department of Justice are in agreement that the present military situation does not at this time require the removal of American citizens of the Japanese race."[48]

Before McCloy could voice an opinion on the press release, Gullion heatedly objected to the final sentence and demanded that DeWitt be consulted before any statement was given to the press. Rowe replied that DeWitt had assured him, at the Presidio conference on January 4, that he was "very much opposed to any mass evacuation" and questioned Gullion as to whether DeWitt had changed his mind. Noting that over the past month DeWitt had "traveled up and down the West Coast" and had conferred with Governor Olson and other state officials, Gullion stated that it was his "understanding that General DeWitt does favor mass evacuation" of Japanese Americans. McCloy ended the impasse with the suggestion that Biddle hold up issuance of the press release until DeWitt had a chance to submit a written recommendation on the evacuation question. Biddle's agreement ended the acrimonious meeting.[49]

Whether or not Rowe and Ennis expected that Stimson would sign the proposed press release and authorize its publication, they succeeded in planting doubts in McCloy's mind about the rush to endorse the congressional campaign for evacuation. After reporting to Stimson on Monday, February 2, the results of the Justice Department conference, McCloy informed Gullion and Bendetsen that he would meet with them in Stimson's office the following day to canvass the situation. Before he met with his civilian superiors, Gullion called DeWitt at the Presidio to secure approval for a claim that DeWitt backed a mass evacuation program. "I haven't gone into the details of it," DeWitt replied, "but Hell, it would be no job as far as the evacuation was concerned to move 100,000 people."[50]

Gullion led off the meeting with Stimson and McCloy on February 3 with an assertion that acts of espionage by Japanese Americans required their evacuation from the West Coast. Stimson recorded in his diary later that day Gullion's report that DeWitt "thinks he has evidence that regular communications are going out from Japanese spies . . . to submarines off the coast assisting in the attacks . . . which have been made upon practically every ship that has gone out." Gullion then argued that an evacuation limited to Japanese aliens, conceded by the Justice Department to be legally permissible, would offer little protection against espionage and sabotage. It was the Nisei, Gullion explained, who "are probably a more dangerous element at the present time than their unnaturalized parents." At a minimum, he urged Stimson, the War Department should authorize DeWitt to carry out "the evacuation of the Japanese of the area surrounding the intensely important area at San Diego, Los Angeles, San Francisco, and Puget Sound, where are located some of the most important airplane factories and naval shipyards."[51]

This meeting marked Stimson's first direct exposure to the Army's evacuation arguments. Hardly an introspective man, Stimson laid out in his diary a balance sheet of the competing claims. "If we base our evacuations upon the ground of removing enemy aliens," he recorded on one side of the ledger, "it will not get rid of the Nisei who are . . . the more dangerous ones." But if "we evacuate everybody including citizens," Stimson put on the other side, "we must base it as far as I can see solely upon the protection of specified plants." Stimson's bottom line reflected his ingrained constitutional concerns: "We cannot discriminate among our citizens on the ground of racial origin."[52]

Stimson made clear to Gullion his opposition to the mass evacuation of Japanese Americans. The outcome of the War Department conference on February 3 was a temporary truce between the civilian and military officials. "We talked the matter over for quite a while," Stimson wrote in his diary, "and then postponed it in order to hear further from General DeWitt who has not yet outlined all of the places that he wishes protected." At the meeting's end, McCloy called DeWitt to pass on Stimson's instructions. DeWitt "should not take the position even in your conversations with political figures out there," McCloy told the general, that the War Department "favors a wholesale withdrawal of all Japanese citizens and aliens from the Coast, for the reason that it may get us into a number of complications which we have not yet seen the end of." Mass evacuation raised "so many legal questions involved in discrimination" between citizens and aliens, McCloy cautioned, that he and Stimson felt that "perhaps the best solution . . . is to limit the withdrawal to certain prohibited areas."[53]

DeWitt remained skeptical about this suggestion. "Out here, Mr. Secretary," he replied to McCloy, "a Jap is a Jap to these people now." DeWitt added that he had met the day before with Governor Olson and Tom Clark, whom Biddle had recently designated as liaison between the Justice Department and the Army, and suggested to McCloy an alternative evacuation plan drafted by the three officials. Under this plan, all adult males in the Japanese American population would be moved from the "combat zone" on the coast to "resettlement projects" located in agricultural areas within California to work as farm laborers. McCloy reminded the general that such a plan required voluntary participation, since no legal basis existed for compulsory relocation. "The bad ones, the ones that are foreign agents, that are sympathetic with Japan," McCloy suggested, "will not volunteer, will they?" The Nisei group that Gullion had described to Stimson as the dangerous element, and that DeWitt had claimed were committing acts of espionage, were unlikely to volunteer for relocation. What did the state officials propose to do if this group resisted Olson's appeals to relocate, McCloy asked. "Then I don't know how they're going to handle it," admitted DeWitt.[54]

Agreeing that DeWitt could continue to explore with Olson the feasibility of the voluntary resettlement plan, McCloy proposed as an interim measure that the Army designate as "military reservations" the areas surrounding major defense plants and installations. The War Department would then "exclude everyone—whites, yellows, blacks, greens—from that area and then license back into the area those whom we felt there was no danger to be expected from." The licensing power would be applied to citizens and aliens alike. "Everyone but the Japs," McCloy added, could be licensed to remain in these military reservations. "You see," he explained to DeWitt, "then we cover ourselves with the legal situation . . . because in spite of the constitution you can eliminate from any military reservation" both citizens and aliens. Such a scheme could be imposed "without suspending writs of Habeas Corpus and without getting into very important legal complications," McCloy added in a bow to Stimson's constitutional qualms.[55]

McCloy's idea struck DeWitt as a logistical nightmare if the Army were required to process license applications on an individual basis. "It would be a big administrative job," McCloy conceded. "I think you might cut corners," he proposed, by announcing that all residents of these reservations were automatically licensed to remain with the exception of Japanese Americans. "In the meantime the Japs would have to be out of there," McCloy noted. The genesis of this scheme lay in Rowe's offhand comment to Bendetsen on January 30 that military edict might justify the evacuation of citizens from "prohibited zones." DeWitt agreed to consider McCloy's proposal and to continue working with state officials in Olson's voluntary resettlement plan.[56]

The lengthy conversation between McCloy and DeWitt on February 3 ended without any consensus on a program that would satisfy both DeWitt's military demands and Stimson's constitutional concerns. The two officials did agree, however, that DeWitt would frame a formal recommendation on the evacuation issue within ten days for presentation to Stimson. February 13, 1942, thus became a crucial date for Japanese Americans, anxious about the mounting press and political campaign against them but still free to live and work on the West Coast.[57]

3

"*Be As Reasonable As You Can*"

THE FINAL ROUNDS in the evacuation debate began with the War Department meeting between John J. McCloy and Karl Bendetsen on February 3, 1942. Official approval came sixteen days later, on February 19, with the signing by President Roosevelt of Executive Order 9066. Unprecedented in its impact on civilians during wartime, Roosevelt's order authorized Secretary of War Stimson to exclude "any or all persons" from specified "military areas" within the continental United States.

Armed with the authority conferred on him by Stimson, and with the prod of criminal penalties handed to him by Congress the following month, General DeWitt wasted no time in directing the mass evacuation of Japanese Americans from their West Coast homes. Designed initially to encourage the "voluntary" migration of Japanese Americans to inland states, DeWitt's evacuation program soon encountered objections from officials of these states and was quickly replaced with an internment program. DeWitt gave the Japanese Americans no choice. Aside from the small number who had fled to sanctuary outside the West Coast states, Japanese Americans were quickly herded at gunpoint into "relocation centers" scattered from California to Arkansas.

This chapter will examine separately each of the four debates that led to the ultimate internment decision. The first of these ended on February 13, with the drafting of DeWitt's "final recommendation" on evacuation; the second on February 19, with the signing of Executive Order 9066; the third on March 19, with congressional enactment of Public Law 503; and the fourth on April 7, with the showdown between federal and state officials over the migration of Japanese Americans to the Rocky Mountain states. In one sense, however, the separation of these debates over the fate of the Japanese Americans is artificial. Their eventual outcome was in fact settled by a document drafted on February 3 by the most junior official who took part in these debates, Karl Bendetsen.

Bendetsen was not, of course, solely responsible for the evacuation and internment decision; officials of greater rank shared that responsibility. Provost Marshal Gullion, General DeWitt, Assistant Secretary of War McCloy, Secretary Stimson, and President Roosevelt all stood above Bendetsen in the chain of command. On paper, Bendetsen simply executed the orders of his hard-nosed superior, General Gullion, the most persistent advocate of internment. As the emissary of both Gullion and McCloy, however, Bendetsen assumed an independent and aggressive role both in eroding the doubts expressed by DeWitt about evacuation and in framing the "final recommendation" of the cautious and fearful West Coast commander. The crucial role of this recently mobilized Army officer and lawyer illustrates the power exercised by lower-echelon but strategically placed officials in affecting the decisions of superiors who are distracted by other duties and who are dependent on their subordinates for information and advice.

The memorandum that Bendetsen drafted on February 3 and handed to Gullion the following day constituted the first detailed discussion of "the so-called 'Japanese problem' " prepared within the War Department. Bendetsen based his memorandum on the assumption that members of the Nisei group constituted a greater threat than did the alien Issei. "Many citizens who enjoy the privileges and immunities accorded by the Bill of Rights are potential saboteurs," Bendesten asserted. Without any citation to sources, Bendetsen further argued that "by far the vast majority of those who have studied the Oriental assert that a substantial majority of Nisei bear allegiance to Japan, are well controlled and disciplined by the enemy, and at the proper time will engage in organized sabotage, particularly, should a raid along the Pacific Coast be attempted by the Japanese."[1]

Although Bendetsen had earlier pressed for the designation of "prohibited" and "restricted" areas around defense plants and military installations from which alien enemies would be excluded, he dismissed these measures as inadequate. Exclusion of aliens from such limited areas "does not reach the subversive individual and the potential saboteur who is a citizen," Bendetsen told Gullion. The "safest course to follow" in dealing with Japanese Americans, he suggested, would be "to remove them all from the West Coast and place them in the Zone of the Interior in uninhabited areas where they can do no harm under guard." Bendetsen pointed out that this plan "has the widest acceptance among the Congressional Delegations and other Pacific Coast Officials."[2]

Despite his personal advocacy of "mass evacuation" as a course which would "largely relieve the necessity for eternal vigilance" over the Japanese Americans, Bendetsen shied away from a formal recommendation that Gullion propose such a program to Stimson and McCloy. Two factors stood in the way. An evacuation and internment program "overlooks the serious dislocation of economic life and the loss of vital perishable produce" from farms operated by Japanese Americans, Bendetsen first noted. The second obstacle posed a more difficult problem. Bendetsen admitted that "no one has justified fully the sheer military necessity for such action." Since Bendetsen urged, in the "final recommendation" he prepared for DeWitt just ten days later, that mass evacuation was required "by reason of military necessity," this concession in his February 4 memorandum stands out as a striking disparity.[3]

As a lawyer, Bendetsen knew that the War Department lacked legal authority to order the evacuation of Japanese American citizens from the entire West Coast area. His February 4 memorandum to Gullion accordingly proposed "the designation of islands surrounding all vital installations in the Western Defense Command" and the exclusion of aliens from such areas. The next step would be "a temporary internment of all alien enemies involved in such move with an open offer to the families of such alien enemies to accompany them in internment facilities to be provided by the Army." Bendetsen finally proposed "resettlement on a merit basis . . . of all those persons who could show that they had a bona fide place to go" outside of the restricted zones. This evacuation program, he estimated, "will involve approximately 30,000 people."[4]

Bendetsen recommended to Gullion "that the necessary action be taken to seek Presidential approval" of this program. "Drafts of the necessary Executive Order . . . are in the course of preparation and will be submitted should this recommendation be approved," he informed Gullion, who promptly set to work on the bureaucratic lobbying campaign that Bendetsen's proposal required for ultimate War Department and White House approval.[5]

The path between Gullion's office in the War Department and the Oval Office in which Roosevelt sat was strewn with potential roadblocks.

Gullion first encountered skepticism from within the military establishment. While Bendetsen's memorandum was being typed on February 4, Gullion received a call from General Mark Clark, an aide to General George C. Marshall, the Army Chief of Staff. "I've got to go to represent General Marshall up at a Congressional meeting this morning," Clark told Gullion. Following the lead of their House colleagues, West Coast members of the Senate had met on February 2 and set up two *ad hoc* committees: Republican Senator Rufus C. Holman of Oregon chaired the Committee on Defense, and Senator Monrad Wallgren, a Washington state Republican, chaired the Committee on Alien Nationality and Sabotage. Holman's committee had scheduled a Capitol Hill meeting on February 4 with a battery of high-ranking military officers that included Clark and Admiral Harold Stark, the Chief of Naval Operations.[6]

"I anticipate some questions on this enemy alien thing," Clark said in his call to Gullion. "I wondered if you could bring me up to date just generally on that situation," he asked. Gullion responded with a denunciation of Attorney General Biddle for having said, at the February 1 meeting in Biddle's office, that "the Department of Justice would be through if we interfered with citizens" on the West Coast. Biddle had agreed to the exclusion of aliens from "restricted areas," Gullion reported. "Now that doesn't touch citizens at all," he told Clark, "and personally I don't think that is going to cure the situation much." Clark then asked about the attitudes of Stimson and McCloy, and Gullion confessed that "they are just afraid DeWitt hasn't enough grounds to justify any movements" of citizens. Since "the War Department's position is of course what Stimson's and McCloy's position is," Gullion acknowledged, the two civilian officials stood in the path of mass evacuation. Bendetsen then joined the conversation and attempted to persuade General Clark that the evacuation of citizens was essential. Merely "moving the alien enemies and then saying to the others, we ask that you move voluntarily," Bendetsen told Clark, was unlikely to "get rid of all undesirables" from the West Coast. Clark listened politely to Bendetsen's argument but remained noncommittal. "I've gotten the big picture and I appreciate the time you have given me," he said in ending the call.[7]

Clark went to the meeting with Senator Holman's committee unconvinced by the arguments of Gullion and Bendetsen. According to Holman's notes, Clark assured the committee that "the defense facilities already provided in the Pacific coastal area are considerable and are being steadily augmented and approved." Admiral Stark expressed equal confidence that the West Coast was well defended. Well aware by now that the Japanese offensive in the Pacific was directed toward the Philippines and territory to its south, Stark discounted the threat of a mainland invasion. It would be "impossible for the enemy to engage in a sustained attack on the Pacific Coast at the present time," Stark flatly stated. Sporadic air raids on the West Coast were possible and "perhaps even probable," he conceded, but would have "little, if any, bearing on the course of the war." Between them, Clark and Stark offered no support to the mass evacuation campaign.[8]

Bendetsen entered the fray himself on February 5 at a meeting of the committee chaired by Senator Wallgren. As he had twice in the past week, Bendetsen encountered opposition from Justice Department lawyers. Wallgren had also invited Attorney General Biddle, who brought Edward Ennis and James Rowe with him. Buttressed by an FBI report submitted to Biddle on February 1 by J. Edgar Hoover, discounting the Army's claims of sabotage and espionage on the part of Japanese Americans, Ennis argued to the senators that the "ABC" roundup had effectively neutralized any threat to military security. As Rowe had hinted to Bendetsen a week earlier, however, Biddle opened a crack in the door that led to evacuation and internment. "The military must determine the risk and undertake the responsibility for evacuation of citizens of Japanese descent," Biddle told the committee.[9]

Bendetsen quickly shouldered his way through this inviting opening. Attributing to DeWitt a position the general had explicitly denied in his talk with McCloy the day before, Bendetsen assured Wallgren and his colleagues that the "military judgment on the West Coast on whether or not this evacuation should take place was positively in the affirmative." Bendetsen backed off, however, from advocacy of immediate evacuation, citing the logistical problems that housing the Japanese Americans and the disruption of food production presented. But with the statement that "it is better to do it now than to wait until an attack occurs," Bendetsen left no doubt that he would welcome the addition of political pressure to the Army's evacuation campaign. Unlike their House counterparts, the members of both informal Senate committees limited their function to fact-finding and held off any formal proposals to President Roosevelt. Bendetsen thus returned to Gullion's office empty-handed, although encouraged by Biddle's concession of power to the War Department.[10]

Gullion's chagrin at the lack of enthusiasm shown by the Senate committees was compounded by a report from his West Coast deputy, Colonel Archer Lerch, who reported "a decided weakening" of DeWitt's support for evacuation. Fearful that the War Department leaders might shut the door that Biddle left ajar, Gullion sent an apocalyptic letter to McCloy on February 6, "If our production for war is seriously delayed by sabotage in the West Coastal states, we very possibly shall lose the war. . . . From reliable reports from military and other sources, the danger of Japanese inspired sabotage is great." Gullion dismissed in his letter the doubts expressed by Bendetsen and Stimson: "No half-way measures based upon considerations of economic disturbance, humanitarianism, or fear of retaliation will suffice. Such measures will be 'too little or too late.' " McCloy's response to these fervent but unsupported warnings neatly fit into Gullion's lobbying campaign. On February 7, six days before the deadline for DeWitt's report, McCloy dispatched Bendetsen to the West Coast "to confer with General DeWitt in connection with mass evacuation of all Japanese" and to assist in drafting the recommendations McCloy had requested.[11]

With Bendetsen en route to the Presidio, Attorney General Biddle reconsidered his previous neutrality and took his concerns for the first time to the White House. Over lunch with Roosevelt on February 7, Biddle "discussed at length with him the Japanese situation" and told the President "that we believed mass evacuation at this time inadvisable, that the F.B.I. was not staffed to perform it," and that the Army had offered "no reasons for mass evacuation" as a military measure. Biddle subtly underscored the political hazards of giving in to West Coast pressures. "I emphasized the danger of the hysteria, which we were beginning to control, moving east and affecting the Italian and German population in Boston and New York," he told Roosevelt. Significantly, Roosevelt concluded the discussion by saying that he was "fully aware of the dreadful risk of Fifth Column retaliation in case of a raid." This cryptic comment seemed to signal that Roosevelt accepted without question the sabotage and espionage charges made earlier by Navy Secretary Knox and repeated in the Roberts Commission report on Pearl Harbor.[12]

Biddle hardly could have interpreted Roosevelt's comment as an encouragement to stand in the Army's way. Pressed hard by Rowe and Ennis to remain firm but unwilling to challenge Stimson and Roosevelt, the Attorney General took the unusual step of soliciting an opinion on the constitutionality of evacuation from a trio of lawyers outside the Justice Department. The senior member of this legal troika, Benjamin V. Cohen, had long been a valued New Deal legislative draftsman and a quiet but influential White House advisor. Overshadowed by his ebullient partner, Tommy Corcoran, as one of the "Gold Dust twins," Cohen had worked since 1934 from an obscure post as general counsel to the National Power Policy Committee in the Interior Department. In preparing a memorandum for Biddle, Cohen enlisted two lawyers in the Office of Emergency Management, Oscar Cox and Joseph Rauh.[13]

A few days after Biddle's meeting with Roosevelt, the Attorney General received from the three lawyers a seven-page memorandum headed "The Japanese Situation On the West Coast." Cohen's careful hand was evident in the balancing of conflicting constitutional claims: "It is well to remember that unnecessarily harsh action is not justified just because the legal power to take such action exists. On the other hand it is important to bear in mind that action truly necessary for the national safety cannot lightly be assumed to be barred [by] constitutional constructions which would make our Constitution in time of war either unworkable or non-existent." What tipped the balance against the Japanese Americans, in the view of Biddle's unofficial advisors, were the Army's "military necessity" claims and their assumptions about Orientals. "In time of national peril any reasonable doubt" about the loyalty of Japanese Americans "must be resolved in favor of action to preserve the national safety," Cohen and his colleagues wrote.[14]

"Persons of Japanese descent constitute the smallest definable class upon which those with the military responsibility for defense would reasonably determine to impose restrictions," the three lawyers stated. "Since the Occidental eye cannot readily distinguish one Japanese resident from another, effective surveillance of the movements of particular Japanese residents suspected of disloyalty is extremely difficult if not practically impossible." As Caucasians, Biddle's legal advisors considered it unnecessary "to bar the millions of persons of German or Italian stock from either seacoast area," since "the normal Caucasian countenances of such persons enable the average American to recognize particular individuals by distinguishing minor facial characteristics."[15]

The amateur anthropologists shrank, however, from an endorsement of forced internment for the indistinguishable Japanese Americans. "Special reservations should be provided at safe distances from the West Coast," they recommended, "where American citizens of Japanese extraction could go voluntarily and where they could be usefully employed and live under special restrictions." This plan, essentially identical to Governor Olson's proposal for agricultural labor camps, did not specify what "special restrictions" might be imposed on Japanese Americans or how to deal with those who refused the relocation offer.[16]

None of the lawyers who signed the memorandum favored a forced evacuation. Joseph Rauh later stated that "the memorandum was the final effort by the three of us to prevent evacuation and internment." He also recalled Cohen's later reaction to the evacuation ordered by General DeWitt. "When I went into his office one night a couple of months later," Rauh said, "he showed me a newspaper picture of a little Japanese American boy leaning out of the evacuation train window and waving an American flag. Mr. Cohen had tears in his eyes."[17]

Rowe and Ennis, whose constitutional objections to evacuation the outside lawyers had dismissed, reacted to the memorandum with scorn. Rowe attributed authorship of the opinion to Oscar Cox. "He was a great dabbler," Rowe later said, "and he may have gotten Rauh and Cohen to do it. It was none of his damn business." Ennis was equally annoyed at this incursion on his turf. "You know, Francis," Ennis replied when Biddle showed him the memorandum, "constitutional law on a high level is politics. You, as the Attorney General, should oppose this." Despite the remonstrances of his staff, however, Biddle read the memorandum as a constitutional endorsement of evacuation and subsequently rejected arguments from Rowe and Ennis on this score.[18]

Although the Cohen-Cox-Rauh memorandum salved Biddle's constitutional doubts, the Attorney General remained skeptical about the necessity for evacuation. He objected strenuously to DeWitt's interim proposal to designate all the major West Coast cities as "restricted zones" from which Japanese Americans would be excluded. The responsibility for approving this proposal rested with Biddle as a result of the agreement reached by Rowe and DeWitt at the Presidio conference in early January. Biddle withheld his approval and explained his reasons in a February 9 letter to Stimson. "No reasons were given for this mass evacuation," Biddle complained, and added that the Justice Department "is not physically equipped to carry out any mass evacuation." He concluded with an implied request to be relieved of responsibility: "The proclamations directing the Department of Justice to apprehend and, where necessary, evacuate alien enemies do not, of course, include American citizens of Japanese race. Should they have to be evacuated, I believe that this would have to be done on the military necessity in the particular area. Such action, therefore, should in my opinion be taken by the War Department and not by the Department of Justice."[19]

Stimson had little desire to catch the hot potato that Biddle tossed to him and had more doubts about the legality of evacuation than his cabinet colleague. The day he received Biddle's letter, Stimson met with McCloy to examine the maps of the areas that DeWitt wanted evacuated. "The second generation Japanese can only be evacuated as part of a total evacuation, giving access to the areas only by permits," Stimson noted is his diary, "or by frankly trying to put them out on the ground that their racial characteristics are such that we cannot understand or trust even the citizen Japanese. This latter is the fact but I am afraid it will make a tremendous hole in our constitutional system." The lack of a persuasive and documented "military necessity" argument for evacuation obviously concerned the Secretary of War.[20]

With the deadline for DeWitt's "final recommendation" imminent, doubts in Washington were matched by determination on the West Coast. On February 10, the day that Stimson and McCloy met to discuss the proposal to evacuate the West Coast cities, Bendetsen presented to DeWitt a memorandum headed "Evacuation of Japanese from the Pacific Coast." Outlining for DeWitt the options available to him, Bendetsen began with an assumption of "the necessity for placing all Japanese in the same category" regardless of citizenship status. "It is generally accepted that the danger from the American citizen of Japanese ancestry," Bendetsen wrote, was greater than that posed by aliens. The only question was that of the scope of evacuation. "The Secretary of War is inclined to the view that such an evacuation should be from selected areas surrounding vital installations," Bendetsen reported. "It is highly improbable that the Secretary will accept the recommendation of the entire evacuation from the coastal strip."[21]

Bendetsen made clear in the February 10 memorandum his personal commitment to mass evacuation from the entire West Coast. Significantly, he balanced the claims of "military necessity" against competing economic considerations. The "military necessity" argument that Japanese Americans posed dangers of espionage and sabotage, Bendetsen wrote, "can be developed only after a consideration of all the factors such as loss of vegetable production which may be consequent, and other economic dislocations which may ensue" from evacuation. "If from the military standpoint, the military disadvantage involved in the loss of vegetable production which may result from a complete evacuation from the Pacific Coast is sufficiently great to outweigh the military advantage, then and only then should the recommendation for evacuation be confined to selected areas." General Gullion was prepared to implement a mass evacuation, Bendetsen assured DeWitt, and was "compiling a list of available shelter in the zone of the interior" for housing Japanese Americans.[22]

Back in Washington, Secretary of War Stimson continued to wrestle with the evacuation question. General Gullion, after a telephone discussion with Bendetsen, relayed to McCloy on February 10 the news that General DeWitt was disposed toward the mass evacuation that Bendetsen had proposed. McCloy then set up the second meeting in two days with Stimson to review the situation. On the morning of February 11, Stimson sat down with McCloy and General Mark Clark to discuss DeWitt's proposal. "This is a very stiff proposition," Stimson noted in his diary. "General DeWitt is asking for some very drastic steps, to wit: the moving and relocation of some 120,000 people including citizens of Japanese descent." Stimson questioned the ability of the Army to manage the logistical problems that mass evacuation would entail. "This is one of those jobs that is so big that, if we resolved on it, it just wouldn't be done," he wrote. Stimson's immediate decision reflected his earlier order to DeWitt: "I directed [DeWitt] to pick out and begin with the most vital places of army and navy protection and take them on in that order as quickly as possible."[23]

The realization that DeWitt's "final recommendation" would undoubtedly propose evacuation of all Japanese Americans from the West Coast left Stimson uneasy. He had full authority to reject such a plan and to insist that DeWitt limit evacuation to the "restricted zones" already approved. Stimson's doubts about the constitutionality of a plan based on the "racial characteristics" of one minority group, and the Army's inability to back up its "military necessity" claim with hard evidence, disposed him against mass evacuation. The growing pressures from Gullion and from West Coast politicians, however, showed no signs of yielding to tolerance and a cool-headed assessment of the waning threat of Japanese invasion or attack. Confronted with the necessity of choice, Stimson decided at his meeting with McCloy on February 11 to put the question before the President.

Stimson called the White House that morning and asked for an appointment with Roosevelt. Having been told that he was too busy to schedule a personal meeting, Stimson called the President in the early afternoon. Their conversation was guided by a memorandum, hastily drafted with the aid of McCloy and General Clark, that posed one basic question: "Is the President willing to authorize us to move Japanese citizens as well as aliens from restricted areas?" If Roosevelt's answer was yes, Stimson proposed to ask the President to choose between three alternatives: first, evacuation of Japanese Americans from the entire West Coast; second, evacuation from the major coastal cities; and third, evacuation only from areas that surrounded "airplane plants and critical installations."[24]

Asking Roosevelt to settle the question effectively sealed the fate of the Japanese Americans, aliens and citizens alike. Temperament and timing both militated against the display of any special sensitivity on Roosevelt's part to the problems of a small, isolated, and feared minority. Despite his basically humanitarian impulses, FDR was no Eleanor Roosevelt; his record as President reflected a limited awareness of and attention to the plight of racial minorities. Black Americans in particular suffered from Roosevelt's political dependence on the Southern racists who dominated Congress. And the fact that word of the surprisingly easy Japanese conquest of Singapore, the last Allied stronghold on the mainland of Southeast Asia, reached the White House on February 10 could hardly have disposed the President to sympathize with Japanese Americans.

Stimson did not get a direct answer to any of his questions. With the President so preoccupied that he could not fit into his schedule a meeting with the Secretary of War, it is not surprising that Stimson found the problem thrown back at him with only the vaguest instructions. According to Stimson's diary, Roosevelt told him "to go ahead on the line that I myself thought the best." Stimson did, however, gather from this conversation that Roosevelt had a "very vigorous" desire for a prompt resolution of the problem and would be willing to back up any action taken by Stimson with an executive order conferring on the War Department the authority that Biddle was eager to relinquish.[25]

The significance of this conversation lay in its transmittal to the West Coast. Although Roosevelt had expressed no opinion on mass evacuation, McCloy quickly put through a call to Bendetsen at the Presidio reporting that "we have carte blanche to do what we want to as far as the President's concerned." If the Army's proposal "involves citizens, we will take care of them too," McCloy added in his account of Roosevelt's quick comments. "He states there will probably be some repercussions, but it has got to be dictated by military necessity, but as he puts it, 'Be as reasonable as you can.' " Bendetsen made clear his interpretation of the word "reasonable" within a hour, in calling Gullion in Washington to relay the news of Roosevelt's "carte blanche along the Coast" and his willingness to sign an executive order that would authorize the evacuation of Japanese American citizens. In this talk, Bendetsen suggested an evacuation program that would involve roughly 101,000 people, three times the number he floated with DeWitt the day before. Mass evacuation was now on the move.[26]

With the assurance of White House approval, Bendetsen quickly prepared for DeWitt's signature the "final recommendation" requested by McCloy. The resulting memorandum, completed on February 13, called for mass evacuation on the basis of an argument that lumped together racial stereotypes about Japanese Americans and conspiratorial fears of an imminent outbreak of sabotage. "In the war in which we are now engaged racial affinities are not severed by migration," Bendetsen wrote. "The Japanese race is an enemy race and while many second and third generation Japanese born on United States soil, possessed of United

States citizenship, have become 'Americanized', the racial strains are undiluted." In Bendetsen's opinion, there was no doubt "that along the vital Pacific Coast over 112,000 potential enemies, of Japanese extraction, are at large today."[27]

The danger posed by the Japanese Americans, Bendetsen claimed, lay in their concentration in areas that surrounded West Coast defense installations and other vulnerable facilities. From the Boeing Aircraft factory in Washington state to the defense plants in Los Angeles, large numbers of "Japanese live and operate markets and truck farms adjacent to or near these installations," Bendetsen noted. He cited as "possible and probable enemy activities" the prospect of Japanese naval attacks on shipping and the shelling of coastal cities, air raids on the area that extended two hundred miles inland, and the sabotage of defense plants and power, communications, and transportation facilities. Bendetsen flatly predicted that Japanese Americans would assist such enemy action: "Hostile Naval and air raids will be assisted by enemy agents signaling from the coastline and the vicinity thereof; and by supplying and otherwise assisting enemy vessels and by sabotage." The lack of evidence that any sabotage had occurred in the two months since Pearl Harbor did not deter Bendetsen. "The very fact that no sabotage has taken place to date is a disturbing and confirming indication that such action will be taken," he baldly claimed.[28]

The "final recommendation" followed the course suggested by Bendetsen in his February 4 memorandum to General Gullion. Over DeWitt's signature, Bendetsen proposed that "the Secretary of War procure from the President direction and authority to designate military areas in the combat zone of the Western Theater of Operations, (if necessary to include the entire combat zone), from which, in his discretion, he may exclude all Japanese, all alien enemies, and all other persons suspected . . . of being actual or potential saboteurs, espionage agents, or fifth columnists." Bendetsen contemplated that DeWitt would proclaim a "designated evacuation day" on which all Japanese American aliens would be rounded up and placed under military guard in "internment facilities" prepared by the Army. Those with American citizenship would be "offered an opportunity to accept voluntary internment, under guard," along with the aliens. Bendetsen recommended that citizens "who decline to accept voluntary internment, be excluded from all military areas, and left to their own resources," with an offer of federal and state assistance for "resettlement outside of such military areas. . . ."[29]

At the time he prepared the "final recommendation" for DeWitt, Bendetsen did not envision long-term internment of all Japanese Americans. He suggested that "mass internment be considered as largely a temporary expedient pending selective resettlement'' of those in the citizen group unwilling to remain under guard with their alien families and friends. The initial goal of evacuation was simply to clear the West Coast of the Japanese Americans, with their later disposition left open. One aspect of the plan, however, represented a clear break with the earlier Army proposals approved by Attorney General Biddle: implementation of the ''final recommendation'' required that citizens be uprooted from their homes and removed from the West Coast under legal compulsion.[30]

With a copy of this document in his briefcase, Bendetsen took a plane back to Washington. As the primary author of the ''final recommendation,'' Bendetsen was in the best position to present its details and conclusions to his War Department superiors. Anticipating Bendetsen's arrival in Washington on February 17, Gullion arranged in advance a meeting with Stimson and McCloy for that afternoon. Jumping the gun, Gullion also secured McCloy's approval of a telegram to West Coast military commanders alerting them to ''orders for very large evacuation of enemy aliens of all nationalities predominantly Japanese'' within the next forty-eight hours.[31]

Even before Bendetsen's return, Stimson came under additional pressure on both sides of the evacuation question. DeWitt himself prompted one source of this pressure. On the morning of February 12, the Washington *Post* (and hundreds of other newspapers across the country) carried a column by Walter Lippmann, the nation's most prestigious political commentator. Under the headline ''The Fifth Column On the Coast,'' Lippmann deplored ''the unwillingness of Washington to adopt a policy of mass evacuation and mass internment of all those who are technically enemy aliens.'' Without revealing that he had met with DeWitt at the Presidio, Lippmann repeated almost verbatim the evacuation argument made in the ''final recommendation'' by Bendetsen. ''It is a fact that communication takes place between the enemy at sea and enemy agents on land,'' Lippmann asserted. He dismissed the ''fact that since the outbreak of the Japanese war there has been no important sabotage on the Pacific Coast'' with the conspiracy theory advanced by Bendetsen: ''It is a sign that the blow is well-organized and that it is held back until it can be struck with maximum effect.''[32]

At DeWitt's urging, Lippmann placed his prestige behind the evacuation of citizens as well as aliens. ''Nobody's constitutional rights include the right to reside and do business on a battlefield,'' he wrote. ''And nobody ought to be on a battlefield who has no good reason for being there. There is plenty of room elsewhere for him to exercise his rights.'' Three days after this column appeared, the *Post* carried an echo from Westbrook Pegler, a columnist as noted for vitriol as Lippmann was for soothing punditry. "Do you get what he says?" Pegler asked his readers in quoting from Lippmann's column. "This is a high-grade fellow with a heavy sense of responsibility." Pegler added his own prescription: "The Japanese in California should be under armed guard to the last man and woman right now—and to hell with habeas corpus until the danger is over."[33]

Justice Department lawyers, in a final effort to block the evacuation that seemed imminent, responded with a last-ditch appeal to Roosevelt that matched Pegler in rhetorical pyrotechnics. James Rowe drafted for Biddle a letter to Roosevelt sent to the White House on February 17, the day of the final showdown over evacuation. Lippmann and Pegler, Biddle's letter noted, "recently have taken up the evacuation cry on the ground that attack on the West Coast and widespread sabotage is imminent." In terms that reflected Rowe's hostility to evacuation, the Justice Department letter blasted the columnists as "Armchair Strategists and Junior G-Men" for predicting Japanese attack and West Coast sabotage "when the military authorities and the F.B.I. have indicated that this is not the fact. It comes close to shouting FIRE! in the theater; and if race riots occur, these writers will bear a heavy responsibility."[34]

Both the desperate tone of this letter and its date show that Rowe had only the faintest hope that he could block the evacuation decision. While Rowe was drafting this letter in his Justice Department office, in fact, Secretary of War Stimson was conducting a dress rehearsal in his office of the final confrontation between the advocates of evacuation and their opponents. Within hours of Bendetsen's arrival in Washington from the West Coast, Stimson presided over a War Department strategy session in preparation for a meeting on the evening of February 17 with Justice Department officials. Backed by McCloy, who by this time had abandoned the last of his legal doubts, Stimson overrode Mark Clark's protest that mass evacuation would tie up troops needed for combat. Clark had sent Stimson a memorandum on February 12 stating that "I cannot agree with the wisdom of such as mass exodus" as that proposed by DeWitt. "We must not permit our entire offensive effort to be sabotaged in an effort to protect all establishments from ground sabotage," Clark added in his futile dissent. Stimson recorded the outcome of the afternoon meeting in his diary: "A proposed order for the President was outlined and General Gullion undertook to have it drafted tonight. War Department orders will fill in the application of this Presidential order. These were outlined and Gullion is also to draft them."[35]

The final act in the evacuation drama was played out in the incongruous setting of Biddle's living room. Six men, all of them lawyers, gathered to decide the fate of the Japanese Americans. McCloy, Gullion, and Bendetsen represented the War Department and faced Biddle, Rowe, and Ennis of the Justice Department. Rowe later described the scene: "The argument waxed hot and though the Attorney General did not back Ennis and me with much force, he at least did not argue against us, and we had refused every Army demand successfully." Unaware of the meeting earlier that day in Stimson's office, Rowe and Ennis confronted their adversaries with the constitutional arguments against evacuation. They were astounded, Rowe recalled, when Gullion suddenly "reached into his pocket and pulled out a slip of paper which contained an order giving the War Department power to remove citizens and aliens."[36]

Gullion's sudden move, the product of a hasty drafting session with Bendetsen, evoked from Rowe a characteristic reaction of those surprised by an unpleasant ultimatum. "I laughed at him. The old buzzard got mad. I told him he was crazy, and I immediately perceived that he was pulling the old Army tactic of attacking when on the defense. But in another minute I thought that I was crazy." Rowe did not know that the Attorney General had called the President before the meeting and had agreed to support Stimson on the evacuation issue. Biddle's assistants were astounded a second time to learn that "the Attorney General immediately wanted to get to work polishing up the order." The Justice Department lawyers were devastated. "Ennis almost wept," Rowe later said. "I was so mad that I could not speak at all myself and the meeting soon broke up."[37]

The evacuation battle was over. With Biddle's surrender in hand, McCloy and Gullion exacted from the Attorney General his participation in "polishing up the order" for final approval by Stimson and delivery to the White House for Roosevelt's signature. After some last-minute tinkering, the two delegations met in Stimson's office the following morning, February 18. Stimson recorded in his diary that he considered the draft "a good piece of work" about which he "made a few suggestions and then approved it." According to Rowe, Edward Ennis resisted to the bitter end, "arguing with Stimson and Biddle and getting absolutely nowhere because his own boss was against him." During their cab ride back to the Justice Department, in fact, Rowe later said he "had to convince Ennis that it was not important enough to make him quit his job."[38]

The document that emerged from this final conference—on which were based the military curfew and exclusion orders issued by General DeWitt in the next few months—rested for legal authority on the President's dual constitutional roles as chief executive and commander-in-chief of the armed forces. Premised on the unassailable claim that "successful prosecution of the war requires every possible protection against espionage and against sabotage" of defense installations, it went on to authorize the Secretary of War and his military subordinates to "prescribe military areas . . . from which any or all persons may be excluded" and to place further restrictions on "the right of any person to enter, remain in, or leave" such areas at the discretion of military authorities. The order additionally authorized the War Department to provide "transportation, food, shelter, and other accommodations" to those affected by evacuation orders, and directed all federal agencies to assist in this task. On its face, the order made no reference to Japanese Americans or any other group. It simply offered General DeWitt a blank check to be filled in as he thought best, a fact that later sparked a heated legal debate.[39]

Following approval by Stimson and Biddle, the task of guiding the order to Roosevelt's desk fell to James Rowe, experienced in White House procedures. Rowe took it to Harold Smith, the longtime budget director whose duties included clearance of all presidential orders. "He didn't know what the hell it was all about," Rowe recalled. "I said, 'it's all been cleared, Harold. Justice has cleared it, and the Secretary of War has cleared it. Now take it to the President.' And he did, rather reluctantly." On February 19, 1942, Roosevelt signed the order without ceremony. When the President lifted his pen from Executive Order 9066, the rights of more than a hundred thousand Japanese Americans to remain on the West Coast became subject to military edict.[40]

The surrender of Attorney General Biddle to the War Department ended the month-long evacuation battle. Congressional pressure, the impact of the Roberts Commission report on Pearl Harbor, the press campaign against the Japanese Americans, Biddle's deference to Stimson, the Cohen-Cox-Rauh memorandum, Roosevelt's insensitivity to the plight of racial minorities—all these factors combined to make the objections voiced by Rowe and Ennis a futile gesture. In the end, however, the balance between constitutional concerns and military demands was tipped by the dogged efforts of two Army officers, General Allen Gullion and Colonel Karl Bendetsen. Gullion's single-minded commitment to the evacuation crusade and Bendetsen's supporting role in shaping the "final recommendation" signed by General DeWitt added to these factors the indispensable elements of bureaucratic determination and strategic deployment. At a time of military and civilian fear of a "second Pearl Harbor" and against a backdrop of Japanese advances in the Pacific, constitutional qualms fell before the military offensive that demanded evacuation as a mainland line of defense.

With the signing of Executive Order 9066, the evacuation debate shifted to a pair of unresolved questions: implementation and enforcement. Two memoranda prepared on February 20 initiated this subsequent round of debate. Secretary of War Stimson sent to General DeWitt, along with a letter signed by John J. McCloy, a formal designation of DeWitt "as the Military Commander to carry out the duties and responsibilities" for evacuation on the West Coast. Stimson made clear his opposition to an immediate evacuation: "Removal of individuals from areas in which they are domiciled should be accomplished gradually so as to avoid, so far as it is consistent with national safety . . . unnecessary hardship and dislocation of business and industry." DeWitt was instructed to submit "detailed plans for evacuation" to the War Department and to encourage the "voluntary exodus of individuals" before he announced any evacuation orders. To assist DeWitt in this task, McCloy dispatched the well-traveled Bendetsen to the Presidio on February 23 with instructions to draw up a detailed evacuation plan.[41]

Enforcement of DeWitt's forthcoming evacuation orders required the participation of both Congress and the Justice Department. Attorney General Biddle, either unaware of or hoping to evade the legal issues that enforcement of Executive Order 9066 raised, tried to wash his hands of the problem in a February 20 memorandum to Roosevelt. The powers granted to the War Department, Biddle wrote, could be "exercised with respect to Japanese, irrespective of their citizenship." Biddle assured the President that in acting under his "general war powers," evacuation could proceed "without further legislation."[42]

Biddle's motives in suggesting that enforcement legislation was not necessary are puzzling. Without some form of penalty as a prod to compliance, the Army's evacuation orders would be left in a legal limbo. The Attorney General certainly knew that only Congress had the power to back the Executive Order with criminal sanctions. Perhaps he wished to place on the War Department the onus of asking Congress to establish the penalties that would face any Japanese Americans who refused to obey evacuation orders. In any event, War Department lawyers soon moved to fill the enforcement vacuum that Biddle had created. Karl Bendetsen in particular reacted with contempt to what he considered Justice Department weakness on the enforcement issue. According to Bernard Gufler, a State Department official with whom he talked on

February 21, Bendetsen "displayed great bitterness toward the Department of Justice" for "passing the buck" to the War Department. The Justice Department "should remember that the Army's job is to kill Japanese not to save Japanese," Bendetsen told Gufler.[43]

Bendetsen took on himself the task of drafting an enforcement statute. On February 22, three days after Roosevelt signed Executive Order 9066, he submitted to McCloy the draft of a bill that would make it a felony for any person to "enter, leave, or remain in any military area or military zone" in which residence by aliens or citizens was proscribed by military order. In proposing penalties of a $5,000 fine and a maximum prison term of five years, Bendetsen passed on to McCloy the recommendation of General DeWitt that prison terms be mandatory. Pointing out that "you have greater liberty to enforce a felony than you have to enforce a misdemeanor," Bendetsen quoted DeWitt as saying that "you can shoot a man to enforce a felony."[44]

McCloy shrank from this trigger-happy proposal, and changed the statute that Bendetsen had drafted to reduce the crime of violating a military order to a misdemeanor with a maximum penalty of imprisonment for a year. With the scope of evacuation still undecided, McCloy held off congressional consideration of the enforcement bill while Bendetsen returned to the West Coast to assist DeWitt in preparing the detailed plans that Stimson had requested. On March 2, after hurried preparation by DeWitt's staff of maps of the coastal area and examination of Census Bureau figures that showed the location of the Japanese American population, DeWitt issued the first in what would become a deluge of military orders prepared under Bendetsen's supervision.

Public Proclamation No. 1 did not order the evacuation of any of the Japanese American residents of the West Coast. This document paved the way for subsequent evacuation by designating as Military Area No. 1 a broad coastal strip that included the western halves of California, Oregon, and Washington, and the southern half of Arizona. The remaining area of these four states was designated as Military Area No. 2, in which were included ninety-eight "military zones" that surrounded defense plants, military bases, and public utilities. DeWitt's initial proclamation warned "such persons or classes of persons" he would later specify that they "will by subsequent proclamation be excluded" from these areas. DeWitt made his intentions clear in an accompanying press release: "Eventually orders will be issued requiring all Japanese including those who are American-born to vacate all of Military Area No. 1." Following Bendetsen's earlier suggestion, DeWitt held out the carrot of "voluntary resettlement" as an alternative to compulsory internment. "Japanese and other aliens who move into the interior out of this area," the Army's press release hinted, "in all probability will not again be disturbed."[45]

DeWitt's plea for a voluntary exodus from the West Coast rested in part on the lack of facilities to house those willing to accept internment rather than migration to inland areas. Several factors help to explain why few of the Japanese Americans who lived within Military Area No. 1 took the hint and moved out: Many of them assumed that the calls for forcible evacuation would soon blow over; the freezing of their bank accounts left most without the financial resources that resettlement would require; few of them had relatives or friends outside the West Coast willing to help in finding jobs and housing; and newspapers reported a growing hostility in these interior areas toward Japanese Americans. DeWitt later cited "the fact that the interior states would not accept an uncontrolled Japanese migration" as the reason for the adoption of mass internment. In the end, fewer than ten thousand of the Japanese Americans affected by DeWitt's initial proclamation moved from Military Area No. 1, and most members of this group resettled within Military Area No. 2 and were later caught in the internment trap that snapped shut in both areas.[46]

A second reason that DeWitt did not demand an immediate evacuation reflected the lack of criminal penalties for noncompliance. A week after Public Proclamation No. 1 put Japanese Americans on notice that they would eventually be forced into exile, either voluntary or compulsory, McCloy moved to secure from Congress the criminal penalties necessary to punish violations of subsequent military orders. On March 9, McCloy sent his version of the bill drafted by Bendetsen to the chairmen of the House and Senate armed services committees. In accompanying letters, Secretary of War Stimson urged prompt action with the argument that "General DeWitt indicated that he was prepared to enforce certain restrictions at once . . . but did not desire to proceed until enforcement machinery had been set up."[47]

The congressional railroad ran on schedule for the War Department. Senator Robert R. Reynolds, the North Carolina Democrat who chaired the Senate Military Affairs Committee, presided at a one-hour hearing on March 13 at which the only witness was Colonel B. M. Bryan, who represented Provost Marshal General Gullion. Whether intentionally or not, Bryan led the committee to believe that the bill applied only to aliens, stating that "the bill we are considering is authority over these aliens that we are proposing to move." Bryan's only reference to "American citizens of Japanese extraction" suggested that they were "dual citizens" under Japanese law and thus fell in the alien category. Assured by Bryan that McCloy considered the bill "sufficient to cover the violation of curfew and similar restrictions," the Senate committee approved it unanimously.[48]

House consideration of the bill took even less time. In a half-hour appearance before the House Committee on Military Affairs on March 17, Colonel Bryan repeated his instructions from McCloy that the War Department "was particularly anxious that the committee be informed that General DeWitt proposed to impose curfew restrictions and wants the legislation broad enough to cover the violation of any such restrictions." Like its Senate counterpart, the House committee sent the bill to the floor with its unanimous endorsement.[49]

In the subsequent race for enactment, the House barely nosed out the Senate. Only five members spoke during a ten-minute session on the morning of March 19 at which the House passed the bill by voice vote. Representative Andrew J. May, the Kentucky Democrat who chaired the House Committee on Military Affairs, easily handled the questions put to him during this perfunctory debate. Representative E. A. Michener, a Michigan Republican, suggested that legislation "interfering with . . . the rights of citizens" should be "thoroughly understood and debated before their passage." His committee "gave very careful consideration" to the bill, May assured his colleague. Reflecting the assurances given to his committee by Colonel Bryan, May answered another question as to whether "citizens of this country" might be prosecuted for unknowingly entering proscribed military areas with this flat statement: "Citizens of this country will never be questioned about them, as a matter of fact."[50]

Senate passage of the bill that afternoon took longer only because Senator Reynolds indulged his long-winded proclivities with a speech that denounced Japanese Americans as "fifth-column" agents and saboteurs. Reynolds repeated without question the charges made by Navy Secretary Frank Knox and by the Roberts Commission report that espionage and sabotage on the part of Japanese Americans had aided the attack on Pearl Harbor. Without attribution, Reynolds claimed that in Hawaii "canefields were cut in the form of arrows pointing to military objectives," that Japanese American saboteurs had "wrecked cars and otherwise obstructed traffic" in the vicinity of Pearl Harbor, and that "Japanese pilots shot down above Pearl Harbor were found to be wearing Honolulu high school insignia and United States college rings." Reynolds relied for these allegations on sensational but erroneous press accounts, perhaps unaware that an exhaustive FBI investigation had concluded that each of these charges had been totally unfounded.[51]

Like his House counterpart, Reynolds led those few members of the Senate who were present on the floor to believe that the War Department bill "deals primarily with the activities of aliens and alien enemies" and was designed to "provide protection for American citizens" against the sabotage of war industries. Aside from Reynolds, only two senators participated in the debate, and one simply sought assurance that the military orders would be published in order to provide notice to those affected by them. Senator Robert Taft, the conservative Ohio Republican, raised the sole objection to the bill. "I think this is probably the 'sloppiest' criminal law I have ever read or seen anywhere," Taft said. "It does not say who shall prescribe the restrictions. It does not say how anyone shall know that the restrictions are applicable to that particular zone. It does not appear that there is any authority given to anyone to prescribe any restriction." Taft professed his resignation that the bill "would be enforced in wartime" but put his constitutional qualms on the record: "I have no doubt that in peacetime no man could ever be convicted under it, because the court would find that it was so indefinite and so uncertain that it could not be enforced under the Constitution."[52]

Taft knew he was wasting his breath, and Reynolds did not bother to answer the objections of his principled colleague. Thirty seconds after Taft sat down, the bill passed by voice vote without any recorded dissent. Two days later, President Roosevelt put his signature on the enforcement bill as Public Law 503. Having authorized the War Department a month earlier to issue military orders that "excluded" Japanese Americans from their West Coast homes, Roosevelt now placed on the Justice Department, as the federal government's law-enforcement agency, responsibility for enforcing these orders through criminal prosecution. Given the background of discord between the two departments, this division of authority for implementation and enforcement of the evacuation program created the prospect of additional conflict.[53]

At the time Roosevelt signed Public Law 503 on March 21, the initiative rested with General DeWitt, who had begun to assemble the machinery of mass evacuation well before the congressional action on enforcement. The issuance of Public Proclamation No. 1 on March 2 provided the blueprint for the evacuation apparatus. During a West Coast trip early in March, John J. McCloy suggested that DeWitt set up two new branches of the Western Defense Command, the Civil Affairs Division and the Wartime Civil Control Administration, to organize and carry out the evacuation program. As the architect of DeWitt's "final recommendation," Karl Bendetsen became the logical candidate for the post of evacuation engineer. In appointing Bendetsen on March 12 to head these agencies, DeWitt instructed him to "provide for the evacuation of all persons of Japanese ancestry" from the West Coast "with a minimum of economic and social dislocation" and with a directive to encourage "voluntary migration" as an alternative to forcible internment.[54]

Although the Army gave lip service to the "voluntary migration" concept for another month, Bendetsen's first moves in his new positions made clear his intention to locate and construct the facilities for mass internment from the outset. DeWitt began early in March with instructions to establish two giant "Reception Centers" through which Japanese Americans would be funneled out of Military Area No. 1. Located in barren areas of the Owens Valley in eastern California and the Colorado River Indian Reservation in Arizona, these two camps—Manzanar and Parker—were designed "to provide temporary housing for those who were either unable to undertake their own evacuation, or who declined to leave until forced to." Each camp was constructed to house some ten thousand evacuees. On March 16, Bendetsen dispatched two site-selection teams of federal officials with instructions to locate facilities capable of housing 100,000 people. Within four days these teams reported back to Bendetsen, listing between them seventeen potential sites. After a quick review, DeWitt ordered the Army's Engineer Corps on March 20 to proceed with construction of fifteen "Assembly Centers" for the housing of evacuees, and gave the Corps a deadline of April 21 for making the camps ready.[55]

Shortly after evacuation became official policy through the issuance of Executive Order 9066, War Department officials urged that they be provided with assistance from civilian agencies. The sheer magnitude of the evacuation program, they argued, required the establishment of a new agency to cope with its logistical problems. Secretary of War Stimson took the lead in this effort at a February 27 cabinet meeting. President Roosevelt, in Stimson's account of this meeting, "showed that thus far he has given very little attention to the principle task of the transportation and resettlement of the evacuees." Stimson was dismayed by the "general confusion" displayed by his cabinet colleagues and their reluctance to undertake the task. Attorney General Biddle broke the impasse by suggesting that "a single head should be chosen to handle the resettlement," and Roosevelt immediately decided to establish a new agency with a civilian head.[56]

In signing Executive Order 9102 on March 18, Roosevelt created the War Relocation Authority as the agency jointly responsible with the War Department for the evacuation program. Since it was understood that evacuated Japanese Americans would be relocated to rural areas, and since about half of them operated various kinds of farms, the obvious choice of a director for the new agency was an official from the Agriculture Department. After a brief search and considerable prodding, Milton S. Eisenhower agreed to assume the position as WRA director. A forty-two-year-old native of Abilene, Kansas, Eisenhower had been trained as a journalist and had served in the Agriculture Department since 1926, most recently as director of information. He had no military background, but the fact that his brother Dwight was a fast-rising and popular Army general helped to convince War Department officials that Eisenhower could work well with DeWitt and Bendetsen in carrying out the evacuation program.[57]

Within days of Eisenhower's appointment, he discovered that Bendetsen had no enthusiasm for the "voluntary migration" plan that WRA officials had assumed would form the basis for evacuation. Eisenhower had been in office less than a week when Bendetsen unilaterally announced the first moves toward mass internment with two orders issued on March 24. Over DeWitt's signature, Bendetsen announced Public Proclamation No. 3, which directed all alien enemies and Japanese American citizens to remain in their homes between the hours of 8:00 P.M. to 6:00 A.M. This curfew order additionally restricted the movements of Japanese Americans to a five-mile radius from their homes and places of work during non-curfew hours. On the same day, DeWitt issued the first of an eventual 108 "exclusion orders" directing Japanese Americans to leave their homes and report to assembly centers.[58]

Civilian Exclusion Order No. 1, issued after intense pressure from the Navy, required the fifty-four Japanese American families who lived on Bainbridge Island in Puget Sound (close by the Bremerton Naval Base) to report by March 30 to the Puyallup Assembly Center, located on the state fairgrounds south of Seattle. The printed "Instructions to All Japanese Living on Bainbridge Island" tacked onto walls by Army troops informed the evacuees that they could take with them only bedding, toilet articles, clothing, eating utensils, and other possessions "which can be carried by the family or the individual" in their arms.[59]

DeWitt and Bendetsen quickly followed this initial exclusion order with a directive that virtually ended voluntary migration. Public Proclamation No. 4, issued on March 27 and effective two days later, forbid those Japanese Americans who lived within the boundaries of Military Area No. 1—some 90 percent of those who resided on the West Coast—from leaving the area without permission. Fewer than ten thousand had moved before this date, most of them into Military Area No. 2 in eastern California. Trapped by the "freeze order," those who remained could only wait helplessly for the inevitable exclusion order that would force them into an assembly center. All three of these directives—the curfew, exclusion, and freeze orders—were backed by Public Law 503 and the threat of criminal prosecution.[60]

Although the freeze order was issued by General DeWitt, it had been recommended by Milton Eisenhower as a means of halting the unsupervised flow of Japanese Americans into the interior states. Eisenhower apparently feared that those who moved on their own would encounter violence and hostility, and intended to prevent further migration until the Army completed the construction of assembly centers and the WRA had a chance to develop a resettlement program in cooperation with state officials. To implement this plan, on April 2 Eisenhower announced a five-point program based on a combination of public and private employment for the Japanese Americans. The WRA program envisioned that most of those willing to relocate would be settled in rural areas and would work on sugar-beet farms.[61]

Eisenhower's plan went up in smoke within days, as it hit a fire storm of resistance from officials of the western states. Any hope that the detention of Japanese Americans in assembly centers would be a brief stop on the road to resettlement ended at a meeting called by Bendetsen in Salt Lake City on April 7. The governors, attorneys general, and other officials of all the western states but California attended this crucial conference, which Eisenhower opened with a heart-felt endorsement of the loyalty of Japanese Americans and a plea for state cooperation with his resettlement plan. After outlining its provisions, the WRA director asked the assembled governors for "any frank comments they might have regarding the proposed program." The barrage of racism that greeted his appeal for tolerance and assistance literally stunned Eisenhower.[62]

What the governors wanted from the Army and the WRA, they made clear to Bendetsen and Eisenhower, was a concentration camp regime for the Japanese Americans. Governor Herbert Maw of Utah led off with a demand that evacuees "be put into camps" and compelled to work as agricultural laborers. Complaining that the federal government was "much too concerned about the constitutional rights of Japanese-American citizens," Maw suggested that "the constitution could be changed" to provide for internment. Governor Chase Clark of Idaho then demanded that Japanese Americans "should be put in camps under guard" and returned to California after the war. The next speaker, Governor Nels Smith of Wyoming, stated that his constituents "have a dislike of any Orientals, and simply will not stand for being California's dumping ground." He had recently met with a delegation of Japanese

Americans who proposed that they buy land on which to resettle evacuees, Smith added. "There would be Japs hanging from every pine tree" in Wyoming if such a plan were attempted, Smith reported telling the delegation.[63]

According to Bendetsen's notes of this conference, the "greatest extreme in sentiment" was voiced by Bert Miller, attorney general of Idaho. Miller advocated that "all Japanese be put in concentration camps, for the remainder of the war, and that no attempt should be made to provide work for them." Miller made no effort to hide his racism: "We want to keep this a white man's country," he stated bluntly. Perhaps unwilling to associate themselves with this blatant expression of prejudice, officials from Arizona and Washington offered their general support for Eisenhower's program. Bendetsen, however, sensed the depth of hostility toward Japanese Americans and assured the state officials that evacuees would remain "under military police guard" in assembly centers and relocation camps.[64]

With his resettlement plan reduced to ashes by the flames of racism, Eisenhower ended the meeting with a brief statement of surrender. Acknowledging "the consensus of the meeting that the plan for reception centers was acceptable to the states as long as the evacuees remained within the reception centers under guard," he agreed with Bendetsen that Japanese Americans would remain in relocation centers under Army control. On his return to Washington from this meeting, Eisenhower informed Secretary of War Stimson that the WRA would accept military control of the relocation camps then being constructed under Bendetsen's suprevision.[65]

Resettlement gave way to internment, and to the harsh regime of barbed wire and armed guards, with Stimson's report to President Roosevelt on April 15 that the "acute hostility of the people" in the western states required that Japanese Americans "must remain under the general control of the Army" for an indefinite period. "As time goes on, the prejudice will gradually die down," Stimson added hopefully. On his part, Eisenhower was unwilling to wait for a gradual end to the racism that had unnerved him at the Salt Lake City conference. Increasingly unable to sleep at night, Eisenhower finally submitted his resignation as WRA director on June 13. In an anguished letter to Roosevelt, he predicted that "a genuinely satisfactory relocation of the evacuees into American life" could only come at the end of the war, "when the prevailing attitudes of increasing bitterness have been replaced by tolerance and understanding."[66]

Eisenhower's departure from the WRA to a less stressful job as deputy director of the Office of War Information forced on Roosevelt a quick search for a successor. Turning once again to the Agriculture Department, the President drafted Dillon S. Myer, a fifty-year-old agronomist who had worked in the Soil Conservation Service since 1935. Although Myer had no record of military service, he brought to his position a reputation as an experienced administrator and an even-tempered and patient negotiator who had worked for close to three decades in both state and federal government. During his four years as WRA director, Myer survived the storms of hostility toward the Japanese Americans and criticism of the WRA with an equanimity that Eisenhower had found impossible.[67]

Even before the shift of command in the WRA, the Army Engineers who worked under Bendetsen's supervision had been busy whitewashing the horse stalls of the assembly centers and hammering together the barracks of the ten relocation centers located from California to Arkansas. While this construction proceeded, Army troops posted on walls and windows in Japanese American communities the 107 exclusion orders that followed the initial evacuation of Bainbridge Island. Skipping up and down the West Coast, these orders successively ordered Japanese Americans, in groups of roughly one thousand at a time, to dispose of their property within a week and to report to assembly centers. As quickly as barracks opened in the relocation centers, convoys of trains, trucks, and buses transported the evacuees and those possessions they could stuff into suitcases to their dusty, barren destinations.

The last of the exclusion orders that required the departure of Japanese Americans who resided within Military Area No. 1 took effect on June 7, 1942, six months after Pearl Harbor and two days after the stunning American naval victory in the battle of Midway Island. By that date, some 97,000 residents of the coastal strip that lay within this area had been herded behind barbed wire. Over the next five months, the five thousand who lived within Military Area No. 2 and the ten thousand who had earlier sought refuge in this inland area were forced by military order to join their fellow evacuees in relocation camps. With statistical exactitude, Bendetsen's staff later calculated that precisely 111,999 "persons of Japanese ancestry" had been placed under guard in relocation centers by October 30, 1942.[68]

Camp conditions were spartan in the extreme. Laid out in blocks of jerry-built tar paper and pine barracks, the camps had been designed with no thought for family life and privacy. The walls that separated the barracks compartments were made of thin plywood and failed to contain the noise of children and family squabbles. The barracks set aside for single people had no walls, and bunks were divided only with sheets and blankets. Older residents were particularly disturbed by the communal bathing and toilet facilities, things entirely foreign to their culture. Forced to live in a virtual fishbowl, camp residents often lost their traditional reserve and good manners. "As time went on," Yoshiko Uchida later wrote of her experiences in the Central Utah Relocation Center, "the residents of Topaz began to release their frustrations on others in acts that seemed foreign to the Japanese nature. Internal squabbling spread like a disease."[69]

Physical hardships added to the discomfort of crowded living conditions. In later recollections, camp residents almost unanimously cited their revulsion at the dust and sand that blew across the camps and seeped through the cracks of their barracks. Lillian Tateishi had a vivid memory of the camp in Manzanar, California: "Those awful sandstorms. The sand would blow right through the floor. Several times every night we had to get up and wash off. Sometimes we had to wear goggles. Some people just cried."[70]

John McCloy, whose directive to General DeWitt in February 1942 set the internment program in motion, claimed forty years later that "the whole operation was as benignly conducted as wartime conditions permitted." McCloy also asserted that conditions in the camps he visited during the war were "very good and very pleasant." Those who lived in the camps, and who spent an average of 900 days behind barbed wire, did not share McCloy's sentiments. The fact remains that Japanese Americans reported for internment virtually without exception. Had the internment been ordered forty years later, there is no question that more than a handful of Japanese Americans would have refused to obey General DeWitt's military orders. Looking back, however, it is hard to fault those who chose to endure two or three years of barbed wire and sandstorms as an alternative to prison.[71]

4

"Am I an American or Not?"

JAPANESE AMERICANS first confronted the regime of military edict on March 28, 1942, the effective date of the curfew imposed on them by General DeWitt. Congressional enactment of Public Law 503 exposed curfew violators to criminal prosecution and possible imprisonment. The fusillade of exclusion orders that began on March 29 also relied on this statute as an enforcement threat. Faced with DeWitt's orders, Japanese Americans were forced to make unenviable choices. Compliance led inexorably to internment, first in "assembly centers" and then in "relocation centers" ringed with armed guards. Resistance seemingly led with equal inevitability to internment, either as a form of sentencing or after release from jail, with the lasting stigma of a criminal record branded on violators. With a choice of barbed wire or prison bars, it is hardly surprising that all but a handful of this frightened and almost friendless minority complied with the curfew and dutifully reported for internment.

Were there in fact no alternatives to eventual internment? Among the 120,000 Japanese Americans subject to DeWitt's orders, a mere dozen looked to the legal system for redress. This chapter will introduce the four young Nisei whose challenges to the various military orders ultimately reached the Supreme Court, and whose cases are followed to their conclusion in this book. Only the barest sketch of these challengers emerges from the Court's opinions in their cases, a consequence of the depersonalization of the legal process. One purpose of this chapter is to remove what John Noonan has called the "masks of the law" and to reveal the faces of this disparate quartet. Looking behind these masks we see four unique individuals, each with a separate path to resistance and a different reason for challenging DeWitt's orders. What we view is less a group portrait than a collection of snapshots in the Supreme Court's album of opinions.[1]

Literally the only link that joined the four challengers was the shared circumstance of their Japanese ancestry. The related factors of race and national origin provide a second focus for this chapter and raise a preliminary question of great significance: Why did such a tiny number of the Japanese Americans choose resistance over compliance? Including those whose cases failed to reach the Supreme Court, only one in ten thousand of this group directly challenged the curfew and exclusion orders. The inevitable prospect of detention helps to explain why the vast majority chose to remain with family and friends over the alternative of separation and stigma. The total sweep of the military dragnet also differentiates the response of this minority to legal apartheid from that shown in later decades by others, in particular the black Americans who courted arrest and went to jail by the thousands as a form of protest.

The wartime setting of this forced choice, however, does not fully answer the question posed above. Certainly more than a dozen of the Japanese Americans considered resistance at some point before reporting for internment. We cannot even guess at their number and can only speculate about why they rejected the course of resistance. Some clues come from conversations with those who did resist about their friends and families. The prospect of indefinite separation from their families and close-knit communities quite naturally deterred most of those who thought of resistance. Lack of familiarity with the legal system and the scarcity of lawyers who served the Japanese American population were additional deterrents.

Several factors made it easier for the civil rights activists of the 1950s and 1960s to engage in mass resistance to the laws and customs of a segregated society. It took courage, of course, to face police dogs and cattle prods as well as vigilante terror in the Deep South. But the jailed demonstrators could return to their families and hometowns after serving sentences that were generally short, however unpleasant the conditions to which they had been subjected. Black lawyers were in short supply, but a dedicated contingent of white lawyers—most of them volunteers—filled the breach. On the local and state levels, judges and jurors alike were almost uniformly hostile to civil rights defendants. Federal judges, however, particularly those who sat on the Fifth Circuit Court of Appeals whose jurisdiction spanned the Deep South states, took their constitutional oaths seriously and reversed most of the convictions brought before them. The Supreme Court as well, having placed its legal and moral authority behind the assault on official racism in its

1954 decision in *Brown* v. *Board of Education*, subsequently struck down most of the civil rights convictions presented to the justices.

The factor that most sharply divided the Japanese Americans from black Americans, however, was that of leadership. This crucial factor rests in turn on the links between the younger and older leaders in the respective minority groups. Most of those who assumed the leadership of civil rights movements in the 1950s and 1960s were young and lacked experience when they were thrust into the front ranks by their impatient followers. When he was abruptly drafted to lead the Montgomery, Alabama, bus boycott in 1955, Martin Luther King, Jr., was barely twenty-six years old. King had behind him, however, not only a determined mass movement but the support of an older and more experienced generation of black leaders which included his father. Although few of the black ministers and lawyers who advised the young militants were themselves willing to face beatings and arrest, their advice on strategy and tactics proved invaluable to the emerging leaders of groups such as the Southern Christian Leadership Conference and the Student Non-Violent Coordinating Committee.[2]

In contrast to the generational ties that fostered a continuity of leadership within black communities and organizations, Japanese Americans confronted evacuation and internment almost bereft of direction. Before the outbreak of war, the older Issei had provided their communities with a measure of cohesion and continuity. However, the sudden roundup of the Issei on the Justice Department's "ABC" list had deprived Japanese Americans of leadership at a critical time. Cut off from their elders, the younger Nisei faced the evacuation campaign and DeWitt's orders as political neophytes. Only one organization, the Japanese American Citizens League (JACL), tied together the Nisei scattered along the West Coast when the war began. Pulled together from a loose confederation of Nisei clubs in 1930, the JACL was an avowedly assimilationist and patriotic organization. The JACL's limitation of membership to American citizens, and its requirement that members sign a profession of loyalty to the United States, drove an additional wedge between the younger and older generations of Japanese Americans.

Two young men, Saburo Kido and Mike Masaoka, shared the responsibility for shaping the JACL's response to evacuation pressures and DeWitt's orders in the months after Pearl Harbor. Opposites in appearance and temperament, Kido and Masaoka complemented each other in approach and training. Slight in build and serious in demeanor, Kido was a Hawaii native who came to the mainland in 1921 at the age of nineteen. After his graduation from the Hastings Law School in 1926, he established a marginal practice near the "Japantown" area of San

Francisco. His interests soon shifted, however, to the efforts to build an effective Nisei organization. Kido attended the JACL's founding convention and in 1934 he assumed the office of executive secretary. After six years in this post, during which he traveled endless miles in organizing several dozen JACL chapters along the coast and across the country, Kido was elected in 1940 to a two-year term as president. While he served in this largely honorific position, Kido retained his role as executive secretary until August 1941.[3]

Drained of energy by incessant travel and concerned about the inroads on his law practice and income, Kido turned his organizational post over to Mike Masaoka just four months before Pearl Harbor. Only twenty-five at the time, Masaoka was a burly, cocky, and articulate counterpart to his predecessor. Born in Fresno, California, in 1915 and the fourth of eight children, Masaoka moved with his family three years later to Salt Lake City, where his father operated a small fish market before his death in 1924. Masaoka majored in speech at the University of Utah, where his skills as a debater and his friendship with Elbert Thomas, then a political science professor and later a Democratic Senator, helped him land a job as instructor of speech. A relative newcomer to the JACL, Masaoka made up in drive and brashness what he lacked in experience and contacts with the Japanese American communities along the West Coast.[4]

Under the leadership of Kido and Masaoka, the JACL and its 15,000 members confronted an agonizing dilemma in responding to the political campaign for evacuation that followed Pearl Harbor. In a sense, the JACL's eagerness to demonstrate the patriotism and loyalty of Japanese Americans made it difficult if not impossible to launch an effective effort to block evacuation. Professions of willingness to share the "sacrifices" of other Americans placed the JACL in a bind: resistance to evacuation on a mass basis would fuel the charges that Japanese Americans constituted a "disloyal" group and represented a fifth-column threat. As an alternative to resistance, and with the hope of heading off more Draconian measures than voluntary migration, the JACL adopted a strategy of collaboration with government intelligence officers. This policy, established well before the outbreak of war, in effect made the JACL a hostage of the intelligence agencies through the enlistment of its leaders as informers on Japanese Americans suspected of "disloyalty." Collaboration in adding names to the "ABC" lists fatally compromised the JACL. Regardless of motive, such informing put the JACL at the mercy of officials who could easily discredit the organization and its leaders. Resistance thus became futile once evacuation and internment became a reality.

The links that bound the JACL to the government's intelligence network were forged in March 1941 at a dinner hosted in Los Angeles by Lieutenant Commander Kenneth D. Ringle, the Naval Intelligence officer delegated to investigate the loyalty of Japanese Americans. JACL vice-president Ken Matsumoto headed the Nisei delegation and Ringle brought with him an Army Intelligence officer and Los Angeles County Sheriff Eugene Biscailuz. Ringle's later reports vouching for the loyalty of the vast majority of Japanese Americans relied in large part on the eager cooperation of JACL leaders in fingering both Issei and Nisei considered sympathetic to Japan. In the months before Pearl Harbor, those who informed perhaps had no idea that the names they provided the FBI and military intelligence would be added to the "ABC" lists as candidates for arrest and internment. But with the "ABC" roundup underway JACL leaders appealed to fellow Japanese Americans to become volunteer informers. Togo Tanaka, editor of the Los Angeles newspaper *Rafu Shimpo*, spoke to Nisei in a radio broadcast on the evening of Pearl Harbor: "As Americans we now function as counterespionage. Any act or word prejudicial to the United States committed by any Japanese must be warned and reported to the F.B.I., Naval Intelligence, Sheriff's Office, and the local police."[5]

JACL leaders in Los Angeles moved from informal to formal collaboration with the FBI soon after Pearl Harbor. Under the leadership of Fred Tayama the Southern California chapters formed an Anti-Axis Committee on December 7, 1941. Two weeks later a Committee delegation met with Richard B. Hood, who directed the FBI's Los Angeles office. Hood chided his visitors for their earlier reluctance to "furnish any specific derogatory information concerning any organization or individual." Unlike Ringle, FBI agents had viewed the names and information provided before Pearl Harbor as little more than gossip. Members of the Anti-Axis Committee admitted the truth of this reproof but assured Hood that "they were now willing to inform on all individuals who appeared to be a danger to this country."[6]

Over the next month the Committee met frequently with Hood and his staff and furnished the FBI with detailed information. In a report to J. Edgar Hoover on January 20, 1942, Hood listed a dozen "ardent supporters of the Japanese cause" fingered by the Anti-Axis Committee. This list included Kaoru Akashi, director of the Japanese Chamber of Commerce and Industry in Los Angeles. "A presidential warrant has been requested for the apprehension of this individual," Hood noted to Hoover. Committee members also turned over to Hood the membership list of the Kibei Division of the Los Angeles JACL, and the names of "pro-Japanese" Kibei Leaders. Other JACL leaders joined the Anti-

Axis Committee in providing information to the FBI, and "expressed no objection" to Hood's intention to share this material with other intelligence agencies. Fred Tayama paid a heavy price for his role as a government informer after his internment in the Manzanar Relocation Center. On the night of December 5, 1942, reported Bill Hosakawa, "six masked men invaded Tayama's barracks room and beat him so badly that he had to be hospitalized." The ringleader of the Kibei suspects was arrested, and during a rock-throwing melee that followed a Kibei protest demonstration military police shot and killed one young man and wounded several others.[7]

The consequences of collaboration, and of the bind in which protestations of loyalty put the JACL, became evident during the period that preceded DeWitt's internment orders. In his March 1942 testimony before the congressional Tolan Committee, Mike Masaoka struggled to reconcile the conflicting pressures of patriotism and revulsion from the racist motives behind internment. "With any policy of evacuation definitely arising from reasons of military necessity and national safety," he assured the congressmen, "we are in complete agreement. . . . But, if, on the other hand, such evacuation is primarily a measure whose surface urgency cloaks the desires of political or other pressure groups who want us to leave merely from motives of self-interest, we feel that we have every right to protest and to demand equitable judgment on our merits as American citizens."[8]

Masaoka's acceptance of the "military necessity" rationale for evacuation left him defenseless as the Tolan Committee members pressed him for an endorsement of evacuation. Congressman John Sparkman of Alabama demanded to know whether "in the event the evacuation is deemed necessary by those having charge of the defenses, as loyal Americans you are willing to prove your loyalty by cooperating?" His professions of JACL loyalty left Masaoka trapped. "Oh yes, definitely," he answered Sparkman, adding that "if the military say 'Move out,' we will be glad to move, because we recognize that even behind evacuation there is not just national security but also a thought as to our own welfare and security because we may be subject to mob violence and otherwise if we are permitted to remain."[9]

Saburo Kido found himself in the same trap when he addressed an emergency meeting of the JACL National Council in Salt Lake City on March 8. "Today we are preparing to go into temporary exile from the homes in which we were born and raised," Kido said in his emotional leave-taking. As a lawyer, he denounced evacuation as a violation of "fundamental rights" guaranteed by the Constitution to all citizens and predicted that "the day is coming when those who are responsible for these outrageous violations of our rights will be ashamed of their conduct." Kido nonetheless expressed "implicit confidence" in President Roosevelt and the gratitude of the JACL "for the fairness with which our case has been handled. We are glad that we can become the wards of our government for the duration of war."[10]

Dictated by the policy of collaboration adopted before Pearl Harbor and carried out through informing on fellow Japanese Americans after war began, the JACL's acceptance of evacuation and internment precluded any possible strategy of mass resistance. Another consequence of this policy, however reluctantly adopted, was that the JACL found itself unable to offer support to those who resisted DeWitt's orders as individuals.

One minute after midnight on March 28, 1942, Japanese Americans on the West Coast became subject to criminal penalties for violation of the curfew imposed by General DeWitt on "all persons of Japanese ancestry." Later that same day, five hours after the 6:00 P.M. curfew took effect, Minoru Yasui walked into a Portland, Oregon, police station and demanded to be arrested for curfew violation. This early act of resistance gave Yasui the distinction of raising the first legal test of DeWitt's orders among the entire Japanese American population.

Min Yasui was in many ways an unlikely candidate for this distinction. The path that ended in the Portland drunk tank on that Saturday night had passed through training as an Army officer, education as a lawyer, employment in a Japanese consular office, and active involvement in the Japanese American Citizens League. In pursuing his challenge to the Supreme Court, Yasui nonetheless accepted the basic legality of Roosevelt's executive order and the congressional statute that enforced it. Even the ordeal of nine months in solitary confinement failed to shake Yasui's avowed "110 percent" patriotism and his commitment to military obedience. In a final touch of irony, Yasui volunteered his services to the Justice Department in a futile campaign to dissuade imprisoned Japanese American draft resisters from continuing their own objections to military orders.[11]

Perhaps the best explanation of the apparent contradiction between Yasui's roles as a law violator and law enforcer lies in his thoroughly American upbringing. Born in October 1916 to parents who settled in Hood River, Oregon, after their migration from Japan, Min Yasui was the second of seven children. Masuo Yasui raised his children as Methodists, sent them to public schools, and put them all through college.

The owner of an apple orchard in the fertile Hood River Valley, Masuo was accepted into the largely white leadership of the apple growers' association, while at the same time he acted as a leader of the six hundred Japanese Americans in the valley. As a youngster, Min attended the local Japanese language school for three summers but never achieved fluency in his ancestral tongue. Even then he was a stubborn student. "I was kicked out before I finished Book Three for being a bad boy," he later said with obvious relish.[12]

Min entered the University of Oregon at Eugene in 1933. After two years of compulsory military training, he volunteered for the final two years of reserve officer training. Forced to wait until his twenty-first birthday, he received a commission as Second Lieutenant in the Army Infantry Reserve on December 8, 1937. Min then entered the University's law school, where he studied under Wayne Morse, then the nation's youngest law school dean and later a maverick member of the United States Senate. Morse later provided an incisive but telling thumbnail sketch of Yasui's personality in a 1943 letter to ACLU director Roger Baldwin. He held a "relatively high opinion" of Yasui as a law student, Morse wrote, "but on many occasions I detected a streak of blind stubbornness in him. . . ." This was a characterization that others who knew and dealt with Yasui would not dispute.[13]

Yasui found it difficult to land a job as a lawyer following his law school graduation in 1939. His father, who had been decorated by the Japanese government for his leadership of the Hood River Valley community, was a close friend of the Japanese consul in Portland. Through the intercession of his father, Yasui secured a position as an attaché of the Japanese consulate in Chicago. As an American citizen, he duly registered with the State Department as a foreign agent. Yasui later described his work as primarily clerical. Under questioning at his trial, however, he admitted having defended Japanese policies in Asia in speeches before Rotary clubs and similar civic groups in the Chicago area. But he insisted that in none of these speeches had he acted in opposition to the interests of the United States.[14]

The day after Pearl Harbor, while the Japanese consul hurriedly burned cables and codes, Yasui received a telegram from his father: "NOW THAT THIS COUNTRY IS AT WAR AND NEEDS YOU, AND SINCE YOU ARE TRAINED AS AN OFFICER, I AS YOUR FATHER URGE YOU TO ENLIST IMMEDIATELY." Responding to this parental request on his own patriotic impulse, Yasui immediately resigned his consular post. When he went to the Chicago railroad station to buy a ticket to Portland, he discovered that the agents would not sell a ticket to anyone of Oriental appearance. Only after he received a telegram from the Army a few days later, ordering him to report for duty at the Vancouver barracks across the Columbia River from Portland, was Yasui able to buy a train ticket. When he reported to Fort Vancouver, Yasui was placed in command of a platoon of soldiers. The next day, before his formal induction, Army officers told Yasui he was unacceptable for service and ordered him off the base. This rebuff on purely racial grounds triggered Yasui's streak of stubborn determination. He returned eight times to Fort Vancouver with an offer to serve and was turned away each time.[15]

A few days after he rejoined his family, Yasui's father was arrested for membership in the "ABC" list and sent to the Justice Department internment camp in Missoula, Montana. At loose ends after his father's arrest and his rejection by the Army, Yasui moved from Hood River to Portland and hung out his shingle as a lawyer. In the atmosphere of uncertainty and fear within the Japanese American community, few clients appeared in his office. Concerned about his father's fate, Yasui traveled to Missoula early in February and requested permission from Justice Department lawyers to represent his father and several of the Issei internees from Portland at their loyalty hearings. But these hearings were conducted without legal counsel and Yasui's request was rejected.

"So far as my father was concerned," Yasui later said, "I was permitted to sit in as a member of the family. The hearing was a complete farce. They produced some very childish maps of the Panama Canal, and they were saying, 'Do you know what these are?' Dad looked at them and said, 'They look like maps of the Panama Canal.' 'How did you get them?' he was asked. 'Well, my kids drew these maps in school.' The maps were illustrations of how the locks worked. The questioner said, 'This shows how you were really trying to disguise a nefarious plot to blow up the Panama Canal.' Dad said, 'Of course not; I had no such intention.' 'Well, prove that you didn't have such an intention,' they replied." Classified as "disloyal" on the basis of this colloquy and his prewar decoration by the Japanese government, Masuo Yasui remained in detention until 1945.[16]

Within two weeks of Min Yasui's return from Missoula to Portland, President Roosevelt signed Executive Order 9066. "A lot of rumors were flying back and forth," Yasui recalled. "They were going to take the Nisei, they were not going to take the Nisei, they were going to draft everybody and put them into labor camps, all sorts of rumors." Hoping even before the curfew and the first evacuation orders to find a legal means to block internment, Yasui consulted Earl F. Bernard, a leading Portland lawyer and at the time only a casual acquaintance. Bernard, a stolid and conservative lawyer in his early fifties, advised

Yasui that no challenge was possible until the government issued orders backed with criminal penalties. However, Bernard did offer to represent Yasui in the event that he later raised a challenge to the anticipated orders.

Never shy about approaching those in authority, Yasui also met with Frank Nash, a Portland FBI agent and a former law school classmate, and with Carl Donaugh, the local United States attorney. "We had a lot of discussions about what the government could do and could not do," Yasui recalled of these meetings. "I said to Donaugh, 'Look, if this ever happens, we're going to start a test case on this.' " Meeting with fellow Nisei in Portland, Yasui plotted a strategy to find an appealing test case. "We were going to find a Nisei who'd served in the Army and had an honorable discharge, with two or three little kids, and we thought that would be an ideal test case. So I talked to my friends, but none of them were willing to undertake it. I had a few bucks, so I said, 'Look, I'll put up the money, you guys be the guinea pigs.' But it's hard to tear yourself away from your family and friends. I knew I was not an ideal test case, but somebody had to do it."[17]

Yasui did not wait for the evacuation orders he felt were inevitable. Reports in the newspapers that a curfew would begin on the night of March 28 impelled him to resist. The decision to violate the curfew and to court arrest stemmed in part from Yasui's resentment at the internment of his father and his rejection by the Army. He had no quarrel with the curfew order on general principle, or with one applied only to aliens. "But Military Order Number 3 applied to all persons of Japanese ancestry. I said, 'There the general is wrong, because it makes distinctions between citizens on the basis of ancestry.' That order infringed on my rights as a citizen."[18]

Yasui wasted no time in offering himself as a test case. "I had my secretary call the police on March 28th, a Saturday night, and report that 'There's a Japanese walking up and down the streets, arrest him.' I had an awful time getting arrested. I was getting tired walking around town, and I approached a policeman at eleven o'clock at night. I pulled out this order that said all persons of Japanese ancestry must be in their place of abode, and I pulled out my birth certificate and said, 'Look, I'm a person of Japanese ancestry, arrest me.' And the policeman said, 'Run along home, you'll get in trouble.' I actually had to go down to the Second Avenue police station and talk to the sergeant and tell him what I wanted to do. He said, 'Sure, we'll oblige you.' So they threw me in the drunk tank until Monday morning, which was a miserable experience." In his eagerness to institute a test case, Yasui forgot that persons arrested on Friday and Saturday nights languished in the lockup over the weekend. He remained behind bars until Earl Bernard arrived on Monday morning to bail him out.[19]

Coming only two weeks after Mike Masaoka had assured the Tolan Committee that Japanese Americans were willing to "move out" on military order, Yasui's curfew challenge precipitated a crisis in the JACL. His role as an apostate JACL member provoked a personal attack from Masaoka, who described Yasui as "a Nisei attorney who worked for the Japanese consulate in Chicago as late as last December 7th, registered with the State Department as a propaganda agent for a foreign government" in a bulletin circulated to all JACL chapters on April 7, 1942. Masaoka was obviously concerned that Yasui's example might prompt other Nisei to resist the Army's curfew and evacuation orders. What especially bothered Masaoka was that Yasui "is 'out' on bail and is said to be circulating a petition among the Portland chapter members demanding that the National Organization take some definite stand on the question of the constitutional rights of the Japanese Americans."[20]

Even one resister undercut the JACL's promise to the Tolan Committee that Japanese Americans would "move out" at DeWitt's direction. Masaoka feared that Yasui's act might arouse further public hostility toward the group. "Even though we should win a legal victory," he wrote in the April 7 bulletin, "if the people at large resent our activities, it might have been better either to have lost or not to have attempted a contest." The JACL did "not intend to create any unnecessary excuses for denouncing the Japanese as disloyal and dangerous." Masaoka quoted from a letter to the San Francisco *Examiner* as evidence of such an excuse: "Yasui took advantage of an American education, going to the University of Oregon, and paid that back with the usual treachery." He made it clear that Yasui could not expect support or sympathy from the JACL: "National Headquarters is unalterably opposed to test cases to determine the constitutionality of military regulations at this time."[21]

Masaoka's effort to brand him as a renegade left Yasui unshaken. His response in this internal polemical battle took the form of a point-by-point rebuttal circulated on April 17. Yasui took care not to criticize those who felt compelled to obey DeWitt's orders: "The National JACL is to be commended on its attitude of cooperation with the Federal Government." He also disclaimed "advocacy of mass violation of the orders of the duly constituted Army authorities." Yasui emphasized that he had acted as an individual in bringing a test case and had no desire to create dissension within the JACL.[22]

Masaoka had urged that Japanese Americans accept a "temporary suspending or sacrificing some of our privileges and rights of citizenship'' as a show of wartime patriotism. This appeal failed to budge Yasui, who refused to surrender his constitutional rights as a test of patriotism. If the JACL ''is willing to sacrifice certain fundamental rights of citizenship,'' he asked Masaoka, ''then is it not possibly contributing to the destruction of the very fundamental basis of this country?'' Yasui rested his challenge to the curfew on the narrowest legal point raised by DeWitt's order: its failure to distinguish between aliens and citizens. When Army orders ''place us in a less favorable position than that of an *enemy* alien,'' he wrote, ''surely there is basis for protest and redress of our grievances.'' The fact that Yasui had worked for the Japanese government obviously colored the vehemence of his response to Masaoka. It seems clear in retrospect that Yasui's legal test of the curfew stemmed in large part from an eagerness to reclaim and defend his status as an American citizen.[23]

Notwithstanding his constitutional challenge to the curfew, Yasui never abandoned his professions of patriotism or his attachment to the Army. Yasui also retained his allegiance to the JACL. Following his conviction for curfew violation and his subsequent internment in the Minadoka, Idaho relocation center, Yasui patched up his quarrel with Mike Masaoka and the JACL. Along with Masaoka's older brother, Joe Grant, Yasui undertook in 1944 to quash the resistance movement to the government's belated decision to require Selective Service registration of the young Japanese Americans in internment camps.

''As part of the JACL program,'' Yasui recalled, ''Joe Grant Masaoka and I decided that it would be wise to talk to these young people in jails and try to have them change their minds.'' Yasui referred to the fifty-nine young men—all from the Heart Mountain Relocation Center in Wyoming—who had been jailed after refusing to submit to preinduction draft physicals. Years later, Yasui vividly recounted his visit to the Cheyenne County Jail. ''I remember talking to this 18-year-old kid and saying, 'Look, it doesn't do any good to refuse, it will just hurt you and your record.' This kid was gripping the bars with tears streaming down his face. He said, 'The government seized my father, they put him in camps. Who's going to take care of my mother and sister if I go off to war?' I told him, 'You fulfill your obligations, otherwise you're not being true as an American citizen.' He said, 'If the government recognizes my rights, I'll recognize my obligations.' And we said, 'You don't bargain with the government. You fulfill your obligations, and *then* you demand your rights.' ''[24]

Yasui's recollection of these interviews matches the report he and Joe Grant Masaoka submitted to the Denver JACL office in May 1944. Yasui wrote that the two men hoped to ''straighten out these boys'' and persuade them to abandon their resistance. He added that ''such repudiation would have some effect upon the draft-resistance group in the centers, and tend to dissuade others from following the same course of action." Yasui and Masaoka subsequently gave copies of their report to the FBI agent in Denver, who informed J. Edgar Hoover that "their purpose in visiting the Heart Mountain draft delinquents was to ascertain their reasons for refusing to report for the pre-induction physical examinations as ordered."[25]

On the surface, Yasui's stance in 1942 as a curfew resister seems incompatible with his 1944 efforts to dissuade the jailed draft resisters. A comparison of Yasui's earlier exchange with Mike Masaoka and his later JACL report abounds with ironies. Masaoka had denounced "self-styled martyrs who are willing to be jailed in order that they might fight for the rights of citizenship." Yasui had responded to this denigration of his stand as "unacceptably condescending." Two years later, he wrote condescendingly of the Heart Mountain resisters: "Some display manifestations of a martyr complex, some are sullen and resentful, and in others, traces of self-pity can be discerned." Masaoka had expressed fear that Yasui's act of resistance might erode the last vestiges of public sympathy for the plight of Japanese Americans. "Surely, the American citizen who qualms before the possible criticism of unthinking people is certainly a poor American," Yasui replied scornfully. Two years later, he directed his scorn at the draft resisters. "Boomeranging of good will toward persons of Japanese ancestry," he wrote in 1944, was "seemingly of secondary concern to the boys in jail."[26]

What appear as contradictions, however, actually help to define Min Yasui's unique role among those who challenged General DeWitt's orders. Distinctions between citizens on the grounds of ancestry offended Yasui's conception of the Constitution. He refused to obey the curfew because it "infringed on my right as a citizen" to be treated without regard to race. The military draft, on the contrary, offered Japanese Americans the chance to fulfill their obligations of citizenship alongside those of other races.[27]

The motivations of people whose cases reach the Supreme Court and shape constitutional doctrine are sometimes simple, and their acts are often inadvertent. The factors that underlay Min Yasui's curfew challenge were complex, and his act of resistance was deliberate. Yasui emerges from the apparent contradictions of his statements and behavior as a distinctive type of constitutional challenger: the legalist.

More than six weeks passed before Min Yasui was joined by a second challenger to DeWitt's military orders. On the morning of May 16, 1942,

Gordon Kiyoshi Hirabayashi arrived at the FBI office in Seattle, accompanied by a local lawyer, Arthur Barnett. Then a twenty-four-year-old University of Washington senior, Hirabayashi had been required by Civilian Exclusion Order No. 57 to report to the Maryknoll Mission House in Seattle's University District on May 11 to register for evacuation on May 16.

Barnett had earlier called the FBI office to announce that he and Hirabayashi were coming, and the two men were met by Special Agent Francis V. Manion on their arrival. Hirabayashi handed to Manion a neatly typed four-page statement headed "Why I refused to register for evacuation." Phrased in terms that were rooted in his Quaker faith and colored by his exposure to the pains of evacuation, Hirabayashi's statement expressed both anguish and determination: "This order for the mass evacuation of all persons of Japanese descent denies them the right to live. It forces thousands of energetic, law-abiding individuals to exist in a miserable psychological and a horrible physical atmosphere. This order limits to almost full extent the creative expression of those subjected. It kills the desire for a higher life. Hope for the future is exterminated. Human personalities are poisoned."[28]

The statement went on to objections to evacuation based upon civics-lesson precepts. "Over sixty percent are American citizens," Hirabayashi wrote of his fellow Japanese Americans; yet their rights "are denied on a wholesale scale without due process of law and civil liberties which are theirs." He concluded on a defiant note: "If I were to register and cooperate under those circumstances, I would be giving helpless consent to the denial of practically all of the things which give me incentive to live. I must maintain my Christian principles. I consider it my duty to maintain the democratic standards for which this nation lives. Therefore, I must refuse this order for evacuation."[29]

Special Agent Manion read through the statement, but did not tell the serious young man that the FBI already had a copy. The day before, running to catch a bus, Hirabayashi had dropped a copy on the sidewalk in front of the Sears Roebuck store; the woman who picked it up promptly called the FBI, which dispatched an agent to collect the copy. While Hirabayashi and Barnett waited in the FBI office, Manion conferred with Assistant U.S. Attorney Gerald Shucklin, who advised him to give Hirabayashi a chance to register for evacuation. Manion then drove with Hirabayashi to the Maryknoll Mission House, where the Army officer in charge offered him the registration forms. When Hirabayashi refused to complete them, Manion called Shucklin and was told to file a complaint for violation of the evacuation order. After returning to the FBI office, Manion completed the necessary paperwork and then took his charge to the nearby King County Jail.[30]

The next day, Hirabayashi was visited in jail by Captain M. A. Ravisto, adjutant of the Wartime Civil Control Administration in Seattle. Ravisto's effort to change Hirabayashi's mind proved futile. Three days later, on May 20, Hirabayashi appeared before United States Commissioner Harry Westfall for a preliminary hearing on the evacuation violation charge. "Subject admitted his failure to comply with the Exclusion Order and was bound over to the Grand Jury under bond of $5,000," Manion reported to FBI headquarters in Washington. The setting of bail was academic, since Commissioner Westfall conditioned Hirabayashi's release from jail on his transfer to the Puyallup fairgrounds near Tacoma, where his fellow Japanese Americans were being held. Despite this chance to join his family and friends, Hirabayashi turned down the offer on principle and remained behind bars in the King County Jail.[31]

Unlike Min Yasui, who had been raised in a thoroughly "American" setting and who welcomed military training, Gordon Hirabayashi grew up in an unconventional family. Born in 1918 in Auburn, a town twenty miles south of Seattle where his father ran a roadside fruit market, Hirabayashi absorbed the pacifism of his parents, Japanese natives who belonged to a sect called "Friends of the World." Similar in organizational form and beliefs to the Quakers, of which it was a Japanese offshoot, this group worshipped without ministers and rejected military service and war. Eager for contact with young people outside the small Japanese American community in his home town, Hirabayashi served as president of the nondenominational Auburn Christian Fellowship during his high school years.[32]

When he entered the University of Washington in Seattle in 1937, Hirabayashi became active in the student religious and social-action groups that contended with the dominant fraternity and sorority atmosphere of the conservative campus. He assumed a leadership role in the student YMCA and the Japanese Student's Club, and also joined the Seattle chapter of the Japanese American Citizens League. Shopping around for a religious home, Hirabayashi and his roommate, Bill Makino, attended in turn the University Temple ("because they had an excellent choir"), the Unitarian Church, and finally the University Quaker Meeting. "We liked that setting," he recalled. "We found ourselves gravitating over there more frequently, and after a while we weren't shopping around."[33]

As a YMCA officer, Hirabayashi traveled to New York City in the summer of 1940 to attend the "President's School" held jointly at Columbia University and the affiliated Union Theological Seminary. Here he was exposed in seminars and discussions to the social activism and pacifism preached by A. J. Muste, Evan Thomas (brother of Socialist

Party leader Norman Thomas), and John Nevin Sayre, all members of the pacifist Fellowship of Reconciliation (FOR). This experience proved to be a turning point in the young student's life. "I guess I was ready for that philosophy," Hirabayashi later said. "It all made sense, and the fact that my parents belonged to this non-conformist, non-church Christian group from Japan made these things at home to me." Hirabayashi joined the FOR, which advocated nonviolent but militant resistance to war and military service, during his summer in New York. On his return to Seattle, he registered with his local draft board as a conscientious objector and was granted that status without objection.[34]

Precarious family finances had forced Hirabayashi to alternate quarters of study at the University with work as a houseboy and farmhand during his first two years of school. At the age of twenty-four, he had just begun his senior year when the curfew on Japanese Americans became effective in March 1942. Hirabayashi was then living with a dozen other students in a dormitory at the campus YMCA. The issuance of the first Civilian Exclusion Order on March 29, which required the evacuation of the Japanese American residents of nearby Bainbridge Island, prompted Hirabayashi to drop out of school. "I knew I wasn't going to be around very long," he recalled, "so I just didn't register for the spring quarter and volunteered with the fledgling American Friends Service Committee [AFSC] in Seattle." Headquartered in Philadelphia, the AFSC was the social-service branch of the Quakers. Working with AFSC director Floyd Schmoe, Hirabayashi helped Japanese American families subject to exclusion orders in finding storage space for their furniture and in transporting them to the Puyallup Fairgrounds. His family had not yet been ordered to the assembly center, but Hirabayashi felt anguish at the plight of those he helped to dispose of their household goods and pets and whom he drove to Puyallup center. "I fully expected that when the University District deadline came up I would be joining them," he later said, "and those that saw me waving goodby to them all expected to see me within a few weeks."[35]

Like all Japanese Americans, Hirabayashi had been subject to General DeWitt's curfew order since March 28, 1942. He obeyed the curfew until the evening of May 4, unaware of Min Yasui's challenge to it more than a month before. "I expected like every citizen to obey the law, and I did," he recalled. "There were twelve of us living in the YMCA dorm, and they all became my volunteer timekeepers—'Hey, it's five minutes to eight, Gordy'—and I'd dash back from the library or the coffeeshop. One of the times I stopped and said, 'Why the hell am I running back? Am I an American or not? Why am I running back and nobody else is?' "[36]

Hirabayashi began keeping a diary of his activities on May 4, when he first broke the curfew. His friend Helen Blom had come to the YMCA dormitory that night to return his raincoat. "Helen lives one half block west of Roosevelt—the 'line that mustn't be crossed,' " his first entry read. "Though it was 8 P.M. I walked over to the line and back with her. Peculiar, but I received a lift—perhaps it is a release—when I consciously break the silly old curfew."[37]

Gordon and Bill Makino made dozens of trips to the Puyallup fairgrounds in the course of their AFSC work. Hirabayashi's diary recorded his revulsion at conditions in the center. "All morning Bill and I hauled baggage to the pick up places," he wrote on May 9. "Gosh!—something seems wrong there; helping people to go behind barbed wires and flimsy shacks, etc. What a mixed-up life this is—the American way. Went over to the Schmoes with Bill and had a waffle and little pigs dinner. Stayed over in spite of curfew regulations."[38]

During the weeks that preceded the order to evacuate the University District, Hirabayashi and Makino talked for hours about a joint stand against evacuation. Both young men encountered opposition from their parents. Hirabayashi later recounted these arguments: "My mother said, 'I know you're right, I agree with you and I admire this stand of yours. But we don't know if we'll ever see each other again. Why stick to a principle? Stick with us.' She used tears and everything, but I couldn't do it. Dad was physically able, so I didn't have that worry. But Bill was the only son of parents who were at least ten years older than my parents and this pressure was very strong. I didn't want to have someone who would be having remorse all the way through, and I figured we were going to have serious problems. So I told him, 'You should think this thing through very carefully, and if there's any way you could persuade yourself to go with your family you should do that. You should come with me only if you can't go and you have to object. Then I welcome you.' He thought about it and decided he'd just have to stick with his family."[39]

Before he made a final decision to resist, Hirabayashi sought legal advice from Arthur Barnett, a thirty-five-year-old lawyer and fellow member of the Friends Meeting. Word of his stand also reached Mary Farquharson, a lawyer who represented the University District in the state senate. Although not a Quaker, her efforts on behalf of interned Japanese Americans kept her in touch with Arthur Barnett. She was also a member of the small local chapter of the American Civil Liberties Union, which had decided to back any of the Japanese Americans who might refuse to report for evacuation.

"Mary Farquharson came to see me," Hirabayashi recalled. "She said, 'I'm checking up on a rumor that you are intending to object to evacuation; is that true?' I said, 'Yes, I've already made a stand, and I've written a statement.' She said, 'Are you planning to make a test case of this?' 'Well, I know that's a possibility,' I said, 'but I don't know very much about law and I don't have any money. I'm making a personal stand. I don't know what's going to happen as a result of it and I've made no plans.' 'If you've made no plans,' she said, 'there's a group here including myself who are very upset about what's happening to our civil liberties and the status of citizenship. We've been looking for a case to object to these things, and we haven't been able to find one. Do you have any objections to a group of us using your case as a vehicle to fight for citizens' rights?' "[40]

Hirabayashi was delighted with this offer of support, and Farquharson quickly organized an informal committee to provide legal advice and to raise money for bail in anticipation of his arrest. Arthur Barnett volunteered his legal services, although he suggested that a lawyer more familiar with constitutional issues and with more prestige be recruited to act as trial counsel. Ray Roberts, a former YMCA secretary in China who owned a Chinese goods store in Seattle, offered to act as treasurer and to put up Hirabayashi's bail. Gordon then met several times with Arthur Barnett to discuss the legal steps that lay ahead and to polish the statement he intended to give the FBI.

When he and Barnett arrived at the FBI office on May 16, Hirabayashi intended simply to initiate a test case of the evacuation order. Had he not brought with him a briefcase that contained his incriminating diary, it is unlikely the FBI would have learned of his repeated curfew violations. FBI agent Manion, however, confiscated the briefcase. After filing the complaint charging Hirabayashi with violation of the evacuation order, and taking him to the King County Jail, Manion went through the briefcase and discovered the diary. On May 24, Manion visited Hirabayashi in jail and secured from him a five-page statement admitting three curfew violations from May 4 to May 10. Gordon refused to sign the statement because his lawyer was not present, but Manion turned it over to the U.S. attorney's office. Four days later, after amendment of the initial complaint, the federal grand jury in Seattle returned an indictment that charged Hirabayashi with two violations of Public Law 503, the first for failure to report for evacuation and the second for curfew violation.[41]

Legal training and frustrated patriotism underlay Min Yasui's challenge to the curfew. Gordon Hirabayashi came to resistance from a contrasting background of social activism and religious pacifism. Added to the basic moral underpinning of his decision to offer himself as a test case, however, was a sketchy but real knowledge of the constitutional rights of citizenship. "I knew something of court cases as a student," he later said. "I had read of World War I and the constitutional cases," referring to the trials of Socialist Party leader Eugene V. Debs and other war objectors, "but it wasn't a high priority in forming my decision."[42]

The report that Manion sent to FBI headquarters of his initial meeting with Hirabayashi accurately recorded the amalgam of these motivations: "He stated . . . that it was the principle of the Society of Friends that each person should follow the will of God according to his own convictions and that he could not reconcile the will of God, a part of which was expressed in the Bill of Rights and the United States Constitution, with the order discriminating against Japanese aliens and American citizens of Japanese ancestry."[43]

These forceful words, and the statement that Hirabayashi handed to Manion in the FBI office, bear a remarkable similarity to the letter composed two decades later by Martin Luther King in the Birmingham City Jail. Religious conviction and constitutional concerns are separately powerful. Joined in struggles against discrimination, they lead to acts of legal significance. In expressing through his act of resistance the separate commandments of the Christian and constitutional decalogues, Gordon Hirabayashi exemplified a second type of challenger: the moralist.

The third Japanese American whose violation of DeWitt's orders reached the Supreme Court had not intended to offer himself as the subject of a test case. On the afternoon of May 30, 1942, the police in San Leandro, California, picked up a young man walking down the street with his girlfriend. Under questioning by Lieutenant A. B. Poulsen at the San Leandro police headquarters, the young man produced a draft registration card that identified him as "Clyde Sarah." The suspect claimed to be of Spanish-Hawaiian origin. He had been born in Las Vegas, the suspect told Poulsen, and his parents had been killed in a fire that burned their house to the ground. The young man's story quickly fell apart. He spoke no Spanish, and his draft card had been clumsily altered with ink eradicator.

Poulsen could not persuade the suspect to reveal his name, although he did admit that he was of Japanese descent. His identity came out by chance: "One of the girls who worked in the office seemed to recognize me, and so I finally said who I was." The slim young man told Poulsen that his name was Fred Toyosaburo Korematsu. He was a welder and had lived until recently in nearby Oakland, where he had been born in 1919, with his Japanese-born parents and three brothers. Korematsu told Poulsen that the other members of his family had reported to the Tanforan assembly center—located south of San Francisco in a converted race track—three weeks earlier on May 9. This was the effective date of Exclusion Order No. 34, to which all Japanese Americans who lived in Oakland and San Leandro were subject.[44]

The San Leandro police apprehended Korematsu on a Saturday afternoon and transferred him the following day to the Alameda County Jail in Oakland. Lieutenant Poulsen had notified the San Francisco FBI office of Korematsu's arrest, and he was intensively questioned on May 31 and June 1 by Special Agent Oliver T. Mansfield. The FBI agent encountered a cooperative prisoner who no longer held back the details of his life or of his violation. After graduation from Oakland High School in 1938, Korematsu told Mansfield, he entered Los Angeles City College but dropped out after only one month for financial reasons. He then attended the Master School of Welding in Oakland and worked as a shipyard welder following this training. The Navy turned down his attempt to volunteer for service in June 1941; the next month he was classified 4-F by his draft board because of gastric ulcers. Korematsu had belonged to the Boiler Makers Union, which expelled its members of Japanese descent after the Pearl Harbor attack. He lost his shipyard job as a result and had worked before his evacuation order at a series of short-term welding jobs.[45]

After taking down this history, Mansfield turned the questioning to the circumstances of Korematsu's arrest. The San Leandro police had given their prisoner no hint of how he had been spotted on the street. Korematsu was convinced that his arrest was not accidental. "The way I got caught," he later said, "was that I went into a drugstore to get some cigarettes and the pharmacist recognized me. He was the one who called the police; otherwise I don't think I would have been recognized."[46]

What gave Korematsu confidence that he would not be recognized in San Leandro as a Japanese American, three weeks after the evacuation deadline? Mansfield's initial report to FBI headquarters illustrated why this confidence was misplaced. The report described Korematsu as a member of the "yellow race" and included this observation: "Scars or marks—Cut scar on the forehead, lump between eyebrows on nose." Asked about these recent scars, Korematsu confessed that he had undergone plastic surgery in an effort to conceal his racial identity.[47]

This is the statement that Korematsu dictated to Mansfield the day after his arrest to explain why he had tried to alter his appearance: "I am of Japanese ancestry. I have lived all my life in Oakland . . . with my folks until four weeks before we had to evacuate. Then I left home telling them I was going to Nevada. Then instead I stayed in Oakland to earn enough money to take my girl with me to the Middle West. Her name is Miss Ida Boitano. She is a different nationality—Italian. Between the time I left home and the date before evacuation I lived 2 wks in San Francisco during an operation on my face and 2 wks in Oakland with a Friend. The operation was for the purpose of changing my appearance so that I would not be subjected to ostracism when my girl and I went East."[48]

Under subsequent questioning by FBI agent G. E. Goodwin, Korematsu gave a fuller account of his plastic surgery. About a month before the May 9 evacuation order, he said, he had noticed an advertisement in the San Francisco *Examiner* placed by a Dr. Masten, offering facial operations at low prices. According to Goodwin, Korematsu "discussed the matter with his fiance, Ida Boitano, and they decided that if he had the operation performed, it might be possible for them to go to Arizona and get married without anyone suspecting that subject was Japanese. He continually reiterated that he feared violence should anyone discover that he, a Japanese, was married to an American girl." When he visited Masten's office, the doctor asked no questions and offered to perform plastic surgery on his eyes and nose for $300. Korematsu replied that he could pay only $100, and Masten "agreed this to be payment in full."[49]

FBI agents quickly located and interviewed Dr. Bennett B. Masten at his office in downtown San Francisco and reported that the elderly physician was "quite cooperative." An unidentified "confidential source"—most likely an official of the local medical society—had earlier told the agents that Dr. Masten "engages in various unethical practices" and was considered "entirely untrustworthy." The FBI informant added that "he has had numerous complaints that Masten's work was highly unsatisfactory but that he was unable to take any action on such a matter." Armed with this knowledge and with derogatory reports from a San Francisco credit-reporting agency, FBI agents paid a visit to Dr. Masten.[50]

The agents reported that Masten told them that Korematsu "first came to his office on March 4, 1942, and stated that he wanted an operation on his facial characteristics and had seen the doctor's card in a San Francisco paper." Korematsu had explained to Masten "that he was American-born of Japanese parents and that he was married to an American girl. He desired to have his Oriental facial features changed so that he and his wife would not be subjected to comment and embarrassment.'' Masten informed the agents that he had explained to Korematsu ''that he could build up his nose and remove the folds from the inner corner of his upper eyelids but that he could not make the subject look like an American.'' On March 18, Masten performed an operation on Korematsu's nose, for which he received $75. Six days later, he operated on Korematsu's eyelids and charged him an additional $25. Masten did not charge his patient for removing the final dressings on March 30.[51]

FBI agents also questioned Ida Boitano, who expressed remorse about her relationship with Fred Korematsu. ''She said that she was originally engaged to subject and had intended to marry him,'' the agents reported, ''but that she now realized that such a marriage was impossible and that she had made a big mistake, particularly after the law regarding evacuation went into effect.'' The young woman, who worked in a San Leandro biscuit factory, told the agents that she had met Korematsu during a trip to the mountains in 1939. Korematsu had later visited Ida to take piano lessons from her. Ida's parents objected to these visits, and the two young people had continued their budding romance away from the Boitano residence.[52]

Korematsu's decision to undergo plastic surgery had led to conflict between the young couple, the FBI agents reported. Ida ''tried to talk the subject out of having an operation performed,'' they wrote, ''because she feared he would get into some trouble with authorities over this.'' However, Korematsu ''continually assured her that if he was unable to go to Arizona with her and marry her that he would surrender himself for evacuation.'' She was now sorry, Ida assured the FBI agents, ''that she did not report subject to proper authorities when he refused to give himself up.'' The engagement was definitely over, the agents reported dryly: ''Miss Boitano stated that subject had recently written her a personal letter from Tanforan and that she had answered him telling him not to write her anymore.''[53]

Fred Korematsu was not the only person of Japanese ancestry picked up in the evacuation dragnet. FBI records show that local police arrested nine other Japanese Americans in the San Francisco area and six in Sacramento. The day after Korematsu's arrest in San Leandro, the San Francisco police found Koji Kurokawa in the basement of the house where he worked as a houseboy. Kurokawa had hidden out, sneaking upstairs at night to find food, for three weeks before his apprehension. Food had run out and Kurokawa was weak from hunger when his employer discovered him and called the police. Taken to the hospital before he was sent to jail, Kurokawa told the police he had decided on May 9 not to report for evacuation. ''I am an American citizen,'' he explained to a newspaper reporter from his hospital bed. John Ura, who was then a college student in Atlanta, had been arrested when he returned to San Francisco to pick up his typewriter.[54]

A few days after their arrests, these three young men received a visit from Ernest Besig, a lawyer who directed the San Francisco office of the American Civil Liberties Union. Besig had learned of the arrests from newspaper reports, and came to the San Francisco County Jail—Korematsu's fourth stop behind bars—looking for a test case volunteer. Koji Kurokawa and John Ura both met briefly with Besig and politely declined his offer of legal assistance. The two men later pleaded guilty to violations of Public Law 503 and were sentenced to short terms at the Federal Prison Camp in Dupont, Washington.[55]

Besig was surprised to find a willing client in Fred Korematsu. The ACLU official knew from press accounts of his arrest that Korematsu had undergone plastic surgery, and he encountered a shy and reticent young man. Outlining the legal steps that lay ahead, Besig made clear that chances of ultimate victory were slim. Wartime hysteria, prejudice against Japanese Americans and judicial reluctance to upset military decisions all made a challenge to General DeWitt's orders an uphill battle. Besig also warned Korematsu that he would be exposed to the glare of publicity, and that the press would undoubtedly focus on his altered features. This blunt advice failed to deter Korematsu, who assured Besig he was willing to endure public scrutiny and to pursue his challenge to the Supreme Court.[56]

On the surface, Korematsu seemed an unlikely candidate for a test case. He had neither the legal training of Min Yasui nor the background of religious and social activism that motivated Gordon Hirabayashi. From the time of his arrest to the present, accounts of his case have uniformly portrayed Korematsu as a young man impelled by romance alone, and whose effort to change his features was a bizarre response to DeWitt's exclusion order. The decision of the Supreme Court to uphold Korematsu's conviction reflected, at least in part, these assumptions. "After notice of his proposed exclusion," Justice Hugo Black wrote in the first draft of the Court's opinion, Korematsu "moved from his home to another place in Oakland" and had "an operation on his face" in order to "conceal his identity as a person of Japanese ancestry."[57]

Black had second thoughts about the propriety of these personal references and removed them from his final opinion. However, they show that Black had misread the record in the case. The FBI reported accurately that Korematsu had moved from his home and had undergone plastic surgery several weeks before the exclusion order was issued. Korematsu had first intended to take advantage of DeWitt's short-lived offer of "voluntary" migration from the West Coast and had altered his features so that he and Ida Boitano could move "to some spot in the Middle West where they could live as normal people." It is unlikely that Black's errors in chronology affected the Court's decision in the case, but they certainly reflected an error in judgment about Korematsu's motivation.[58]

Min Yasui and Gordon Hirabayashi both turned themselves in for arrest and intended from the outset of their cases to raise constitutional challenges to DeWitt's orders. Fred Korematsu, in contrast, hoped to evade the exclusion order and seemed to be motivated solely by personal interest. The ties of romance, depleted finances, and the naive belief that he could escape detection as a Japanese American were among the reasons he remained behind and risked arrest. These factors help to explain why Korematsu failed to report for evacuation. They offer little help, however, in explaining the quiet but firm determination that Ernest Besig discovered in his first jailhouse visit with Korematsu. There is considerable evidence, in fact, that this shy young man shared with Yasui and Hirabayashi an equal devotion to constitutional principle in offering himself as a test case challenger.

FBI records provide part of this evidence. According to Special Agent Goodwin, Korematsu "stated that he believed that the statute under which he is imprisoned was wrong . . . and that he intended to fight the case even before being approached by the Civil Liberties Union." This interview took place after Korematsu's transfer from jail to the Tanforan assembly center, where he finally joined his parents and three brothers. Before he left his family's home early in March 1942, however, Fred had spent hours in debate over the impending evacuation with his eldest brother, Hiroshi. As chairman of the Committee on Alien Resettlement of the San Francisco YMCA, Hi Korematsu had worked before the evacuation and internment to mitigate its impact on Japanese Americans. On February 20, 1942, the day that newspapers reported President Roosevelt's approval of the evacuation program, Hi sent a letter to Attorney General Biddle expressing the YMCA's concern about the "growing critical problem of caring for the dispossessed aliens" already held in Justice Department camps. Fred and Hi differed in their individual responses to DeWitt's exclusion order, but the two brothers had discussed their obligations at length before their temporary separation.[59]

After his arrival at Tanforan, where he had been sent to await trial, Fred resumed his debate with Hi over the effect of his test case on the interned Japanese Americans. "My older brother arranged a meeting in Tanforan," Fred recalled. "I asked whether I should go ahead and fight the case or not. Some people said, 'We're in here now, why make it worse.' And other people said, 'It's up to you.' They left everything up to me, because I'm fighting the case and they're not. So I decided to go ahead and see the thing through." FBI agents learned of the meeting from an informant on the Tanforan staff. The FBI informant reported that few of those at the meeting offered support to Korematsu "due to the fact that most of them desired to be cooperative with the United States government."[60]

Forced to stand almost alone, Korematsu did not back down from his challenge to internment. During one of Ernest Besig's visits to Tanforan, he handed the ACLU official a statement that expressed his position in words that made up in conviction what they lacked in grammar: "Assembly Camps were for: Dangerous Enemy Aliens and Citizens; These camps have been definitely an imprisonment under armed guard with orders shoot to kill. In order to be imprisoned, these people should have been given a fair trial in order that they may defend their loyalty at court in a democratic way, but they were placed in imprisonment without any fair trial! Many Disloyal Germans and Italians were caught, but they were not all corralled under armed guard like the Japanese—is this a racial issue? If not, the Loyal Citizens want fair trial to prove their loyalty! Also their [*sic*] are many loyal aliens who can prove their loyalty to America, and they must be given fair trial and treatment! Fred Korematsu's Test Case may help."[61]

The statement that Korematsu gave to Besig lacked the polish of the one Gordon Hirabayashi had composed, and the young welder could not match Min Yasui in legal sophistication. As a resister, Korematsu more resembled Rosa Parks, the footsore seamstress whose refusal to yield her seat in the "white" section of a city bus sparked the Montgomery, Alabama, bus boycott in 1955. Rosa Parks later explained her decision to risk arrest for her lone protest: "It just happened the driver made a demand and I just didn't feel like obeying his demand." Fred Korematsu later explained his refusal to leave his home in similar terms: "I figured I'd lived here all my life and I was going to stay here."[62]

Korematsu took a unique path to resistance, one which set him apart from Yasui and Hirabayashi as challengers who had planned their arrests. He shared with them, however, an equal commitment to his rights as an American citizen. In refusing to obey the exclusion order, Fred Korematsu personified a third type of constitutional challenger: the loner.

A fourth Japanese American joined these three young men in bringing a challenge to General DeWitt's orders before the Supreme Court. Mitsuye Endo differed from them, however, not only in sex but in the form of her challenge. Endo did not test the curfew and exclusion orders that preceded internment, nor did she risk the criminal penalties provided in Public Law 503. Her challenge to internment began after she reported to the Tanforan assembly center and was based on the civil procedure of a habeas corpus petition. Despite a lengthy delay in the lower courts, the petition brought on behalf of Mitsuye Endo eventually forced the Supreme Court to confront the internment issue directly.

Endo's case actually began several months before she reported to Tanforan, and well before the decision to intern Japanese Americans had been made. James Purcell, a thirty-six-year-old San Francisco lawyer, received a telephone call late in January 1942 from his friend, Saburo Kido. The two lawyers had worked together on earlier cases that involved Japanese American clients. Kido had called Purcell from Sacramento, the state capital, where he had gone in response to rumors of an impending purge of state employees of Japanese ancestry.[63]

Kido had found a state of near-panic among the civil servants with whom he met in Sacramento. They had suddenly been ordered by the State Personnel Board to complete lengthy questionnaires that probed their past and present activities in detail. Despite the fact that all the affected workers were American-born citizens, the questionnaire seemed to be predicated on the assumption that they were citizens of Japan under that country's "dual nationality" law. The forms asked for details about past visits to Japan, knowledge of the Japanese language, and membership in organizations with ties to Japan. A firm statement by California attorney general Earl Warren that dismissals on the basis of race would be illegal had failed to deter the personnel board. News reports of a resolution of the California state senate calling for the firing of the state's Nisei employees added to their concern.[64]

Kido met with the apprehensive state workers both as a lawyer and as president of the Japanese American Citizens League, and assured them that the JACL would provide legal support. Until the personnel board actually moved to dismiss any of the Nisei, he added, informal efforts to block the anticipated firings offered the only avenue of redress. Assuming that a purge was imminent, Kido decided to recruit a lawyer who was not of Japanese ancestry, with the hope of deflecting prejudice at personnel board hearings and in the courts. After he failed in repeated efforts to enlist a lawyer from one of the well-connected San Francisco firms, he approached James Purcell, who practiced in a two-man office. Purcell agreed to take the assignment without fee and soon traveled to Sacramento, where he advised a group of Nisei state employees to hold tight while he tried to convince members of the personnel board to rescind their dismissal efforts.[65]

Against a background of increasing pressure for mass evacuation, Purcell was given a cold shoulder by the personnel board. Days after President Roosevelt signed Executive Order 9066 on February 19, Nisei employees were "advised" to stay home from work, although they were not formally dismissed. On April 2, with the evacuation program underway, the personnel board notified these employees of their immediate suspension and that charges would soon be filed against them. Wayne Miller, secretary of the personnel board, sent to each Nisei employee on April 13 an identical seven-page statement of charges. Cast in the form of an indictment, the board's statement alleged "failure of good behavior, fraud in securing employment, incompetency, inefficiency, and acts incompatible with and inimical to the public service" as grounds for dismissal.[66]

All of the charged Nisei employees were native-born American citizens, a requirement of California law. Each was nonetheless first charged with being "a citizen of the Empire of Japan, and a subject of the Emperor of Japan." Each "defendant" in the dismissal proceedings was additionally charged with the ability to "read and write the Japanese language," having attended "a Japanese school conducted by the officials of the Buddhist Church," and with being "a member and officer of certain Japanese organizations" which were "violently opposed to the Democratic form of Government of the United States and to its principles." The necessary exposure of the public to state employees of Japanese descent, claimed the personnel board, had "created discord, hostility, unfriendliness, opposition, antagonism, disharmony [and] truculency. . . ."[67]

The patent absurdity of such broadside charges encouraged Purcell to believe that "we'd have no difficulty meeting the charges as they were originally filed." He and Kido quickly began work on a suit to challenge the dismissals, which the two lawyers intended to file in a state court. Their effort was sidetracked, however, by the rapid pace of General DeWitt's exclusion orders. Before Purcell completed the complaint he planned to file on behalf of his new clients, they had been forced by DeWitt's orders to report to assembly centers along with all the other Japanese Americans who lived in California.[68]

Faced with this situation, Purcell visited those of his clients who were held in the Tanforan assembly center, located in a converted racetrack near San Francisco. The conditions under which his clients were held appalled Purcell and sparked his sensitivity to injustice. "I grew up in Folsom prison," he later said. "My father was a guard there. I know a prison when I see it, and Tanforan was a prison with watch towers and guns." The Army staff at Tanforan required Purcell to meet with his clients in their living quarters rather than in an office. "They'd put a family in a stall big enough for one horse, with whitewash over the manure," he recalled. "Guards with machine guns stood at the gates. I couldn't understand why innocent citizens were being treated this way."[69]

Purcell returned to his San Francisco office after these meetings determined to find an interned state employee willing to challenge his or her detention in Tanforan. With his clients now under Army control, Purcell shifted his legal strategy. Aware that a challenge to dismissal of the Nisei state workers would most likely be dismissed quickly by a state court, Purcell now hoped to find an interned state employee on whose behalf he could file a habeas corpus petition in federal court. The ground for such a petition would be that unlawful detention by the Army had deprived a state employee of the right to report for work. In pursuing this strategy, Purcell put together his own questionnaire, closely modeled on the form circulated by the state personnel board. He asked more than a hundred interned state workers whether they could read or write the Japanese language, had ever been to Japan, considered themselves dual citizens under Japanese law, subscribed to Japanese language newspapers, or belonged to Japanese clubs and organizations.

Although he had no specific client in mind, Purcell scrutinized the completed questionnaires with a careful eye. He finally picked out Mitsuye Endo as a "perfect type" of plaintiff for a habeas corpus petition. A twenty-two-year-old clerical worker in the California Department of Motor Vehicles in Sacramento, Endo had been raised as a Methodist, did not speak or read Japanese, and had never visited Japan. Best of all, she had a brother serving in the Army. Purcell had not previously met with Mitsuye Endo and secured permission to file suit on her behalf by correspondence. On July 12, 1942, Purcell filed a habeas corpus petition with the federal district court in San Francisco under the caption of *Endo* v. *Eisenhower,* asking the court to require Milton Eisenhower, as director of the War Relocation Authority and as the person responsible for her detention, to show cause why Mitsuye Endo should not be released from internment.[70]

In a way, Mitsuye Endo resembled the "picture brides" who were picked from photo albums and sent from Japan to marry earlier immigrants to the United States. Purcell met his client only once during the entire course of her case, during an interrogation conducted by WRA solicitor Philip Glick, who offered to release her from internment in return for an agreement that she would not return to the "restricted area" of the West Coast, which included all of California. Despite this offer to escape from internment, made as part of the government's effort to avoid a Supreme Court test of its powers to detain Japanese Americans, Endo refused to abandon her legal challenge and remained behind barbed wire for another two years.[71]

Aside from this brief meeting with the lawyers on both sides of her case, Endo remained an anonymous litigant. She never appeared in court during the judicial proceedings and disappeared from public view after the Supreme Court ruled on her case. In this respect, Mitsuye Endo exemplified a unique type of constitutional challenger: the recruit.

Purcell's action in filing the habeas corpus petition completed the roster of cases that would reach the Supreme Court as tests of the three stages of the internment program: curfew, evacuation, and detention. Behind the "masks of the law" that concealed them from the high court, the four young Japanese Americans who brought these test cases emerge as individuals who differed markedly in background and motivation.

Much like runners who complete the first leg of a relay race, the four challengers left the track after they passed the baton to their lawyers for the subsequent laps through the courts. Although the three criminal defendants testified at their perfunctory trials and appeared for sentencing, they then became, like Mitsuye Endo, simply names on legal briefs and opinions. In the legal battles recounted in the following chapters of this book, these four challengers—and the vastly larger group of Japanese Americans confined in internment camps—remained as mute observers of the legal process.

5

"We Don't Intend to Trim Our Sails"

INITIATION of the Japanese American wartime cases ensured that federal courts would rule on the legality of General DeWitt's orders. Lawyers on both sides assumed from the outset that at least two, and possibly all four, of these cases ultimately would be decided by the Supreme Court. Two factors made such an assumption reasonable. Questions about the source and scope of DeWitt's powers, the application of his orders to an entire racial group, and the role of courts in passing judgment on military decisions all raised novel constitutional issues. Lower court judges might well—and in fact did—shrink from ruling on these momentous issues and pass them on to the Supreme Court. The fact that these cases involved the separate phases of the internment program—curfew, evacuation, and detention—also made it likely that the Supreme Court would review the orders at issue in the individual cases.

Even in cases that seem tailor-made for eventual resolution of important and unsettled legal questions by the Supreme Court, the lawyers involved must first prepare for the initial steps in the litigation process: hearings and trials in the lower courts. The Japanese American test cases were no exception. This and the following chapter will recount the legal work that laid the foundation of hearing and trial records upon which the Supreme Court later constructed its opinions in these historic cases. That work was preceded and accompanied, however, by sharp and often bitter disputes among the lawyers on both sides, disputes that stemmed from conflicts both of personality and policy. Since these internecine legal battles vitally affected the test cases, from their inception through the final Supreme Court rulings, a recounting of the initial skirmishes forms a second focus of this chapter.

Close to forty lawyers participated at some stage of these four cases over their three-year course. Given this large number, the emergence of disputes among them is hardly surprising. Lawyers are, after all, disputatious by definition. There are several factors, however, which explain the unusual depth and endurance of the conflicts that split the shaky legal teams on both sides. One set of factors reflects the same issues that confronted the courts. Differing attitudes toward military authority over civilians during wartime, official discrimination against racial minorities, and the proper balance of powers between the branches of government existed among lawyers as well as judges. The debate that raged between Justice and War Department lawyers over the weeks preceding Executive Order 9066 displayed the wide range of positions on these issues within the government's ranks. And, although most of the lawyers who represented the Japanese Americans rejected the military's claims, a surprising number refused to challenge Roosevelt's order as fundamentally unlawful.

A second set of factors behind these internal conflicts arose from divisions of authority within the contending legal camps. Attorney General Biddle directed the government's lawyers, at least on paper. The nature of the test cases, however, required the participation of a separate force of War Department lawyers commanded by Assistant Secretary McCloy and another platoon headed by Philip Glick, solicitor of the War Relocation Authority. The dictates of the adversary system now forced Justice and War Department lawyers into an uneasy alliance, but the divisions among them remained deep.

Relations among lawyers for the Japanese Americans were equally divisive. Lawyers affiliated with the American Civil Liberties Union represented both Gordon Hirabayashi and Fred Korematsu. Roger Baldwin, the longtime ACLU director, contended both with a deeply split board of directors and a San Francisco branch that resisted dictation from ACLU headquarters in New York. The ACLU's lack of control over the independent lawyers who represented Minoru Yasui and Mitsuye Endo also complicated the coordination of strategy in the test cases.

Against this backdrop of internal conflict, we will examine below the legal politics that accompanied the search for and selection of test cases, the disputes over enforcement of General DeWitt's orders, the debates over constitutional issues, and the preparation on both sides of the legal fence for the initial hearings and trials in the cases.

While it is inaccurate to say that Roger Baldwin *was* the American Civil Liberties Union, it is not misleading to characterize the ACLU as an extension of the personality and concerns of this lifelong activist. Although he lacked formal legal training, Baldwin left his mark as ACLU director on virtually every major civil liberties battle that erupted between World War I and the Vietnam War. Born to a family of wealthy Boston Brahmins in 1884, he attended Harvard and first worked as a juvenile court officer and civic reformer in St. Louis. Opposition to impending American involvement in World War I, less political than pacifist in origin, brought Baldwin to New York as director of the Civil Liberties Bureau of the American Union Against Militarism (AUAM), a loose coalition of respectable socialites, political radicals, religious pacifists, and lawyers and law professors concerned with the rights of war objectors.[1]

Charged with defending conscientious objectors against their harsh treatment in Army prisons, Baldwin exploited his Harvard and Park Avenue contacts in gaining access to War Department officials on behalf of the COs. Unwilling to act only as an advocate, he later refused to obey his own draft order and served a one-year prison term. During the rabid Red Scare period that followed the war, the AUAM split over the question of whether to defend the communist and anarchist targets of the notorious Palmer Raids. The more radical wing of the AUAM, along with many of those trained in law, met in January 1920 to found the American Civil Liberties Union and appointed Baldwin as director.[2]

Wartime negotiations with high-level federal officials over the treatment of COs, and later efforts to secure amnesty for imprisoned radicals and aliens, taught Baldwin how to negotiate the maze of government corridors in bureaucratic Washington. He worked over the next two decades on innumerable legal battles over free speech rights, labor organization, and the protection of black Americans against lynching and official discrimination. Despite his personal flirtation with Popular Front politics during the 1930s, Baldwin remained a flexible, pragmatic operator and a master at moderating the conflicts among an ACLU board of directors whose membership spanned the political spectrum. At the outbreak of World War II, despite a dues-paying core of barely more than five thousand members, the ACLU exerted considerable influence in Washington, due in large part to Baldwin's political skills and personal contacts.[3]

The Japanese attack on Pearl Harbor did not elicit any immediate response from the ACLU on behalf of Japanese Americans. Editorial calls for tolerance initially persuaded Baldwin that this minority would escape the retribution and repression that German Americans suffered during World War I. Late in January 1942, however, he picked up rumors that growing public pressure for mass evacuation had gained Army support. On one of his frequent trips to Washington for informal consultation with government officials about issues of concern to the ACLU, Baldwin learned that General DeWitt "has recommended moving the whole Japanese population eastward from the seacoast area"; this he reported on January 20 to Ernest Besig, who directed the ACLU branch in San Francisco.[4]

Provided by Justice Department lawyer James Rowe, this inside information was in fact prescient. DeWitt was then waffling on the issue and did not formally recommend mass evacuation until almost a month later. Rowe's accurate prediction nonetheless left Baldwin "rather fearful that some move may be made, if the emergency should appear great," he wrote Besig, that "would virtually suspend civil rights" on the West Coast.[5]

Baldwin also learned during his meeting with Rowe of the forthcoming dispatch to the West Coast of the congressional committee headed by Representative John Tolan. Rowe had engineered the formation of the Tolan Committee in hopes that members of the panel, exposed to testimony that Japanese Americans were overwhelmingly loyal and posed no danger to the country, would report to Congress that mass evacuation was not necessary. Because of the mounting public hostility toward Japanese Americans, Baldwin did not share Rowe's optimism.

On January 30, Baldwin conveyed to Dr. Clinton J. Taft, the Methodist minister who directed the ACLU branch in Los Angeles, his fear that "any action by the Tolan Committee would come too late to be of any practical good." Baldwin's pessimism reflected in part the intervening impact of the Roberts Report, which claimed that Japanese Americans in Hawaii had aided the Pearl Harbor attack. Confronted with growing public pressure for evacuation, Baldwin seemed at a loss. His only suggestion was that the West Coast ACLU branches sponsor "public meetings in San Francisco or Los Angeles which might increase tolerance" toward Japanese Americans. This proposal did result in the formation of an *ad hoc* group of California educators and ministers who called themselves the Committee on National Security and Fair Play. This group proved no more successful in blocking the evacuation, however, than did Rowe's instigation of the Tolan Committee.[6]

Baldwin's ineffectual efforts shifted to more concrete plans in the wake of Executive Order 9066. On March 1, he suggested to the directors of the California branches a two-pronged strategy: first, that they meet with General DeWitt and offer "to assist in protecting the civil rights of Japanese-American citizens"; and second, that they "confer with representatives of Japanese-American organizations" and offer the ACLU's aid in bringing court challenges to the impending evacuation orders. Nothing came of either suggestion. DeWitt's staff ignored the

ACLU's overtures for meetings, and Taft and Besig found no sympathy among their Japanese American contacts for any legal challenges.[7]

Baldwin had undertaken his initial Washington consultations and his futile efforts to mobilize opposition to evacuation on his own. Although his role in founding the ACLU and his personal magnetism conferred on him considerable latitude in conducting the Union's day-to-day operations, Baldwin remained subject to the policy decisions of the ACLU's board of directors. John Haynes Holmes, the minister of New York's nondenominational Community Church, then chaired a twenty-five-member board composed of New York City residents and almost evenly divided among religious leaders, social activists, and lawyers. Despite the prestige that Baldwin had earned outside the ACLU over the past two decades, political splits and personality conflicts among the board members forced him to tread softly in forging and implementing ACLU policy. One recent incident in particular, the expulsion in 1940 of the board's only acknowledged communist member, Elizabeth Gurley Flynn, had exacerbated tensions among board members and had eroded Baldwin's support from those who resented his role as prosecuting attorney in the stormy board "trial" that culminated in Flynn's expulsion.[8]

Reporting on his meeting with James Rowe and the suggestions he had sent to the West Coast branches, Baldwin first brought the Japanese American issue before the ACLU board at its weekly meeting on March 2, 1942. The board was then divided roughly into factions led by the two lawyers who shared the title of ACLU general counsel. These two men presented a striking contrast in personality and politics. Arthur Garfield Hays, a compatriot of Baldwin since the founding of the ACLU, was a veteran of the Sacco-Vanzetti case and the Scopes trial of the 1920s and shared with Baldwin an absolutist attitude toward free speech and assembly issues. Hays also brought to his legal work a visceral suspicion of governmental actions. The board faction that looked to Hays for leadership included Socialist Party leader Norman Thomas, Oswald Garrison Villard, editor of *The Nation,* and John Finerty, who combined work as a corporate lawyer on behalf of railroads with a fiery Irish nationalism. Finerty had prepared an unsuccessful last-minute writ seeking a stay of execution for Sacco and Vanzetti and had represented Tom Mooney before the Supreme Court in a celebrated case of labor militance.[9]

Morris Ernst headed the opposing faction of the ACLU board. Abrasive and publicity-hungry, Ernst practiced in a law firm that specialized in representing labor unions and basked in a long-standing friendship with Franklin D. Roosevelt. Much like Felix Frankfurter, with whom he had collaborated in several labor cases, Ernst peppered the

White House with unsolicited policy suggestions and offers of political help. His faction of the ACLU board included vice-chairman Walter Frank, a former garment manufacturer whose law firm represented many of his fellow businessmen, and Whitney North Seymour, the board's token Republican and a partner in a prestigious Wall Street law firm. Baldwin later recalled Seymour as "a wise if cautious counselor" who gave the board "a right-wing balance—often too right to suit me." Although they differed in partisan attachment, Ernst and Seymour generally displayed a similar reluctance to challenge the exercise of governmental authority.[10]

Caught in the middle of these board divisions, and temperamentally above the battle, was Osmond K. Fraenkel, whom Baldwin later described as "our leading constitutional authority, scholarly, balanced and endlessly devoted." Despite his admitted "political bias for the left" and his role as an officer of the left-leaning National Lawyers Guild, Fraenkel retained within the ACLU a reputation for fairness and objectivity on legal questions. His involvement in the Guild "never seemed to me to influence his legal judgments," Baldwin later said of Fraenkel.[11]

These factional differences did not surface during the board's initial discussion of the Japanese American issue. With little to act upon but the rumors that Baldwin relayed from James Rowe, the ACLU board ratified the two suggestions Baldwin had already made to the West Coast branches: first, the "creation of influential national and California committees to secure modification" of military orders; and second, "an immediate court test of the legality" of the expected orders. Later in March, Baldwin drafted for the board a public letter to President Roosevelt setting out the ACLU's concern that Executive Order 9066 was "open to grave question on the constitutional grounds of depriving American citizens of their liberty and use of their property without due process of law." Baldwin's letter also urged that the government establish a system of individual loyalty hearings for the Japanese Americans subject to evacuation orders.[12]

Although at its March 23 meeting the board approved the letter to Roosevelt that Baldwin had drafted, five members registered their dissent. Those who objected to Baldwin's questioning of the constitutionality of the President's order had not often agreed on ACLU policy. Morris Ernst and Raymond Wise, a former federal prosecutor, represented the board's conservative faction and had supported the expulsion of Elizabeth Gurley Flynn. Corliss Lamont, heir to a railroad fortune but a vocal left-wing gadfly, had clashed bitterly with Ernst over the expulsion issue. The negative votes cast by Ernst and Wise reflected their sentiments as adamant Roosevelt loyalists, while Lamont's vote stemmed not from partisan attachment but from his fellow-traveling position of unquestioning support for Roosevelt as leader of a nation now in wartime alliance with the Soviet Union.[13]

This unlikely coalition of ideological opponents failed to block the decision of the board's majority to send Baldwin's letter to the White House. The loyalist minority also failed to prevent the board from directing Baldwin to "submit the first case which in his opinion might be the basis for a test of the constitutionality of the President's order." Over the next three months, Baldwin's search for test cases was complicated by the continuing efforts of Ernst and Lamont to reverse the board's initial stand on Executive Order 9066.[14]

Baldwin faced another problem in carrying out the board's directive. The loose structure and limited resources of the ACLU made the national office dependent on its scattered branches for the initiation and funding of test cases. The New York office functioned largely as a clearinghouse for branch activities, and Baldwin then relied on a single full-time staff lawyer, Clifford Forster. A young Yale Law School graduate who joined the ACLU staff in 1941, his main tasks were to screen the cases submitted by the ACLU's network of volunteer lawyers around the country and to deal with the day-to-day legal work in the office. Baldwin later spoke highly of the young lawyer's skills: "His energy, brains, initiative and judgment gave our legal service a vitality it had never had before." However, Forster had only sporadic personal contact with the ACLU's staff and lawyers outside New York and played no direct role in policy formation.[15]

Baldwin was hampered in his search for test cases by the ACLU's weakness on the West Coast. Although it maintained skeleton branches in several West Coast cities, only those in Los Angeles and San Francisco had enough dues-paying members to support offices and a full-time staff, and even these two branches operated on a shoestring. In addition, the national board exercised no control over the staffing of ACLU branches, and those in Los Angeles and San Francisco exhibited marked differences in responding to dictates from New York. Clinton Taft, who directed the Los Angeles branch, looked to Baldwin for guidance and rarely disputed board policy. As the largest and most affluent West Coast branch, Los Angeles also retained a part-time lawyer, Al Wirin.

Born in Russia in 1901 and renamed by his parents after their migration to Boston in 1909, Abraham Lincoln Wirin (who detested his adopted name and used only his initials) displayed an early concern for civil liberties as a schoolboy. Early in World War I, his vocal protest against an assault on antiwar marchers by a group of sailors resulted in a $5 fine for breach of the peace. Financial sacrifices by his parents helped Wirin through Harvard College and Harvard Law School; after graduation he worked in the ACLU's national office and developed a close friendship with Roger Baldwin. Wirin moved to Los Angeles in 1931 and established a partnership with J. B. Tietz that combined civil liberties work with bankruptcy law, which during the Depression years was one of the few sure sources of income for lawyers. Although he later praised Wirin as "probably the most energetic, daring and successfully skillful practitioner we ever had anywhere," Baldwin increasingly considered him a liability to the ACLU for his private representation of the Communist Party and its members. Wirin consistently denied party membership or sympathy with its aims, but the confusion of his private practice and role as ACLU counsel raised hackles within the national board. Along with Clinton Taft, however, Wirin considered himself bound in his ACLU work to board policy.[16]

In contrast, Ernest Besig directed an ACLU branch in San Francisco that was marked by iconoclasm and independence. Like Wirin an expatriate easterner, he moved to Los Angeles two years after his 1928 graduation from Cornell Law School. Besig worked with the ACLU branch in Los Angeles for several years, particularly on cases that involved labor-organizing battles. In the wake of the bitter and bloody general strike in San Francisco in 1934, Besig moved to that city to help organize an ACLU branch and became its executive director in June 1935. Unlike the more affluent Los Angeles branch, the San Francisco office could not afford even a part-time staff lawyer. Besig was not a member of the California bar and depended on volunteer lawyers to represent ACLU clients. "We were a piddling outfit," he later said. "We needed money that we didn't have, and we had no staff counsel. I was the executive, with a part-time stenographer, and you can't very well operate on that basis."[17]

Another contrast between the two California branches was that Besig habitually treated directives from New York with disdain, a consequence in part of his strained relations with Roger Baldwin. Political conflict between the two men added to their continuing personality clash. "My sharp differences with Roger arose in 1935," Besig later said, as a result of Baldwin's insistence that the San Francisco branch add "fellow travellers" to the local ACLU board. This dispute arose during the years of Baldwin's involvement in Popular Front activities, with which Besig vehemently disagreed. Baldwin retained a grudging admiration for Besig's devotion to the ACLU and later described him as "a young zealot for civil liberties, self-sacrificing, tactless, uncompromising, obstinate, immensely hard-working."[18]

Baldwin had suggested to Taft and Besig that they explore the possibilities of test cases well before the directive from the ACLU's national board on March 23, 1942. Despite their differences in attitude toward national ACLU policy, the two West Coast branch directors responded to Baldwin's inquiry with equally negative results. Taft reported the willingness of the Los Angeles branch to sponsor a test of Executive Order 9066 "if a good case arises," but he added that "thus far the Japanese themselves have been unwilling to cooperate with us in making such a test." Besig similarly reported to Baldwin on March 13 that he had attended a meeting of the Japanese American Citizens League and had been told that the JACL "had definitely instructed its people not to contest any action by the local, state or federal authorities."[19]

Although the Los Angeles area included the largest concentration of Japanese Americans, Baldwin heard nothing more from the branch there about potential test cases for almost three months, after the completion of mass evacuation. The news from San Francisco was also unpromising. On March 20, Besig informed Baldwin that a poll of the branch's executive committee and local membership showed majority support among both groups for Executive Order 9066 and General DeWitt's evacuation program. By narrow votes of 9-to-8 and 103-to-96, each group rejected an ACLU test of the orders, although substantial majorities favored the establishment of hearing boards for Japanese American citizens. Besig continued his efforts to find a test case despite the disapproval of such action by his governing board and membership, but to no avail. "Frankly," he wrote to Baldwin on April 4, "I think it will be a miracle if we do get a legal case testing DeWitt's orders. When it comes to a showdown, without exception the Japanese refuse to resist." To Baldwin's chagrin, opposition to evacuation appeared to be a cause without a client.[20]

Baldwin's contacts outside California were so skimpy and scattered that he learned of the first courtroom test of DeWitt's orders only months afterward. On April 13, 1942, former state judge Austin Griffiths filed a habeas corpus petition in the Seattle federal district court on behalf of Mary Asaba Ventura, a native-born Japanese American whose husband was a Philippine citizen. Ventura alleged that DeWitt's curfew order unlawfully restrained her liberty of movement and threatened her with arrest for violation. Griffiths filed the petition on a Monday morning and the case was argued that evening before Judge Lloyd L. Black, who issued an oral opinion from the bench two days later.

Judge Black's background disposed him to support the military. An Army reserve officer and former American Legion post commander, he adopted a tough "law and order" stance as prosecuting attorney of Snohomish County from 1917 to 1919. Black sided in his legal role with the lumbermen who resisted the efforts of the radical Industrial Workers of the World (the famed "Wobblies") to organize the logging camps in this forested area north of Seattle, and he prosecuted dozens of Wobblies accused by the "loyal" press and public of hindering the war effort.[21]

In ruling on Ventura's petition, Black began with a holding that she had improperly sought relief from the curfew through habeas corpus because she was not being held in custody. "So far as I know," Black said in an aside from the bench, "she may be in the hall to the court room listening to this opinion through the open door." This aspect of Black's opinion rested on solid precedent and legal doctrine. But since Griffiths had argued that the curfew constituted "constructive custody" of Ventura and other Japanese Americans who were required to remain in their houses during curfew hours, Black added that he felt compelled to decide the legality of DeWitt's order.[22]

Griffiths was unprepared for the vehemence with which Black defended DeWitt's order and questioned the loyalty of Japanese Americans. Waving aside Ventura's profession of loyalty, Black raised the specter of "fifth columnists . . . pretending loyalty to the land where they were born" but who might "become enemy soldiers over night." He asked rhetorically "how many in this court room doubt that in Tokyo they consider all of Japanese ancestry though born in the United States to be citizens or subjects of the Japanese Imperial Government? How many believe that if our enemies should manage to send a suicide squadron of parachutists to Puget Sound that the Enemy High Command would not hope for assistance from many such American-born Japanese?"[23]

Judge Black's opinion escaped notice in the ACLU national office. Given the premature status of Ventura's habeas corpus petition, the case was hardly promising as a test of DeWitt's orders in any event. However, the case was significant in its relation to the first potential test case that came to Roger Baldwin's attention, the curfew challenge brought by Minoru Yasui in Portland, Oregon. Government lawyers took the Yasui case seriously, not only because Yasui's act in courting arrest had removed the complications of the Ventura case but also because they knew that he was willing to pursue his case through the Supreme Court if necessary. With these factors in mind, Justice Department officials had sent Charles Burdell, a Special Assistant to the Attorney General, to Seattle to participate in the Ventura case. Burdell had made a point of suggesting to Judge Black that Japanese Americans posed a fifth-column threat, and he quickly incorporated large chunks of Black's opinion in the brief that he prepared for the initial hearing in the Yasui case.[24]

Although Baldwin remained unaware of the connection between the two curfew cases, word of Yasui's challenge initially sparked his interest. Portland lawyer Gus Solomon, who had volunteered his services to the ACLU in several cases, first informed Baldwin about the Yasui case in late April, 1942. The ACLU director turned Solomon's report over to Clifford Forster. Two factors in the case led Forster to recommend to Baldwin that the ACLU adopt a hands-off attitude. One was that Yasui had already secured a lawyer, Earl Bernard, who had not himself approached the ACLU with a request for assistance. The other, perhaps more important to Forster, was the report that Yasui had worked for the Japanese consulate in Chicago before the Pearl Harbor attack. Neither of these facts disturbed Ernest Besig, who had learned of the case in San Francisco from newspaper accounts and had passed on to New York his belief that the ACLU should offer support to Yasui. However, Forster replied to Besig on June 1 that the ACLU "is in no wise interested in the Yasui case."[25]

Another potential test case *did* excite Baldwin. Al Wirin reported from Los Angeles that Ernest and Toki Wakayama had approached the ACLU branch in April, shortly after the imposition of DeWitt's "freeze order" of March 29. The Wakayamas had asked Wirin for help in challenging their impending evacuation. Wirin had responded that the only avenues open were to refuse to report to the assembly center, which would risk arrest and jailing, or to report as ordered and then to bring a habeas corpus petition seeking their release from detention. Unwilling to abandon their children, the Nisei couple duly reported to the assembly center at the Santa Anita racetrack. In terms of expected public reaction and judicial sympathy, the Wakayamas promised to be an ideal test case. A native of Hawaii and a former post office worker, Ernest Wakayama was an Army veteran of World War I and an American Legion officer. He had been an active Republican precinct officer in Hawaii and after his move to California was elected secretary-treasurer of the fisherman's union on Terminal Island. As early as June 1940, Wakayama had sent to Representative Lee Geyer a formal declaration of patriotism adopted by the union and his own vow to "be the first one to report to the Government authorities should I discover any persons who are detrimental to our beloved country for immediate arrest."[26]

Wirin's plan to pursue what he told Baldwin was a "perfect" test case soon ran into legal barbed wire. Shortly after Wakayama reported to Santa Anita, camp authorities arrested him and several others for conducting a "secret" meeting in the Japanese language to organize a protest against camp conditions. Wirin held off filing his petitions while he struggled to secure Wakayama's release from the Los Angeles County Jail. The arrests embarrassed government lawyers, who privately agreed with Wirin's claims that internal camp regulations could not be enforced through federal prosecutions. The government finally dropped the charges and shipped Wakayama and his family to the Manzanar relocation camp. Wakayama's arrest, however, unsettled the ACLU national office. Clifford Forster advised Wirin on June 29 that he saw nothing "arbitrary or unreasonable" in the disputed regulations and suggested that the publicity generated by the arrests would "undoubtedly weaken" the appeal of any habeas corpus petitions.[27]

These objections did not impress Wirin, who filed the petitions in the Los Angeles federal district court in August 1942. Ernest Wakayama was so embittered by his incarceration, however, that early in 1943 he applied for repatriation to Japan despite his American citizenship. Wirin had become emotionally involved in the case as the expression of his own revulsion at the internment of Japanese Americans. Wirin pressed the case for more than a year, and forced a series of inconclusive hearings, until Wakayama's insistence on repatriation and lack of support from New York finally persuaded him to withdraw the petitions. Admitting to Baldwin "how bitter a personal disappointment" he felt in abandoning the case, Wirin expressed reluctance to begin the search for a substitute.[28]

Shortly after he learned of Ernest Wakayama's arrest, and even before Wirin had filed the habeas corpus petitions, Baldwin decided to look for an additional test case that would challenge internment. He delegated this task to Forster, who wrote to Ernest Besig in June 1942 asking that he find a camp resident "who would be willing to have us sue out a writ of habeas corpus in his behalf." The motivation behind this request was largely self-serving. Besig had reported to ACLU headquarters a few days earlier that James Purcell intended to file a habeas corpus petition on behalf of Mitsuye Endo, and had made it clear that Purcell would not ask for ACLU support. Baldwin considered the internment issue to be far more important as a legal challenge to Executive Order 9066 than the curfew, and hoped for a test case under ACLU control. However, Besig respected Purcell and had no desire to bring what might be considered a competing internment case. Besig's refusal to act ended the efforts of Baldwin and Forster to find an alternative to the Wakayama case. In the end, the ACLU wound up with no case of its own that tested internment and could only tag along as a "friend of the court" in the Endo case.[29]

Despite these setbacks, the ACLU could claim as its own the test cases initiated by Gordon Hirabayashi and Fred Korematsu. Baldwin learned of Hirabayashi's plan to refuse evacuation before the young Quaker turned himself in for arrest. Mary Farquharson wrote Baldwin from Seattle on May 14, 1942, outlining the case and asking for "suggestions regarding procedure" and the names of sympathetic lawyers. Baldwin replied quickly and enthusiastically. "I hope your Japanese boy will stick," he responded on May 18. "He sounds like a man who would—Christian and a C.O." Hirabayashi's background struck a responsive chord in Baldwin, himself a former conscientious objector. "Of course we will pay any expenses of a test suit," he assured Farquharson. Lacking legal contacts with ACLU experience, Baldwin suggested several Seattle lawyers he thought might be willing to help. "Lawyers get intrigued with questions like this even when they are not too sympathetic," he added hopefully. On the same day, the ACLU board adopted Baldwin's recommendation that it support the case.[30]

Farquharson had asked Baldwin for the names of Seattle lawyers because Arthur Barnett, with whom Hirabayashi consulted before his arrest, considered himself too inexperienced to handle an unprecedented constitutional case. The task of finding competent and willing counsel, however, soon encountered snags. Baldwin's list began with the law firm headed by George F. Vanderveer, a civil liberties hero for his role in the showcase trial in Chicago during World War I of the entire national leadership of the Industrial Workers of the World. John Geisness, a partner in the firm, initially agreed to represent Hirabayashi but dropped out within a month. The ostensible reason was that Geisness demanded a fee of $1,000, twice as much as Farquharson felt able to raise for the trial. Farquharson reported to Baldwin in mid-June her belief that "Geisness would have been willing to come down on the fee," but she added that "Vanderveer objected strenuously to any member of his firm being connected" with the case. "Vanderveer of all people!" she exclaimed in frustration.[31]

Barnett and Farquharson both suspected that behind the withdrawal of Geisness lay Vanderveer's close association with the Teamsters Union and its powerful Seattle leader, Dave Beck. Vociferously in favor of Japanese American internment, the Teamsters were a leading client of Vanderveer's firm. Forced to search for a substitute lawyer, Barnett finally enlisted Frank L. Walters, a respected corporate lawyer but one with little experience in constitutional cases. A fifty-year-old graduate of the University of Michigan Law School, Walters was stolid and formal in appearance. Barnett approached him largely because of his American Legion membership, hoping that this fraternal tie would appeal to Judge Lloyd Black, who had earlier decided the Ventura case and to whom Hirabayashi's trial had been assigned.[32]

The ACLU's representation of Fred Korematsu raised similar problems in finding a suitable lawyer. Ernest Besig's duties as director of the San Francisco branch and his lack of California bar membership precluded any courtroom role in the case. Besig first recruited Clarence Rust, a branch board member, to represent Korematsu at his initial arraignment. Because of the demands of his busy practice, however, Rust acted only in a stand-in capacity. Besig then turned to Wayne M. Collins, a young San Francisco lawyer with a practice so marginal that he shared a secretary with the firm from which he rented a room. Both in temperament and legal approach, Collins presented a contrast with Frank Walters. Intense and impatient, he ruffled feathers among adversaries and allies alike. "Wayne was a little fox terrier, with a machine-gun delivery of speech," Besig recalled. Despite their personal friendship and longtime ACLU relationship, Besig and Collins clashed in legal style. "Wayne's approach was sort of a shotgun approach, which is not my way of doing business," Besig later said. "I like to use the big weapons and not to muddy up the waters with all the little arguments that could possibly be made."[33]

Within days of his recruitment to the Korematsu case, Collins moved to force a courtroom confrontation over the constitutional issues raised by DeWitt's exclusion order. He began work immediately on a motion to dismiss the charge against Korematsu, which was due for filing on June 20, only three weeks after his client's arrest. Roger Baldwin was familiar with Collins's "shotgun" style and reputation as a "lone wolf" lawyer. On June 8, Baldwin reminded Besig that the issues presented in the case were "of such importance that the case should be exceedingly carefully prepared." Between the lines of this letter was a hint that Besig should keep a watch over Collins's shoulder. Unwilling to act as a legal censor, Besig assured Baldwin that "Collins is going to great pains" in drafting his motion. He admitted, however, that in looking for every possible argument against DeWitt's order Collins intended to "drag in most everything from soup to nuts."[34]

Baldwin's instinctive sympathy with Gordon Hirabayashi led him to recommend that the ACLU national board support the Seattle test case without reservation. In addition to his concern about Collins, the ACLU director viewed Fred Korematsu with skepticism as a potential recipient of the board's support. Before submitting the case to the board, Baldwin wrote Besig on June 8 that he would "like to know a little more about the client—his attitude, background, connections and patriotism." Besig replied that Korematsu "has no political connections and is patriotic in the conventional sense." Baldwin had expressed concern that Korematsu's act in undergoing plastic surgery might complicate the case, at least in terms of public support. Besig assured him, however, that he saw "nothing in the facts to jeopardize our chances of success."[35]

The roster of potential test cases was completed on July 12, 1942. On that date the dockets of federal courts along the West Coast included five cases brought by challengers of DeWitt's military orders: Gordon Hirabayashi in Seattle, Min Yasui in Portland, Fred Korematsu and Mitsuye Endo in San Francisco, and Ernest and Toki Wakayama in Los Angeles. Advising the ACLU national office of the latest developments in these cases, Ernest Besig expressed satisfaction that "we ought to be able to reach the Supreme Court one of these days."[36]

Roger Baldwin, however, viewed the lineup of cases with less enthusiasm. The ACLU exercised no control over the Yasui and Endo cases, while Ernest Wakayama's arrest for violation of camp rules had complicated the habeas corpus petitions and threatened to derail Al Wirin's "perfect" test of the internment program. The Hirabayashi case appealed to Baldwin, but the choice of Frank Walters as a second-best lawyer disturbed him. Finally, the Korematsu case—on paper the strongest and most significant of the five—was being handled by a lawyer in whom Baldwin had little confidence. But with internment virtually completed, and with more competent lawyers unavailable, Baldwin and the ACLU had little choice but to press ahead with these less-than-ideal cases.

Initiation of the test cases found the government's lawyers, if anything, even more divided than their opponents. One source of friction reflected the diffusion of responsibility for a program carried out under War Department orders, administered by the War Relocation Authority, and enforced by the Justice Department. Divisions of geography and bureaucratic function within each agency further complicated the task of coordinating the government's legal work. The necessity of forging a unified position on the test cases rubbed additional salt into wounds opened during the internal debate that preceded Executive Order 9066; conflict among Justice and War Department lawyers over constitutional issues continued unabated behind the façade of external agreement.

As noted earlier, Attorney General Francis Biddle held on paper the reins of the legal troika responsible for the test case litigation. He delegated to Edward Ennis, however, the primary role in these cases for the Justice Department. As director of the Alien Enemy Control Unit, Ennis had no direct jurisdiction over cases that involved citizens, but his role in drafting the initial alien-enemy proclamations and regulations made him a logical choice for this supervisory task. Ennis looked for assistance on the test cases to two of the lawyers on his small staff, John L. Burling and Nanette Dembitz.

Burling in particular played a crucial role in the Japanese American cases. Only thirty at the time, Burling was a Harvard Law School graduate who had spent his first two years after graduation working under Thomas E. Dewey in the New York County district attorney's office, where he was exposed to Dewey's aggressive style as a prosecutor of gangsters and grafting public officials. He then joined the staff of the U.S. attorney in New York City at the time Ennis headed the civil division of that office, and moved to Washington in 1941 when Ennis became general counsel of the Immigration and Naturalization Service. Burling presented a sharp contrast in personality with the gregarious, politically astute Ennis. Described by one former colleague as "brilliant but erratic" and by another who had known him from childhood as "wearing his nerve endings outside his skin," Burling suffered both from physical afflictions that included debilitating attacks of asthma and eczema and from a painful shyness that could erupt into explosions of rudeness.[37]

As the junior member of his legal staff, Ennis had recruited Nanette Dembitz, a 1938 graduate of Columbia Law School and a niece of former Supreme Court member Louis D. Brandeis. In her limited but still important role in the test cases, Dembitz spent much of her time in the Justice Department library, conducting legal research and drafting memoranda and briefs.[38]

Several other Justice Department lawyers also participated in the Japanese American cases. Local U.S. attorneys assumed responsibility for the cases at the initial stages of hearings and trials, and were assisted by lawyers assigned to the cases by Attorney General Biddle. Tom Clark, who then headed the department's Antitrust Division on the West Coast, had been delegated by Biddle early in 1942 to provide liaison with General DeWitt's legal staff. Clark in turn assigned lawyers on his staff to assist the U.S. attorneys in the prosecution of the three criminal cases, and these lawyers also worked with the Criminal Division of the Justice Department, headed by Assistant Attorney General Wendell Berge. As might be expected, the plethora of Justice Department lawyers from different divisions produced confusion during the initial hearings and trials in the test cases and complicated the work of the lawyers who took over at the appellate level.

Since it was assumed that one or more of the test cases would reach the Supreme Court, Solicitor General Charles Fahy and his staff became involved at an early stage. Although the primary role of the Solicitor General's office, one of the smallest units of the Justice Department, was that of preparing and arguing before the Supreme Court those cases in which the federal government was a party, Fahy and his staff also were responsible for cases brought before the federal courts of appeals. Fahy had an additional role in the Japanese American cases as director of the War Division of the Justice Department, which Biddle created in June 1942 to supervise all the cases that stemmed from wartime laws and regulations.

Much like Whitney North Seymour as a member of the ACLU national board, Charles Fahy added a conservative and patriotic voice to internal debates over the test cases. A fifty-year-old native of rural Georgia and a Georgetown Law School graduate, Fahy came to the Justice Department in 1940 after five years as general counsel of the National Labor Relations Board. He gained a reputation during his NLRB service as a meticulous legal craftsman, concerned more with the exactitude of his briefs and with winning cases than with policy questions. Slight in build and dapper in appearance, Fahy had been nicknamed "Whispering Charlie" by the press for his soft-spoken courtroom ways. But he could explode in dressing down his subordinates for sloppy work. Fahy had been a naval pilot during World War I and demonstrated throughout his government career a decided deference to military judgment.[39]

Practical considerations rather than legal necessity dictated that Justice Department lawyers maintain close if not cordial relations with their War Department colleagues. Although not formally a party to any of the Japanese American cases, the War Department had initiated the evacuation and internment programs and General DeWitt had issued the military orders challenged in the cases. Within the department, Assistant Secretary McCloy exercised civilian control over a military legal staff headed by Judge Advocate General Myron C. Cramer, who had replaced General Allen Gullion in this post just six days before the Pearl Harbor attack. Cramer had also served with General DeWitt in the Philippines during the 1930s. Not surprisingly, the Army's top lawyer shared with his old friends a hard-line position on the Japanese American cases.[40]

From his War Department headquarters, Cramer directed a West Coast legal staff headed by Colonel Joel F. Watson, Judge Advocate of the Western Defense Command. Watson's deputy, Captain Herbert E. Wenig, would play a critical behind-the-scenes role in the test cases. A graduate of Stanford Law School, Wenig was a reserve officer who reported to the Presidio from the office of California attorney general Earl Warren. One of his last tasks as Warren's assistant had been to compile the data on "Japanese encirclement" of military installations presented in the argument for mass evacuation that Warren made to the Tolan Committee in February 1942. During the entire course of the test cases, Wenig shuttled between the Presidio and his former state office with DeWitt's approval, and helped to draft the "friend of the court" briefs submitted to the courts by the West Coast states. Wenig and his superiors concealed this dual role from the Justice Department, no doubt because judicial rules forbid such a conflicting status.[41]

McCloy balanced his dependence on Cramer's military viewpoint with exposure to the moderating opinions of the lawyers on his personal staff. Two young lawyers drafted into military service, both Harvard Law School graduates, filled in turn the position of executive assistant to McCloy. Captain John M. Hall, who worked under McCloy from mid-1942 until early 1943, had practiced in the prestigious Boston law firm founded by his grandfather before he was recruited to McCloy's staff by his friend Harvey Bundy, Secretary Stimson's personal aide. Hall later said that McCloy "deputized the Japanese American situation into my hands" and had made him the primary liaison with Justice Department lawyers, a job that led to clashes with John Burling. Hall's successor was Captain Adrian S. Fisher, who had clerked for both Louis Brandeis and Felix Frankfurter at the Supreme Court before he joined the legal staff of the State Department in 1941. Fisher wound up in McCloy's office after a short stint as an Army Air Force navigator, when Frankfurter prevailed on him to take the post on a short-term basis. Neither of these young lawyers in uniform had much enthusiasm for internment, but each loyally carried out McCloy's orders at the occasional cost of abuse from their Justice Department counterparts.[42]

The legal staff of the War Relocation Authority (WRA) constituted the third platoon of government lawyers in the test cases. In their role as a legal quartermaster corps, WRA lawyers shouldered two burdens. First, in serving the agency that administered the internment camps, they oversaw the drafting of WRA and camp regulations and they dealt with the legal problems of camp residents. WRA lawyers also volunteered at the outset of the test cases to undertake the legal research on which the Justice Department briefs and arguments would be based.

Philip M. Glick supervised these separate tasks as Solicitor of the WRA. Born in Russia in 1905, he was a 1930 graduate of the University of Chicago Law School who became one of many urban Jewish lawyers to find a Depression-era haven in the Agriculture Department. Between 1933 and 1942, Glick rose to become chief of the Land Policy Division and also served as the department's Assistant Solicitor, working closely in both positions with Milton Eisenhower. When Eisenhower was drafted to head the WRA, Glick accompanied him to the new agency and brought along the nucleus of a legal staff. Diminutive and soft-spoken, Glick presented a contrast in personality with Edward Ennis and John McCloy but stood his ground in the internal battles over the test cases.

Glick displayed an equally firm resolve in defending the WRA in the cross fire of charges over the agency's treatment of the interned Japanese Americans. Almost from the outset of internment, West Coast politicians and their press allies claimed that the WRA was "coddling" the camp residents. At the same time, the WRA was accused of treating camp residents harshly and abusing their civil rights. Glick's most insistent and acerbic critic on this score was ACLU official Ernest Besig. The initial clash between the two lawyers illustrates the conflicting loyalties of strong-willed men who both professed devotion to civil liberties and to the interests of Japanese Americans. Their continuing battle began in June 1942 over the WRA's move in segregating those Japanese Americans considered "disloyal" or sympathetic to Japan in the Tule Lake Relocation Center in northern California.

After he had been turned away by WRA officials when he appeared at Tule Lake to meet with camp residents who had complained to the ACLU of mistreatment, Besig fired off an angry letter to Glick. Passing on to WRA lawyer Edwin Ferguson, who headed the agency's regional office in San Francisco, the suggestion that he meet with Besig to "establish friendly and sympathetic contact" with the ACLU official, Glick expressed sympathy with Besig's aims. "We are just as much interested in protecting the civil liberties of the evacuees as is the American Civil Liberties Union," Glick wrote.[43]

Glick's intervention with Tule Lake officials finally resulted in permission for Besig to meet with the complaining camp residents. At the same time, however, Glick launched an effort to persuade the ACLU to withdraw the habeas corpus petitions that challenged the WRA's internment powers. He first dispatched Maurice Walk, the agency's assistant solicitor, to the West Coast with instructions to ask that Besig appeal to

James Purcell that the petition filed on behalf of Mitsuye Endo be abandoned. "I am sorry to observe that Besig did not appear to be impressed by this argument," Walk reported to Glick on July 24, 1942. Unfazed by this rebuff, Glick met two weeks later with ACLU director Roger Baldwin and renewed his request. Baldwin reported to Besig after this meeting that the WRA solicitor was "quite opposed to our court cases" on the ground that the ACLU challenges would damage the WRA's efforts to convince the War Department that "loyal" Japanese Americans should be allowed to leave the internment camps. The condition that Glick placed on this offer—that Endo and other concededly "loyal" camp residents agree to comply with WRA "leave regulations" and to move away from the West Coast—failed to persuade either Baldwin or Besig.[44]

Well before this imbroglio with the ACLU officials, Glick had staffed his office with an eye toward an eventual court test of General DeWitt's military orders. He first recruited Maurice Walk as assistant solicitor. Walk had been Glick's jurisprudence professor in law school and left a lucrative Chicago law practice to advise his former student on the constitutional issues raised by internment. "He went to work at once," Glick later said of Walk, "guessing what kind of challenges would be made, what kind of suits we would face, what should be the position of the WRA, and outlining and roughing up drafts of possible briefs."[45]

As a self-proclaimed constitutional liberal, Walk harbored serious doubts about the WRA's legal power to hold "loyal" Japanese Americans in the internment camps. His initial research on the Endo case left him "convinced that the Supreme Court will not sanction wholesale detention of citizens without hearing or imputation of crime for an indefinite period of time," Walk confessed to Glick in July 1942. Perhaps in response to this negative assessment, Glick later recruited a second constitutional advisor, James McLaughlin. Walk soon found himself at odds with McLaughlin, whose brusque manner and hard-line defense of internment led to acrimony between the two lawyers when the test cases reached the appellate stage. Walk's resignation in August 1943, ostensibly to return to his busy law practice, stemmed in part from these personal and policy conflicts. Before he left, however, Walk shaped the basic legal strategy that the Justice Department adopted in the test cases and followed through their argument before the Supreme Court.[46]

Among the divided ranks of the government's lawyers, positions on the legal issues raised by the Japanese American cases had hardened well before the first court proceedings. Within the Justice Department, Edward Ennis and John Burling made no secret of their convictions that General DeWitt lacked the constitutional authority to issue military orders with the force of law. Only two weeks after Min Yasui challenged DeWitt's curfew order, Ennis argued to James Rowe that "the statute by permitting military commanders as a practical matter to pass criminal laws probably is an unconstitutional delegation of legislative power." Ennis struck at the heart of Public Law 503, on which enforcement of DeWitt's orders depended, in making what would be to laymen an abstruse legal argument. What he meant, in essence, was that Congress had not laid down in the statute a sufficiently precise standard on which officers of the executive branch—including DeWitt—could base orders that were legally enforceable. Without such congressional guidance, the subsequent military orders would lack constitutional sanction.[47]

War Department lawyers predictably took a hard-line position on the test cases. Their approach to the legal issues, however, ignored the delegation question that bothered Ennis and rested largely on claims that considerations of "military necessity" and the "disloyalty" of Japanese Americans as a group provided justification for DeWitt's orders. Colonel Joel Watson, who served as Dewitt's chief legal advisor, presented these claims in a September 1942 speech to the Oregon state bar association. There is little doubt that Watson's speech had been drafted by Captain Herbert Wenig, since it included substantial chunks, almost verbatim, from the statement Wenig had prepared for Earl Warren six months earlier.

The evacuation and internment of Japanese Americans had been required, Watson told the Oregon lawyers, because their proximity to military installations and defense plants "threatened not only the security of the states along the coast, but the production effort and defense of the entire nation." Not only could this factor "not be overlooked by General DeWitt" in framing defense measures, Watson added, but the "racial differences" that separated Japanese Americans from other West Coast residents made it impossible to determine their loyalty. "Their mental and emotional responses are understood by but few of our people and in general the individual Japanese presents an inscrutable personality," concluded Watson.[48]

Colonel Watson's speech touched only briefly on the constitutional origin of DeWitt's orders in the "war powers" conferred on the President in his dual roles as chief executive and commander-in-chief of the armed forces. The question of the scope of this amorphous and unspecified grant of powers to the President, and its relation to the due process and equal protection rights accorded by the Constitution to individual citizens, lay at the heart of the Japanese American test cases. Even before his appointment as WRA solicitor, however, Philip Glick had recognized the centrality of this question and had prepared a series of legal memoranda designed to provide his staff with arguments in cases that might challenge the WRA's powers to detain citizens in the internment camps. In sending these memoranda to Justice Department lawyers, Glick presented them with ready-made briefs that could be fashioned, with a little cutting and pasting, to the criminal cases as well.

Glick first addressed the "constitutional validity of wartime restraints upon persons in the United States" in a memorandum he sent to Milton Eisenhower on April 15, 1942. His analysis admitted no doubt about the balance between the "war powers" and individual rights in this constitutional conflict: "Citizens may be detained, or other restraints placed upon them, to whatever extent is necessary to the national safety in wartime. The war power to that extent overrides the constitutional guarantees in the Bill of Rights." In reaching this conclusion, Glick analogized the war powers doctrine to that of the "police powers" exercised by the states. "It is well established," he wrote, "that any measure that has a substantial relationship to promotion of the health, safety, or general welfare of a State may be properly undertaken as an exercise of the State police power, and that constitutional limitations against the deprivation of liberty or property without due process of law do not apply in such a case."[49]

Glick foresaw the difficulty in applying the police power doctrine, under whose sheltering umbrella he placed the war powers doctrine, to a situation in which one class of citizens was singled out for discriminatory treatment. Supreme Court precedent that stretched back for almost a half-century had made clear that the police powers of the states—applied in areas such as public health and safety—could be exercised only on a basis that did not discriminate on grounds of race. As early as 1886, in its opinion in the *Yick Wo* case, the Court had struck down as a violation of due process—the doctrine that citizens must be treated equally and fairly by the government—a San Francisco ordinance that discriminated against Chinese laundrymen. The complaining Chinese in this case had been uniformly denied licenses to operate laundries in wooden buildings while their Caucasian competitors had all received dispensations from the law.[50]

The only possible exception to the doctrine of the *Yick Wo* case was that other constitutional provisions provided support for the discrimination against the racial group singled out for separate treatment. Reaching out for support to the war powers doctrine, Glick performed a feat of legal legerdemain in his memorandum to Eisenhower. It followed from his analysis, Glick asserted, "that restraints may discriminate between certain classes of persons, so long as the classification is related to a genuine war need and does not under the guise of national defense discriminate against any class of persons for a purpose unrelated to the national defense." Glick admitted that the determination of what would constitute a "genuine war need" turned on questions of fact and thereby opened to judicial scrutiny the reasonableness of restraints on Japanese American citizens. He was confident, however, that "the courts will give great weight to legislative determination of need, and will not substitute their judgment for that of the law-making authority in doubtful cases." Glick ignored in his initial analysis the troubling question of whether the "law-making authority" was Congress, which had rushed through Public Law 503 with only perfunctory and one-sided hearings, or General DeWitt, whose "judgment" reflected military concerns alone. Behind this question lay the delegation problem that bothered Edward Ennis, but which Glick would leave to the courts for resolution.[51]

Glick proposed reliance in prospective internment cases on three kinds of "facts" to justify the detention of Japanese Americans. He first raised the prospect of vigilante violence against this racial minority. Detention as a precautionary measure against "bloodshed and violence that cannot readily be controlled by police protection," he argued, "would be reasonable if the prevention of the consequent disorder could be shown to be related to the war effort." Second, he claimed that "resident Japanese cannot well be distinguished from a disguised Japanese soldier landed by parachute or from small boats along the coast." Glick's third proposition was that Japanese Americans were "much more likely to engage in sabotage and fifth column work than any other class of resident," which would make it reasonable to take preventive measures against all citizen Japanese and thus to distinguish between them and other American citizens." Assuming that such "facts" could be established in test cases, Glick concluded, "the removal of all Japanese from vital defense localities, and restrictions of their movements in other areas within range of feasible sea or air attack, is justified."[52]

This hastily drafted memorandum was designed to provide WRA lawyers with a legal strategy in defending challenges to the agency's internment powers. Glick and his staff, however, worked closely with Justice Department lawyers in preparing for the trials in the criminal prosecutions. Glick's initial memorandum, and the material assembled by the WRA staff to flesh out the "facts" he proposed to present to the courts, handed to government lawyers a detailed blueprint of the strategy they followed from the trials through the Supreme Court. This strategy included two arguments, one constitutional and the other factual. Government lawyers would first urge on the courts an expansive reading of the President's vaguely defined war powers, justifying the application of DeWitt's orders to a single ''class'' of citizens by analogy to the police powers of the states. The factual basis for the orders would rest on the argument that the distinctive ''racial characteristics'' of Japanese Americans predisposed them to disloyalty and the commission of sabotage and espionage, thereby supporting the ''military necessity'' claim on which the orders rested.

WRA lawyers moved quickly to search out material to buttress the ''facts'' asserted in Glick's memorandum, although three months would pass before the Endo case first directly involved the WRA in litigation. On April 22, 1942—the day of Min Yasui's indictment for curfew violation—Edwin Ferguson asked for research help from Edwin Bates, head of the WRA's Information Service Division. ''We have no way of knowing when some disgruntled citizen Japanese may seek to test his rights,'' wrote Ferguson. Noting that ''the chief legal work involved in defending the constitutionality'' of internment ''will lie in assembling and marshalling facts,'' he requested material bearing on the loyalty of Japanese Americans. ''The keystone of our defense in any litigation will be the proof of facts showing disloyalty or possibility of disloyalty among the Japanese to an extent justifying the special precaution of detention,'' he reminded Bates.[53]

Among the ''evidence'' he wanted on this issue, Ferguson included data on the ''dual nationality'' of native-born Japanese Americans under the laws of Japan, the education of the Kibei group in Japan, ''evidence of non-absorption of Japanese into the American culture,'' evidence of ''suspicious activities'' of Japanese Americans around military installations, and ''evidence of specific acts of disloyalty among citizen Japanese or Japanese aliens'' such as the holding of reserve commissions in the Japanese armed forces. Ferguson noted that much of this ''evidence'' might be inadmissable in court as hearsay, but he asked Bates to track down the names and addresses of persons ''who might be able to testify from personal knowledge'' about these questions.[54]

With the first test case—the trial of Min Yasui—set to begin in Portland on June 12, 1942, Glick and his staff had hammered out both a strategy and supporting material that they handed ready-made to their Justice Department counterparts. Discord among their ranks was concealed from the courts and the lawyers who represented the Japanese American challengers. Edward Ennis and John Burling, the most adamant opponents of Glick's constitutional arguments, confined their objections to the pages of memoranda that remained in filing cabinets. At least on the surface, government lawyers approached the courts with a uniform position.

The dictates of the adversary system had forced government lawyers to close ranks behind a single constitutional position in the Japanese American cases, despite the discord that had raged for months among them. The approach of the test case trials failed, however, to heal the equally divisive split within the American Civil Liberties Union. Debate over the March 1942 letter to President Roosevelt, expressing the "grave" concern of the ACLU's national board over the constitutionality of Executive Order 9066, had first split the board. Rather than concede their defeat, the coalition of Roosevelt loyalists and legal conservatives who lost this initial vote dug in their heels and renewed their campaign to place limits on the constitutional arguments open to ACLU lawyers in the test cases.

Board member John Finerty, who had voted with the majority in the March debate, brought the issue of the ACLU's position in the test cases to a head on May 4. Finerty presented a resolution at the board's weekly meeting that would have placed the ACLU on record as opposing, "in the absence of immediate military necessity, any order by the government of the United States investing either military or civilian authorities with power to remove any citizen or group of citizens" from their homes. The board took no immediate action on Finerty's resolution. Pressing the issue, Finerty offered a follow-up resolution at the board's next meeting. This resolution stated that the provision of hearing boards to determine the loyalty of Japanese Americans on an individual basis, suggested in the board's earlier letter to Roosevelt, "would not cure the constitutional violations" that mass evacuation and internment had produced.[55]

Heated objections to Finerty's two resolutions led board chairman John Haynes Holmes to appoint a five-member committee charged with drafting a referendum for submission to the ACLU's national committee. This group included more than seventy ACLU members spread across the country, who acted in an advisory capacity on issues that divided the national board. Morris Ernst and Whitney North Seymour, although divided by partisan sympathy, represented those on the ACLU board who supported the constitutionality of Roosevelt's order. John Finerty and Arthur Garfield Hays represented those who opposed the order, while Osmond Fraenkel provided a moderating and mediating voice on the committee. Holmes asked the committee members to meet with ACLU director Roger Baldwin, not to resolve their differences but to draft an opposing pair of resolutions for submission to the national committee.[56]

After consultation with Baldwin over the week that followed the May 11 board meeting, the committee polished the language of two resolutions. One combined Finerty's two resolutions into one that reiterated opposition both to the evacuation of citizens and to the provision of hearing boards as a constitutional curative. The countering resolution had been drafted by Walter Frank and Nathan Greene, the latter a long-time friend of Supreme Court member Felix Frankfurter. The Frank-Greene resolution supported the government's right during wartime "to establish military zones and to remove persons, either citizens or aliens, from such zones when their presence may endanger national security, even in the absence of a declaration of martial law." This resolution added, however, the qualifying condition that the ACLU would support evacuation "only if directly necessary to the prosecution of the war or the defense of national security" and only if evacuation was "based upon a classification having a reasonable relationship to the danger intended to be met."[57]

Although neither resolution directly attacked the constitutional basis of Executive Order 9066, Finerty's version authorized ACLU support for challenges to orders that imposed restraints on citizens without a showing of "immediate military necessity." The Frank-Greene resolution, in contrast, implied ACLU support for Roosevelt's order on a showing that a "reasonable" basis existed for the removal of Japanese Americans from the West Coast. In essence, the first placed the burden of proof on the government while the second shifted it to the challengers. The Frank-Greene resolution in fact echoed Philip Glick's earlier memorandum on this crucial issue.

Roger Baldwin withheld action on the pending test cases for a month, while members of the ACLU board and national committee considered the opposing resolutions sent to them on May 22. When finally tabulated on June 16, the referendum result produced a clear victory for those who would subordinate civil liberties to wartime considerations and political loyalties. The ACLU's governing bodies approved the restrictive Frank-Greene resolution by a precise 2-to-1 vote of the seventy-eight members who indicated a choice. The board members in the new majority included ideological opponents such as Morris Ernst and Corliss Lamont, literary notables such as Van Wyke Brooks, John Dos Passos, Elmer Rice, and Max Lerner, and Whitney North Seymour and Osmond Fraenkel, lawyers who often clashed on civil liberties issues.

Among those who backed the losing side were ACLU chairman John Haynes Holmes and general counsel Arthur Garfield Hays, socialist leader Norman Thomas, and pacifist minister John Nevin Sayre, whose social gospel had influenced Gordon Hirabayashi to challenge the curfew and evacuation.[58]

The ACLU board promptly moved to enforce the new policy. Baldwin was instructed on June 22 to inform the West Coast branches that "local committees are not free to sponsor cases in which the position is taken that the government has no constitutional right to remove citizens from military areas." The only legal argument open to lawyers who acted in the test cases under ACLU auspices was that DeWitt's orders had unlawfully singled out Japanese Americans on racial grounds. Should any of the lawyers refuse to bow to the board's dictate, they would be forced to withdraw as ACLU counsel. Perhaps in anticipation of resistance, the board also directed Baldwin to "advise the defendants in the test cases already brought to arrange, if they desire, for counsel who will be free to raise other constitutional issues."[59]

Baldwin dutifully passed on the board's directives in identical letters to Al Wirin, Mary Farquharson and Ernest Besig. The defendants "ought to be able to raise any constitutional question they wish," he admitted, "but we cannot participate except in challenging the evacuation order as it applies to Japanese-Americans on the ground of race discrimination." Swallowing his own objections to the new policy, he suggested that the test case lawyers act as individuals "without association" with the ACLU and that independent committees be set up to support the cases "without using the name of the Civil Liberties Union." Confessing that the policy switch "will cause a little trouble," Baldwin held out the prospect of financial backing from outside sources. Funds had been provided in other cases by foundations and well-heeled friends of the ACLU, and Baldwin expressed his willingness to tap these sources for the Japanese-American cases.[60]

Reaction to Baldwin's letter ranged from submission to rejection. Al Wirin, who had not yet filed the habeas corpus petitions on behalf of the Wakayamas, replied from Los Angeles that he had no desire to challenge the constitutionality of Executive Order 9066. On the contrary, he wrote, "it is our judgment that such blanket attack would hurt the effective presentation of the case both legally and psychologically." Wirin intended rather to challenge his clients' detention as "imprisonment without a hearing of any kind" and as "imprisonment resulting from race or ancestry." This approach fit neatly within the board's policy; it also reflected Wirin's role as an ACLU loyalist and his status as a lawyer on retainer.[61]

Mary Farquharson acted as a volunteer in the Hirabayashi case and displayed no compunction in writing Baldwin from Seattle that she "was very much disappointed—and shocked—to learn of the action" of the ACLU board. After consulting with Frank Walters and Hirabayashi's local supporters, however, she reported to Baldwin that "it seems impossible to think of doing anything but carrying on in the best way possible and I think your suggestion of an independent committee is a good one." With the help of Ray Roberts, she organized the Gordon Hirabayashi Defense Committee and set out to raise funds from local sources.[62]

In his reply to Baldwin on July 2, Ernest Besig first adopted a conciliatory tone. With only two dissents, he reported, the executive committee of the San Francisco branch had agreed that "insofar as any new cases are concerned, we must consider ourselves bound by the change in policy." But he refused to back down in the Korematsu case. Speaking for his local branch, Besig wrote that "we feel compelled to proceed as before, because we cannot in good conscience withdraw from the case at this late date." In rejecting Baldwin's proposal that an independent committee be set up to support Korematsu, Besig pointedly reminded the ACLU director that "at the time of our intervention in this case we were acting in complete accord with the Board's position." Besig's argument against the retroactive application of the new policy rested on the letter the ACLU board had sent to President Roosevelt in March 1942. While the letter had not directly challenged the constitutionality of Executive Order 9066, in expressing the ACLU's "grave" concern on this issue the board had implied that such a challenge might later find support from the ACLU.[63]

Besig added fuel to the smoldering conflict when he sent Baldwin a copy of the brief Wayne Collins had prepared for the initial hearing in the Korematsu case. Collins included in his brief a direct attack on Executive Order 9066 as an unconstitutional exercise of the "war powers" delegated to the President. Without the imposition of martial law, the contentious lawyer argued, restraints on the movements of *any* civilian were unlawful. Baldwin sent the brief to Osmond Fraenkel with a request that he report to the board on its compliance with the new policy. This task was simple, and Fraenkel duly reported that Collins had gone "even beyond the position originally authorized by the Board." At the same time, Fraenkel sympathized with Besig's claim that his branch had acted within the limits of ACLU policy when it initially agreed to represent Korematsu. Walter Frank, who was then acting as board chairman in the absence of John Haynes Holmes, privately agreed with Fraenkel that "the San Francisco committee could not be stopped although it was raising many points not authorized by the Board and others that were legally foolish.''[64]

Notwithstanding his private views, Frank fired off a telegram to San Francisco on July 8, repeating the board's demands that Besig set up an independent defense committee and replace Collins with a lawyer who had no ACLU affiliation. Besig replied to this second edict as he had to the first. After quickly convening his local board for a vote of confidence, he answered on July 10 with a tone of defiance. ''We don't intend to trim our sails to suit the Board's vacillating policy,'' Besig wrote to Clifford Forster, adding a threat to force the issue to a referendum vote of the entire national membership. The San Francisco branch director acted within his rights as a local official in proposing a national vote on board policy. The prospect of a wider schism over the Korematsu case did not appeal to Roger Baldwin. ''That would be most unfortunate and should be avoided at all costs,'' he warned Walter Frank. ''We must come to an agreement with them,'' Baldwin added firmly.[65]

The ACLU board did not share Baldwin's sympathy for the position of the San Francisco branch. After a lengthy discussion of the conflict on June 20, the board instructed ACLU secretary Lucille Milner to send Besig an order that Collins drop his ''wholly indefensible position'' in the Korematsu case. Milner also relayed for a third time the demand that the branch pursue the case through an independent committee. Besig simply ignored these demands, although he also dropped his threat to provoke a national referendum. The trial of Fred Korematsu took place on September 8, 1942. Besig's refusal to answer mail from New York for more than two months left relations between him and the ACLU board at a standoff.[66]

The first round in the courtroom battle over the Japanese American cases began with Min Yasui's trial in Portland on June 12, 1942. Hearings and trials in the other test cases took place in each of the next four months, while Yasui was finally brought from solitary confinement in the Multnomah County Jail to hear the judgment of conviction against him on November 16. The following chapter will recount the initial judicial proceedings in these cases. Worth mention at this point, however, is that none of the lawyers who represented the Japanese Americans had the backing of the national ACLU. This fact raises a puzzling question: What factors led the only independent organization dedicated to defending the rights of racial and political minorities to withhold support from those who challenged the uprooting of an entire racial group from its homes? Put another way, the question requires explanation of the outcome of the referendum on the Frank-Greene resolution: Why did the ACLU by a 2-to-1 margin refuse to sanction direct challenges to the President's power to authorize the military orders directed at Japanese Americans?

The outcome of the struggle over ACLU policies in wartime cases suggests that principled support for civil liberties was a veneer worn thin by the rub of conflicting pressures. Evidence for this view—and expression of these pressures—comes from the report in Osmond Fraenkel's diary of an informal meeting of the ACLU board on October 12, 1942. Board chairman John Haynes Holmes, obviously concerned about the acrimony within the board over the past six months and hoping to ventilate the steam of personal and policy disputes in a relaxed setting, had called the meeting held at Walter Frank's home. Holmes had circulated in advance a list of topics for discussion that included the Japanese American cases. More pressing on the board's agenda, however, were the pending sedition prosecutions of pro-Axis agitators such as William Dudley Pelley, whose band of "Silver Shirts" preached Hitler's brand of "Aryan" racial supremacy. The ACLU board at the time was closely divided on providing legal support to the alleged seditionists.

Holmes led off the board's discussion with the provocative suggestion that "perhaps some of the members were actuated by considerations other than devotion to civil liberties." This challenge seemed to touch raw nerves. According to Fraenkel, the playwright Elmer Rice shot back that "the Union should not assist anyone who aided the enemy; he was for America and against anyone who opposed the American way." Whitney North Seymour then announced his intention to submit a resolution at the next board meeting that would limit the ACLU's support in sedition cases to issues of procedural regularity. Morris Ernst added to these expressions of wartime patriotism his partisan view that the ACLU "should assist the government in formulating its policy." The ACLU was "losing our influence," he claimed, because it was "not taking an affirmative position" on the government's side. When Fraenkel proposed supporting sedition case defendants "except where their utterances interfered with the war effort within the clear and present danger rule," he was dismayed that "no one appeared to agree."[67]

A handful of board members did voice concern about the erosion of support for civil liberties. Reverend Allen Knight Chalmers told his fellow members that "we were too fearful and anxious to remain respectable." Arthur Garfield Hays, who shared with Ernst the post of ACLU general counsel, "was astonished to hear so much talk against civil liberties" among the organization's leaders. Perhaps the most ominous reaction to the debate was Roger Baldwin's statement that "there might be situations in which he would be unable to act in carrying out the Board's orders and in which he might, independently, feel he must take contrary action.'' Even the prospect of rebellion by the ACLU director—who had served the organization and the cause of civil liberties for more than two decades—did not seem to faze the board's adamant majority.[68]

Patriotism and partisan attachment, however, do not fully explain the board's attitude toward the wartime cases, those of Japanese Americans and alleged seditionists alike. During the ''Red Scare'' that followed World War I, the ACLU had battled the prosecutions of anarchists and communist supporters of the Russian revolution, despite the sympathy of many ACLU members for the administration of Woodrow Wilson. In fighting for the rights of black Americans during the 1930s, the ACLU had also criticized President Roosevelt for his failure to support anti-lynching legislation.[69]

What seems to have produced the ''shift in opinion within the Board'' that so distressed Osmond Fraenkel was the nature of World War II as a global crusade against Nazi and fascist aggression and terror. Like most other Americans, members of the ACLU board were willing to countenance every effort to win the war. Separated by a continent from the bulk of the Japanese American population, the board members—all of whom lived in New York—placed their hatred of the Axis above their civil liberties concern. The man who authorized the evacuation was not only the President but Commander-in-Chief of the troops who fought to preserve democracy. Those in the ACLU who supported the Japanese American challengers thus confronted the visceral sentiments of their fearful colleagues.[70]

6

"We Could Have You Inducted"

THE TRIAL of the first Japanese American to challenge General DeWitt's orders began in the federal courthouse in Portland, Oregon, on a Friday morning, June 12, 1942. Brought to the courtroom from his cell in the Multnomah County Jail, the slight, intense defendant had already spent several weeks in solitary confinement while he awaited trial. "United States of America, plaintiff, versus Minoru Yasui, defendant," intoned Judge James Alger Fee. "The defendant is ready for trial, your Honor," replied Earl Bernard. "The Government is ready, your Honor," answered United States Attorney Carl Donaugh.[1]

In truth, neither lawyer was fully prepared for a trial that would involve an untested congressional statute, unprecedented wartime orders, and uncharted constitutional waters. They knew that it would take little time to establish the facts of Yasui's curfew violation. Since his client admitted these facts, Bernard had advised him to waive his right to a jury trial and to place the legal issues squarely before Judge Fee. Both lawyers also knew of Fee's reputation as a judicial maverick who often conducted his own interrogation of witnesses from the bench. An Oregon native who was graduated from Columbia Law School in 1914, Fee had worked as a War Department lawyer in 1919 and 1920 and had been a state court judge before his appointment to the federal bench in 1931 by President Hoover.

As soon as Bernard and Donaugh voiced their readiness to proceed, Fee introduced an unusual twist to normal trial practice. Sitting in the spectator's section of the courtroom were eight of Portland's leading lawyers. He had asked the members of this legal panel "to appear as friends of the Court in this proceeding on the constitutional issues" raised by the Yasui case, the judge explained. Bernard and Donaugh knew from earlier discussions with Fee of his doubts about two of the crucial questions in the case: Whether Yasui had forfeited his American citizenship by working for the Japanese consulate in Chicago before the war; and whether Public Law 503 was constitutional as applied to citizens. Confronted in effect with a jury of lawyers on these issues, Bernard and Donaugh bowed to Fee's judicial innovation.[2]

The two lawyers responsible for arguing the case approached Yasui's trial with quite different goals, aside from their divergent interests in its outcome. Earl Bernard's commitment as a lawyer was to one client and his single goal was to win the case, either at trial or on appeal. Assuming he prevailed on the issue of Yasui's contested citizenship, Bernard hoped to persuade Judge Fee that Executive Order 9066, as the legal foundation of the curfew order, was unconstitutional, and he intended to use every available argument in making this attack. With no ties to the American Civil Liberties Union—which had refused in any event to support his client—Bernard would not be constrained by the ACLU resolution limiting the grounds of such an attack. Yasui's trial thus proceeded, on Bernard's part, without any connection to the other test cases.

For the government, however, this first judicial test of Executive Order 9066 assumed an importance that extended far beyond the curfew issue alone. Carl Donaugh certainly hoped to secure Yasui's conviction at trial. His task depended, of course, on a favorable ruling by Judge Fee on the constitutional question. While a ruling against the presidential order could be appealed and would have no weight as precedent, a loss in the initial test case would place an added burden on the lawyers who prosecuted the later cases. Donaugh had another goal than that of upholding the curfew order. The Yasui case formed an essential element in the government's long-range strategy in defending the evacuation and internment programs in which the curfew had been the first step. Yasui's trial offered government lawyers a chance to try out the courtroom tactics on which the strategy was based. The success or failure of these tactics in the first trial would thus shape the approach to the subsequent test cases.

The division of authority among government lawyers would normally have given the task of framing the test case strategy and trial tactics to the Justice Department. Responsibility for Yasui's prosecution rested with this agency, and Donaugh's role in the case stemmed from his position as U.S. attorney in Oregon. The test case strategists came, however, from the War Relocation Authority, an agency with no direct connection to the case. The WRA played no part in the enforcement of the curfew and was limited to administration of the internment camps. Nonetheless, WRA lawyers eagerly volunteered for duty in the Yasui case and in fact wrote the script for the trial. Their goal was to utilize this first trial as a dry run for a later, and legally more significant, courtroom test of the WRA's power to hold Japanese Americans in the barbed-wire camps. Victory in this initial case would set the stage, WRA lawyers hoped, for a successful defense of detention.

WRA solicitor Philip Glick and his legal staff had begun their preparation of the test case strategy even before they learned of Yasui's curfew challenge. Glick's memorandum to Milton Eisenhower in April 1942 had outlined a prospective legal strategy based on claims that Japanese Americans were "much more likely to engage in sabotage and fifth column" activities than other West Coast residents. Concrete evidence that Japanese Americans had committed such acts would obviously help in securing convictions of those who challenged DeWitt's orders. Like other government lawyers, however, Glick knew of no such evidence. Assuming that it existed in War Department files, military intelligence records that might substantiate such charges were hardly likely to be offered as evidence in a public trial.[3]

Given these limitations, the strategy devised by WRA lawyers depended on the argument that the "racial characteristics" of Japanese Americans predisposed them to the commission of subversive acts. The follow-up work of the WRA staff in "assembling and marshalling facts" to support this argument was thus intended to present the courts with a substitute for direct evidence in future test cases. Soon after they learned of Yasui's impending trial in Portland, WRA lawyers volunteered their assistance to Carl Donaugh. Two weeks before the trial date, Donaugh responded to a letter from Maurice Walk that urged him to press this argument at the trial. Donaugh needed no prompting. "In so far as the rules of evidence permit," he assured Walk, "I wish to introduce evidence to support the proclamation of the Western Defense Command . . . affecting the Japanese by reason of their racial characteristics and belief which stamp and distinguish them from other nationalities."[4]

In a lengthy letter to Donaugh on June 6, Walk presented the prosecutor with a detailed blueprint of the trial tactics that flowed from the WRA strategy. Granting that DeWitt's curfew order subjected citizens of Japanese ancestry to racial discrimination, Walk suggested that "the facts relied on to vindicate the legality of this differential treatment are not susceptible of proof by the ordinary types of evidence." Walk noted that Donaugh would thus "be compelled to rely greatly on the doctrine of judicial notice" in presenting evidence. Designed to avoid the need for testimony on questions such as the wording of statutes, this doctrine required that evidence submitted for judicial notice be limited to undisputed factual issues.[5]

Walk proposed that Donaugh employ the judicial notice doctrine to make the government's "military necessity" and "disloyalty" arguments. The supposed link between these separate elements of the claim that the curfew orders were lawful rested on Walk's premise that Japanese Americans had organized a "fifth column" of saboteurs and espionage agents. Walk conceded that the government could not provide direct evidence of the existence of a shadowy and secret group which "gives no inkling of its plans or of its membership." To require that the government present such evidence, he argued, "would place upon the State an intolerable burden of proof at a time when it is struggling for survival." The lack of witnesses able to present this missing proof did not, however, dissuade Walk from urging that Donaugh ask that Judge Fee take judicial notice of eleven "propositions," which the WRA lawyer called "matters of public knowledge and general notoriety."[6]

Central to these propositions was the following claim: "There is a Japanese fifth column in this country of undisclosed and undetermined dimensions. It is composed of American citizens of Japanese descent, and will be used as an instrument of espionage and of sabotage." Walk did not explain to Donaugh why, if the existence of the fifth column was a matter of public knowledge, proving this claim through the testimony of witnesses would place an "intolerable burden" on the government. Evading this question, Walk submitted a list of "propositions" that supposedly showed that Japanese Americans were predisposed to join or support the secret fifth column. He first conceded that the "great majority" of this group was loyal to the United States, but then echoed DeWitt's claim that "it is impossible during this period of emergency to make a particular investigation of the loyalty of each person in the Japanese community." The proposition on which this claim depended—and which Walk suggested that Judge Fee notice judicially as an undisputed fact—laid bare the racist foundation of the "racial characteristics" argument that underlay the entire test case strategy: "Such an investigation would be hampered in any case by the difficulties which the Caucasian experiences with Oriental psychology."[7]

Walk divided his remaining propositions into two categories. Those in the first reflected a mixture of fact and racial stereotyping. Noting the facts that some members of the Japanese American population had been educated in Japan, that others belonged to the Emperor-worshipping cult of Shinto, and that some claimed dual nationality under Japanese law, Walk concluded that "it is impossible to predict how these persons will act if a Japanese army of racial brothers were landed upon our shores."

Under the doctrine of judicial notice, of course, such a prediction would need to be evident and undisputed. Walk's second category of propositions rested on the "protective custody" argument that government lawyers also pressed during the course of the test cases. The first of these propositions summed up the argument: "The presence of persons of Japanese descent in strategic areas has caused widespread public suspicion and animosity among the general public and creates the danger of disturbances to the civil peace and order of such areas, as well as a hazard to the safety of such persons."[8]

Walk made no secret in his letter to Donaugh that WRA lawyers viewed Yasui's trial as a laboratory in which to experiment with the judicial notice strategy. Their ultimate goal was success in a case that challenged the WRA's power to hold Japanese Americans in the internment camps. "It is of great importance to us," Walk emphasized, "in planning the strategy of a case which will necessarily involve the validity of the detention of Japanese-Americans as well as their exclusion from military areas, to know just how far we are likely to get with the doctrine of judicial notice." Walk concluded with the hope that Donaugh would "find it possible to urge the foregoing considerations upon the Court in the approaching trial of Minoru Yasui."[9]

Perhaps because he suspected that Judge Fee might object to a case that depended entirely on this strategy, Donaugh began a search for witnesses who might support the "racial characteristics" argument with direct testimony. However, he accepted the basic outline of the trial that Walk had prepared. Charles Burdell, the young Justice Department lawyer who sat at Donaugh's side during the trial, applied further pressure for the adoption of Walk's strategy. As a Special Assistant to the Attorney General, Burdell had assisted Donaugh's counterpart in Seattle during the argument of the Ventura case before Judge Lloyd Black in April 1942. Burdell had been assigned to this task by Tom Clark, the Justice Department lawyer who acted as liaison on the West Coast with General DeWitt's legal staff.

Before he left Seattle to work on the Yasui case in Portland, Burdell had drafted for submission to Judge Fee a brief that included the government's "racial characteristics" argument. Burdell did not mince words. "Jap citizens are inevitably bound, by intangible ties, to the people of the Empire of Japan," he wrote. "They are alike, physically and psychologically." Burdell then elaborated his genetic theory of loyalty. "Even now, though we have been separated from the English people for over 100 years, we still take pride in the exploits of the R.A.F. over Berlin, and the courageous fighting of the Aussies in Northern Africa. Why? Because they are people like us. They are Anglo-Saxons." Burdell's theory equally fit the Japanese Americans. "Who can doubt that these Japs in this country, citizens as well as aliens, feel a sense of pride in the feats of the Jap Army—this feeling of pride is strong in some, weak in others, but the germ of it must be present in the mind of every one of them."[10]

When the trial of Min Yasui began on the morning of June 12, Carl Donaugh had four witnesses ready in the courtroom. Two were there to establish that Yasui had knowingly violated the curfew order. The other two had been recruited to make the "racial characteristics" argument through direct testimony. Although he agreed with the outline of the trial strategy that Maurice Walk had drafted, Donaugh considered it safer to rely on live witnesses in making this argument, since Judge Fee might balk at the tactic of asking that he take judicial notice of Walk's "propositions" on the basis of documents alone.

Donaugh opened his case against Yasui with the testimony of Portland police sergeant William H. Mass. Yasui came into the downtown police station at 11:20 on the night of March 28, Mass related, "and he told me that he wanted to be arrested, he wanted to test the constitutionality of that alien curfew law. He said he had been down in the North End; he asked several policemen down there to arrest him, but they wouldn't do it, and so he came into the Station." Bernard declined his chance to cross-examine Sergeant Mass, and Donaugh then put on the stand an agent of the Portland FBI office. Yasui had showed up in his office on Monday, March 30, Special Agent Ray Mize told the court, "for the purpose of being questioned as to violation of the curfew regulation." Mize said that he had asked Yasui why he had deliberately courted arrest, and testified that Yasui answered that he felt that the curfew order "was unconstitutional, in that it was a discrimination against one group of United States citizens" in singling out Japanese Americans. "I asked him if he felt that during these particular times his action would reflect very favorably on the Japanese colony," Mize added, "and Mr. Yasui stated that when thinking it over he did not think that it would be a very good reflection and that he in a certain sense was sorry that he had taken the action that he had." Mize concluded his testimony by relating an admission Yasui made during their conversation: "I asked Mr. Yasui what he would do if he was in charge, in command of the West Coast here, and an invasion of this country was very probable . . . and Mr. Yasui said, 'Well, that is a rather hard question at this time,' but after due hesitation he finally stated that 'I feel that I would intern all Japanese aliens and Japanese citizens.' "[11]

When Mize stepped down from the witness stand and concluded the government's case against Yasui, Charles Burdell took over from Donaugh in questioning Yasui. Donaugh had introduced, without objection from Bernard, the form Yasui had signed in 1940 when he registered with the State Department as an agent of the Japanese government. Burdell had hardly begun to press Yasui on the question of his allegiance to Japan when Judge Fee jumped in and took over the interrogation. Announcing first that the application of the curfew order to citizens "makes me doubt its constitutionality," Fee added that the issue of Yasui's citizenship status was the reason he had asked the eight Portland lawyers "to be present here as friends of the court to determine whether or not" Yasui retained his citizenship.[12]

Judge Fee surprised Yasui with an unanticipated line of interrogation. "What is Shinto?" he abruptly asked. Yasui was clearly puzzled by the question. "Shinto? As I understand, Shinto is the national religion of Japan." "Do you give adherence to its precepts?" Fee continued. "My mother and father were Methodists in Japan," Yasui replied, "and I myself have been a Methodist in this country and I don't know the precepts of the Shinto religion." Fee pressed on doggedly. "Was not Shinto practiced in your household?" "No, sir," Yasui answered. Barely concealing his disbelief, and advertising his preparatory research on the issue, Fee persisted in his judicial inquisition. Did Yasui "accept divine pretentions on the part of the Emperor of Japan?" "No, sir, I do not," Yasui replied. "Were offerings ever made in the graveyard or before the grave of any of the people of your family?" Fee then asked. "Offerings? Floral offerings, yes, on Memorial Day and on Sundays." Fee was still not satisfied: "Were there not food offerings placed?" "There were no food offerings placed," Yasui relied. "Both my father and mother are good, devout Methodists. They are really Christians."[13]

Confronted with this adamant disavowal by Yasui of the state religion of Japan, Fee abruptly shifted his line of questioning. "Do you believe in the sanctity of an oath?" he demanded to know. "I do, sir," Yasui affirmed. With Bernard sitting in reluctant silence, Fee proceeded to impugn Yasui's patriotism and motivations in challenging the curfew order. He extracted from Yasui the embarrassing admission that he could not repeat the oath he took at his induction as a reserve Army officer three years earlier. "I cannot repeat it," Yasui conceded, although he strained to recall that its substance was "to obey the commands of the commanding officer upon proper authority in time of active service, or something to that effect." Fee demanded to know whether Yasui "thought there was no special obligation on you to obey this particular order?" In his answer, Yasui attempted to distinguish his obligations as a military officer from his rights as a citizen. He had held himself in readiness "for active service at any time," Yasui said, "but I feel that, after all, this country is dedicated to the proposition that all men are created equal, that every American citizen has a right to walk up and down the streets as a free man, and I felt that these regulations were not constitutional."[14]

Unable to extract a concession that Yasui considered his military oath of allegiance and promise of obedience as paramount to his rights as a citizen, Fee finally abandoned his role as a judicial Torquemada and returned the questioning to Bernard. Explaining his statement to Ray Mize about the necessity for internment as a protection against sabotage and espionage, Yasui said he had agreed with Mize that internment was "the only sure way, but that is purely a theoretical question." Yasui's answer hardly eradicated from Fee's mind the impact of his admission, and the judge took over again with questions that indicated doubt about the sincerity of Yasui's professions of loyalty. With the conclusion of Fee's questioning, Bernard displayed a perceptible sense of relief. "The defendant will rest his case, your Honor," he eagerly stated as Yasui left the witness box.[15]

As soon as Bernard sat down, Burdell jumped up to exercise his right of rebuttal. Judge Fee had made clear his doubts about Yasui's citizenship status, but he had also expressed doubt about the constitutionality of the curfew order. Fee's questioning of Yasui on the topic of Shintoism, Burdell assumed, had opened the door to the "racial characteristics" argument, and he had witnesses in the reserve on this issue.[16]

Burdell first called as a rebuttal witness the business agent of Local 3 of the Lumber and Sawmill Workers union in Oregon, Gerhard Goetze. Burdell got no further than to ask Goetze whether he had "recently been asked to settle certain disputes which arose among the laborers and their employers concerning the employment of Japanese" when Bernard objected to the question as "wholly immaterial to any issue in this case and as not being proper rebuttal testimony." In calling Goetze as a witness, Burdell was acting on the suggestion from Maurice Walk that he present evidence that the "presence of persons of Japanese descent in strategic areas has caused widespread public suspicion and animosity among the general public" and thus presented a danger to the Japanese Americans themselves. Burdell had not, however, laid a foundation for this issue in direct testimony, an omission that escaped neither Bernard nor Judge Fee. Asked by Fee to explain the purpose of Goetze's proposed testimony, Burdell lamely argued that "the Japanese people themselves realize that their own safety demands that there be a certain type of regulation, of restriction of this nature, and that is what I propose to show. . . ." Bernard expressed indignation in his response to Burdell's offer of proof. "If Your Honor pleases," he said to Fee, "this is the first time we ever heard that advanced as an argument for the violation of the due process of law clause of the Constitution . . . that that violation would be justified because in the opinion of the Government the defendant would be benefited by it." Fee sustained Bernard's objection, and Goetze left the witness box.[17]

Burdell had one witness left. Without identifying him, Burdell described his mystery witness as "a man who is familiar, by reason of long residence and contact, with the Orient, and in particular the Japanese people, a distinguished scholar, educator, who is available to testify as to . . . the Japanese as a race of people and their ideals and culture and their type of loyalty . . . under circumstances such as the present conditions of war between Japan and the United States." This effusive introduction whetted Fee's appetite for testimony, but in the face of Bernard's anticipatory objection that "what some of the Japanese might do under certain conditions . . . is not a subject of expert testimony at all," Fee informed Burdell that he could "produce this man and ask him some questions" but that "if the other side wants to object . . . the Court will rule." As a lawyer experienced in the rules of evidence, Donaugh saw the handwriting on the wall and stepped in to save Burdell from an exercise in futility. "The government rests, your Honor," he interposed.[18]

Whatever his curiosity about the identity of Burdell's mystery witness, Bernard had no desire to give the government a last shot at Yasui. He immediately asked Fee to issue a judgment of not guilty, arguing that the government had conceded in its indictment the fact of Yasui's citizenship and that the curfew regulations "are void as to him, for the reason that they deprive him of his liberty and his property without due process of law." Fee then helpfully prompted Bernard that he "had better include the other grounds of your motion, and that is that it deprives him of equal protection of the law." Bernard thanked the judge for noting his oversight, and Fee in turn thanked the eight lawyers who sat through the day-long proceedings; he adjourned court with Yasui's fate left undecided. Tried first, Yasui would become in the end the last of the three criminal defendants to learn whether or not he would be convicted.[19]

While they awaited a ruling in the Yasui case and prepared for the Hirabayashi and Korematsu trials, government lawyers suddenly confronted the Endo case and shifted their attention to the San Francisco courtroom of Judge Michael J. Roche. In directly challenging the government's power to detain citizens in internment camps, the Endo case struck WRA lawyers in particular as more threatening than the three criminal cases. The first and most decisive phase of the internment program, the herding of Japanese Americans into assembly centers, had been virtually completed by the time James Purcell filed a habeas corpus petition on behalf of Mitsuye Endo on July 13, 1942, and it seemed unlikely that further challenges to the curfew and exclusion orders would arise after this date. As preliminary steps in the overall internment program, these orders imposed less drastic restrictions on the liberties of Japanese Americans, and would more likely appear to be genuinely related to emergency needs, than would detention for an indefinite period. Their basis in Executive Order 9066 as measures designed to provide an "immediate solution" to the dangers of espionage and sabotage convinced government lawyers, as one put it, that "no district court on the Coast would take upon itself the responsibility for upsetting military action at the present time."[20]

The Endo case, in contrast, filled government lawyers with a sense of foreboding. Given the wording of Executive Order 9066, they recognized that it would stretch legal doctrine to its limits to argue that the power to exclude Japanese Americans from a military zone carried with it a concomitant power to intern the entire group. WRA lawyer Maurice Walk had made clear to Philip Glick his belief that "the Supreme Court will not sanction wholesale detention of citizens" for an indefinite period. Walk's gloomy prognosis prompted him to urge that Glick draft and implement, as quickly as possible, WRA furlough regulations that would grant some freedom of movement to camp residents willing to move away from the West Coast and able to convince WRA officials that "there was no reason for distrusting their loyalty or that they constituted no danger to the military effort." Such regulations, Walk argued, were "essential in my judgment to gain judicial acceptance of our program."[21]

Even before he learned of the Endo petition, Glick had begun drafting a set of temporary regulations that permitted camp residents who could show a "specific job opportunity" in an area outside the West Coast to apply for release from detention, provided they were certified by the WRA as loyal and agreed to remain outside the restricted military zones. Although the regulations placed on applicants for leave the burden of proving their loyalty, a reversal of the traditional legal presumption of innocence, Glick hoped to appease the courts on the due process issue and to convince them that detention was a temporary and necessary intermediate step in the "sifting" of loyal Japanese Americans from the disloyal minority. Glick issued these temporary regulations on July 20, 1942, the same day Judge Roche scheduled the first hearing in the Endo case.[22]

Among the panoply of procedures available to those who challenged their detention by the government, the writ of habeas corpus, by requiring that the government promptly produce the "body" of the person held in confinement before a judge for a decision on the legality of detention, promised the most expeditious way to test such detention. In the Endo case, this procedure began without delay. Purcell appeared before Judge Roche, just a week after filing his petition, expecting that Roche intended to set a subsequent date for a hearing on the petition. Roche shocked both Purcell and his courtroom adversary, deputy U.S. attorney Alfonso J. Zirpoli, by demanding that they proceed immediately with constitutional arguments on the detention issue.[23]

"Your Honor," Purcell replied, "I understood the hearing this morning was for the purpose of setting a time for argument." Purcell had understood correctly, Roche said, and *right then* was the time set for argument. "He tried to catch me unprepared," Purcell recalled. "Fortunately I had done my homework." Roche's abrupt move was in character with his nickname of "Iron Mike" and his reputation as a gruff, crusty courtroom martinet. Born in Ireland in 1878, Roche had been a state court judge before his appointment by President Roosevelt to the federal bench in 1935, and his lack of patience with lawyers who raised technical legal arguments was notorious.[24]

With barely a chance to catch his breath, Purcell launched into a denunciation of detention as a violation of due process and as a measure unsupported by statutory sanction. The only record of the argument was a report prepared by WRA regional attorney Edwin Ferguson, who attended the hearing to advise Zirpoli on the details of WRA procedures. Ferguson gave Purcell a mixed review in his report to Philip Glick, describing him as "a young man, who talks quite well in getting his points across, although in my mind his material was not too well organized and he lacked judgment in that he spent too much time discussing cases that were not too relevant to the main issues." Ferguson gave Purcell credit for stressing that "the President and the military had no authority to order evacuation and detention of citizens except pursuant to an act of Congress" and for noting that Public Law 503 conferred no authority on General DeWitt to order the detention of Japanese Americans. Anticipating that Zirpoli would raise a "military necessity" claim in defending detention, Purcell cited the report of the congressional Tolan Committee "to show that there was no sabotage in Hawaii before, during, or after the Pearl Harbor attack. . . .'' Purcell's ''strongest point'' in attacking detention, Ferguson reported, was his contention that ''there had never been a Supreme Court decision upholding the power of a military commission to try a citizen or permitting the military to detain a citizen.''[25]

In making this argument, Purcell relied on the 1866 opinion of the Supreme Court in *Ex Parte Milligan* to support his propositions that ''only by act of Congress could the writ of habeas corpus be suspended, and that no military action could be taken except under martial law conditions.'' Not only in the Endo case, but in the criminal cases as well, this old Civil War case bedeviled government lawyers. Lambdin Milligan, a Copperhead sympathizer of the Confederacy in Indiana, had been arrested on military order in 1864, tried and convicted by a military tribunal for the statutory offense of conspiracy to overthrow the government, and sentenced to hang. Congress had earlier authorized President Lincoln to suspend the writ of habeas corpus ''whenever, in his judgment, the public safety may require it,'' but had limited suspension to cases in which operation of the civil courts had become impossible. ''Martial law can never exist,'' the Supreme Court majority held in *Milligan,* ''where the courts are open, and in the proper and unobstructed exercise of their jurisdiction.'' Military rule and its implementation through edict, the Court further held, ''cannot arise from a *threatened* invasion. The necessity must be actual and present; the invasion real, such as effectively closes the courts and deposes the civil administration.''[26]

In painting detention as a form of undeclared martial law, and by stressing the *Milligan* opinion as a precedential barrier, Purcell confronted Zirpoli with an acute dilemma. It was obvious that Mitsuye Endo had been detained by military order and without a hearing, and that the civil courts were open on the West Coast. It was equally apparent that, whatever General DeWitt's fears about a possible Japanese invasion, the mainland had not been subjected to actual attack. By hammering away at these facts, Purcell forced Zirpoli to take a stand on *Milligan* as a precedent. If Zirpoli argued that detention was not an exercise of martial law and that *Milligan,* which involved suspension of habeas corpus, was inapplicable to the Endo case, he would necessarily be forced to specify another constitutional basis to support this delegation to the military of the power to determine persons to be detained, and then to defend such detention of civilians by the military without due process. On the other hand, if Zirpoli described the detention as a species of military rule, he faced the inevitable rebuttal that such rule was improper, since the civil courts had remained open throughout and held jurisdiction in the case.

Purcell's argument lasted through the morning session of court, and as the noon recess approached, Judge Roche let Purcell know that he had scored telling points. "When this matter was first brought up," Roche admitted, "I was of the opinion that it was a frivolous action. I am no longer of that opinion." Roche then turned to Zirpoli and warned him of his task in rebuttal: "Be prepared to answer when court is resumed at 2 o'clock." Faced with this unexpected display of judicial skepticism, Zirpoli spent the recess poring over the *Milligan* case. He also put in a hurried call for reinforcements. When Purcell returned from lunch, he found the courtroom half filled with lawyers in uniform, recruited from the office of the Judge Advocate General. Judge Roche was equally surprised. "To what do we owe the honor of the presence of this array of military brass?" he quizzed Zirpoli. One of the military lawyers answered this question when he approached Purcell during a mid-afternoon recess. "Jim, you know we have one sure way of beating this case," Purcell recalled his old college friend saying. "We can have you inducted." Purcell assured him that "you'll have an easy time finding me. It will either be in the brig or the hospital," and he ended the exchange with a warning: "I hope you're joking, because I'd hate to have to tell the judge you're trying to intimidate me."[27]

Fortified with his lunchtime research, Zirpoli opened the afternoon session on an aggressive note that met Purcell head-on and that pleased Edwin Ferguson. According to Ferguson's report to Glick, Zirpoli "first sketched in the background for the evacuation program—112,000 Japanese on the Coast in strategic areas, inability to tell loyal from disloyal, possibility of sabotage and fifth column"—and urged that Judge Roche "judicially notice the factual background" as a justification for the detention that followed evacuation. Answering Purcell's sarcastic dismissal of Judge Black's opinion in the Ventura case as "judicial drivel," Zirpoli engaged in a bit of legal flag-waving by telling Roche that "in these times a court should be reluctant to take any action that would undo what the Executive and military deem necessary."[28]

Zirpoli then disconcerted Ferguson by taking a position on the *Milligan* case that risked judicial disaster. In effect, Zirpoli suggested that Judge Roche overrule the Supreme Court majority in *Milligan,* an argument hardly calculated to appeal to a district court judge. In "relying heavily on the minority opinion in the *Milligan* case," Ferguson reported, Zirpoli "went into a discussion of martial law, explaining the difference between military law, military government, and martial law; arguing that there could be 'qualified' as well as 'absolute' martial law, and that if it was necessary to drag in martial law concepts this was a proper case for the application of qualified martial law." Zirpoli also argued "that to the extent necessary military exigencies during war time overrode the Bill of Rights." He based this claim on the statement by Chief Justice Salmon P. Chase, writing for the *Milligan* minority, that in a "theatre of military operations . . . constantly threatened with invasion," military government could legitimately displace a functioning civil government. So long as either Congress or the President determined that "such great and imminent public danger exists as justifies the authorization of military tribunals," Chase had written in dissent, "the civil safeguards of the Constitution" had no force.[29]

To counter the risk inherent in suggesting that a district court judge adopt a Supreme Court dissent, Zirpoli offered to Judge Roche a law review article fresh off the press. In the June 1942 issue of the *Harvard Law Review,* in discussing General DeWitt's military orders, Stanford Law School professor Charles Fairman dusted off and refurbished the argument made by Chase in his *Milligan* dissent. "When one considers certain characteristics of modern war—mobility on land, surprise from the air, sabotage, and the preparation of fifth columns—it must be apparent that the dictum that 'martial law cannot arise from a threatened invasion' is not an adequate definition of the extent of the war power of the United States," Fairman wrote in belittling the *Milligan* majority and in contrasting the Civil War and World War II. Acknowledging that neither evacuation nor detention of the Japanese Americans "is defensible on any other basis than prevention," Fairman credited DeWitt with having "doubtless acted on such intelligence as was available" about Japanese American disloyalty and with "the express sanction of the President and the Congress." Fairman also, without citation of supporting evidence, made the "racial characteristics" argument pressed by WRA lawyers. "Fundamental differences in mores have made them inscrutable to us," Fairman wrote about Japanese Americans. "Because of the absence of that frank interchange by which human personality is revealed," he asserted, "the Nisei have remained largely unknown to their fellow-citizens."[30]

In his attack on the *Milligan* majority, Fairman rejected as outmoded and dangerous a distinction between unvarnished martial law and civilian supremacy. Citing the "shelling of Santa Barbara" by a Japanese submarine in February 1942 as proof of "the reality of the danger" that confronted General DeWitt, Fairman concluded that the possibility that a Japanese American might "signal to a submarine would add up to a sufficient reason for evacuating" all members of the group. In judging the legality of "vigilant precautions" against such dangers, Fairman urged, it was "the duty of the courts" to grant "the necessity for the commander's assuming control of the functions of civil government." Zirpoli's offer of the Fairman article as support for detention sufficiently intrigued Judge Roche that he asked for a copy to follow the argument from the bench. What was not revealed to Roche was that Fairman, identified in the article only by his academic affiliation, was then in active military service as a Colonel on the Judge Advocate General's staff.[31]

Even with the imprimatur of the *Harvard Law Review*, Zirpoli's implicit invitation to Judge Roche to overrule the Supreme Court encountered judicial skepticism. Roche's questioning of Zirpoli led Ferguson to report that the judge "raised in my mind the feeling that he questioned the doctrine of 'qualified' martial law. In my opinion Zirpoli should not have gotten into the martial law discussion, since it served only to cloud the real issues." Ferguson added that he deplored Zirpoli's departure from the WRA strategy of pressing for judicial notice of the "racial characteristics" argument. "I do not believe he dealt long enough or as persuasively as . . . can be done on the judicially cognizable facts showing the military necessity—the heart of the whole matter."[32]

At the conclusion of the hearing, Zirpoli moved that Judge Roche dismiss the habeas corpus petition. Zirpoli cited in support of his motion the WRA furlough regulations that became effective the day of the hearing. Under normal practice, a habeas corpus petitioner needed to demonstrate that she had exhausted all available administrative remedies reasonably imposed by the government. At the time of Endo's initial detention, no administrative avenue provided an escape route from confinement. Given the effective date of the WRA regulations, Endo could hardly have complied with them, let alone have learned whether WRA approval would follow a leave application. These facts did not dissuade Zirpoli from contending that "the petition was defective on its face because it did not show the administrative remedies had been exhausted," reported Ferguson. Even if they had, Zirpoli added, "the documents and facts of which the court should take judicial notice clearly justified the detention of the petitioner and the petition should be dismissed."[33]

Neither Purcell nor Zirpoli expected an immediate ruling on the motion, despite the unexpected length of the preliminary hearing. Following normal practice in habeas corpus cases as an emergency procedure, Judge Roche asked that both lawyers submit briefs within ten days and "indicated that he would decide this question five days thereafter." In the event Roche denied Zirpoli's dismissal motion, both sides expected the judge to set a date for a full-scale hearing on the petition. With the rights of 70,000 Japanese American citizens confined in internment camps hanging in the balance, a prompt ruling on the Endo petition seemed likely. Purcell and Zirpoli hastened to meet the deadline set by Judge Roche. After filing their briefs on the dismissal motion, both lawyers set to work preparing for the subsequent hearing.[34]

Astonishingly, weeks stretched into months with no ruling by Judge Roche on the dismissal motion and no notice of a hearing date. Mitsuye Endo remained behind the barbed wire of the Tule Lake internment camp in northern California while judicial inaction turned into interminable delay. Satisfied with the status quo, Zirpoli had no interest in pressing for a decision. But even Purcell, despite the continuing confinement of his client, aquiesced in the situation. ''We [the United States military forces] were getting the hell kicked out of us in 1942,'' he later explained, ''and I wanted to let some time pass.''[35]

The only person to express indignation was Edward Ennis. In late December 1942, Ennis informed Solicitor General Charles Fahy that the Endo petition, as well as those filed by Al Wirin on behalf of Ernest and Toki Wakayama, ''have been pending undecided for approximately six months. The statutes and the decisions regulating the issuance of this great writ,'' Ennis reminded Fahy, ''emphasize that expedition is required and that procrastination and trifling with this remedy is prohibited.'' Noting that the Justice Department had ''responsibility to see to it that these writs are disposed of one way or the other,'' Ennis asked Fahy whether ''we should approach the courts and enquiry when they are likely to be decided.'' In his laconic response, Fahy displayed no sense of urgency or assumption of responsibility. ''I do not think we should approach the courts,'' he penned at the bottom of Ennis's memorandum. ''If the petitioners initiate such approach we could then appropriately give our views that such cases should be decided promptly.''[36]

Another six months passed before Purcell abandoned his cursory inquiries of the court clerk and matched Ennis in concern. By this time, all three criminal cases had been tried and decided by the district courts, argued before the Court of Appeals, and certified for review by the Supreme Court. ''I communicated with the Judge,'' Purcell wrote to Clifford Forster on June 23, 1943, ''informing him that I desire that the Endo case be ruled on. He, however, felt that he should await the determination of the Supreme Court in the cases which have been referred to it.'' Once his excuse for inaction was removed by the Supreme Court decisions that upheld the convictions of Hirabayashi and Yasui, Judge Roche took the guidance given him by the Supreme Court. On July 3, 1943, ten days shy of a year since Purcell filed his habeas corpus petition, Roche issued an order granting Zirpoli's dismissal motion, unaccompanied by explanation.[37]

In contrast to the judicial caution of Judge Fee and the virtual paralysis of Judge Roche, the judges who conducted the trials of Gordon Hirabayashi and Fred Korematsu moved quickly once the cases came to trial. Both trials, in fact, became perfunctory exercises in legal formality, with their outcomes a foregone conclusion once the courts disposed of constitutional challenges to the indictments.

Wayne Collins, joined by Clarence E. Rust in representing Korematsu before trial, wasted little time in using the "shotgun" approach in his attack on the charge against Korematsu. On June 20, 1942, three weeks after Korematsu's arrest, Collins and Rust filed in the federal court in San Francisco a demurrer that fired a volley of sixty-nine shots at the government. Their challenge to Executive Order 9066, Public Law 503, and the Civilian Exclusion Order that prohibited Korematsu from remaining in San Leandro, included citations to three articles of and nine amendments to the Constitution. Some of these claims of unconstitutionality bordered on the frivolous, such as the charge that Public Law 503 constituted a "grant of Title of Nobility by the United States to all citizens whose birth or lineage makes them 'Aryan,' 'White,' 'Pink-Complexioned," . . . to the exclusion of citizens of Japanese ancestry who are descended from a mythical Sun-Goddess. . . ." Others reflected a lack of legal knowledge, such as the invocation of the Fourteenth Amendment, applicable only to actions of the states. Among the shots aimed closer to the target, Collins and Rust raised the Fifth Amendment issue that the government sought to deprive Korematsu of his liberty without a hearing or other due process protections, that the singling out of Japanese Americans for exclusion violated rights to equal protection of the laws, and that DeWitt's exclusion order violated the "delegation" doctrine.[38]

Collins and Rust had the bad luck of having the Korematsu case assigned to federal judge Martin I. Welsh. A twenty-five-year veteran of service in the California state courts before his appointment to the federal bench by President Roosevelt in 1939, Welsh was a fervent Democratic loyalist and a member of the Native Sons of the Golden West, a group notably hostile to Japanese Americans and other Orientals. Welsh had a reputation as an impetuous and lazy judge whose political ambitions colored his judicial behavior. Although Northern California ACLU director Ernest Besig had little faith in the federal judiciary in general as protectors of civil liberties, he also reflected a common opinion when he said that "Judge Welsh is not much of a lawyer." In the first round of the Korematsu case, Collins argued his demurrer before Welsh on August 31, 1942. As he had in the Endo case, Alfonso Zirpoli represented the government in opposition. Eager to begin his vacation, Judge Welsh summarily denied the demurrer from the bench in a twenty-eight-word order that discussed none of the issues raised by Collins. Welsh did not bother to follow his order with a written opinion. He did, however, set a trial date for September 8, just eight days later.[39]

With Welsh on vacation, the Korematsu case fell to Judge Adolphus F. St. Sure for trial. Both in background and philosophy, St. Sure offered both a contrast with Welsh and hope for a more fair and sympathetic proceeding. Nearing retirement at the age of seventy-three, St. Sure had been appointed to the federal bench by President Coolidge in 1925 after three decades in private practice and a two-year stint as a state judge. A Bull Moose Republican, St. Sure displayed independence in his rulings and showed no partiality to the government. Both Collins and Zirpoli acknowledged their respect for St. Sure by waiving their rights to a jury trial in the Korematsu case. Given Judge Welsh's earlier denial of the demurrer, however, there seemed little chance that St. Sure might find Korematsu not guilty, since the only issues remaining for trial were the factual questions of whether DeWitt's exclusion order applied to Korematsu and whether he had violated it.

Proceeding first at the trial as prosecutor, Zirpoli presented only one witness, FBI agent Oliver Mansfield. In rapid-fire fashion, Mansfield first produced the two written statements Korematsu made on the two days that followed his arrest, in which Korematsu admitted knowledge of the exclusion order and his violation of it. Mansfield then testified that Korematsu had confessed his forgery of the draft card listing his name as "Clyde Sarah" and that he had undergone plastic surgery. Precisely and dispassionately, Mansfield recounted the explanations given by Korematsu "that he had wanted to remain in Alameda County and in Oakland and in San Leandro because of friendly relationships with people there; that he considered himself an American and did not want to be evacuated; that he wanted to disguise his identity because his name 'Korematsu' would give him away as Japanese and that for said reasons he adopted the name of Clyde Sarah." After introducing as government exhibits Korematsu's forged draft card and his birth certificate, Zirpoli rested his case.[40]

Collins had not objected to the introduction of Korematsu's statements to Mansfield and passed up as equally pointless his chance to cross-examine the FBI agent, whose testimony had been direct and emphatic. Since this testimony effectively proved the government's factual case, Collins looked toward an eventual appellate decision on the constitutional issues in moving for a judgment of acquittal on the grounds raised in the demurrer. St. Sure predictably denied the motion and Collins made his exception for the record. These formalities concluded, Collins then put Korematsu on the stand, less to counter the government's irrefutable case than to convince St. Sure of Korematsu's sincerity and possibly to secure a light sentence.[41]

Hesitant and soft-spoken, Korematsu made an effective witness. He sketched for St. Sure his background and schooling, noting that he had spent three months as a chemistry student at Los Angeles City College. "I had to work after school hours to earn my way through college," he said, "but was compelled to abandon my studies because of inability to earn sufficient funds to support myself." After returning to Oakland to work in his father's nursery, Korematsu said, he had applied for military service but was rejected on medical grounds. "As a citizen of the United States I am ready, willing, and able to bear arms for this country," he affirmed. Collins drew from Korematsu his lack of attachment to Japanese culture: he had never been to Japan, did not claim dual citizenship, did not read Japanese, and spoke the language poorly. "As my mother does not understand my broken speech," Korematsu explained, "my elder brother interprets my English into Japanese for her." Under gentle cross-examination by Zirpoli, Korematsu confirmed his efforts to evade the exclusion order through forging his draft card, assuming the name of Clyde Sarah, and undergoing plastic surgery. His description of the doctor's bargain-rate surgery drew smiles in the courtroom: "I don't think he made any change in my appearance for when I went to the Tanforan Assembly Center everyone knew me and my folks didn't know the difference."[42]

Korematsu's forthrightness impressed Judge St. Sure. After denying a second motion for acquittal offered by Collins for the record, he pronounced Korematsu guilty and sentenced him to a five-year probationary term. St. Sure unexpectedly declined to impose the sentence, a move that left the case in a state of legal limbo and later confounded the Court of Appeals. When Collins then announced his intention to file an appeal, St. Sure obligingly set bail of $2,500, which Ernest Besig promptly offered to post on behalf of the ACLU. There followed, however, what may be one of the few incidents in the history of the United States of armed revolt by the military against duly constituted judicial authority. It must certainly have been a bizarre scene to witness.

With his bail posted, Korematsu was technically free to remain at liberty pending his appeal, but a military policeman immediately grabbed him. "I was supposed to be free to go," Korematsu recalled, "but the MP got all excited. He wasn't going to let me out on the street and he pulled a gun on me and said he's not going to let me go. The judge was all excited, he didn't know what to do." Confronted with this tense tug-of-war, St. Sure ordered that bail be raised to $5,000, but Besig quickly offered negotiable stocks to cover this amount. The military policeman insisted that he had orders to take Korematsu into custody, and St. Sure finally gave in. Korematsu left the courtroom under armed guard, taken first to the Presidio and then escorted back to the Tanforan internment camp.[43]

As the last of the criminal defendants to face trial, Gordon Hirabayashi languished in the King County Jail in Seattle for five months before he was escorted to the courtroom of Judge Lloyd D. Black on October 20, 1942. Black had already made clear to Frank L. Walters, who represented Hirabayashi, that the shifting tide of the Pacific war—shown most dramatically in the decisive American naval victory in the Battle of Midway—had not softened his fears of a Japanese attack on the U.S. mainland. A month before Hirabayashi's arrest in May, Black envisioned in his Ventura opinion the prospect of a Japanese "air armada that would rain destroying parachutists from the sky" and of "fifth columnists" among Japanese Americans willing to conceal these airborn invaders. On September 15, Judge Black reiterated these fears in more apocalyptic terms in an opinion overruling the demurrer that had been filed by Walters and was argued on June 29.

In his demurrer to Hirabayashi's indictment, Walters adopted a sharpshooter's stance, in contrast to the shotgun blast leveled by Wayne Collins in the Korematsu case, and aimed his fire directly at the Fifth Amendment target. The curfew and evacuation orders challenged by Hirabayashi, Walters argued, violated both the due process clause of the Fifth Amendment and the rights of Japanese Americans as a racial minority to equal protection of the law. This latter point, buttressed by citation to scores of the 130-odd cases included as precedent in the brief that Walters submitted to Judge Black, rested on the assertion that the equal protection clause of the Fourteenth Amendment, proscribing legislative discrimination by the states, had been "incorporated" into the Fifth Amendment as a similar bar to similar discriminatory acts by the federal government. However solidly based as a reading of congressional intent in enacting the Fourteenth Amendment, Walters' argument that the principle of equal protection would now not allow discrimination even by the federal government had little support in precedent. Two decades would pass, in fact, before the Supreme Court, responding to the civil rights movement, formally "incorporated" the equal protection language of the Fourteenth Amendment into the due process guarantees of the Fifth Amendments.[44]

Black's written opinion on the demurrer forecast his conduct of the Hirabayashi trial. Dismissing the "mass of citations" offered by Walters in his brief as a judicial burden that could not be met "without most tediously extending this opinion," Black declined the task of legal analysis. In its place he substituted patriotism and paranoia. "It must not for an instant be forgotten," Black wrote, "that since Pearl Harbor last December we have been engaged in a total war with enemies unbelievably treacherous and wholly ruthless, who intend to totally destroy this nation, its Constitution, our way of life, and trample all liberty and freedom everywhere from this earth." As he had in his Ventura opinion, Black expressed fears of airborne attack and fifth column support: "Of vital importance in considering this question is the fact that the parachutists and saboteurs, as well as the soldiers, of Japan make diabolically clever use of infiltration tactics. They are shrewd masters of tricky concealment among any who resemble them. With the aid of any artifice or treachery they seek such human camouflage and with uncanny skill discover and take advantage of any disloyalty among their kind."[45]

Black dealt with the Fifth Amendment challenge raised by Walters in one sentence. The "technical interpretation" of the due process clause offered as an objection to the curfew and evacuation orders, he ruled, "should not be permitted to endanger all of the constitutional rights of the whole citizenry" in balancing the rights of an individual. Black additionally made clear his approach to the Hirabayashi trial: "At the close of the oral argument counsel were advised that my views" in the Ventura case "were quite at variance with the defense arguments in this case and that unless I came to the conclusion that I was then mistaken that of necessity my decision would be adverse to defendant's contentions now before me. It suffices to say that I am still of the opinion that my views as contained in that decision are correct."[46]

Duly warned of the burden he faced, Frank Walters prepared for the Hirabayashi trial with the same purpose shown by Wayne Collins in the Korematsu case, that of perfecting a record for appeal. Walters took a more aggressive stance, however, insisting on a trial by jury and interposing frequent objections to Black's rulings on evidentiary issues and legal points. Testimony in the trial began on an odd note. After Judge Black empaneled and swore in an all-male and largely elderly jury, Assistant U.S. Attorney Allan Pomeroy called Hirabayashi's father as a prosecution witness. His apparent strategy was to counter the jury's possible sympathy with Gordon Hirabayashi, as an articulate and sincere defendant, by an appeal to their prejudice against an "alien enemy" who spoke English haltingly. If so, Pomeroy's ploy backfired. "Dad understood English," Hirabayashi recalled, "but he'd never been in court and he was kind of intimidated up there and hesitating in his answers. Although he was a government witness, Frank Walters popped up and said, 'Your Honor, I think we should have an interpreter for him.' The judge said, 'Okay, is there anybody here who could do it?' Nobody in the audience stepped forward, so I said, 'Well, I could interpret for him if it's proper.' " Neither Judge Black nor Pomeroy objected to this somewhat unusual procedure, and Hirabayashi translated into English the testimony by his father, Shunto, that he and his wife Mitsu had both been born in Japan and were Gordon's parents. Those two questions having met Pomeroy's purpose, he turned the elder Hirabayashi over to Walters for cross-examination.[47]

"I had just gotten into questions concerning what I wanted Mr. Hirabayashi to testify about," Walters later said, "probably the third or fourth question, and Gordon turned around to me and said, 'Mr. Walters, I don't understand nor can I speak the Japanese language sufficiently to interpret for my father.' I turned to Mr. Pomeroy and asked him where his doctrine of indoctrination of the Japanese through the language school was. It went out the window right then with that statement." Reverting to halting English, Shunto Hirabayashi then testified that he and his wife arrived in the United States in 1909 and 1914, that neither had been back to Japan, and that both had become Christian converts before their departure from Japan.[48]

Pomeroy called as his next witness FBI agent H. H. McKee, who recounted that Hirabayashi had said he "could not voluntarily obey the evacuation orders because he believed them unlawful and that they deprived him of his rights under the Constitution as an American citizen." In a seemingly perverse move, Pomeroy then called as prosecution witnesses Floyd Schmoe, a Quaker activist and the father of Hirabayashi's fiancée, and Arthur Barnett, the lawyer Hirabayashi consulted before turning himself in for arrest. In light of Judge Black's ruling on the demurrer, Pomeroy's purpose in permitting these witnesses to attest to Hirabayashi's constitutional convictions is hard to fathom.[49]

Even with these openings, however, Walters encountered judicial roadblocks during his cross-examinations. Tom G. Rathbone, who headed the Civil Control Station to which Hirabayashi had been directed to report for evacuation, told Walters that Hirabayashi had said, after McKee brought him to the evacuation center, that his constitutional rights "would be violated if he obeyed the orders, registered and submitted to the unlawful evacuation orders." Walters then demanded to know whether Hirabayashi had been "given an opportunity to have an appearance before an impartial jury" before receiving the order. Over objection to this question from Pomeroy, Judge Black made clear the limited scope of cross-examination permitted Walters: "The Court has ruled very clearly that it was his duty to report, his duty to obey the curfew. It is a matter for the Court's decision. The jury should not be asked to interpret the Constitution."[50]

The courtroom was filled with Hirabayashi's fellow students and members of the Seattle Quaker community when Walters called him to the stand. Hirabayashi told the jury of his background as a Boy Scout and as a Quaker, explained that he had spent three years at the University of Washington, and affirmed that he "never had any connection with Japan or corresponded with anyone there." "What was the training given by your parents, Gordon?" asked Walters. "All my training has been to be a good American according to Christian principles," Hirabayashi answered. Noting the testimony of government witnesses that "you wouldn't voluntarily obey the registration for evacuation," Walters asked Hirabayashi to explain the grounds for his refusal. "It was my feeling at that time," Hirabayashi explained, "that having been born here and educated and having the culture of an American citizen, that I should be given the privileges of a citizen—that a citizen should not be denied such privileges because of his descent. I expressed my thoughts that I had a right to stay."[51]

On cross-examination, Pomeroy asked Hirabayashi only one question: did he knowingly violate the curfew order and did he fail to report for evacuation as ordered? Hirabayashi admitted both acts. As a final character witness, Walters called M. D. Woodbury, who directed the university YMCA where Hirabayashi had lived for three years. "I would say that Gordon is one of the best liked students at the YMCA since I have been there," Woodbury said. "He has lived a life based on real Christian principles." Walters then rested his case and moved for the record that Judge Black dismiss the indictment and issue a judgment of acquittal. With the jury excused for argument on these motions, Black repeated the fears expressed in his earlier opinions. What justified the orders Hirabayashi violated, Black said, was that "in attacks by plane that might come overnight the government didn't have time to sift out the chaff from the wheat." Reports from Asia demonstrated that "Japanese soldiers were adept at concealing themselves among those of Japanese descent; if they were allowed to be here during parachute attacks they could be unwitting protection for such invaders."[52]

Before Black recalled the jury for closing arguments and his legal instructions, he warned Walters that "I am going to have to instruct them that if this defendant did what he admits he did, they will have to follow the Court's instructions. I cannot see what the jury could do but bring in a verdict of guilty." Walters bowed to the inevitable. When the jury returned, he began his summation on a note of submission: "The Court has indicated to you what he is going to instruct you. I have been advised what these instructions are going to be by the Court and therefore I cannot make any particular appeal. I would not make a sentimental appeal anyway because I am not in this case representing a criminal. I am not representing a man who violated a valid law of the United States. He explained to you in very plain language what his reasons were—that he believed his constitutional rights . . . have been denied him and for him to voluntarily be evacuated—be interned—would be an acceptance of these orders and violate the rights which he believes he is entitled to as American citizen."[53]

In concluding his summation, however, Walters stepped over the legal line Black had drawn between the bench and the jury box with an appeal to the ancient tradition, stemming back to Colonial opposition to British rule, of jury nullification of unpopular laws. "I don't expect you to disobey the instructions of the Court," he began disarmingly. "But in every criminal trial it is your province and your province alone, to say whether the defendant is guilty or not guilty. If you believe the defendant here was justified in refusing to be evacuated it is your duty not to wilfully violate your oath and the right to trial by jury in the United States."[54]

Pomeroy answered this appeal to conscience in his summation by reminding the jury of its narrow function. "It is your duty to obey the instructions of the Court. If we don't win this war with Japan there will be no trial by jury." He painted Hirabayashi as a pawn in the hands of groups of suspect patriotism. "If the pressure groups in this case had left Gordon alone he would have done what his father and mother would have done." The only questions open for jury decision, Pomeroy stressed, were these: "Did Gordon Hirabayashi on Monday, May 11th report at the civilian control station? He said he didn't. Did he obey the curfew law? He says he didn't. I want to tell you what the law is. You as American citizens are bound to obey the laws of the Court."[55]

In his formal instructions to the jury, Judge Black echoed Pomeroy's attack on the jury nullification appeal made by Walters. "You are instructed that in this case," Black said, "it is your duty to accept the laws as stated by the Court, despite any opinion of your own that the law should be different." He further instructed the jury that both Public Law 503 and General DeWitt's orders were "valid and enforceable" laws, and he ordered jury members to find as matters of fact that Hirabayashi was of Japanese ancestry and therefore subject to the curfew and evacuation orders, that he had violated the curfew, and that he failed to report for evacuation. Based on these findings, Black concluded, "you are instructed to return a finding of guilty, and if you will not you are violating your oath." While the jury retired for deliberation, Walters entered for the record his protest that Black's instructions "amounted in effect to instruction to the jury to bring in a verdict of guilty on both counts, which it was improper for the court to do," a motion Black promptly denied. The jury returned in ten minutes with a verdict of guilty on both counts of the indictment.[56]

Hirabayashi returned to court the following day for sentencing. Under existing rules, the five months Hirabayashi had spent in jail awaiting trial could not be credited against his sentence. "I'm going to take that into consideration," Black told Hirabayashi in his recollection of this proceeding, "and I'm going to sentence you to thirty days on count one and thirty days on count two, to be served consecutively." Black then asked whether Hirabayashi had anything to say before imposition of sentence. "I've been advised by jail-experienced people," Hirabayashi replied, "that if I want to serve my time outside of cellblocks I have to serve at least ninety days; they won't bother to process all the paperwork for anything less than that." He was willing to accept a longer sentence, Hirabayashi explained, in exchange for a chance to serve his time in the outdoors setting of a roadcamp. "I could accommodate that," Black replied with a smile. "Why don't we simplify it and instead of having two consecutive sentences, why don't we just say ninety days for count one and ninety days for count two, to be served concurrently." Without realizing the consequences, Hirabayashi accepted Black's offer, to which neither Walters nor Pomeroy objected. In their eagerness to spare Hirabayashi further confinement in jail, none of those present in court anticipated that the Supreme Court would seize on this legal accident, eight months later, as an excuse to avoid ruling on the legality of Hirabayashi's conviction for refusing to report for evacuation.[57]

Hirabayashi's conviction and sentence did not conclude the first round of judicial proceedings in the Japanese American test cases. Still outstanding were a ruling by Judge Fee in the Yasui case and the status of the Korematsu case, left hanging by the failure of Judge St. Sure to impose sentence as a precondition to appeal. Obviously awaiting both the outcome of the Hirabayashi trial and the research efforts of the eight Portland lawyers he had appointed as friends of the court, Fee finally issued his ruling on November 16, 1942. In an exhaustive, ten-thousand-word opinion that canvassed American history from the Revolutionary court-martial of Major John Andre in 1780 through the Supreme Court decision, issued just two weeks earlier on October 29, upholding the court-martial convictions of the eight Nazi saboteurs caught after their landing by submarine on the East Coast, Fee separated for decision two issues raised in the Yasui case. He devoted all but the last two pages of his opinion to the constitutionality of General DeWitt's curfew order as applied to American citizens, finding the order unconstitutional in this application. Fee then found Yasui guilty, holding that his service as a Japanese consular agent constituted a forfeiture of his American citizenship and subjected him to the curfew order as an "enemy alien."[58]

In reaching his first conclusion, Fee relied largely on his reading—or that of his legal panel—of the Supreme Court majority in the *Milligan* case. Denouncing as a "pernicious doctrine" the theory of "partial martial law, unproclaimed and unregulated except by the rule of the military commander," Fee blasted it as "a complete surrender of the guarantees of individual liberties confirmed by the Constitution of the United States." Without an express presidential suspension of habeas corpus and congressional declaration of martial law, Fee held, DeWitt's issuance of "regulations binding indiscriminately upon citizen and alien" alike had no force as applied to the former group. Anticipating in his opinion the "incorporation" of the Fourteenth Amendment's equal protection clause into the due process protections of the Fifth Amendment, Fee found unconstitutional on this ground the provision of DeWitt's curfew order that discriminated between citizens on the basis of "color or race" and its enforcement through Public law 503. So long as DeWitt allowed "a civil court to remain open to try violations of his orders, without support by force," Fee concluded, "military necessity cannot be so imperative that the fundamental safeguards" of the Constitution "must be abandoned."[59]

Having dissected the *Milligan* case and its application to DeWitt's curfew order with Jesuitical precision and Talmudic length, Fee then disposed of the question of Yasui's citizenship in almost cursory fashion. Fee accepted without dispute the proposition that, despite the fact that his American birth conferred citizenship on Yasui, "he was also a citizen of Japan and subject to the Emperor of Japan." Although Fee acknowledged that Japanese law conferred on Yasui the right of election of citizenship at the age of majority, and that the record disclosed no such election of Japanese citizenship, he found more persuasive "the nativity of his parents and the subtle nuances of traditional mores engrained in his race by centuries of social discipline."[60]

Perhaps aware of the casuistry of this reasoning in its application to citizens of Japanese but not those of German or Italian ancestry, Fee moved to anchor his finding in the facts of Yasui's background. Yasui had vehemently denied at trial any election of Japanese citizenship, but Fee nonetheless concluded that election was a "mental act" that might be "found in a criminal case contrary to the sworn evidence, protestations and declarations of a defendant." Having thus assumed the role of a forensic psychologist, Fee plumbed Yasui's mind. Citing as support Yasui's service as a Japanese consular employee, and the fact that "Yasui remained as a propaganda agent until after the declaration of war by this country against Japan and after the treacherous attack by the armed forces of Japan" on Pearl Harbor, Fee concluded that Yasui "only resigned when it seemed apparent that he could no longer serve the purposes of his sovereign in that office" and decided he could better further the interests of Japan as "an officer of the armed forces of the United States on active service." The facts that this conclusion flew in the face of documentary evidence presented at Yasui's trial without challenge by the government did not dissuade Judge Fee. "Since Congress provided for the punishment of persons violating the proclamations" issued by General DeWitt, and since Yasui "is an alien who committed a violation of this act," Fee held, "the court finds him guilty."[61]

Fee imposed sentence on Yasui two days later, on November 18, 1942. Given the chance to address the court before imposition of sentence, Yasui responded in his characteristic lawyerly and patriotic way. Proclaiming "no intent to plead for leniency for myself or to request a mitigation of the punishment that is about to be inflicted upon me," Yasui pointedly took issue with Fee's decision on his citizenship status. "I am confident that I can establish in law and in fact," Yasui said, "that I am an American citizen, who is not only proud of that fact, but who is willing to defend that right. When I attained majority," Yasui added in reference to his military commission, "I swore allegiance to the United States of America, renouncing any and all other obligations that I may have unknowingly owed." Affirming his willingness to enter military service, Yasui concluded on a note of defiance: "I can say that I have never, and will never, voluntarily relinquished my American citizenship." Judge Fee sat impassively through this peroration and then sentenced Yasui to the maximum penalty of one year in prison and a fine of $5,000. Earl Bernard promptly announced his intention to appeal Yasui's conviction.[62]

A month later, Wayne Collins appeared before Judge St. Sure in

San Francisco, hoping to untangle the procedural snarl complicating the appeal in the Korematsu case. Collins had filed a notice of appeal in the Circuit Court of Appeals on October 11, but Alfonso Zirpoli had countered with a motion to dismiss on the ground that no final sentence had been imposed. His dilemma, Collins explained at the December 23 hearing, was that a recent Supreme Court decision held that a probationary sentence did not constitute a final judgment and precluded appeal. Failure to impose sentence "would keep the matter pending here for five years, during which time no appeal could be taken," Collins said, "and we could not attack the constitutionality of the statute." Collins then moved that St. Sure impose a minimal sentence of five or ten days in jail, suspend execution of the sentence, and again place Korematsu on probation.[63]

"I don't know why I should do that," St. Sure responded. "The judgment rendered was one I thought proper in that case. I did not wish to send that man to jail." Collins hastened to assure the judge that his request would not place Korematsu behind bars. "I am not asking that you send him to jail. I am asking it for the purpose of testing this matter on appeal." St. Sure remained adamant. "I am not going to help you make one," he replied. "Do you know any reason why I should, Mr. Zirpoli?" The government lawyer was eager to keep the case from the appellate courts. The Supreme Court opinion Collins had cited, Zirpoli replied, showed that "the judgment as imposed is not an appealable judgment" and thus left him "in no position to join in the request" made by his adversary. This exchange on procedural technicalities left St. Sure confused and unwilling to budge. "I don't see any reason why I should make any change in my order," he told Collins, "to enable you to take this matter up on appeal." He would read the Supreme Court opinion on the issue," the judge assured Collins, "but I am indicating to you now I shall probably deny the motion."[64]

As the year that followed Pearl Harbor drew to a close, the status of the test cases remained uncertain. The lawyers who represented Min Yasui and Gordon Hirabayashi had filed appeals from their convictions with the Court of Appeals in San Francisco. Within the American Civil Liberties Union, however, continuing divisions over the test cases prompted a third round of debate over the ACLU's role in them. The refusal of Judge St. Sure to rule on the motion that he impose sentence on Fred Korematsu left that case in a legal limbo, while Judge Roche's inaction on the habeas corpus petition filed by Mitsuye Endo blocked any action in that case. The New Year of 1943 began on a note of conflict among the lawyers who represented the test case challengers.

7

"These Cases Should Be Dismissed"

GOVERNMENT LAWYERS won convictions at the trials of the three Japanese Americans charged with violations of General DeWitt's military orders. Among their ranks, however, reactions to these judicial victories differed widely. War Department lawyers were predictably pleased with the vindication of the orders they had drafted. Those in the War Relocation Authority, who had drawn the blueprint of the trial strategy, were equally pleased but looked ahead to the Endo case for an ultimate test of their legal powers to hold Japanese Americans behind barbed wire. With the three criminal cases now before the Court of Appeals in San Francisco, Justice Department lawyers broke ranks with an unusual proposal that the government abandon the prosecutions.

Edward Ennis laid out this proposal in a memorandum to Solicitor General Fahy on December 26, 1942. "I think that these cases should be dismissed if possible," Ennis urged, "particularly in view of the fact that the evacuation has been completed and there are no Japanese either to be evacuated or to whom the curfew can apply . . . now DeWitt has lifted the curfew." Ennis balanced his suggestion with an admission that the test cases raised "the first great constitutional issue arising out of the second World War," a factor that argued for a definitive Supreme Court resolution of the conflicting constitutional principles at issue in the cases.[1]

In proposing that Fahy approve the dismissal of the criminal cases, Ennis acted as the Justice Department lawyer who would be responsible for their argument before the Court of Appeals. On his part, Solicitor General Fahy held the power of review over the government's cases at the appellate level. This division of roles, complicated by their divergent views on the legality of DeWitt's orders, placed the two lawyers in the uncomfortable position of scorpions in a bottle. Fahy knew that Ennis had consistently denounced the orders as unconstitutional, but he also knew that Ennis had loyally defended before the Court of Appeals other military orders that he opposed on constitutional grounds. In making his case for dismissal of the criminal charges against the Japanese American defendants, Ennis knew that Fahy was intensely concerned with his won-lost record in the courts and harbored an antipathy to internal discord and to sloppy work by lawyers under his supervision.

Complicating the choice that Ennis had forced on Fahy was the need for a quick decision. Briefs in all three of the criminal cases were due in the Court of Appeals in mid-January 1943, with oral argument scheduled for the following month. Ennis took the initiative in pressing for dismissal of the cases. On January 2, he sent Fahy a copy of the brief drafted by the U.S. attorney in Seattle in the Hirabayashi case. Ennis shrewdly appealed to Fahy's sense of legal craftsmanship in suggesting that the brief was "probably inadequate" in its argument on the "war powers" doctrine as a defense of DeWitt's curfew and evacuation orders.[2]

In criticizing the Hirabayashi brief, Ennis referred Fahy to a decision handed down less than three weeks earlier by the Court of Appeals in San Francisco in a case that Ennis had personally argued and won. This case involved the regime of martial law that had been imposed in Hawaii on the day of the Pearl Harbor attack. Military officials had subsequently arrested and interned Hans Zimmerman, a German alien suspected of subversive activities. Despite the suspension of habeas corpus by military edict, Zimmerman filed a writ in the federal district court in Honolulu, seeking his release on the ground that the civil courts were functioning. Officials of the War Department, against whom the writ was directed, knew that Ennis doubted that suspension of habeas corpus was constitutional in this situation but approved his assignment to argue the case.

In upholding the district judge's denial of the writ, the Court of Appeals agreed that the Hawaiian Islands "are particularly exposed to fifth-column activities" and that "detention by the military authorities of persons engaged in disloyal conduct or suspected of disloyalty is lawful in areas where conditions warranting martial rule prevail." As Ennis had anticipated in his appellate argument, however, this judicial language barely concealed the skepticism of the court's majority that the "war powers" doctrine could be extended to the mainland, where martial law had not been imposed, a position clearly stated in a heated dissent in the case. This recent experience prompted Ennis to predict to

Fahy that the Court of Appeals, "which has already indicated a difference of opinion on military power in the Zimmerman case," might reject the "war powers" argument made in the Hirabayashi brief.[3]

Ennis continued his campaign to persuade Fahy of the inadequacy of the Hirabayashi brief by enlisting the support of Philip Glick, solicitor of the War Relocation Authority. The WRA lawyer "thinks the Government's brief is weak and hopes we can get more time from the court to write a stronger one in which his agency would like to participate," Ennis reported to Fahy. Ennis hoped, in recruiting the WRA's chief lawyer to his lobbying effort, to bring to the Solicitor General's attention the split within the WRA over the scope of the "war powers" doctrine. Confronted with this division over legal doctrine, Ennis reasoned, Fahy might well throw up his hands and agree to abandon the appeals.[4]

Although Ennis had a pragmatic purpose in exploiting the WRA schism, the legal debate refered by Glick took on a theological intensity. Glick had moved in mid-December 1942, shortly after the Court of Appeals placed the three criminal cases on its docket, to secure from Ennis agreement that the WRA would be consulted in writing the appellate briefs. The WRA was not formally a party in any of the cases, and none directly raised the issue of detention present in the judicially stalled Endo case. But in looking ahead to Endo, Glick worried that, without the WRA's restraining influence, Justice Department lawyers might accept the hard-line position of the War Department on the "war powers" question and thus undermine the WRA argument that justified detention as an essentially civilian operation. Glick consequently asked his two advisors on constitutional issues, Maurice Walk and James McLaughlin, for suggestions on ways "to bring our ideas into the brief" in the Korematsu case.[5]

Glick soon discovered that his advisors were fundamentally divided on the "war powers" issue. As a self-proclaimed liberal, Walk distrusted military authority and rejected the argument that the courts lacked the power during wartime to review the reasonableness of military orders. He particularly deplored the idea that the Constitution lumped together the President's separate powers as chief executive and as commander-in-chief of the armed forces. "I suppose if we were Medievalists," Walk wrote to Glick in a sarcastic dismissal of this concept, "we would borrow the reasoning of the Nicean Council on the Athanasian Creed to show how the same individual, the same unity, can combine the attributes of different persons." The only defensible basis for General DeWitt's orders, Walk argued, was that they represented a temporary transfer of civilian authority to the military for the limited purpose of "defending the military establishment against violent interference by civilians in the performance of its constitutional functions." This authority, Walk urged, should be "reviewable in civil courts on the question at least whether there are facts reasonably justifying the assertion of military jurisdiction."[6]

Walk denounced McLaughlin's assertion that the courts should defer in wartime to military judgment in scathing terms. "By setting no conceptual limitations upon military authority over civilians under the war powers," Walk wrote to Glick, "McLaughlin's approach would do nothing to restrain, but would rather encourage, military absolutism in time of war." Speaking on behalf of "liberals within the Government," Walk posed to McLaughlin a question as "one who opposes judicial review of military action" and as an advocate of "the inherent right of the Government and its army officers in time of war to exercise any power they think necessary to win the war." Was McLaughlin, Walk asked rhetorically, "really willing to allow the Colonels to have the final word on the reasonableness of pushing around large minority groups of our citizens?" Walk pointed specifically to Karl Bendetsen as the engineer of the internment program: "Is a Colonel Bendetsen to be the final arbiter of our liberties? It is the mentality of the Colonels that ought to be feared by all liberal thinking men in a time of war."[7]

Responding to Walk's imputation that he advocated a "military dictatorship" immune from judicial review, McLaughlin labeled this argument as "far-fetched" and "phoney." McLaughlin did not conceal his military bias in his rebuttal to Walk. A Captain in the Field Artillery during World War I, McLaughlin (who legally changed his name to MacLachlan in 1948 and who paraded his Scots nationalism) had joined the Harvard Law School faculty in 1924 and had been recruited by Glick from the post of special counsel to the Office of Price Administration. "I am not . . . a liberal," McLaughlin admitted to Glick in distancing himself from Walk. "By asserting a general war power" that linked the President's civilian and military roles, McLaughlin claimed, "I strengthen the civil authority." In contrast to Walk's "strained concept of self defense of the army" as a justification for evacuation, McLaughlin explained to Glick, he would substitute the "simple and direct fact" that the President "needs to protect the country" as a whole. The WRA would be on "firmer ground," McLaughlin concluded, if Glick adopted the position that executive power in wartime drew upon both its civilian and military roots in the Constitution. McLaughlin's clear implication was that searching the Constitution for provisions that separately justified the curfew and evacuation orders on one hand, and the detention program on the other, might well cripple both.[8]

Conscious that Fahy, with his nuts-and-bolts approach to litigation, had little patience for such legal disputes, Ennis spared him the details of the intramural WRA debate and merely alerted him to Glick's doubts about the adequacy of the Hirabayashi brief. Ennis also enlisted Wendell Berge, who headed the Appellate Division of the Justice Department, in his campaign for dismissal of the criminal cases. On January 8 Ennis suggested to Fahy that Berge be authorized to decide "whether it is technically possible to get rid of them altogether." Fahy rejected this suggestion, however, and instructed Ennis to proceed with the appeals. Bowing to this order, Ennis shifted gears and launched a second campaign designed to take control of the briefs away from the local U.S. attorneys and place it in his office.[9]

In seeking this control, Ennis noted to Fahy that he had gone over the brief filed in the Court of Appeals by Frank Walters in the Hirabayashi case. "I am not satisfied," Ennis wrote, "that the Government's brief . . . answers it as well as might be done." Ennis did not specify his objections, but he was concerned that lawyers for the test case defendants might exploit differences on legal issues between briefs filed separately by the U.S. attorneys. A problem that bothered Ennis even more was that members of General DeWitt's legal staff, headed by Colonel Joel Watson, had offered their services to the U.S. attorneys and had placed a hard-line military stamp on the "war powers" arguments made in the draft briefs. Ennis kept these concerns to himself in arguing to Fahy that "this constitutional litigation which is running along so freely without central supervision" be placed under his control. He stressed instead his fear that filing supplemental briefs from Washington, smoothing over disparities between the local briefs, might result in "giving the unfavorable impression that their briefs are inadequate or the cases are extremely doubtful," Ennis told Fahy.[10]

This half-a-loaf tactic succeeded, and Fahy approved the request that Ennis exercise final control over the content of the appellate briefs. Armed with this authority, and with the deadline for submission of briefs to the Court of Appeals impending, Ennis at least had the satisfaction of knowing that he could moderate Colonel Watson's influence over the U.S. attorneys and his insistence that the courts must judge DeWitt's orders as "questions of fact and not law." In a speech to Oregon lawyers, Watson had embraced Charles Fairman's attack on the Supreme Court majority in the *Milligan* case and had argued that decisions by DeWitt on questions of "military necessity" should be immune from judicial review, a position that Ennis considered outrageous. The press of time made it difficult, however, for Ennis to overhaul the draft briefs sent to Washington, and he could only polish their roughest edges before he left for the Court of Appeals arguments scheduled in San Francisco on February 19.[11]

Compared to the divided camps within the government, the legal ranks of the three test case defendants were splintered almost beyond repair as the time for appellate argument neared. As it had before the district court trials, the June 1942 resolution of the national ACLU board, which had proscribed any attack on the constitutionality of Executive Order 9066, created renewed conflict over appellate strategy. On September 14, 1942, a week after Fred Korematsu's conviction at trial, the ACLU board directed Roger Baldwin to inform Ernest Besig that the Union "must be disassociated" in the appeal from any objection to Roosevelt's order.[12]

Besig's response to this expected directive displayed his characteristic hostility to dictation from New York. "My Committee is standing pat on the case," he replied to Baldwin. Wayne Collins had no intention of abandoning his constitutional stand in arguing the Korematsu appeal, Besig reiterated. Unable to exact compliance from Besig with its policy, the ACLU board moved to sidestep his intransigence with an appeal to Bishop Edward Parsons, who chaired the Northern California board. In an effort to smooth over the strained relations between Besig and the national board, Parsons wrote on September 21 to Walter Frank expressing regret that Besig "has given so much concern" to the board. Parsons disavowed any intent to "embarrass" the ACLU and promised that in the future "we shall be entirely loyal to the policy which we now understand."[13]

Over the next three months, communications between New York and San Francisco traveled at two levels. On the high road, Bishop Parsons and members of the ACLU board carried on a polite, conciliatory correspondence designed to reach "an amicable solution of the controversy over the Korematsu case," as board chairman John Haynes Holmes told his colleagues on November 11. Holmes hoped to persuade Parsons and the Northern California branch to withdraw from the Korematsu appeal as counsel and to form an independent committee, the approach reluctantly adopted by the Seattle branch in the Hirabayashi case. Under this proposal, Wayne Collins would represent Korematsu as a private lawyer, with ACLU participation in the appeal limited to a role as amicus curiae. "There is no difficulty between us which cannot be made to yield to resolute and friendly consideration," Holmes wrote to Parsons on November 25 in a spirit of clerical comity. Holmes stressed, in his plea for submission to board policy, that "I am one of the minority on our Board of Directors who are absolutely opposed to the present policy of the Union in the matter of the President's evacuation order. Had I had my way, the Union would have fought that order on every point, beginning most emphatically with the question of its constitutionality."[14]

Holmes confessed that the ACLU policy represented a "serious mistake," but reminded Parsons that he was bound as board chairman "to execute it faithfully. In the same way it is the duty of the local branches to abide by it, and thus preserve that unity of action which can alone make our work effective." On his part, Besig reacted to this homily and similar entreaties with scorn. He rejected out of hand the request that Wayne Collins be divorced by the Northern California branch, noting in a letter to Baldwin that Mary Farquharson in Seattle was "none too happy about what happened in the Hirabayashi case" as a result of the ACLU resolution. Besig made his feelings clear in a subsequent letter to Baldwin: "Frankly, my gullet is just about filled with the constant futile correspondence about the Korematsu case, and I'm writing finis to it. . . . Please don't waste my time on the Korematsu controversy. I refuse to have anything more to do with it."[15]

Despite this outburst of frustration, the dual campaign of missionary appeals to Parsons and the threat of disaffiliation of the Northern California branch finally wore down Besig's unyielding attitude. He wrote to Baldwin on December 14 that the brief filed by Wayne Collins with the Court of Appeals "does not bear the Union's name" and was submitted without an accompanying press release. Besig warned Baldwin, however, that "it is inevitable that the press will associate our name with it since it is public knowledge that our attorneys have been handling the matter as a test case." In this letter, Besig proposed a settlement that represented a major concession on his part: "Our suggestion is that we should carry the case through the Circuit Court and that from then on the National Office should handle it in the way in which they have suggested we might do it." Besig only hinted to Baldwin of the practical reality that underlay this shift of position, in writing that "from your office it would be far easier to secure the right kind of counsel and to finance the thing."[16]

One factor behind Besig's willingness to relinquish control of the Korematsu case in the event it reached the Supreme Court reflected his fear that Wayne Collins lacked both the temperament and competence to prepare an adequate brief and to make a persuasive argument before the Court. Besig never wavered in public from his support of Collins, but the "shotgun" strategy adopted by Collins both at trial and on appeal clashed with Besig's legal approach. Anticipating a defeat in the Court of Appeals, or at least a lengthy delay over the issue of Judge St. Sure's refusal to impose sentence on Korematsu, Besig also realized that the additional costs of appeal would strain his skimpy budget. Baldwin controlled the purse strings for these expenses, having reached beyond the ACLU's own limited resources to enlist the financial largesse of an unlikely angel. Utilizing his Boston ties, Baldwin had secured funding for the Korematsu case from Godfrey Lowell Cabot, an octogenarian manufacturer of carbon black and a certified Boston Brahmin. Cabot extended an open checkbook to Baldwin, conditioning his support on assurances of anonymity, and ultimately poured several thousand dollars into the case. Besig had no comparable source of funds, and reluctantly bowed to this fiscal reality. He insisted, however, that Baldwin and the ACLU board refrain from any interference with Collins until the Court of Appeals ruled on the case.[17]

Baldwin duly reported Besig's concession and its conditions to the ACLU board, which responded on December 21 with a resolution that "expressed regret" over the refusal to withdraw from the Korematsu case before the Court of Appeals, while it accepted Besig's "suggestion that the national office assume responsibility for handling an appeal to the Supreme Court." On this note of uneasy accommodation, the conflict over the case ended with a truce that lasted less than six months. Wayne Collins, it soon became obvious, had no intention of making a gracious withdrawal from the case. For the time being, however, his inability to persuade Judge St. Sure to impose sentence on Korematsu shunted Collins to the legal sidelines.[18]

At the same time that it adopted an implicit vote of no confidence in Wayne Collins, the ACLU board created consternation on the West Coast with moves that intimated more sympathy for General DeWitt and WRA director Dillon Myer than for the Japanese American defendants. On October 8, 1942, the ACLU issued a press release commending Myer for his announcement of WRA regulations permitting "indefinite leaves" from internment camps for those Japanese Americans certified as loyal and willing to relocate away from the West Coast. In praising Myer for his "far-sighted statesmanship in developing a policy of absorbtion of the Japanese into American life," the ACLU board ignored the fact that the habeas corpus petition filed by James Purcell on behalf of Mitsuye Endo, then pending before Judge Roche, rejected such leave conditions as an unconstitutional imposition on one class of citizens. The fact that Purcell had brought his petition without support from the ACLU contributed to the obvious conclusion on the part of the press and the public that the Union conceded the constitutionality of detention and was seeking only to mitigate the hardship to the Japanese.[19]

The ACLU compounded its complicity in the internment program by sending to General DeWitt on November 11 (the same day that Besig sent his letter of capitulation to Baldwin) a letter that "congratulated the War Department for the efficient manner in which it completed" the evacuation of Japanese Americans from the West Coast. In a message signed by board chairman John Haynes Holmes, general counsel Arthur Garfield Hays, and Roger Baldwin, the ACLU officially commended DeWitt for his role in the evacuation, finding in it "testimony to a high order of administrative organization that it was accomplished with so comparatively few complaints of injustice and mismanagement." The facts that under DeWitt's direction the evacuation program had been conducted without brutality, and that the ACLU made clear "its opposition to the wholesale removal of racial groups by military order," could hardly conceal the Union's implied rebuff of the Japanese Americans who challenged DeWitt's orders.[20]

The ACLU board matched its commendations of Myer and DeWitt with its refusal to support the appeals of Minoru Yasui and Gordon Hirabayashi. Earl Bernard had represented Yasui from the outset without ACLU support, but Ernest Besig urged that the Union file an amicus brief with the Court of Appeals as a sign of solidarity with all three defendants. The Yasui appeal fell victim, however, to an ACLU resolution proposed by Whitney North Seymour designed to disassociate the Union from the sedition prosecutions brought by the Justice Department against alleged Nazi sympathizers under the World War I espionage statute. On October 19, 1942, the ACLU board unanimously adopted a resolution that precluded support for cases where "there are grounds for a belief that the defendant is cooperating with or acting on behalf of the enemy, even though the particular charge against the defendant might otherwise be appropriate for intervention by the Union." Only cases "where the fundamentals of due process are denied" were excepted from the blanket proscription of the Seymour resolution, which represented a turnabout from the ACLU's defense of the First Amendment in the Espionage Act cases brought during World War I and the "Red Scare" that followed the war.[21]

A month passed between adoption of the Seymour resolution and Judge Fee's opinion holding that Yasui had renounced his citizenship through service in the Japanese consulate in Chicago. On the basis of press reports of the opinion, the ACLU board quickly moved, by a 10-to-4 vote at its November 23rd meeting, that Yasui's "connection with the Japanese government as a registered propaganda agent'' precluded support of his appeal, even in an amicus role.[22]

The board's vote, and its reliance on sketchy press accounts of Fee's opinion rather than on a reading of the full document, disturbed Milton Konvitz, a lawyer and political science professor then acting as ACLU staff counsel in place of Clifford Forster. Konvitz immediately conveyed his doubts about this precipitous action to ACLU general counsel Osmond Fraenkel, who replied on November 27 that his interpretation of the Seymour resolution ''is that we should have nothing whatever to do with cases which involve enemy agents,'' a category in which Fraenkel placed the Yasui case. Fraenkel promised, however, to read the full opinion and to reopen the case before the ACLU board if he decided that Judge Fee had wrongly concluded that Yasui had in fact renounced his citizenship. After reading the opinion, Fraenkel found himself in agreement with Fee and declined the request from Konvitz that the board review its vote.[23]

Konvitz dropped out of the Yasui controversy when Forster returned as staff counsel at the beginning of 1943. Since Earl Bernard did not ask for ACLU support, the issue remained dormant until early February, when Ernest Besig persuaded his local board to authorize the filing of an amicus brief with the Court of Appeals. With the appellate argument set for February 19, Besig promptly wired Baldwin in New York to inform him of this action and to seek reconsideration of the earlier ACLU board vote. Baldwin wired back his disapproval of the request, noting that federal law ''provides many grounds for losing citizenship.'' Without specifying the grounds on which Yasui might have lost his citizenship, Baldwin added that civil liberties issues were ''involved only in cases of opinions or discrimination evidently not present in Yasui case.''[24]

In this daily exchange of telegrams, Besig wired Baldwin on February 2 to remind him that Yasui had not renounced his citizenship ''but is being expatriated solely because of associations. No question would have been raised had he worked for and registered as agent of British consulate. Decision makes citizenship from which many civil rights flow very insecure.'' The flaw in Judge Fee's opinion, Besig told Baldwin in a telegram sent the next day, was its basis not in federal but international law. This judicial choice of law, Besig argued, undermined constitutional supremacy and additionally rested on a dubious reading of Japanese law. Besig followed up his barrage of telegrams with a letter to Baldwin on February 4, informing him that the Northern California branch ''has voted unanimously to file an amicus curiae brief in the Circuit Court in the Yasui case, on the issue of dual citizenship.'' Besig added that he had "read the record in the Yasui case most carefully" and was "more convinced than ever that the Board should intervene." In deciding that "a native born citizen, who in some manner has acquired dual citizenship, may lose his American citizenship" through perfectly lawful employment with a foreign government, Besig argued, Judge Fee's decision "opens the way for a wholesale expatriation of American-born citizens whom other nations claim."[25]

Baldwin remained unwilling to commit the ACLU to support of the Yasui appeal. He reminded Besig on February 8 that "a very large majority" of the ACLU board had decided the previous November that Yasui's employment with the Japanese consulate "brought his case clearly under the October 19 resolution." Admitting the futility of an order that the Northern California branch withdraw from its role as amicus, Baldwin cautioned Besig that "if your attorneys go into the case independently of the Union no reference should be made officially or otherwise to any participation or endorsement by the Union." The next day, on the motion of playwright Elmer Rice, the ACLU board voted "to reaffirm the position previously taken not to intervene in the case of Minoru Yasui."[26]

The irony of the board's renewed refusal to support Yasui was that Besig soon converted both Forster and Baldwin to his claim that Judge Fee's opinion was wrong on the citizenship issue. On February 17, just two days before the Court of Appeals argument, Forster replied for the first time to a succession of lengthy letters from Besig. Fee's "application of so-called international law to determine the rights and disabilities of American-born citizens does, in my opinion, raise substantial civil liberties questions," Forster wrote. As expiation for his sins, Forster promised to ask Baldwin to bring the case before the board once again. By this time, of course, it was too late for the ACLU to endorse the Yasui appeal before the Court of Appeals. In a letter to Forster the day after the appellate argument, Besig wryly conveyed his gratitude that "you and Roger now concur with us that the matter presents civil liberties questions." Besig also pointedly noted that, in contrast to the ACLU's doubts on the issue, "the Government is not defending Judge Fee's expatriation theories."[27]

Compared to the fireworks in the Korematsu and Yasui cases, the role of the ACLU in the Hirabayashi appeal produced only a faint spark of controversy. Not once before the appellate argument did Frank Walters, who resented his second-best choice as Hirabayashi's lawyer, ask for ACLU support. Difficulties in raising funds for the appeal, however, prompted Mary Farquharson and Arthur Barnett to approach affluent Quakers in Philadelphia for financial assistance. Roger Baldwin had not offered, as he had in tapping Godfrey Cabot for funds in the Korematsu case, any similar aid to the Seattle committee set up outside the ACLU to defend Hirabayashi. One of the Quakers solicited by Barnett was Harold Evans, a prominent Philadelphia lawyer and a friend of Baldwin's. A month before the Court of Appeals argument, Evans wrote to Baldwin seeking advice on Barnett's request for funds. Evans informed Baldwin that there was "a good bit of sympathy" in Quaker circles for Hirabayashi, whom he described as "a high type of man." Without specifying the source of his doubts, Evans questioned Baldwin whether "a good record has been made at the trial" and noted that "much depends on whether the appeal is to be handled by able counsel. . . ." Baldwin did not respond to this inquiry before the appellate argument, perhaps intending that Evans interpret his silence as an implied disavowal of Walters.[28]

A formal request that the ACLU board endorse an amicus brief on behalf of Hirabayashi came at the last minute from an unlikely source, Al Wirin of the ACLU's Southern California branch in Los Angeles. Frustrated by the decision by Ernest and Toki Wakayama to abandon the habeas corpus petitions he had doggedly pressed over the past six months, Wirin had shifted his attention to the Hirabayashi case. Wirin first attempted without success to persuade the Japanese American Citizens League to file an amicus brief in the case, traveling to the JACL's biennial convention in Salt Lake City early in February 1943 for this purpose. Rebuffed by the JACL in his quest for a test case role—he later admitted to Clifford Forster his "selfish interest" in "playing a part in the oral arguments before the Supreme Court"—Wirin immediately appealed to the ACLU office in New York for permission to file an amicus brief in the Hirabayashi appeal. Forster informed him in a telegram on February 13 that the board "will not sanction brief in Hirabayashi case as we have already publicly dissociated ourselves from it."[29]

At the time of the Court of Appeals session, then, the national ACLU had no formal role in any of the test cases. Through its resolutions of June and October 1942, and ACLU board had turned its back on the Japanese American defendants and could make no claim of sympathy for their challenges to the constitutionality of Executive Order 9066. In the Hirabayashi and Korematsu cases, however, control of funding for the expected and expensive appeals to the Supreme Court placed the ACLU in the driver's seat. Whether and how the ACLU would exercise this control depended on the decisions of the Court of Appeals. Determined to retain their independence to the end, the three West Coast lawyers entered the courtroom in San Francisco united in their constitutional convictions. In their own minds—if not in those of the ACLU board majority—Executive Order 9066 and General DeWitt's curfew and evacuation orders were an affront to the Constitution.

The judges of the Court of Appeals convened to hear arguments in the test cases on February 19, 1943. None of the lawyers who spoke noted the irony of this date, the first anniversary of Roosevelt's order. Conscious of the gravity of the issues raised by the cases, the court had decided that, rather than the usual practice of having appeals heard by three-judge panels, all seven members of the court would sit in an en banc proceeding. Adding to the drama of the situation was the awareness of all the lawyers present that two members of the court were so at odds in politics and personality that their mutual animosity almost guaranteed a split over the test cases.

Chief Judge Curtis D. Wilbur, who presided over the session, was a crusty and conservative judicial veteran at the age of 74. An Iowa native, he had been graduated from the U.S. Naval Academy in 1888. Wilbur resigned from the Navy after two years of service and had moved to Los Angeles, where he began law practice in 1890 as a law office apprentice. After four years as a county prosecutor, Wilbur joined the California state bench in 1903 and rose to become chief justice of the state Supreme Court in 1922. President Coolidge appointed him Secretary of the Navy in 1924—in which post he served while on leave from the court—and in 1929 he joined the Ninth Circuit bench on the nomination of President Hoover.[30]

Although he sat next to Wilbur on the bench, Judge William Denman barely concealed his contempt for the chief judge. Five years younger at 69, Denman was a San Francisco native and a Harvard Law School graduate who had served stints in private practice, in government service, and in teaching law school before his nomination to the court in 1935 by President Roosevelt. A more partisan Democrat than Wilbur was as a Republican, Denman had avidly supported Roosevelt's ill-fate "court-packing" plan in 1937 and claimed a share of its authorship.[31]

Both on and off the bench, Denman was a tortured man. Described later by one government lawyer as a "twisted personality" who moved from "flights of genius to some very weird positions" in his judicial opinions, Derman brought to the test cases an obsession of almost psychotic proportions. He had harbored since the disastrous San Francisco earthquake and fire of 1906 a deep suspicion that military officials were lax in their civil defense planning, and the prospect of Japanese air raids on the city unleashed from him in 1942 a barrage of warnings to General DeWitt. Unsatisfied by the replies to his letters, the judge filed a formal grievance against DeWitt and John J. McCloy with Secretary of War Stimson in July 1942, which was ignored. McCloy refused to engage in a public battle with Denman but privately complained that he "gives me a sharp pain in my backside."[32]

Denman's irascible temperament and his long-standing feud with Wilbur promised sparks from the bench during the test case arguments on February 19. Before Wayne Collins rose to lead off in the Korematsu case, however, the court first dealt with another case that involved Japanese Americans. Those in the courtroom were exposed to a bizarre and almost comic legal sideshow. Despite their differences, Wilbur and Denman listened with equal incredulity to the argument made by Ulysses S. Webb in a case entitled *Regan* v. *King*. Webb, who had preceded Earl Warren as California's attorney general, was a longtime activist in the American Legion and the Native Sons of the Golden West. That day he was in court to represent a group of white voters in a suit against state election officials. Their claim, already rejected by the federal district court in San Francisco, was that the enrollment of citizens of Japanese ancestry on the voting rolls unconstitutionally diluted the voting strength of the Caucasian majority.[33]

Webb's argument in this case rested on constitutional fantasies and outright racism. The Supreme Court had ruled in 1898, in the *Wong Kim Ark* case, that native-born persons of Oriental descent were entitled to citizenship under the provisions of the Fourteenth Amendment. All such persons were entitled to vote and to exercise all the other attributes of citizenship. Webb claimed, however, that the Supreme Court was "in error" and that the amendment was "an abortive act of Congress." The framers of the Constitution, Webb claimed, intended to establish "a government of, for and by white people." Looking to General DeWitt for support, Webb cited the evacuation of Japanese Americans as evidence of their implied renunciation of citizenship. "Dishonesty, deceit and hypocricy are racial characteristics" of Japanese Americans, Webb told the court. "A Japanese born in the United States is still a Japanese," he added in words almost identical to those used by DeWitt.[34]

Although Justice Department lawyers considered the *Regan* case a joke and expected that the Court of Appeals would reject it, Webb's racist attack on Japanese Americans nonetheless worried them. Edward Ennis breathed a sigh of relief in the courtroom when Chief Judge Wilbur, after Webb concluded his polemics and even before the state's lawyer could rise in rebuttal, upheld the district court's dismissal of the case and sent Webb packing. This abrupt move left Al Wirin, who had been granted thirty minutes to argue on behalf of the JACL as an amicus, without a chance to speak. Ernest Besig, present to observe the test case arguments, reported to Clifford Forster that the judges "left Al with one untried speech on his hands, which he would be willing to deliver at the drop of a hat. Poor Al!"[35]

After this short-circuited episode, Wayne Collins led off for the test case defendants. In effect, all the arguments before the Court of Appeals constituted a reprise of those made earlier before the district court judges on the separate demurrer motions; by judicial rule and tradition, arguments before appellate courts are supposed to focus exclusively on issues of law as opposed to those of fact. Behind this practice is the assumption that judges or juries at the trial level, with their firsthand exposure to trial testimony, can better observe the demeanor of witnesses and weigh their credibility on questions of fact. Even at the most abstract constitutional level, however, questions of law depend for their resolution on the factual record of the case and draw on issues of executive implementation as well as legislative intent. In practice, lawyers mix issues of fact and law in arguments to appellate courts and often give them an emotional tinge. These realities of appellate argument affected both Collins and his colleagues, and the government lawyers who opposed them.

Speaking on behalf of Fred Korematsu, Wayne Collins devoted little of his time to the procedural issue of whether Judge St. Sure's imposition of a probationary sentence constituted an appealable order. Collins hammered away instead at the issue of martial law, cloaking himself in the mantle of the *Milligan* majority and pointing the appellate judges to the 1932 decision of the Supreme Court in the *Sterling* v. *Constantin* case. In this case, which involved the imposition of martial law by the governor of Texas in an attempt to prevent violence in the East Texas oil fields, the Supreme Court affirmed in clear-cut terms the holding of the *Milligan* majority that martial law decisions by military authorities were subject to judicial review. "What are the allowable limits of military discretion," wrote Chief Justice Charles Evans Hughes, "and whether or not they have been overstepped in a particular case, are judicial questions."[36]

Despite the certitude of this holding, neither *Milligan* nor *Sterling* gave Collins much support; both involved actual martial law conditions, and Collins' attempt to analogize DeWitt's orders to them failed to impress the Court of Appeals judges. Sticking doggedly to his "shotgun" strategy, Collins also undermined his argument with irrelevant issues pressed on the court with unyielding belligerence. Mary Farquharson later passed on to Roger Baldwin the comments of Caleb Foote, who attended the session as an observer for the American Friends Service Committee. Collins "didn't do nearly as good a job as I'd hoped," Foote reported, "acting as if he had a chip on his shoulder. . . . He also raised a new—and I don't think very good—argument that DeWitt's proclamation preventing citizens from having contraband violated the second amendment guaranteeing the right of all citizens to carry arms."[37]

Arguing next in the Hirabayashi appeal, Frank Walters presented a stark contrast with Collins both in demeanor and approach. Walters framed his argument almost solely around the equal protection issue, claiming that in singling out Japanese Americans as the only group subject to the curfew and evacuation orders, DeWitt had violated the Fifth Amendment requirement that the federal government impose equal burdens on all classes of citizens. Walters put the issue before the judges in words that joined his American Legion patriotism and his concern for racial equality: "If these things can be done to one minority group, such as the Japanese, they can be done to other minority groups, merely because they happen to be Chinese, or Negroes, or Jews or Catholics. We do not want our boys to come home from foreign fronts and find that the very liberties for which they fought have been dissipated during their absence."[38]

However heartfelt as an expression of Walters' convictions, this appeal for judicial sympathy lacked support in existing precedent. In addition, his submissive attitude and stumbling response to questions from the bench appalled courtroom observers. "I confess I am very much disappointed at the way the cases have gone," Besig reported the next day to Clifford Forster. "Mr. Walters was so inadequate in his argument that it was pitiful." Caleb Foote added that when an unidentified judge (most likely Denman) helpfully "asked a question as to whether there was proof of the fact that pressure groups had caused the evacuation," Walters could offer none. In passing up this perfect opening for an attack on the "military necessity" claim, Walters overlooked the repeated expressions of pressure-group hositility to Japanese Americans that permeated the hearings and the report of the congressional Tolan Committee, even though government lawyers quoted liberally from these documents and offered them to the court as support for the evacuation program under their "judicial notice" campaign. "Lots of us in the courtroom could hardly keep from 'prompting' Walters" on this point, a dispirited Caleb Foote wrote.[39]

Earl Bernard's low-key and workmanlike argument in the Yasui appeal escaped critical comment by the courtroom observers. Bernard occupied the doubly advantageous position of defending Judge Fee's finding that the curfew regulations were unconstitutional as applied to citizens, and of having in hand the government's agreement that Yasui had not in fact renounced his citizenship. Edward Ennis, in response to a question from the bench on this issue, helped Bernard with a formal waiver of the point.[40]

As a matter of protocol, Ennis had offered to share his time at the podium with A. J. Zirpoli, who represented the three U.S. attorneys who prosecuted the test cases. The ostensible allies actually displayed before the court quite antithetical positions on the justification for DeWitt's orders. Zirpoli began, late in the afternoon, with an argument based on the "racial characteristics" and "protective custody" claims fashioned before the district court trials by Maurice Walk and Philip Glick of the WRA. Asserting as matters subject to judicial notice, but without supporting evidence, Zirpoli repeated the claims that the alleged inability of Caucasians to distinguish loyal from disloyal Japanese Americans, and the need to protect Japanese Americans from "danger of bloodshed and riot," constituted essential elements of military responsibility to devise effective measures against sabotage and espionage.[41]

Ennis had little sympathy for these back-door claims of support for the "military necessity" argument. When he spoke before the court on Saturday morning, in a session made necessary by the length of the arguments the day before, Ennis showed no compunction in distancing himself from Zirpoli on these points. When Judge Denman asked him whether there had been "a single case from Pearl Harbor to the evacuation" where any Japanese American had been "found by competent authority to be a menace" to military security, Ennis admitted without hesitation that he knew of none. Ennis felt himself constrained, however, to give Zirpoli at least some support on the issue. Answering Denman in what he intended as a hypothetical response, Ennis added that Japanese Americans might have inflicted "incalculable damage" on military installations "even if only a few hundred" had attempted to assist a Japanese invasion.[42]

On this note of speculation and surmise, the test case arguments concluded with both sides sure of the outcome. "I have no doubt," Ernest Besig reported to Clifford Forster, "that the court is going to take judicial notice of the 'military necessity' " argument pressed by Zirpoli. "Ennis tells me that the judges were generally favorable toward the Government in the argument on the three criminal cases," Philip Glick wrote to Maurice Walk. "He told me that he feels quite confident the judgments below will be affirmed." With this unanimity of opinion, and against the backdrop of dismay on the part of Besig and Caleb Foote over the performances of Wayne Collins and Frank Walters, both sides immediately began their planning for the anticipated appeals to the Supreme Court.[43]

Five weeks elapsed between the appellate arguments in the criminal cases and their disposition by the Court of Appeals. While the lawyers on both sides took advantage of this break to feel each other out on the remaining test cases, Al Wirin also stuck his fingers in those awaiting decision. Having learned that Captain Herbert Wenig had prepared the amicus briefs submitted to the appellate court by the West Coast states, Wirin lodged a complaint about Wenig's dual role with Robert Kenny, who had replaced Earl Warren as California's attorney general in January 1943. Wirin suggested to his old friend that Warren had improperly allowed the Army to use his office, and he urged Kenny to stay out of the Hirabayashi and Korematsu cases if they reached the Supreme Court.[44]

Kenny answered with a defense of his predecessor, assuring Wirin that Warren's decision to file the amicus briefs had been "arrived at only after considerable research and a thorough consideration of the problems of civil government and liberties in wartime." Acknowledging the "unfortunate dislocations and inconveniences" imposed on the Japanese Americans, Kenny added that after reviewing the briefs "I am also impressed with the larger question which is before the courts in these cases, namely, that in these days there must be some scope allowed military authorities in critical areas" to deal with security problems beyond the powers of the states. He noted, however, the accuracy of Wirin's complaint "about Wenig being at the bottom of the Warren woodpile while angling for some position with DeWitt." Not only did Kenny dismiss this complaint, but he later signed the amicus briefs prepared for him by Wenig when the Supreme Court heard the criminal appeals. One puzzling aspect of this episode is that Wirin failed to pass on Kenny's admission of Wenig's role in the briefs to the lawyers for the test case defendants, since his activities clearly violated judicial rules.[45]

This exchange raises another question, that of the refusal of the National Lawyers Guild to support the test case challengers. As the only national organization of "progressive" lawyers, the Guild had often worked with the ACLU in civil liberties cases since its founding in

1937. But the Guild actually backed the wartime internment program. One reason for this stand is that Robert Kenny was then serving as the Guild's national president, a post he held from 1940 to 1948. Having signed the amicus briefs supporting (and in fact prepared by) the War Department, he could hardly press the Guild to adopt an opposing position. More important, the Guild's wartime policy was that of "complete support" for Roosevelt and the American-Soviet alliance, which reflected the influence of Communist Party members and fellow-travelers in the organization. One expression of this attitude came from Martin Popper, the Guild's executive secretary, in his speech to the emergency "War Convention" held in February 1943. "We hail the magnificent and unprecedented victories of the Soviet armies," he told the delegates. "We hail the brilliance of its leadership, the unity of its people, and its military successes."[46]

Weighed against the wartime sacrifices of the Soviet people, the plight of the Japanese Americans failed to evoke the Guild's sympathy for the test cases. Writing in the organization's official journal, a Justice Department lawyer dismissed the internment as "a minor item in the heaping quota of human misery which has been produced by the current war." This sentiment illustrates as well the influence of the government lawyers who made up a substantial bloc of the Guild's membership. A telling sign of Guild policy was that the speaker invited to address the "War Convention" on the internment program, Colonel Archibald King, represented the Army's legal staff.[47]

February 1943 was a frustrating month for Al Wirin. Not only did he fail to budge Robert Kenny from his collaboration with the War Department, but Justice Department lawyers also pressured him to abandon the habeas corpus petitions in the Wakayama cases. At a meeting in San Francisco arranged by Edward Ennis, who personally sympathized with Wirin's claim that his clients were being unlawfully detained, Leo Silverstein, the U.S. attorney for Los Angeles, threatened to expose in court the fact that the Wakayamas had requested repatriation to Japan. Afraid that knowledge of this fact would prejudice the judge, Wirin bowed to Silverstein's threat and agreed to withdraw the cases. Roger Baldwin helped to coat this bitter pill by offering Wirin the chance to argue the Korematsu case before the Supreme Court. Through the intercession of Ernest Besig, Baldwin had finally persuaded Wayne Collins to relinquish this round of the case to Wirin, who eagerly grabbed the opportunity to appear at the Court's podium.[48]

Baldwin also explored the possibility that the Endo case might be decided in time to join the other test cases on the Supreme Court docket. On a visit to the Department of Justice headquarters in Washington in mid-March, Baldwin received encouragement from Edward Ennis and John Burling. Their frank discussion with Baldwin, which strained the judicial rules that governed communications out of court between opposing parties, conveyed to Baldwin the opinion that Endo was "the only case the Department feels it will lose" and the suggestion that James Purcell should bypass Judge Roche in seeking a prompt decision. If Purcell desired a ruling in time to reach the Supreme Court with the other cases, Ennis and Burling told Baldwin, he "should go to the [Court of Appeals] and obtain an order requiring the [district] court to decide." In making this suggestion, the two Justice Department lawyers were tipping their hands on behind-the-scenes maneuvers with the Court of Appeals, since it would require an expedited procedure, regardless of which side prevailed in the district court, for the Endo case to reach the Supreme Court before its current term ended in May or June. Perhaps unaware of these procedural technicalities, Baldwin passed on this suggestion to Besig for transmittal to Purcell without any hint of what Ennis and Burling had in store.[49]

What the Justice Department lawyers had been doing behind the backs of Baldwin and the defense lawyers remained concealed from public scrutiny, but their efforts to rush the test cases to the Supreme Court resulted in the unusual action of the Court of Appeals on March 27, 1943. Rather than deciding the three criminal cases, the appellate judges invoked a little-used procedure called certification in asking the Supreme Court to answer constitutional questions raised by the appeals. In dealing with such certified questions, the Supreme Court had three choices: first, it could decline to answer the questions and simply return the cases to the Court of Appeals for decision; second, it could answer the questions, either with a bare yes or no or with an explanatory opinion, and similarly return the cases for decision in light of this guidance; or third, it could relieve the Court of Appeals of its decisional task and order the cases to be brought directly before the Supreme Court for full review and decision. Adopting the last of these alternatives, the Supreme Court ensured that the test cases would be argued and decided before the end of the Court's spring term.[50]

Neither the defense lawyers nor the Supreme Court knew that the Court of Appeals had chosen the certification route at the request of Attorney General Biddle. They also did not know that Edward Ennis, at Biddle's direction, had written the certification statement and framed the questions addressed to the Supreme Court. In undertaking this task without notice to the defense lawyers, Ennis acted outside the rules and proprieties of the courts and the adversary system. His action was prompted, it should be noted, by a desire to put the cases before the Court in a light as favorable to the defendants as to the government.[51]

Ennis hoped in his carefully crafted statement to alert the Supreme Court to the "novel constitutional questions" raised by Public Law 503 and DeWitt's curfew and exclusion orders. Writing in the names of the Court of Appeals judges, Ennis noted their familiarity with earlier Supreme Court decisions "upholding broad exercises of the war powers of the Federal Government." In an even-handed manner, Ennis first admitted for the appellate judges that they knew of "no decisions in which citizens residing in areas not subject to martial law" had been restricted in their movements by military order. "On the other hand," he wrote, "this Court is sensible of the fact that the military authorities held the view that military exigencies of modern warfare" and conditions on the West Coast "at the beginning of the present war were far more grave than any situation hitherto existing in any war with a foreign nation." Given the lack of precedent to guide its decisions, the statement confessed that the question of "whether this exercise of the war power can be reconciled with traditional standards of personal liberty and freedom guaranteed by the Constitution, is most difficult." In phrasing the issue in terms that admitted such serious doubt, Ennis concealed, behind a mask of anonymity, his own conflicts of conscience and duty.[52]

The questions actually posed to the Supreme Court reflected the issues raised separately by the test cases: those submitted in the Hirabayashi case asked the Court to decide the constitutionality of Public Law 503 and DeWitt's curfew and evacuation orders; those in the Yasui case addressed the citizenship issue; while the question asked in Korematsu was whether the probationary sentence constituted an appealable judgment.[53]

This ratification by his colleagues of the Justice Department's desire for a quick Supreme Court review of the test cases struck Judge Denman as an abdication of judicial responsibility, and provoked him to file a heated and almost incoherent dissent to the certification statement. Denman hastily filed on March 27, on the same day that Chief Judge Wilbur issued the court's statement and questions, a short statement of his own. "I dissent from the war-haste with which the question involving the deportation of 70,000 of our citizens, without hearing, is hurried out of this court," he wrote. His initial objection was that "the certificate makes no mention" of "important admissions" made by Ennis at the Court of Appeals hearings.[54]

The following day, Denman sent to the court clerk from his vacation house a 3,000-word dissenting opinion that denounced his colleagues for having "removed from the circuit court of appeals which is best qualified to find them" the factual questions "of the psychology of these deported citizens." Painting himself as an authority on the psychology of "Mongoloid people," Denman cited as "normal reactions" to the legacy of social and legal discrimination against Japanese Americans their "bitter resentment" of such practices. Despite his pique at the court's move, Denman concealed his own position on the cases in listing factors that both supported and argued against DeWitt's orders. On one hand, Denman cited state miscegenation laws, immigration exclusion, proscriptions against ownership of agricultural land, and barriers to union membership as factors that might produce feelings of "racial inferiority" among Japanese Americans and a consequent failure "to perform a citizen's duty in aiding his soldiers against the saboteur or spy." Denman objected as well, however, to the omission from the certificate of "the admission by the Government, at the hearing here, that not one of these 70,000 Japanese descended citizen deportees" had been charged with "espionage, sabotage or any treasonable act."[55]

Denman could not resist adding to his dissent a graphic recounting of the San Francisco earthquake and fire of 1906 and his fears that a fire "started by the Japanese on its windward side . . . well could have the bulk of the city in flames in ten hours." The prospect of a "similar conflagration danger exists in all the Pacific Coast cities," Denman warned, and provided a "rational ground" for a judicial finding that "General DeWitt could well fear the added menace of the saboteur's torches." The point of Denman's dissent, behind his pyrophobia and assertions of expertise in divining the "psychologic impulses" of the "yellow Mongoloid body of citizens" on the West Coast, was that the Court of Appeals "is in a better position than any other to know the effect of such facts on the minds of some of the now deported citizens."[56]

However well taken on procedural grounds as an objection to certification, the vituperative and barely rational tone of Denman's dissent horrified his colleagues, who blocked its publication in the official report of the court's opinions. Denman circumvented this censorship by releasing the dissent to the press, and it reached the Supreme Court through this overground route in time to be read before the Court's weekly secret conference on Saturday, April 3. Acting on the certification request submitted by Chief Judge Wilbur, the justices voted to remove the test cases from the Court of Appeals and to bring the entire records before the Supreme Court for decision, a move announced by Chief Justice Harlan Fiske Stone on April 5. Denman's dissent passed without public comment, but two weeks later Justice Frank Murphy handed a note to his colleague, Felix Frankfurter, while both men sat on the bench listening to arguments: "Two weeks ago—in our Saturday afternoon conference—you were at your peak in your righteous wrath about choking off a judge you have nothing in common with and who was espousing beliefs we probably all disclaim. It seemed to me that while our brethren were not party to it that there was put in motion just what you said—a scheme to gag a judge."[57]

Just as differences of personality and politics separated Wilbur and Denman in the test cases and led to behind-the-scenes maneuvers, similar differences between Frankfurter and Murphy posed the prospect of schism within the Supreme Court. Whether such divisions would emerge, and if so what form they would take, awaited the arguments scheduled before the Court on May 10 and the secret conferences that would follow.

8

"*The Suppression of Evidence*"

THE ABRUPT TRANSFER of the three criminal cases to the Supreme Court confronted the lawyers on both sides with new tasks and a tight deadline. Confined on issues of fact to the skimpy records compiled in the trial courts, and without guidance from the Court of Appeals on the unsettled constitutional issues, both sets of lawyers had only six weeks in which to polish their final briefs and to prepare for oral argument on May 10, 1943. The test cases reached the Supreme Court "at least a year earlier than any of us had assumed," Philip Glick noted at the time. Six weeks was too short a time, it turned out, to heal the wounds the embattled lawyers had inflicted on each other during the months that preceded the unexpected move of the Court of Appeals.[1]

This chapter will first recount the conflicts within the ranks of the defense lawyers, which centered around the struggle of the American Civil Liberties Union to regain control of the Hirabayashi case. The following sections will explore the behind-the-scenes maneuverings of the divided government lawyers over the brief in this case, the most important of the three at this stage. During this short six-week period, Justice and War Department lawyers became embroiled in three episodes that raised serious questions of unethical and unlawful conduct. This round of the test cases led, in fact, to the first suggestion that misconduct on the part of high officials of these agencies had tainted the records submitted to the Supreme Court.

Within the ACLU, Roger Baldwin faced the delicate task of dealing with the reports that Frank Walters had made a "pitiful" argument before the Court of Appeals in the Hirabayashi case. The ACLU director decided that Walters must be replaced as the lawyer who would argue the case to the Supreme Court. His diplomatic skills were tested, however, by the reluctance of Hirabayashi's supporters in Seattle to abandon Walters. The refusal of the ACLU board to approve an amicus brief to the Court of Appeals had also led to resentment among the Seattle group.

Baldwin laid his plans for the campaign to oust Walters from the case with Machiavellian care. His first step was to approach Homer Morris of the American Friends Service Committee in Philadelphia for help in recruiting a prestigious East Coast lawyer as a replacement for Walters. Since the Quaker group had raised most of the funds for Hirabayashi's appeal, Baldwin knew that AFSC support for his move would carry weight. He added leverage by persuading the ACLU board to donate $1,000 to the Hirabayashi Defense Committee for the costs of the Supreme Court appeal; this sum constituted more than a third of the Committee's budget for the appeal. Finally, Baldwin moved to exploit the differences between the two lawyers on the Committee, Arthur Barnett and Mary Farquharson, who had reacted to the criticism of Walters in separate ways.[2]

The Seattle lawyers first learned of Baldwin's campaign from Homer Morris, who sent them copies of a letter Baldwin had sent the AFSC official on March 1, 1943, suggesting that "it would be wise . . . to see that somebody else than Mr. Walters argues the case in the Supreme Court." Mary Farquharson replied directly to Baldwin on March 11. "I have always felt that his ability is mediocre," she wrote of Walters, "and from the very beginning I think all of us on the Committee have hoped that arrangements could be made for a really top-flight attorney to handle it in the Supreme Court." She added, however, that Walters "has been very cooperative" in the case and that "I think it will be rather a delicate situation if he has to be crowded out entirely."[3]

Arthur Barnett left the Committee's relations with Baldwin to Mary Farquharson. But he responded to Baldwin's proposal in a letter to Morris that mixed outrage and conciliation. Professing to be "literally shocked and astounded" by the criticism of Walters' performance in the Court of Appeals, Barnett noted that he had earlier done "quite a courageous and competent job" in dealing with Judge Black's open hostility at Hirabayashi's trial. "Had he been so 'terrible' do you suppose our Local Committee would have retained him as far as the Circuit Court?" Barnett expressed his willingness, however, to defer to the AFSC in adding to the defense team "a competent attorney qualified to take this matter before the Supreme Court." Pointing out that Walters "is thoroughly inculcated with . . . all the evidence and practically all of the law," Barnett urged that he "remain on the job in an advisory sort of capacity'' for the Supreme Court argument. In a later letter to Morris, Barnett made clear his own stake in the issue: ''My own good name and opinions are as much at stake as Walters'.''[4]

Even before he approached Morris for help, Baldwin had tried on his own to recruit a lawyer of national stature. He first sounded out Homer Cummings, a former attorney general under Roosevelt, and John W. Davis, a paladin of the Wall Street bar who had been the Democratic presidential candidate in 1924 and who had argued more cases before the Supreme Court than any lawyer since Daniel Webster. After both men declined his invitation to argue the Hirabayashi case, Baldwin turned to Morris, who suggested Harold Evans, the senior partner in a leading Philadelphia law firm and a prominent Quaker. The fifty-six-year-old Evans had little experience in constitutional cases and agreed to make the argument, he told Baldwin, only as a ''last resort'' in case a better choice could not be found. Baldwin agreed to continue his search, but passed on to the Seattle lawyers through Morris the news that Evans was willing to argue the case.[5]

With the Supreme Court session only a month away, Barnett insisted that Walters remain in the case. The Hirabayashi Defense Committee, he informed Baldwin and Morris on April 9, had given Walters a ''vote of confidence'' and would shortly submit a ''final draft'' of the Supreme Court brief. Barnett pointedly noted that he had worked ''very closely'' with Walters on the brief, adding that any Eastern lawyer selected to argue the case ''will barely have time enough to study the briefs in preparation for his share of the oral argument, let alone spend much time on original research and the study of the record.'' When two weeks passed with no word of a final choice, Barnett expressed his displeasure directly to Evans, writing him on April 22 that the ''search for some nationally known lawyer who would qualify as 'counsel of stature to impress the court' is tending to make me impatient.'' Barnett urged on Evans that Walters ''should definitely participate in some part of the argument because he has been living and breathing the law involved . . . and is a veritable walking encyclopedia in this respect.''[6]

Baldwin failed to find a lawyer more qualified than Evans—or at least one willing to argue the case. He delegated to Evans the decision on whether Walters could participate in the oral argument but warned him that Walters had stumbled badly in the Court of Appeals. Walters had maintained a discreet silence during this episode, undoubtedly embarrassed by the criticism of his appellate argument. After meeting with Walters, however, Mary Farquharson pleaded with Baldwin that he at least be invited to attend the Supreme Court session. ''Unbearable loss of face if he did not,'' she wired Baldwin on April 29. ''Not necessary that he take part in oral argument," she conceded. Baldwin replied the next day with a letter that deprecated the role of trial counsel in Supreme Court argument. "I hardly recollect a single case we have handled in which the same lawyer appeared in the Supreme Court who appeared below," he noted. Doubting that Walters would "lose face by not appearing," Baldwin argued that "a man who has never practiced before in the Supreme Court is at a big disadvantage in a case like this" and reminded Farquharson of "the criticism made of his appearance" before the lower court.[7]

Barnett had more success in this face-saving effort. He wrote Evans on April 30 to urge that Walters be allowed "to delineate the facts of the case" at the argument, adding that Evans "need have no fear of his ability to do a quite creditable job in this respect." Eager to accommodate his fellow Quaker, and perhaps aware that he lacked sufficient time to learn the record in the case, Evans agreed to share his time at the podium.[8]

The Seattle lawyers paid a substantial price for this compromise. They gave up in return their control over the brief that Walters and Barnett had drafted, and became bound to the ACLU resolution that forbid any constitutional attack on Executive Order 9066. Roger Baldwin had won from Walters what Al Wirin, the ACLU lawyer in Los Angeles, had failed to gain in two months of effort to take control of the test case briefs. Frustrated by the recent demise of the Wakayama cases, Wirin admitted his "selfish interest" in "playing a part in the oral arguments before the Supreme Court." In his campaign to reach the Court's podium, Wirin took the tack of suggesting the "coordination" of the test case briefs. On March 29, two days after the Court of Appeals issued its certification statement, Wirin had written to Clifford Forster in New York that "the Government had the better of the argument" before the appellate judges "precisely because the Government's arguments were centralized and hence well organized."[9]

Wirin had sounded out both Earl Bernard and Frank Walters at the Court of Appeals session about his proposal that "I be permitted a hand in the preparation of the first drafts" of the Yasui and Hirabayashi briefs, with inconclusive results. Over the next two months, Wirin pursued his bull-in-the-china-shop approach to both lawyers over the telephone. Surprisingly, in light of his earlier hands-off attitude toward the ACLU, Bernard agreed to share his time before the Supreme Court in the Yasui case with Wirin. Walters, however, remained unreceptive to Wirin's overtures, undoubtedly in reaction to the campaign to displace him from the Hirabayashi case. After repeated calls from Wirin, Walters wrote him on April 7 with the snide comment that "I compliment you on your ambition to become a constitutional lawyer, and add that I think you are well on your way.'' Undeterred by this rebuff, Wirin persisted, but finally reported to Baldwin on April 17 that Walters had rejected his proposal that the briefs be drafted in a collaborative effort directed by the ACLU.[10]

After Baldwin succeeded in his takeover campaign, however, Walters had no choice but to submit to ACLU dictation. The draft brief Walters had sent to New York—which included a constitutional attack on Executive Order 9066—received a failing grade from Clifford Forster, who reviewed the draft for Baldwin. The staff lawyer also objected to several arguments he considered irrelevant to the legality of the curfew and exclusion orders. ''We feel, and so do the Quakers, that Walters' brief which he prepared for the Supreme Court is pretty weak,'' Forster reported to Wirin on April 21. With only two weeks left before the final brief was due in Washington, the ACLU staff turned to general counsel Osmond Fraenkel, a veteran of the brief-drafting process.[11]

With a blue pencil as his scalpel, Fraenkel immediately began legal surgery on Walters' draft brief, cutting out arguments Walters had made before the Court of Appeals. In his dissent to certification, Judge Denman had claimed that it was ''unjust'' to Hirabayashi to omit from the record sent to the Supreme Court three arguments pressed by the Seattle lawyer: that DeWitt's orders constituted a ''bill of attainder'' directed solely at Japanese Americans; that the orders were part of a ''plan to seize [Hirabayashi's] person in violation of the Fourth Amendment''; and that ''the scheme for deporting people from their homes . . . without trial, is a cruel and unusual punishment in violation of the Eighth Amendment.'' By deciding to accept the case for full review, rather than restrict itself to the questions submitted for certification, the Supreme Court had opened itself to argument on all of the constitutional questions raised in the lower court. Fraenkel could thus have dealt with any of these points. But despite Denman's minority support of these questions, Fraenkel excised the first and third from the final brief. His only concession to Walters was to include the claim that the military orders involved an ''unreasonable seizure'' of Hirabayashi's body and thus violated the Fourth Amendment, a claim with little support in precedent.[12]

In a more substantive revision, Fraenkel eliminated the attack on Executive Order 9066 and focused instead on Public Law 503. This may seem on the surface to be a minor distinction, since Justice Department lawyers rested their support for DeWitt's orders on both Roosevelt's order and the congressional statute in equal measure. However, Fraenkel's insistence on making the distinction reflected more than the edict of the ACLU board. In granting the constitutionality of the presidential order, Fraenkel sidestepped the difficult question of whether Roosevelt's "war powers" extended to restraints on civilians. His challenge to the statute and DeWitt's orders made two claims: first, that they exceeded the limits of the presidential directive to protect the West Coast against "sabotage and espionage" under the delegation doctrine; and second, that they involved an unlawful racial discrimination.

On the first point, Fraenkel invoked the doctrine employed by the Supreme Court during the 1930s to strike down broadly worded New Deal statutes. Just as Congress had unlawfully delegated unlimited powers to executive officers in those laws, he argued, in Public Law 503 "Congress has laid down no standard by which the military authorities may be guided either in their definition of military areas or in their determination of what restrictions should be imposed in the movement of civilians in the areas."[13]

Fraenkel encountered more difficulty in making his argument that DeWitt's orders violated the Constitution in singling out Japanese Americans. All prior Supreme Court decisions that struck down racially discriminatory laws rested on the Fourteenth Amendment's equal protection clause, which applied only to the states. The holdings in these earlier cases that race constituted "an improper basis of classification" under state law, Fraenkel wrote, should be extended to the requirement of the Fifth Amendment's due process clause that similar classifications by the federal government have a "reasonable basis" in fact. The "wholesale attribution of disloyalty to a racial group of citizens" simply on the ground that some Japanese Americans "may be under suspicion," he asserted, failed to provide a "rational ground" for the discrimination imposed by DeWitt's orders. Fraenkel could not, however, cite any Supreme Court precedent to support this contention, and he devoted only two pages of the brief to this crucial argument.[14]

The brief submitted to the Supreme Court on behalf of Gordon Hirabayashi—over the signatures of Fraenkel, Walters and Evans—was a traditional and moderate document. Uncompromising in its assault on DeWitt's orders, the brief took a safe road around the constitutional minefield that protected Roosevelt's "war powers" and Executive Order 9066. On the central due process and delegation issues, the brief was short on direct precedent but challenged the Court to apply a body of doctrine established in other legal areas to an unprecedented situation. Fraenkel ended the brief on this note of challenge: "Often the question has been raised whether this country could wage a new war without loss of its fundamental liberties at home. Here is one occasion for this Court to give an unequivocal answer to that question and show the world that we can fight for democracy and preserve it too."[15]

Two additional briefs in the Hirabayashi case, however, broke legal tradition and convention in radically different ways. Both were amicus briefs, one submitted by the Japanese American Citizens League and the other by the San Francisco ACLU branch. The first was drafted at the instigation of Al Wirin and the second was written by Wayne Collins. Roger Baldwin's differing relations with these two lawyers explains why he welcomed the JACL brief and denounced the one submitted by the dissident ACLU branch.

The JACL brief in the Hirabayashi case was an unusual document in two respects. First, it signaled a turnabout of the JACL's policy of withholding support from the Japanese Americans who challenged DeWitt's orders. Wirin helped to engineer this reversal by arranging meetings between Baldwin and Mike Masaoka after the JACL director moved in the fall of 1942 from Salt Lake City to Washington, where he served as a wheeling-and-dealing lobbyist. With the legal rights of Japanese Americans now before the Supreme Court, the ACLU director argued to his young counterpart, an amicus brief would add weight to his own group's effort in the case. Wirin's dual role as counsel to both organizations made him the obvious choice to work with JACL president Saburo Kido in preparing the brief.

Even more unusual was the position of the brief's author. Hidden behind the signatures of Wirin and Kido was the hand of a government employee on the staff of the War Relocation Authority. Morris E. Opler, who then worked as a Community Analyst at the Manzanar Relocation Center in California, came to this job with a doctorate in anthropology from the University of Chicago. A prolific writer on the culture of the Apache and Navaho tribes, Opler had earlier worked for the Bureau of Indian Affairs and taught at the Claremont Colleges in California. Before he joined the WRA staff, Opler had written for Wirin the JACL's amicus brief in the Regan case, the abortive effort of the Native Sons of the Golden West to strip Japanese Americans of their voting rights.[16]

Before the war, Opler had taught Japanese American students and "knew them as kids who were interested in baseball." Part of Opler's motivation in aiding the JACL in the Hirabayashi case stemmed from his objections to the "loyalty" questionnaire imposed by the WRA on camp residents. This mass inquisition, which Opler accurately predicted in April 1943 would become "a basis for repressive action" against those citizens who refused to renounce a nonexistent allegiance to Japan, was underway at the time he volunteered his services to Wirin. Another impetus came from Opler's clashes with Manzanar camp director Ralph Merritt and WRA lawyer J. B. Saks over the causes and consequences of a bloody riot on December 6, 1942. With tensions high on the eve of the first Pearl Harbor anniversary, army guards armed with machine guns fired on an angry crowd gathered to protest the WRA's use of "stool pigeons" and killed two camp residents.[17]

Opler had no legal training and made no effort to match the conventional form of the ACLU brief. He prepared for Wirin, instead, a 126-page document in the tradition of the "Brandeis brief." Lightly salted by Wirin with citations to eleven Supreme Court opinions, Opler's brief ranged widely from anthropological studies—such as Franz Boas's classic book, *The Mind of Primitive Man*—to recent accounts of the cultural assimilation of Japanese Americans. The brief stressed the point that virtually all studies of this racial and national minority agreed that, like other immigrant groups, Japanese Americans sought assimilation and acceptance in American society. Their retention of old-country practices in religion, language, and ceremonial dress did not distinguish them from Greeks, Poles, Italians, or other ethnic groups.[18]

The JACL brief also took aim at General DeWitt. Quoting recent press reports of DeWitt's statement to a congressional committee that "a Jap's a Jap" and that "it makes no difference whether he's an American citizen or not," Opler cited this blatant racism as evidence that the military orders at issue in the Hirabayashi case hid another motive than protection against espionage and sabotage. In his contribution to the brief, Wirin drew the conclusion from Opler's data that DeWitt lacked a "reasonable" basis for the military orders and that they consequently had no constitutional sanction.[19]

Opler's brief failed, however, to sway a single member of the Supreme Court. The unanimous opinion in the Hirabayashi case looked instead to the government's brief and that submitted by the West Coast states for "support for the view that social, economic and political conditions" had prevented the "assimilation as an integral part of the white population" of Japanese Americans. Considering the authorship of these contending briefs, a question to be discussed shortly, Opler clearly had superior qualifications as an expert on this issue. But his identity remained hidden from the Court. Although the WRA was not a party to that case, and although Opler wrote the brief on his own time, his volunteer work for the JACL raised questions of propriety.[20]

Roger Baldwin *did* learn from Al Wirin of Morris Opler's role in the JACL brief and wrote him that "the document comes out better than the ablest briefs I have seen. It constitutes a complete answer to the government's case and provided the Court is willing to take what we regard as a reasonable view it should prevail." Baldwin confessed, however, that "I am fearful that in war-time counter arguments will carry more weight."[21]

Baldwin expressed no such enthusiasm for the amicus brief drafted by Wayne Collins and submitted by the Northern California ACLU branch. In language more suited to a soapbox diatribe than a legal brief, Collins excoriated General DeWitt and bullied the justices of the Supreme Court. Comparing DeWitt to Attila the Hun, Genghis Khan, and Hitler in imposing "brutish slavery" on the Japanese Americans, Collins painted the evacuation program as "a cruelty that evokes horror and beggars description." DeWitt's orders, he claimed, constituted a "military dictatorship." Addressing the Supreme Court from the pages of his brief, Collins wrote for the ACLU branch that "we demand" a reversal of Hirabayashi's conviction. Any member of the Court who voted for "this plot to wreck the lives of these innocent citizens," Collins warned, "will forever be enshrined in the hall of infamy as a symbol of bigotry, intolerance and oppression." Almost lost among this billingsgate was an attack on the constitutionality of Executive Order 9066. Roosevelt's order, Collins wrote, had been issued "in excess of any constitutional power reposed in the President" and additionally lacked congressional approval.[22]

It was less the impassioned language of the brief than its attack on the presidential order that disturbed the ACLU board. Word from Ernest Besig of this defiance of board policy, even before Collins completed his brief, prompted the board on April 26 to warn Besig that it "may be obliged to request disaffiliation" of the disobedient branch. After Collins filed the offending brief two weeks later, the board formally disavowed it and gave the branch thirty days notice that failure to conform to national ACLU policy would result in disaffiliation. This was hardly an idle threat, since the board had recently expelled the Chicago branch and its entire membership for having offered legal support to alleged pro-German seditionists in violation of the board's October 1942 resolution. Only an abject apology from the chairman of the San Francisco branch, Episcopal Bishop Edward Parsons, dissuaded the board from a second wartime expulsion.[23]

As the date set for argument of the three criminal cases neared, Roger Baldwin had few worries about the conduct of the Yasui and Korematsu cases. Earl Bernard's agreement to share his time in the Yasui argument with Al Wirin pleased Baldwin, and the brief Bernard had filed stayed within ACLU policy limits. Baldwin was also relieved that Wayne Collins would not appear before the Supreme Court to argue the Korematsu case. Since the issue before the Court—whether the probationary sentence imposed on Korematsu was an appealable judgment—did not reach the merits of the case, Collins had agreed to let Al Wirin make this argument as well.

Baldwin was deeply concerned, however, about the prospect of discord during argument of the Hirabayashi case. Although precedent existed within the ACLU for the filing of separate briefs by the national office and local branches, never before had the organization exposed to the courts such an open split over constitutional issues. Neither of the lawyers scheduled to argue the case, Harold Evans and Frank Walters, bore any responsibility for the amicus brief Collins had filed, but his intemperate language might provoke resentment on the bench that would find a target in Hirabayashi's lawyers. Evans and Walters also differed over the constitutionality of Executive Order 9066, and sharp questioning from the bench on this issue might turn the uneasy allies into antagonists. The ACLU thus approached the Supreme Court bar both divided and dispirited.

The briefs filed by the ACLU in the Hirabayashi case made the conflicts among its lawyers a matter of public record. Supposedly limited by judicial rules to a single brief, government lawyers nonetheless encountered equally deep, if more private, divisions in framing the Hirabayashi brief filed by the Justice Department. Indeed, in contrast to the two-sided struggle within the ACLU, government lawyers were split into four camps, each with its own ax to grind. Two groups of lawyers jockeyed for position inside the Justice Department, one in the Alien Enemy Control Unit headed by Edward Ennis and the other in the office of Solicitor General Charles Fahy. Lawyers in the War Department, both in the office of Judge Advocate General Myron Cramer and on the staff of Assistant Secretary John J. McCloy, pushed for a hard-line position backing General DeWitt's "military necessity" claims. Philip Glick and his WRA legal staff, looking forward from the Hirabayashi to the Endo case, stood in the shakiest position on the constitutional tightrope; Glick urged simultaneously that Hirabayashi brief defend detention as an integral part of DeWitt's evacuation program and that it distinguish between "military necessity" as a justification for DeWitt's orders and the "protective custody" argument advanced by the WRA as support for detention.

Differences of personality and policy separated Ennis and Fahy over the government's Hirabayashi brief and complicated the task of forging a brief both men would be willing to sign. Ennis made no secret either of his belief that Public Law 503 was unconstitutional or of his distrust of War Department arguments. Fahy "thought the Army was his client and was putting forth the best arguments he could for them," Ennis later said. "The War Department isn't simply our client," Ennis responded. "We're a department of the government of the United States, and we must not put forward everything they tell us." As their debates over the Hirabayashi brief progressed, however, Ennis found that Fahy remained unyielding in his determination to defer to the War Department.[24]

The lawyers assigned by each Justice Department official to the job of writing the Hirabayashi brief reflected these differences at the top. Ennis delegated his part of the task to the most junior member of his staff, Nanette Dembitz. She had turned down job offers with other wartime agencies to join the Alien Enemy Control Unit in search of some legal action. "I was just looking for a job," she recalled, "and this just seemed more interesting and more alive." Her first assignment from Ennis and John Burling had been to draft a memorandum, in preparation for the Yasui and Korematsu trials, supporting the introduction of evidence under the concept of "judicial notice" rather than through the testimony of government witnesses subject to cross-examination. "Eddie felt that if there were a trial in which the government tried to present all the inquities of the Japanese Americans that would be quite inflammatory, with all the groups that were anti-Japanese and pro-DeWitt," Dembitz explained. "If there *had* been trials and really good lawyers contesting the validity of DeWitt's orders, they might have made quite a record."[25]

Working from the Court of Appeals brief as background, Dembitz expanded the "racial characteristics" section considerably by "wading through the card catalogs" at the Library of Congress. Her initial draft of the Hirabayashi brief, in fact, cited extensively from many of the same sources used in Morris Opler's amicus brief. Dembitz cited at length from the record of the Tolan Committee on such topics as Japanese American family structure, education, and religion, works by anthropologist Ruth Benedict, articles in the *Encyclopedia Britannica,* and studies from the fields of history, political science, and sociology. Given its purpose as a piece of partisan advocacy, the draft brief was remarkably even-handed; Dembitz conscientiously noted in the text and footnotes evidence that balanced or contradicted her assertions.[26]

This equivocal approach stemmed in part from Dembitz's awareness that material submitted under the "judicial notice" doctrine "was supposed to represent the consensus of expert opinion, but a lot of this material on Japanese language schools and Shinto temples, for example, really wasn't anything the Court could take judicial notice of." Dembitz also recalled "eliminating all kinds of stuff sent to us by U.S. attorneys on the Coast. I went through a lot of this and concluded it wasn't really respectable." Two other agencies offered their help during the brief-drafting process. "The FBI went through Wayne Collins' wastebasket and told us 'We'll tell you what cases he's going to cite,' " she later said. The staff of the Office of Naval Intelligence offered more information. In later thanking Navy Secretary Frank Knox for this assistance, Attorney General Biddle noted the "mass of factual material pertaining to the Japanese population" provided by Lt. Frederick Welden and Ensign Don C. Gorham.[27]

In final form, however, the Hirabayashi brief made the "racial characteristics" argument in much less equivocal language than Dembitz had proposed. She noted in the draft brief, for example, "the stimulation of prejudice by opportunistic politics and by the sensational press" as sources of hositility toward Japanese Americans and as reasons for their "lack of assimilation" into the dominant Caucasian culture. Dembitz also cited evidence of "assaults and hoodlumism" as explaining the "keen realization" by Japanese Americans of "the fact of discrimination and prejudice against them." Neither of these exculpatory admissions survived the surgery performed on the draft brief. What lasted was simply the conclusion that "an unknown number of the Japanese may lack to some extent a feeling of loyalty toward the United States as a result of their treatment," a statement followed by the unsupported claim that such treatment produced "a consequent tie to Japan" and a "compensatory feeling of racial pride . . . in Japan's achievements."[28]

One reason behind the hardening of position from the draft to the final brief was the blue-pencil power wielded by Arnold Raum, a thirty-five-year-old Harvard Law School graduate who joined the Office of the Solicitor General in 1939. Raum had been delegated authority over the Hirabayashi brief by Solicitor General Charles Fahy, and the two men shared a similar reaction to the Pearl Harbor attack. "The extent of our weakness after Pearl Harbor and of the devastation was never made clear to the public," Raum later said. He then added that fears of sabotage by Japanese Americans were "realistic and not a figment of the imagination." Raum had worked during the 1930s, as had John J. McCloy, on the legal reverberations of the "Black Tom" explosion of

1916, later connected to German sabotage, and considered "the safeguarding of defense plants on the West Coast of enormous importance to the security of the country."[29]

Raum's primary role in framing the final Hirabayashi brief was in putting the "war powers" argument in the strongest terms possible. "Fahy and I were in complete agreement that constitutionally the government could do what it had done" to the Japanese Americans, Raum later asserted. "The general rule is that in undertaking to deal with an evil you sometimes have to go beyond it to make sure you deal with it effectively." Based on this expansive constitutional theory, Raum wrote in the final brief that the war power "requires a far wider latitude for executive judgment and action than is involved in the exercise of ordinary governmental powers." Raum also disparaged the argument that due process doctrine required the granting of individual hearings to citizens of Japanese ancestry, as had been accorded to aliens interned on Justice Department order. Citing without any supporting evidence "the virtually impossible task of promptly segregating the potentially disloyal from the loyal" among Japanese Americans, Raum concluded that "the only certain way of removing [the disloyal] was to remove the group as a whole." This claim, at the heart of the government's brief, had neither been tested at trial nor constituted a subject fit for judicial notice.[30]

During the time that Dembitz and Raum worked on the Hirabayashi brief finally approved by Solicitor General Fahy, three related debates raged within the ranks of government lawyers over issues of direct relevance to the arguments made in the brief. The outcome of each of these debates affected not only the wording of the Hirabayashi brief and the oral arguments made before the Supreme Court by Charles Fahy, but spilled over as well into the briefs and arguments in the Korematsu case when it returned to the Court in 1944. Each episode in this continuing conflict, hidden both from the public and from lawyers for the test case defendants, raised serious questions about the veracity and good faith of War Department officers and lawyers, questions with significant legal consequences.

The first of these internal debates began in January 1943, even before the Court of Appeals heard arguments in the test cases later certified to the Supreme Court. On the surface, the issue was the plan first proposed by Mike Masaoka that the War Department set up a military combat unit composed of Nisei volunteers. Through his contacts with John J. McCloy (who latter claimed credit for the idea), Masaoka persuaded Secretary of War Stimson to establish the 442nd Regimental Combat Team, which fought valiantly in Italy and France and gained renown as the most decorated unit in the Army.[31]

Plans for the Nisei combat unit pleased officials of the War Relocation Authority, who adopted the idea as part of their campaign to secure War Department approval for the gradual release of camp residents to their West Coast homes. Joining the politically popular proposal for the combat unit with the touchy issue of returning Japanese Americans to the Coast seemed to WRA director Dillon Myer an excellent way of defusing opposition to the latter plan. When General DeWitt got wind of these plans, however, he objected vehemently. DeWitt centered his objections on the impact that a release program, based on WRA certification of the loyalty of those permitted to return to the Coast, would have on the pending test cases. In a lengthy memorandum sent to the War Department on January 27, DeWitt reminded his superiors that critics of the evacuation and interment program had "questioned the necessity for mass total evacuation and asked . . . why loyalty boards were not used" as had been done with interned aliens. "These critics were answered by statements that it was substantially impossible to determine the loyalty of Japanese."[32]

If the War Department agreed to the release proposal, DeWitt continued, those "originally critical of mass evacuation will ask: Why was not loyalty determined during the assembly center phase if it can be done now? If the Government will not or cannot justify its position in this regard, critics are certain to force a confession of original mistake in evacuation." DeWitt stressed that government lawyers planned to argue before the Court of Appeals the alleged impossibility of providing individual hearings to Japanese Americans. "The position taken by the Government in the court cases is in some respects contrary to the implications" of the release program, he warned. Although he reluctantly accepted the proposal for a Nisei combat unit, DeWitt drew the line at the border of the Western Defense Command: "None of the excluded persons should be permitted to reenter Military Areas Nos. 1 and 2 at any time prior to the termination of the war." He urged this policy, DeWitt wrote, "in order that the litigation now pending . . . be not hindered or embarrassed" by an implicit confession that the Army's claim on the loyalty-determination question was in error from the outset.[33]

DeWitt's fear that the courts would read a release-and-return program as a sign of weakness on the government's part was countered by the WRA's argument that adoption of such a policy would strengthen the test cases. Dillon Myer sent to Stimson on March 11 a long letter that offered three alternative release plans: Plan A would authorize release only outside the West Coast; Plan B would permit return to the Coast of all camp residents *except* those determined by a government board to be potentially disloyal; Plan C, the middle course that Myer felt most likely to appeal to Stimson, would permit Japanese American citizens cleared for loyalty (but not aliens) to return to the Coast, a much smaller group than that included in Plan B. Myer hoped that the successful return to their homes of these citizens would pave the way for the eventual return of all those certified as loyal.[34]

Myer submitted his proposals to Stimson before the test cases reached the Supreme Court. On April 7, after their certification by the Court of Appeals, WRA solicitor Philip Glick urged Myer to implement Plan C even if the War Department objected. "I strongly believe that an early announcement of Plan C will greatly improve the chances that the Supreme Court will sustain the constitutionality of evacuation." Members of the Court as well as the public recognized, Glick noted, that "since February 1942, when evacuation was decided upon and put into effect, the military situation has changed greatly for the better. The danger of a Japanese invasion of the West Coast has receded very much, indeed." Given this fact, continued internment might strike the Court as unduly harsh and lead it to find DeWitt's orders unwarranted. "The court has no way of knowing that the Government has any other plans for the evacuees than to detain them for the duration of the war," Glick told Myer. "If, however, the Judges will know that when the danger of invasion receded, the Government followed it with the announcement of an important change in plan, that will provide the court with a considerable assurance in the good faith of the Government.[35]

Myer and Glick initially felt confident that Stimson would approve the announcement of Plan C. "We are working on Assistant Secretary of War McCloy and others in trying to get their consent to Plan C," Glick wrote to Maurice Walk on April 8. "Things are beginning to look hopeful." Even such a hard-liner as Judge Advocate General Myron Cramer suggested to McCloy that loyalty screening and the gradual return of Japanese Americans to the Coast might help to win the test cases. "While the question of detention will not be specifically before the Court in the present cases," Cramer wrote on April 26, "the fact that evacuation was a step leading to detention will not be unknown to the Justices." (Government lawyers, incidentally, strenuously denied throughout the test cases that evacuation led to detention.) Should the War Department adopt a policy of "permitting selected detainees to return to their homes," Cramer urged that "the announcement of such a policy before the argument of the cases would show that the measures taken are being reviewed and modified as the military measures appear to the Court, the easier it will be to sustain them."[36]

Against the eager support for Plan C by Myer and Glick and its cautious endorsement by Cramer, DeWitt won the battle to block the return of Japanese Americans to the West Coast. A monumental blunder on McCloy's part contributed to DeWitt's victory. As part of the process by which volunteers for the Nisei combat unit were screened for loyalty, Captain John M. Hall of McCloy's staff drafted a questionnaire that *all* camp residents were required to complete. Questions 27 and 28 on this form asked every interned Japanese American, citizens and aliens alike, and women as well as men, to affirm their willingness "to serve in the armed forces of the United States on combat duty" and to "forswear any form of allegiance or obedience to the Japanese emperor. . . ."[37]

The wording of Hall's questions, and the WRA's decision that all camp residents be required to answer them, understandably created confusion and chaos. Men over draft age, and women in general, shrank from answering yes to Question 27 in fear that they would be impressed into the Army. Aliens felt that a yes answer to Question 28 would strip them of Japanese citizenship and make them stateless persons, while native-born Japanese Americans considered the question a trap designed to elicit an admission of an alliance to Japan they never held. Despite these fears, close to 90 percent of the camp residents affirmed their loyalty and willingness to serve in the Army. Some 7,600 of those forced to answer, however, either checked off a no response to one or both of the questions or qualified their answers to WRA officials in such a way as to brand them as disloyal.[38]

The resulting uproar in the internment camps fueled the growing pressures on Stimson to segregate the "disloyal" Japanese Americans from those willing to affirm their loyalty. In bowing to this pressure by transferring to the Tule Lake interment camp members of the so-called No-No group, Stimson also caved in to DeWitt's demand that the War Department reject the WRA's proposal to permit the return of the "loyal" majority to the West Coast. Stimson held off a reply to Dillon Myer's request that he approve Plan C until after the test cases had been argued before the Supreme Court. His decision to "segregate" members of the No-No group in the Tule Lake camp, Stimson explained to Myer late in May 1943, "renders premature any consideration of relaxing the restrictions in force in the Western Defense Command" on the return of Japanese Americans to the West Coast.[39]

Stimson's rejection of the WRA proposal and of General Cramer's suggestion to McCloy that the War Department "prepare for hearings in individual cases," as a prelude to a release-and-return program, directly affected the wording of the government's brief in the Hirabayashi case. At the time that Japanese Americans were "under complete military control" in the assembly centers, DeWitt had conceded in his "confidential" memorandum of January 27, "there was time to determine loyalty without expanding 50 to 60 millions on relocation centers." Notwithstanding this crucial admission, or perhaps kept from knowledge of it, Arnold Raum claimed in the final Hirabayashi brief that "the identities of the potentially disloyal were not readily discoverable." Even if such individual hearings had been conducted, Raum added, "there is no reason to suppose that they could have solved the problem." Government officials who would be asked in such hearings "to look deep into the mind of a particular Japanese" for evidence of loyalty, Raum told the Supreme Court, could hardly ascertain "the ties of kinship or other intangible forces which might bind him to the members of an invading Japanese army."[40]

A second and more serious debate within the government involved questions not of psychology but of military intelligence. Although the dispute began with material available to General DeWitt and the War Department well before the issuance of Executive Order 9066 in February 1942, it emerged within the Justice Department over a year later. "Last week with our draft of the *Hirabayashi* brief," Edward Ennis wrote to Solicitor General Fahy on April 30, 1943, "I transmitted to Mr. Raum some material which I thought he would find helpful in obtaining a background view of the context of this case." Ennis referred in this memorandum to an article in the October 1942 issue of *Harpers Magazine,* entitled "The Japanese in America, the Problem and the Solution," published under the pseudonymous cover of "An Intelligence Officer."[41]

Intrigued by the article, Ennis tracked down its authorship through contacts in the WRA and discovered that it had been written by Lt. Commander Kenneth D. Ringle of the Office of Naval Intelligence. Ennis discovered and reported to Fahy that Ringle had been loaned by ONI to the War Relocation Authority "to prepare a manual on the background of the Japanese who were being evacuated from an Intelligence or security viewpoint, for the use of WRA personnel." His WRA contacts provided Ennis with a copy of the fifty-seven-page memorandum prepared by Ringle under the title "The Japanese Question in the United States." He had been "most informally, but altogether reliably, advised that both the article and the WRA memorandum prepared by Lt. Com. Ringle represent the views, if not of the Navy, at least of those Naval

Intelligence officers in charge of Japanese counter-intelligence work," Ennis told Fahy.[42]

Ennis did not know at the time he alerted Fahy to the significance of the *Harpers* article and the WRA memorandum to the Hirabayashi brief that both documents stemmed back to a ten-page report submitted to the Chief of Naval Operations on January 26, 1942, under the heading "Report on Japanese Question." Assigned by the ONI under the "delimitation agreement" between the FBI and military intelligence agencies to investigate the loyalty of Japanese Americans on the West Coast, Ringle produced an initial report marked by its uncompromising conclusion. Ringle bent over backward in admitting the "fanatical loyalty" to Japan of the Kibei group educated in Japan, and the pro-Japanese sentiments of those who belonged to such militaristic groups as the "Black Dragon Society" and associations of Japanese army and navy veterans. Granting the potential disloyalty of members of these groups, Ringle nonetheless estimated the number of Japanese Americans "who would act as saboteurs or agents" of Japan as "less than three percent of the total, or about 3500 in the entire United States."[43]

In listing the groups he considered potential threats to military security, Ringle emphasized in his initial report that "the most dangerous are already in custodial detention" as members of the "ABC" group interned on Justice Department order, or were "already fairly well known to the Naval Intelligence service or the Federal Bureau of Investigation" and were consequently subject to immediate apprehension. Ringle summarized his assessment of the loyalty of the Japanese American population in these words: "In short, the entire 'Japanese Problem' has been magnified out of its true proportion, largely because of the physical characteristics of the people [and] should be handled on the basis of the *individual,* regardless of citizenship, and *not* on a racial basis." Ringle specifically proposed, in both the WRA memorandum and the *Harpers* article that followed this report, that residents of interment camps be accorded individual hearings "for the express purpose of deciding, on the basis of logic and reason and in view of the circumstances in each case, whether or not the individual is to be considered in the class of the potentially dangerous."[44]

Ennis had no access to Ringle's initial report, held in ONI files under security classification, nor did he learn that Ringle had masterminded the March 1941 break-in of the Japanese consulate in Los Angeles. He did learn, however, from ONI sources of the prewar "delimitation agreement" and that the Army "agreed in writing to permit the Navy to conduct its Japanese intelligence work for it." In his opinion,

Ennis told Fahy, the Army "is bound by the opinion of the Naval officers in Japanese matters." Ennis pointed out to Fahy that Ringle and the ONI had advocated that only members of the Kibei group, their parents, and those who belonged to "pro-Japanese" military societies be considered for evacuation. These groups included only 10,000 of the total Japanese American population on the West Coast. "Thus, had we known that the Navy thought that 90% of the evacuation was unnecessary," Ennis told Fahy, "we could strongly have urged upon General DeWitt that he could not base a military judgment to the contrary on Intelligence reports, as he now claims to do."[45]

Appealing to Fahy's sense of rectitude and his responsibility as Solicitor General, Ennis argued that "in view of the fact that the Department of Justice is now representing the Army in the Supreme Court of the United States and is arguing that a partial, selective evacuation was impracticable, we must consider most carefully what our obligation to the Court is in view of the fact that the responsible Intelligence agency regarded a selective evacuation as not only sufficient but preferable." Ennis further noted that "one of the most difficult questions" in the Hirabayashi case "is raised by the fact that the Army did not evacuate people after any hearing or any individual determination of dangerousness, but evacuated the entire racial group." Not only had the briefs filed by the test case defendants "particularly pressed the point that no individual consideration was given," he pointed out, but "I regard it as certain that this point will be stressed even more, assuming that competent counsel represent appellants, in the Supreme Court."[46]

Ennis made clear to Fahy the bind in which Ringle's reports placed the government in defending DeWitt's orders before the Supreme Court. On "one of the crucial points" raised in the Hirabayashi case, he noted, "the Government is forced to argue that individual selective evacuation would have been impractical and insufficient when we have positive knowledge that the only Intelligence agency responsible for advising General DeWitt gave him advice directly to the contrary." Ennis phrased his final plea to Fahy in terms that waved a warning flag before the Solicitor General: "I think we should consider very carefully whether we do not have a duty to advise the Court of the existence of the Ringle memorandum and of the fact that this represents the view of the Office of Naval Intelligence. It occurs to me that any other course of conduct might approximate the suppression of evidence."[47]

Submitted to Fahy only days before the final Hirabayashi brief was due in the Supreme Court clerk's office, this memorandum from Ennis raised the first whiff of legal scandal in the test cases. Fahy could, and obviously did, differ with Ennis over the relevance and importance to the brief of the so-called Ringle Report. In his role as Solicitor General, Fahy exercised control over the government's presentation to the Supreme Court, and Ennis's role was technically advisory at this stage of the case. Fahy's reputation as a stickler for accuracy, however, made puzzling the manner in which he and his staff dodged the challenge from Ennis to put this countering evidence before the Court. Arnold Raum, who later asserted that he and Fahy "weren't going to give the Supreme Court anything that wouldn't stand up under the most rigorous scrutiny," also admitted that the Army "knew practically nothing" about the Japanese Americans. Raum knew well that "the Navy had charged itself with intelligence about the Japanese and was opposed to this exclusion as wholly unnecessary."[48]

In light of these admissions, Raum dealt with the material given him by Ennis in a curious way. Raum brushed aside in the Hirabayashi brief Ringle's claim (one emphasized by Ennis also) that individual loyalty hearings were a feasible alternative to mass evacuation. Questions of loyalty were "entirely irrelevant" to the case, Raum wrote. The rationale behind DeWitt's orders was "not the loyalty or disloyalty of individuals but the danger from the residence of the class as such within a vital military area." Such a judgment about the "danger" posed by Japanese Americans as a group, however, necessarily required as the "rational basis" demanded by the due process clause some reasonable estimation of loyalty within the group. In searching for such rationality, Raum retreated to speculation and supposition. Japanese Americans had been "treated as a group," he wrote, because some of them were "thought" to be dangerous. Raum did not identify those who harbored these thoughts, nor did he explain why it would be a "virtually impossible task" to determine loyalty on the basis of hearings.[49]

The Hirabayashi brief also disregarded a second major objection to mass evacuation made by Ringle and pointed out by Ennis in his memorandum to Fahy: "Since the naval officers believe that it was necessary to evacuate only about 10,000 people they could have identified by name, they did not feel that it was necessary to evacuate all of the Japanese." Raum seemed to concede this point in the brief: "If those Japanese who might aid the enemy were either known or readily identifiable, the task of segregating them would probably have been comparatively simple." Despite the clear statement by Ringle that such identification was possible, Raum argued the opposite in the brief, claiming that "the identities of the potentially disloyal were not readily discoverable."[50]

Raum's only citation to the *Harpers* article that Ennis gave him came in a footnote supporting a statement about the Japanese-educated Kibei that "it is probable that many of them are intensely loyal to Japan." Ringle had in fact cast doubt on the loyalty of the Kibei as "a dangerous group." He had noted, however, that their identify "can be readily ascertained from United States government records," a point that Raum neglected to include in the brief. More important, the brief made no mention of the lengthy WRA memorandum that Ennis had offered to Fahy, a document that refuted at almost every point the conclusions drawn by Dembitz and Raum, and adopted by Fahy in his subsequent argument to the Supreme Court, from the material offered to support the "racial characteristics" claims at the heart of the Hirabayashi brief. Neither did the brief acknowledge, as Ennis had urged on Fahy, that the anonymous *Harpers* article represented the views of the ONI.[51]

Rebuffed in his attempt to alert the Supreme Court to the countering views of the Ringle Report and its status as an ONI document, Ennis gave up for the time his objection to Fahy's "suppression of evidence." As a loyal government lawyer, Ennis swallowed his doubts and added his name to the Hirabayashi brief along with those of Fahy, Raum, and Dembitz.

Although government lawyers conducted their debates over the WRA's release-and-return plan and the Ringle Report behind closed doors, the issues were clear to the participants and were decided after relatively open discussion. A third dispute over the Hirabayashi brief, however, took on a conspiratorial cast and left Ennis and his assistant, John Burling, in the dark on an issue that later returned with a vengeance during preparation of the Korematsu brief in 1944. This dispute, the most serious that arose during the short span of the test cases, began in April 1943 with a seemingly innocuous request from Ennis to Judge Advocate General Myron Cramer "to supply any published material in the War Department's possession on the military situation on the West Coast at the time of the evacuation to be used in the Hirabayashi brief in the Supreme Court."[52]

The initial response from Cramer encouraged Ennis. He reported to Solicitor General Fahy on April 19 that Cramer "has today received a printed report from General DeWitt about the Japanese evacuation and is now determining whether it is to be released so that it may be used in connection with these cases." Cramer referred Ennis to Colonel Joel Watson of DeWitt's legal staff for a decision on whether the Justice Department could obtain the report. Watson assured him, Ennis later informed Fahy, "that General DeWitt's report was being rushed off the press and would be available" for use in the Hirabayashi and Yasui briefs. But Ennis never learned, during the War Department's shell game that kept the report hidden from Justice Department lawyers for another year, that this crucial document had already been printed and bound. More important, he also never learned that the version of the DeWitt Report finally offered to the Justice Department was a substitute for the initial version. In one significant respect, the differences between the two versions resulted in misleading the Supreme Court in all three of the criminal test cases that challenged DeWitt's military orders.[53]

On April 19—the same day Colonel Watson told Ennis it was being "rushed off the press"—Assistant Secretary of War John J. McCloy received two printed and bound copies of a massive document titled *Final Report, Japanese Evacuation From the West Coast, 1942*. Ten months in preparation, the evacuation report had been produced at DeWitt's direction by the staff of the Civil Affairs Division headed by Colonel Karl Bendetsen. The bulk of the report consisted of accounts of the mechanics of evacuation and the operations of the Wartime Civil Control Administration, which Bendetsen also headed. These sections depicted evacuation and the interment camps in rosy terms, with eighty pages of photographs that portrayed the camps as bucolic and well-tended places populated with busy and happy residents. These parts of the report, however, had little relevance to the Hirabayashi and Yasui cases and the "military necessity" claim on which the government's justification of the curfew and evacuation orders rested.[54]

The two printed copies of the *Final Report* that arrived in McCloy's office on April 19 were accompanied by a cover letter dated April 15 and signed by DeWitt. Bendetsen had drafted this letter, and in it he acknowledged the importance of the report to the Hirabayashi and Yasui cases. The copies had been shipped to the Pentagon by Air Express, Bendetsen wrote on DeWitt's behalf, "because I am advised that there is an urgent need of the material contained therein for use in the preparation of the Federal Government's briefs in the cases now pending before the Supreme Court of the United States challenging the constitutionality of the entire program."[55]

A hasty review of the *Final Report* left McCloy alarmed and convinced that it was a dangerous document. Two points in particular aroused McCloy's concern that it should not be given to Justice Department lawyers for use in the Supreme Court briefs. The first was that DeWitt had stated flatly in the Foreward to the report his opposition to the return of any Japanese Americans to the West Coast for the duration of the war. DeWitt's objection threatened a split in the ranks, since the War Department's exclusion policy was then under review and since

McCloy himself leaned toward a program of gradual return of those cleared for "loyalty" by the War Relocation Authority. More alarming to McCloy was a paragraph in Chapter 2 of DeWitt's report, which was titled "Need for Military Control and for Evacuation."[56]

The troublesome paragraph included two related claims as justification for the evacuation of Japanese Americans. DeWitt first asserted that it had been "impossible to establish the identify of the loyal and the disloyal with any degree of safety." The next sentence added another claim: "It was not that there was insufficient time in which to make such a determination; it was simply a matter of facing the realities that a positive determination could not be made, that an exact separation of the 'sheep from the goats' was unfeasible." The factors that made such a separation impossible were not specified, but the context of the paragraph and of Chapter 2 as a whole implied that Japanese Americans constituted such a "tightly-knit racial group" that separation by loyalty could not have been accomplished by any means.[57]

Reading this paragraph with a lawyer's eye, McCloy quickly recognized that it seriously undermined the government's position in the test cases. DeWitt's claim that the Army faced an "impossible" task in determining the loyalty of Japanese Americans struck McCloy as damaging in two ways. The West Coast commander had already conceded, in his January 27 memorandum to the War Department, that "there was time to determine loyalty" once this group had been herded into assembly centers. In addition, DeWitt's statement in the printed report smacked of racism.[58]

Equally damaging was DeWitt's admission that lack of time in which to conduct individual loyalty hearings had not been a factor in his decision to recommend evacuation. Justice Department lawyers had argued before the Court of Appeals in San Francisco, however, that Japanese Americans had been evacuated as a group because the Army lacked sufficient time to conduct such hearings in the months after Pearl Harbor. Without this argument as a corollary to the "military necessity" claim, DeWitt's orders became vulnerable to the countering argument that Japanese Americans had been deprived of due process. Lawyers for the defendants had already attacked the "insufficient time" argument by pointing the courts to the English experience, in which hearings had been granted to more than a hundred thousand "enemy aliens" within a few months and without any administrative problems.[59]

McCloy knew that the central paragraph in Chapter 2, if it reached the Supreme Court, might well destroy the government's credibility and risk the outcome of the Hirabayashi and Yasui cases. Working late on April 19 to deal with this unpleasant problem, he placed a call from the

Pentagon to Bendetsen in San Francisco at 11:15 at night. McCloy first expressed displeasure at having received the *Final Report* in printed form. "I thought it was arranged that we were to get a galley of it before you printed it up," he remonstrated. Embarrassed by this dressing-down, Bendetsen assured McCloy that only ten copies had been printed and that "any change that you feel ought to be made, can easily be made." McCloy was not mollified by this offer. "I'm distressed about it," he said of the report's contents. "There are a number of things in it now which I feel should not be made public," he added. Without listing his precise objections, McCloy dismissed the report as "too self-glorifying and too self-serving for the type of document that I think should be perpetuated." Noting that "we have got to send it around to the Department of Justice" before the public release that DeWitt had suggested, McCloy intimated that it might be better to bury the *Final Report*. "I don't know whether we will ever get it out," he told Bendetsen.[60]

Second thoughts about the potential consequences of such a move, and of the likely reaction by General DeWitt, prompted McCloy to order Bendetsen to come to Washington for consultation. McCloy then assigned his legal deputy, Captain John M. Hall, to work with Bendetsen on revisions to the *Final Report*. The collaboration between the two young lawyers went well, but Bendetsen felt inhibited by his responsibility to DeWitt, who was then in Alaska. After meetings with both McCloy and Hall, Bendetsen called Brigadier General James Barnett in San Francisco to pass on the message to DeWitt that the War Department officials were insisting on revisions that "went to the fundamental concept of evacuation." By "urgent" radiogram on April 26 Barnett transmitted to DeWitt the report from Bendetsen that McCloy had objected to the statement in the *Final Report* that "loyalty could not be determined and for that reason mass evacuation was ordered." Bendetsen had told Barnett that he was in "no position" to accept this significant revision. "I told him it was your report," Barnett informed DeWitt, "and that the War Department could not tell you what to say."[61]

In his reply to Barnett on April 27, DeWitt dug in his heels. "My report to Chief of Staff," he radioed his deputy, "will not be changed in any respect whatsoever either in substance or form and I will not, repeat not, consent to any, repeat any, revision made over my signature." Confronted with this adamant stand, Bendetsen found himself caught between loyalty to his commanding officer and pressures from McCloy and Hall. In the ensuing test of wills, McCloy bent over backwards to accommodate DeWitt's resistance to revisions. "I wouldn't want to offend him," he assured Bendetsen. "I wouldn't want him to think that I was trying to tell him what to say.'' Having offered this olive branch, McCloy then said that if DeWitt persisted in his position, ''I would much rather that the report go in to the files and let it go at that.''[62]

Forced to choose between no report and a revised report, Bendetsen became an easy target for the sword that McCloy wielded as a War Department official. Publication of a slightly revised version of the *Final Report,* McCloy argued, ''would be of great use in the pending Supreme Court cases.'' However, the problem with the report in its present form lay in DeWitt's claim that it would be ''impossible'' under any circumstances to determine the loyalty of Japanese Americans. Such a claim ''is fundamentally a different proposition than either the President or the Secretary'' of War could accept, McCloy added. This tactic of throwing out the names of Franklin Roosevelt and Henry Stimson produced the intended effect on Bendetsen. ''I can't find myself feeling that the position he takes is unjustified,'' Bendetsen told General Barnett on April 29.[63]

In a memorandum to DeWitt on May 3, Bendetsen reported McCloy's objection ''to that portion of Chapter II which said in effect that it is absolutely impossible to determine the loyalty of Japanese no matter how much time was taken in the process.'' McCloy had no objection, however, ''to saying that time was of the essence and that in view of the military situation and the fact that there was no known means of making such a determination with any degree of safety the evacuation was necessary.'' Isolated in Alaska, DeWitt tired of what must have seemed an exercise in hairsplitting by lawyers and finally agreed to accept the revisions proposed by McCloy.[64]

Working with Bendetsen, John Hall fashioned a compromise version of the sentence in DeWitt's report that had precipitated this long-distance dispute. Hall's revision broke the offending sentence into two: ''To complicate the situation no ready means existed for determining the loyal and the disloyal with any degree of safety. It was necessary to face the realities—a positive determination could not have been made.'' This editing accomplished both of McCloy's goals: it eliminated the admission that lack of time in which to conduct loyalty hearings had not been a factor in the evacuation decision; and it substituted for the racism of DeWitt's claim that it was ''impossible'' to determine the loyalty of Japanese Americans the explanation that the Army had no ''ready means'' by which to perform this task.[65]

The agreement Hall and Bendetsen reached on this alternative wording ended the intramural dispute between their superiors, McCloy and DeWitt. The War Department lawyers still faced, however, two problems with the *Final Report*. The first was that General Cramer and Colonel Watson had assured Edward Ennis that the Justice Department would have access to the report for use in the Hirabayashi and Yasui briefs to the Supreme Court. The second was that the *Final Report* had already been printed and formally transmitted by DeWitt to the War Department. Under any construction of the promise to Ennis, the printed report fell within his request for "published material" on the evacuation. But if the report reached the Justice Department in its original form, the Supreme Court might well learn of the disparity between the crucial admission on the "insufficient time" issue and earlier representations by government lawyers.

War Department lawyers solved these potentially embarrassing problems in extraordinary fashion. Bendetsen took the first step in the effort to erase the existence of the original report. He ordered John Hall to locate all six copies of the report sent to the Pentagon in April and to return them to San Francisco. Hall also tracked down and removed from War Department files in Washington every trace of the initial submission. On June 7, Hall returned to Bendetsen the original and all copies of DeWitt's first transmittal letter and reported that "War Department records have been adjusted accordingly." McCloy then instructed General DeWitt to submit a second transmittal letter along with a revised and reprinted version of the *Final Report*, as if the first had never existed. DeWitt complied with this order in a letter dated June 15, 1943, again drafted by Bendetsen. In contrast to DeWitt's earlier suggestion that the report be promptly released to the press and public, this substitute letter urged that the report not be released to "any other agency" of the government without the express direction of the Secretary of War.[66]

Bendetsen then ordered the final step in cleansing the files. On June 29, he received a report from Warrant Officer Theodore Smith: "I certify that this date I witnessed the destruction by burning of the galley proofs, galley pages, drafts and memorandums of the original report of the Japanese Evacuation." Every remaining record of this episode was then placed in a "Confidential" file in Bendetsen's office in the Presidio. Not a single piece of paper was left in the Pentagon to show that an earlier version of the *Final Report* had ever existed.[67]

The impact on the Hirabayashi and Yasui cases of the successful effort to withhold DeWitt's report from Justice Department lawyers was evident in their briefs to the Supreme Court. The government's defense of evacuation in the Hirabayashi brief rested on the claim that DeWitt had faced the "virtually impossible task of promptly segregating the potentially disloyal from the loyal" among the Japanese Americans. Had the Army been able to identify those of doubtful loyalty, the brief conceded, "the task of segregating them would probably have been comparatively simple." The brief argued, however, that the Army lacked sufficient time to conduct loyalty hearings: "Many months, or perhaps years, would be required for such investigations." The suppressed version of the *Final Report* included a flat contradiction of this significant argument. Along with the suppression of the ONI report of Commander Ringle, which countered DeWitt's disloyalty assertions, the concealment of DeWitt's report resulted in submission to the Supreme Court of briefs that were tainted with false claims.[68]

One other aspect of the War Department's shell game with the *Final Report* deserves mention. During his effort to obtain access to the report, Edward Ennis and Attorney General Biddle met with McCloy at the Pentagon to press their case in person. According to a later report by Ennis on this meeting, McCloy assured Biddle "that it was not intended to print this report." The Justice Department request was pending at the time DeWitt sent the initial version to the War Department, and remained active when the revised version reached McCloy's office on June 5, 1943. Although this date followed the arguments to the Supreme Court in the Hirabayashi and Yasui cases, it came sixteen days before the Court issued its opinions on them. McCloy took no steps, however, to provide the report to the Justice Department. Protected by a "Confidential" security label, the *Final Report* was not in fact released by the War Department until January 1944, more than seven months after the Supreme Court decided the cases.[69]

War Department lawyers displayed no compunction, however, in leaking the *Final Report* to lawyers outside the Justice Department. In a move that bent the rules of legal procedure, lawyers on DeWitt's staff collaborated with cooperative state officials in placing the *Final Report* on the Supreme Court bench within the covers of an amicus brief.

The trail by which this brief, filed jointly by California Attorney General Robert K. Kenny and his counterparts in Oregon and Washington, reached the Supreme Court remained hidden from both the Court and the Justice Department. Commanding the legal platoon that compiled and wrote the West Coast brief was Captain Herbert E. Wenig, who joined DeWitt's legal staff in July 1942 after serving since 1939 as a key assistant to Kenny's predecessor, Earl Warren. Wenig was perfectly placed, through his close ties with both Warren and Karl Bendetsen, as a link between the California attorney general's office and

DeWitt's office in the Presidio. When Kenny replaced Warren as attorney general in January 1943, after Warren's election as governor, Wenig retained his informal role as liaison between state officials and the Army. His friendship with Bendetsen cemented these ties and helped to camouflage Wenig's mission in the Hirabayashi case.[70]

Judicial rules prohibit the direct participation of a party to a lawsuit in the preparation of amicus brief. Since the War Department, although not named as a party in the Hirabayashi case, was nonetheless an agency of the federal government and bound by this proscription, Wenig's superiors concealed his role from the Justice Department. Robert Kenny acknowledged this undercover arrangement in a letter thanking Colonel Watson, Wenig's immediate superior, for "the assistance being rendered this office" by Wenig, "whom General DeWitt had designated to provide liaison" with Kenny's office. "As you know," Kenny wrote in praising Wenig, "from the outset he has been familiar not only with the facts and issues of the Japanese exclusion litigation, but also with the more general problem concerning the relationships of the military and civilian authorities."[71]

Wenig's familiarity with these issues began with an assignment from Earl Warren, several months before the Pearl Harbor attack, to research the legal basis for the state's powers under civil defense statutes to deal with alien enemies in the event of war. After Congress declared war on Japan, Wenig broadened his research to include the treatment of citizens of Japanese ancestry. The fruits of Wenig's legal and factual research became a major part of Warren's testimony before the Tolan Committee on February 21, 1942. In recommending the mass evacuation of Japanese Americans as a preventive measure against "a widespread simultaneous campaign of sabotage" directed at defense installations, Warren relied on detailed "evidence" of "a close relationship between Japanese associations in California" and the Japanese government and military as proof that these groups "could be utilized for carrying on a program of sabotage and fifth-column activity."[72]

Warren listed in his Tolan Committee testimony the names of dozens of allegedly subversive Japanese American organizations and quoted at length from pro-Japanese statements made by these groups and press reports of their prewar activities. What Warren did not reveal to the Committee was that the bulk of this material, and the conclusions he drew from it of a subversive conspiracy bent on espionage and sabotage, came directly from the files of the notorious House Committee on Un-American Activities, which in turn relied heavily on the amateur sleuthing of right-wing and anti-Oriental groups. Through Wenig and Warren, this biased and paranoid material eventually reached the Supreme Court.

The route over which these charges of conspiracy traveled to the Court began with an obsure Los Angeles organization known as the News Research Service. Adopted by the Un-American Activities Committee headed by Texas congressman Martin Dies, the conspiracy charges picked up military support in DeWitt's *Final Report,* took legal cover in the amicus brief of the West Coast states, and finally emerged in the Supreme Court's opinion in the Hirabayashi case.

It is surprising that Justice Department lawyers failed to notice the spoor left along this trail, since a sharp-eyed member of Congress spotted the tracks that led to the West Coast amicus brief. The first exposure of these connections came in the pages of the *Congressional Record.* On March 27, 1942, Vito Marcantonio, a left-leaning member of the American Labor Party from Manhattan, took the House floor to launch an attack on the "Report of Japanese Activities" recently issued by the Dies Committee. An avowed anti-black and anti-Oriental racist, Dies had designed this report as a rebuke to Attorney General Biddle for having blocked, three months before the Pearl Harbor attack, public hearings on "Japanese propaganda and espionage in the United States." Biddle had, in fact, informed Dies on September 8, 1941, that both President Roosevelt and Secretary of State Cordell Hull "feel quite strongly that hearings such as you contemplate would be inadvisable."[73]

Acknowledging that in "deference to the opinions of these high Government personages" his committee had "abandoned its plans for the public hearings," Dies moved quickly after Roosevelt signed Executive Order 9066 to take his revenge on Biddle. The "vast quantity of documentary evidence" seized by his committee's agents from the files of the Transocean News Service operated by the Japanese government, and the reports of committee "investigators and informers who were acquainted with the Nipponese tongue," Dies claimed in his report, proved that the West Coast was "still in the gravest peril from Japanese espionage and Japanese attack" after Pearl Harbor. In several hundred pages of documentation offered to support this charge, the Dies Committee report discussed the activities of Japanese American veterans organizations, the education in Japan of the Kibei group, Buddhist and Shinto religious groups, and the role of the Japanese American Citizens League.[74]

The Dies Committee report listed under twenty-seven separate headings the purported "evidence" of espionage and sabotage plans prepared before Pearl Harbor by Japanese agents and designed for execution by Japanese Americans. Included on this list were allegations that Japanese-language schools "were inculcating traitorous attitudes toward the United States in the minds of American-born Japanese," that "Japanese in California were occupying tracts of land which were militarily but not agriculturally useful," and that Buddhist and Shinto religious groups were intended as "fifth-column instruments for the forthcoming attack on the United States."[75]

In his speech on the House floor, Marcantonio traced these charges, point-by-point and word-for-word, from the Dies Committee report to their origins in publications of the News Research Service. Marcantonio could not identify the authors of this material. However, he did extract from Noah Mason, an Illinois Republican and a member of the Dies Committee, a confession that "the material that has been quoted from the report and from the News Letter is material that was obtained from the same source and authorized by the same person who gathered it but did not want to be quoted. The source for the News Letter was the same as the source for the reports; they are the same."[76]

Marcantonio could not pry from Mason the original source of this material, or the identity of those who published it anonymously some eight months before its inclusion in the Dies Committee report. Many of the documents cited in both publications came from the Japanese American press, but others (including charges that "maps containing highly important military information" and "aerial photographs of every important city on the west coast" had been passed to Japanese espionage agents) seemed most likely to have come to the Dies Committee and its private sympathizers from government sources. Since the ONI and FBI break-in at the Japanese consulate in Los Angeles took place shortly before the first espionage charges published by the News Research Service, the source of this material might well have been one or both of these intelligence agencies. The elusive answer to this question is less significant, however, than the links between the conclusions of the Dies Committee report and their echoes in Warren's congressional testimony and its later repetition in the *Final Report* and the West Coast amicus brief.[77]

A retracing of this trail reveals dozens of textual identities within these related documents. One example will illustrate their common origin in the Dies Committee report. Dies had announced to the press on July 5, 1941, that he would prove at the hearings scheduled for September that "thousands of Japanese on the west coast are under the direct domination of Japan and [are] cooperating fully with their mother country in fifth column spy and traitor activities." In the report issued after Biddle blocked these hearings, Dies cited in support of his earlier charge the "close integration" of Japanese veterans organizations such as the Military Virtue Society with "other Japanese organizations" in California such as the Buddhist Church, Japanese language schools, and even the "Sakura Baseball Team." As proof of this conspiratorial network, Dies listed the post office boxes shared by these groups. This material turned up in Warren's congressional testimony, with the identical listing of groups and mailing addresses, as a charge that "the Military Virtue Society is closely integrated with other Japanese organizations" in a network "ideally adapted to carrying out a plan for mass sabotage." The same listing and the assertion that the Military Virtue Society was "closely integrated with many other Japanese organizations" and formed part of "a line of control from the Japanese government" became part of DeWitt's *Final Report*. The conclusion that the Military Virtue Society formed part of a "line of control . . . from the Japanese Government" came to rest, without the small-print listing of churches and baseball teams, in the West Coast amicus brief as a fact deserving of judicial notice by the Supreme Court.[78]

The point of this exercise is not to expose Captain Wenig's plagiarism; he may in fact have written the last three of these statements. Two points of greater significance arise from the many threads of similarity among these documents. The first stems, not from the authenticity of the facts piled up in each, but from the stereotyped and conspiratorial conclusions drawn from this material. The Dies Committee report, submitted to Congress by an avowed racist, concluded that "all Japanese" shared an "absolute reverence for Japan" rooted in "the pantheistic teachings of Shintoism." On the fallacious assumption that all Japanese Americans adhered to the state-worshipping tenets of Shinto, the Dies Committee claimed that "no Japanese can ever be loyal to any other nation than Japan" and that the native-born Nisei "cannot become thoroughly Americanized."[79]

The lack of factual support for these sweeping conclusions did not prevent Colonel Bendetsen's staff from adopting them in the *Final Report*. After lengthy but unattributed borrowing from the Dies Committee report, the Army's official report found in this material the basis of the "factors and circumstances with which the Commanding General had to deal" with respect to Japanese Americans. The conclusion that Bendetsen approved in the *Final Report* was that this racial group constituted "a relatively homogeneous, unassimilated element bearing a close relationship through ties of race, religion, language, custom, and indoctrination to the enemy." Finally, and without citation to either of these sources, Wenig presented to the Supreme Court in the West Coast amicus brief the claim that Japanese Americans "represent an unassimilated, homogeneous element which in varying degrees is closely related through ties of race, language, religion, custom and ideology to the Japanese Empire."[80]

Many of the "racial characteristics" claims made in the West Coast amicus brief were based on sources also used in the official government brief filed by the Justice Department. That the cumulative effect of the two briefs worked to authenticate the seemingly solid "documentation" behind the conclusions of the West Coast brief appears evident in the Supreme Court opinion in the Hirabayashi case. Finding that "Japanese nationalistic propaganda," the cultivation of "allegiance to Japan," and the lack of "assimilation as an integral part of the white population" were all facts deserving of judicial notice, the Court discerned in them "a reasonable basis" for DeWitt's imposition of the curfew violated by Hirabayashi and Yasui. A reading of the decision clearly suggests that the "facts and circumstances with respect to the American citizens of Japanese ancestry" offered in the West Coast amicus brief had not escaped the Court's attention.[81]

Edward Ennis did not learn of the use made of the *Final Report* in the West Coast amicus brief until late in 1944, a year after the Supreme Court decided the Hirabayashi case. When he finally discovered this fact, Ennis raised a belated and futile protest. Blaming the deception on DeWitt's staff, Ennis complained to Assistant Attorney General Herbert Wechsler during preparation of the Korematsu brief that "the Western Defense Command evaded the statutory requirement that [the Justice] Department represent the Government [in the Hirabayashi case] by preparing this erroneous and intemperate brief which the States filed."[82]

Although Ennis eventually tracked down the source of the West Coast amicus brief in the *Final Report,* he never learned of Wenig's role in its preparation. This aspect of the episode, perhaps more than the contents of the brief, raises disturbing questions about the actions of War Department lawyers in crossing the line that separates parties to a lawsuit and those who stand as "friends of the court" in an amicus role. Wenig quoted, in the brief signed by California Attorney General Robert Kenny and his counterparts in Oregon and Washington, from virtually every page of the crucial Chapter 2 of the *Final Report.* He refrained, however, from any mention of the allegations made in this chapter that Japanese Americans had committed acts of espionage. When Ennis and John Burling finally gained access to the full text of the *Final Report* in 1944, almost a year after the Supreme Court decided the Hirabayashi case, their discovery of these espionage charges and their efforts to refute them created a furor within the Justice Department.[83]

Divisions within the ACLU resulted in the filing of two briefs with the Supreme Court in the Hirabayashi case. Conflicts within the ranks of government lawyers also produced two briefs, one filed by the Justice Department and the other by the West Coast states in an amicus role. These separate sets of briefs, however, reflected radically different sources of dispute among each group of lawyers. The ACLU lawyers had split into factions over the constitutionality of Executive Order 9066, and their divergent positions on this issue were placed on the record before the Court. In contrast, the battles among Justice and War Department lawyers remained hidden from the Court. Both the alteration and concealment of the *Final Report* of General DeWitt and the participation of Captain Wenig in the amicus brief of the West Coast states took place behind closed doors. The Court met for argument of the test cases, then, with a spotlight on the ACLU's conflicting briefs and with darkness surrounding the opposing briefs.

9

"Something Worthy of the Torah"

Arguments before the Supreme Court in the three cases that challenged General DeWitt's curfew and evacuation orders began on May 10, 1943, late on a Monday afternoon. John P. Frank, present that day as law clerk to Justice Hugo Black, later sketched the scene. The courtroom in "the great marble palace across from the Capitol in which the Court is housed has nothing of intimacy about it," he wrote; "it is a big, cold, richly hung and decorated chamber with the bench itself at one end raised somewhat from the floor." Before the bench, on either side of the podium shared by the opposing lawyers, are plain tables with ink wells and goose quill pens, "placed there for the attorney who may wish to take a few notes and who has forgotten his twentieth-century pen and pencil in the excitement of the occasion. Stretching behind counsel tables are the seats for the other members of the bar, and then the seats of the public."[1]

Promptly at noon, the red velvet curtains behind the bench parted to admit Chief Justice Harlan Fiske Stone and his eight colleagues, who took their swivel chairs on either side of Stone in alternating order of seniority from right to left. After the bailiff intoned the ritual "Oyez, oyez, oyez" that opens each session of the Court, Frank Walters and Arthur Barnett joined a half-dozen other lawyers before the bench to be sworn in by Stone as members of the Supreme Court bar. The six lawyers present to argue the Japanese American cases then patiently waited their turns while they listened to the reading of two opinions—Monday was set aside as "decision day" at the time—and arguments in four prior cases. ACLU general counsel Arthur Garfield Hays, in his role as a private lawyer, represented a notorious New York mobster in a gangland murder case in one of these arguments; NAACP lawyer Thurgood Marshall (also an ACLU board member) appeared for a black defendant in another criminal appeal.[2]

After Marshall concluded his argument, Frank Walters took the podium on behalf of Gordon Hirabayashi. As a brand-new member of the Supreme Court bar, Walters was understandably apprehensive as he faced the bench. His nervousness was compounded by the fact that he had first met Harold Evans, with whom he shared the argument, just half an hour before the court session began. He and Evans had only enough time, Walters recalled, to make "a distribution to each lawyer of that part of the argument that he was going to take." At the order of Roger Baldwin, Walters had been relegated to the essential but unexciting task of stating the facts of the case. Allotted ten minutes for this assignment, he began with a recital of the history of Executive Order 9066 and Public Law 503, the details of DeWitt's curfew and evacuation orders, and the chronology of Hirabayashi's challenge to the orders.[3]

Osmond Fraenkel, who sat next to Hays in the lawyers' section of the courtroom after his fellow ACLU general counsel left the podium, had recently torn apart and rewritten the Hirabayashi brief drafted by Walters. Fraenkel had excised from the draft brief Walters' argument that DeWitt's orders constituted an unconstitutional "bill of attainder" imposed on Hirabayashi and other Japanese Americans; Walters had argued this issue before the Court of Appeals and Judge Denman had noted it in his dissent to the certification of the case to the Supreme Court, but Fraenkel considered it farfetched and frivolous. As Fraenkel looked on, Justice Robert H. Jackson interrupted Walters to ask whether the orders were not bills of attainder. Surprised by the unanticipated question, Walters quickly recovered and agreed with Jackson. However, he later said, Jackson went on to pepper him with questions "in which he inferred that I shouldn't question the power of the military in time of active war." Having led Walters away from his assigned role, Jackson sat back to await the argument continued by Harold Evans.[4]

Evans opened with the claim that Public Law 503 represented an unlawful delegation of legislative power to General DeWitt and was worded too vaguely to provide DeWitt with adequate guidance in framing his military orders. Justice Felix Frankfurter, characteristically too impatient to allow a lawyer to develop his point, broke in to raise another issue. "Then the issue of citizenship is not important," he asked in his rhetorical fashion. "Not so far as this phase of the case is concerned," Evans answered. He held off Frankfurter for the moment by adding that "the discrimination against citizens of Japanese ancestry will be seen when we discuss the proclamations themselves" in the argument on the due process and equal protection challenges to the orders.[5]

Jackson quickly returned to the delegation issue that Frankfurter had cut off. "There is no case holding that it is improper to delegate to the Commander-in-Chief the authority necessary for the conduct of the war," he asked in another rhetorical assertion. Evans could hardly dispute this general proposition, and took the tack of distinguishing the case at hand from Jackson's suggestion that Congress and the President had wartime powers beyond the scope of judicial review. Evans replied that "legislative authority over civilians may not be delegated to the military when the area in question is not a strictly military area." Jackson shot back with a question that ignored the legislative function in statutory delegation of powers: "Can't the President anticipate that certain areas are open to attack and act accordingly?" Evans refused to take the bait. "Those powers that are granted by the Constitution to the President as Commander-in-Chief we do not question," he conceded, "but military control over civilians may not be extended" beyond these powers without congressional specification. Public Law 503 lacked the "definite standards" necessary to guide General DeWitt in determining the classes of citizens subject to his orders, Evans concluded.[6]

Returning to the challenge posed in Jackson's initial question, Evans shifted from the delegation issue to that of the scope of DeWitt's orders. He admitted that "in case of actual invasion or other conditions which might authorize the declaration of martial law," Congress could delegate to the President and the military sufficient power to restrict the liberties of citizens. Evans eagerly grasped the Civil War *Milligan* case in arguing for a distinction between "zones of actual military operation" and areas in which invasion was not imminent. Justice Stanley Reed, a courtly Kentuckian, opened the dialogue on the *Milligan* case. "Then Congress and the President can authorize martial law if the proper conditions exist," Reed stated in laying the foundation for the debate. "Is the distinction in the Milligan case applicable here?" he then asked. "It is certainly to be considered," Evans began. "However, it must be remembered that Hawaii is 2,400 miles from the Coast, Midway 3,300 miles, and Attu 2,600 miles," he added in distancing DeWitt's headquarters from the sites of battle. "It cannot be said because of the military activity in these areas that California was about to be invaded."[7]

This answer to Reed's mild-mannered question provoked Justice William O. Douglas. "Isn't that within the exercise of military judgment?" Douglas retorted. "No," replied Evans. "I submit that the facts speak for themselves." Justice Jackson returned to the debate over military strategy by asking whether the President was required to explain the facts behind military decisions "and put them in the public record for all to read." Before Evans could reply, Justice Wiley Rutledge, who sat at Stone's far left as the Court's junior member, suggested that *Milligan* was a postwar decision and thus less relevant as precedent. Evans stood at the podium, still silent, while Frankfurter burst in with a cryptic comment: "There's a lot in . . . Milligan that will not stand scrutiny in 1943, a lot of talk that is purely political." The most political member of the Court, Frankfurter left his statement hanging without asking a question. "That is for this Court to decide," Evans responded in tossing Frankfurter's challenge back to the bench. On this note of contention, Chief Justice Stone ended the day's proceedings. Evans left the courtroom that afternoon without having raised the due process and equal protection arguments that DeWitt's orders unlawfully discriminated against Japanese Americans as a class.[8]

Earl Bernard opened the argument in the Yasui case at the session that began at noon on May 11. His task was relatively simple, since the government's brief conceded that Judge Fee had wrongly decided that Yasui's employment by the Japanese consulate in Chicago constituted a renunciation of his American citizenship. Uncertain whether the Supreme Court would accept this concession, Bernard stressed that Fee's finding deprived Yasui of his suffrage, his rights as an attorney to practice his profession, and his other citizenship rights. Bernard reminded the justices that Yasui had sworn an oath of allegiance as a reserve Army officer and had never renounced his citizenship. A final attack on Fee's decision, which rested on the "dual nationality" law of Japan, as contrary to the Nationality Act and the "supremacy" clause of the Constitution, concluded Bernard's portion of the argument.[9]

Al Wirin, the insistent interloper in the Yasui case, wasted no time when he replaced Bernard at the podium in launching the equal protection argument that Evans had been unable to make in the Hirabayashi case. Neither Executive Order 9066 nor Public Law 503, Wirin asserted, authorized General DeWitt to single out Japanese Americans as the only citizens subject to his curfew orders. "Do you mean that DeWitt's order was ultra vires?" inquired Justice Douglas, referring to the judicial principle that made unlawful those actions undertaken without any legal basis. "Yes, there was no authority . . . in the Executive Order," Wirin answered. Charging that DeWitt's orders had been "issued in bad faith" and were thus tainted, Wirin labeled him as a puppet of "pseudo-patriotic groups and the economic power groups wishing to acquire Japanese-owned lands at a song." In charging that DeWitt had heeded the "drums of hate against persons of the Japanese race," Wirin rested on the documentation in the JACL brief written by Morris Opler for the Hirabayashi case.[10]

Pounding hard on the facts detailed in Opler's brief, Wirin kept up a drumbeat of denunciation. DeWitt's statement to a congressional committee that "a Jap's a Jap," made just a month earlier in April 1943, provided Wirin with the argument that "race prejudice, not military neccesity, was the reason for these orders" in the first place. Wirin also launched an attack on the report of the Pearl Harbor commission headed by Justice Owen J. Roberts, seated at Chief Justice Stone's elbow as the senior associate justice. The undocumented assertions of the Roberts Commission report that Japanese Americans in Hawaii had committed acts of sabotage and espionage, Wirin told Roberts and his colleagues, had been labeled as "false and misleading" by both Secretary of War Stimson and Attorney General Biddle.[11]

Roberts sat through this rebuke in silence. Hugo Black then took up the thread of Wirin's argument, which led directly to the issue of judicial review of military orders. "To what extent," asked Black, "can we review the decision of a general selected to make those decisions?" Wirin chose as the text for his sermon on judicial review the Court's opinion in the *Sterling* v. *Constantin* case, in which "the Court laid down the three principles of the existence of an emergency, action in good faith, and appropriate steps to meet the emergency." Tested against the record, Wirin said, DeWitt's orders failed to meet each of these standards. Black remained unconvinced. "But wouldn't [your] argument apply to almost every order of a general even in time of actual invasion?" he inquired. "In case of an invasion, martial law would prevail and other standards would govern the situation," Wirin replied.[12]

Justice Jackson returned to the fray with a backhanded defense of General DeWitt. Assuming that DeWitt "might have made an error," Jackson said, much more than the facts in the record before the Court would be required to prove that the General acted in bad faith. Justice Douglas, conceding that "some individuals among those evacuated are loyal Americans," agreed with Jackson that even this fact "does not affect the soundness of the military judgment." Wirin disputed Douglas on this point. The six-month gap between Pearl Harbor and DeWitt's final evacuation order, he replied, showed that the government could have conducted the loyalty screening it claimed to be impossible. Wirin left the podium with the parting shot that "neither color nor race has any military significance."[13]

Charles Fahy then took the podium to present the government's arguments in the Hirabayashi and Yasui cases. His short stature and deferential manner gave the Solicitor General an impression of meekness. John Frank, who often observed Fahy's arguments before the Supreme Court bench, noted that he was "a man not given to gesture, and occasionally in moments of great earnestness he would step away from the speaker's stand and emphasize his point with a slight and slow up-and-down movement of his clenched hands, a movement whose very restraint gave an emphasis greater than if he had shouted and pounded the table." Behind Fahy's quiet demeanor, however, lay a steely determination to win his case; he recorded statistics on the cases he argued and compared his won-lost percentage with those of his predecessors as Solicitor General.[14]

Fahy approached appellate argument with two principles: a meticulous mastery of the factual record, and a focus on the strongest argument in his legal arsenal. He began in the Hirabayashi and Yasui cases by dismissing as "secondary constitutional issues" the charges of vagueness, unlawful delegation, and the lack of congressional sanction for DeWitt's orders. The major issue in the cases, he argued to the Court, related to the war powers of the government; the shared powers of Congress and the President to act in wartime overrode the due process rights of citizens.[15]

Disparaging the charge of statutory vagueness pressed by Harold Evans as merely "grapsing at a straw dispersed by the breath of the words of the statute itself," Fahy defended Public Law 503 as perfectly clear in its one essential purpose. To sustain a conviction, he said, the Court need only to find that the defendant had personal knowledge of the orders and knowingly violated them. Fahy encountered doubt from the bench, however, in gliding quickly over the delegation issue. The heart of the problem was that Congress, in enacting Public Law 503, set out no precise standards for the military orders for which it provided criminal penalties; in effect, the law handed DeWitt a legislative blank check. Reviewing the legislative history of the statute, Fahy argued that Congress had incorporated Executive Order 9066 into the law, and that the reports of both congressional committees that considered the law had specified "curfews and other restrictions" as elements of subsequent military orders. Justice Reed, himself a former Solicitor General and a statutory purist, remained unconvinced. "Does that mean that you are reading the Executive Order into the Act," he asked Fahy. "We are construing the Act in the light of the Executive Order, which forms an important part of its legislative history," Fahy answered. Reed's solitary question and Fahy's claim to have read the mind of Congress concluded discussion of a technical but troubling issue that, in a case involving a less-charged exercise of executive power, would most likely have prompted a detailed dissection of the statute and its history.[16]

Having dealt with these "secondary" issues with somewhat less than his usual precision and forthrightness, Fahy moved on to "the heart of the case," the relation of governmental war powers to the due process requirements of the Fifth Amendment. In approaching this issue, he framed the argument around the evacuation order that constituted the second count in Hirabayashi's conviction; the deprivation of liberty required by evacuation outweighed the more minor restrictions imposed by the curfew order. Fahy's argument was that the wartime emergency shifted the balance of the two constitutional commands. Normally, constitutional provisions that protect the rights of citizens against "arbitrary" or "unreasonable" governmental interference outweigh the positive powers invested in the legislative and executive branches. During wartime, Fahy asserted, the due process clause must give way to the "reasonable discretion" of the military in exercising the war powers "so that both might be given their full meaning."[17]

Fahy's abstract approach to the balancing formula bothered Justice Jackson, another former Solicitor General aware that constitutional principles often obscured pitfalls in the factual underbrush. The obvious racial discrimination imposed by DeWitt's orders troubled Jackson. "We all agree that the Government may not say in peacetime that it is a crime for a descendant of an Irishman to do what would not be a crime if committed by a descendant of another national," he reminded Fahy. "The basis of the discrimination is therefore in the war powers," Jackson continued, his question apparent in the statement. "Certainly this could not be done in peacetime," Fahy agreed. "What makes it reasonable now is the war power and the circumstances of war." The Solicitor General saw the trap laid in Jackson's statement and refused to touch the spring. "We do not admit, however, that there is any discrimination involved."[18]

Moving to the argument that "military necessity" had prompted DeWitt's orders, Fahy took the Court on a verbal tour of the Pacific battlefront and the West Coast. Ignoring the war in Europe and Africa, then nearing its bloody climax, he painted the Pacific war as "the most serious threat" that had ever faced the United States. Fahy stressed the importance of the West Coast defense facilities and the necessity of their protection against sabotage and espionage. But in linking this argument to DeWitt's orders, the Solicitor General relied on the "racial characteristics" claims in the brief prepared by Nanette Dembitz and Arnold Raum. Fahy argued that Japanese Americans "had never become assimilated" and that Japanese-language schools and the presence of Japanese-educated Kibei made it "not unreasonable for those charged with the defense of the West Coast to fear that in case of an invasion there would be among this group of people a number of persons who might assist the enemy." The fear he attributed to General DeWitt "was not based on race but on these other factors," Fahy told the Court in a semantic evasion of the discrimination issue.[19]

In his peroration, Fahy wrapped himself in the mantle of patriotic rhetoric. "During time of war especially," he said in a soft but firm tone, "it is not enough to say 'I am a citizen, and I have rights.' One must also say, 'I am a citizen, and I have obligations.' " Fahy liked these words so well that he repeated them unchanged when he asked the Court, the next year, to uphold Fred Korematsu's conviction.[20]

The Korematsu case brought Al Wirin back to the podium after Fahy concluded his Hirabayashi and Yasui arguments. The issue in this first round before the Supreme Court, as noted earlier, was limited to the question certified by the Court of Appeals as to whether Judge St. Sure's refusal to pronounce the probationary sentence imposed on Korematsu constituted an appealable judgment. Fahy had delegated this argument to John L. Burling, and the ensuing colloquy between the Court and both lawyers more resembled a law-school seminar than an argument between opposing counsel. Only Justice Frankfurter expressed any doubt that Korematsu had a right to appeal his conviction. A probationary sentence placed on a criminal defendant a "social blemish and stigma" comparable to that of a jail sentence, Wirin had argued in answering a question from Justice Reed. "I do not believe that this court reviews social blemishes," Frankfurter cut in with characteristic sarcasm. Burling, however, all but conceded Wirin's claim that judicial suspension of sentence—which the Supreme Court had recently decided was a judgment "final for the purpose of appeal"—and refusal to pronounce sentence should be treated alike. Burling's concession on this issue left no doubt that the Korematsu case would return to the Supreme Court for a second round of argument.[21]

After two days of argument, none of the lawyers on either side harbored any illusions about the outcome of the three cases. Their respective postmortems revealed agreement that Fahy's combination of recital and rhetoric had struck a responsive chord on the Supreme Court bench. "On the whole," Al Wirin admitted to Ernest Besig, "the arguments in the Yasui and Hirabayashi cases went badly for us." Osmond Fraenkel, a veteran of Supreme Court argument and observation, told the ACLU board at its May 17 meeting that "a majority of the justices appeared to be hostile" in grilling the lawyers who represented Hirabayashi and Yasui.[22]

Fahy's effort to console his old friend Harold Evans contained what was most likely an unintended dismissal. "Confidentially, I think it would have been better had you been permitted to have more of the time allotted to your side of the case," Fahy wrote. Philip Glick, who attended the arguments with the pending Endo case in mind, was less charitable in his critique of the lawyers who opposed Fahy. "Of the four," he reported to Maurice Walk without naming names, "two were less than pedestrian and no one of the four was nearly strong enough." In contrast, Glick wrote, Fahy "did a particularly fine job of presenting the Government's case. He was quiet, eloquent, and extremely effective." Like all the lawyers present, Glick was confident of the outcome in the Hirabayashi and Yasui cases. "There is uniform agreement among the lawyers and non-lawyers who sat through the argument," he predicted, "that the Court will hold evacuation constitutional. I agree."[23]

The three Japanese American cases were the only items on the agenda as the nine members of the Supreme Court gathered for a closed-door conference on Monday morning, May 17, 1943. The Court normally met on Saturdays to debate and decide cases argued the preceding week, but the judicial term that began in October 1942 had produced a large number of contentious cases that piled up as the justices neared their summer recess. Continuing disputes among the Court over these cases had necessitated this unusual Monday session. After the traditional exchange of handshakes that signified the bond of fraternity among men who would soon argue heatedly, Chief Justice Stone—also by tradition—opened the conference with a review of the issues in the three cases.

The outcome of the deliberations on May 17 was soon revealed. Two weeks later, on June 1, the Court issued a unanimous opinion that the probationary sentence imposed on Fred Korematsu, even though it had been withheld, constituted a "final and appealable" order and sent the case back to the Court of Appeals for a decision on the legality of the exclusion order. On June 21, after another three weeks, the Court unanimously upheld Min Yasui's conviction for curfew violation. However, the justices agreed with the Solicitor General's concession that Judge Fee had wrongly decided the case on both central issues, that of the constitutionality of the curfew order as applied to citizens and Fee's holding that Yasui had forfeited his American citizenship. Returning the case to the trial court "to afford that court an opportunity to strike its findings" on the latter question, the Supreme Court suggested that Fee resentence Yasui and hinted strongly that it considered a year in prison too harsh a penalty.[24]

Philip Glick had correctly anticipated the disposition of the Hirabayashi case. His prediction that the Supreme Court would uphold the constitutionality of evacuation proved to be wrong, however. In its unanimous opinion, also issued on June 21, the Court seized on Hirabayashi's unintentional error in asking that Judge Black allow him to serve his sentence in a road camp rather than in jail. Black's replacement of the original consecutive sentences on the separate curfew and evacuation charges with concurrent sentences afforded the Court an opportunity to duck the more difficult evacuation issue. The Court's evasion of this question simply put off the debate until the Korematsu case returned from the Court of Appeals the following year.[25]

The outcome of these cases is less important to this account than the process by which Chief Justice Stone forged a unanimous opinion in the Hirabayashi case. As the author of the Court's opinion, Stone not only persuaded his colleagues to confine the holding to the narrowest possible legal ground but he also headed off a passionate dissent in the case. Utilizing to the full his titular and symbolic powers as Chief Justice, Stone began his campaign for unanimity at the May 17 conference, at which he confronted strong-minded men divided both by personal conflicts and divergent views on the function of the judicial role.

When he opened the discussion, Stone looked down the long mahogany table in the Court's conference room at a group dominated by the appointees of Franklin D. Roosevelt. With the exceptions only of Stone and Owen Roberts, the senior associate justice, every member of the Supreme Court in 1943 was a certified New Dealer. After the "Constitutional Revolution" of 1937 had broken the judicial logjam that had frustrated Roosevelt's efforts to cope with the ravages of the Depression, the President had used his appointment power to reconstitute the Court. Stone's elevation to the post of Chief Justice in 1941, after the retirement of Charles Evans Hughes, fit into Roosevelt's plan to project a "bipartisan" image during wartime. Although Stone was a nominal Republican, he had generally voted in the 1930s to uphold New Deal programs.[26]

Roosevelt's expectation that his appointees would vote together as New Dealers had quickly shattered on the shoals of dispute over First Amendment issues. By the spring of 1943, as the Court met to decide the Japanese American cases, the justices had split into two factions whose leaders were barely on speaking terms. Felix Frankfurter, whose charm and wit in public masked an arrogant and abrasive manner in the conference room, brought to the Court on his appointment in 1939 an undeserved reputation as a radical. His defense of real radicals against the paranoia of the "Red Raids" that followed World War I, and his attack on the drive to execute Sacco and Vanzetti in 1927, had made

Frankfurter an anathema to conservatives. In truth, however, he was an apostle of "judicial restraint" and viewed his role on the Court as one of deference to legislative and executive powers. Only in extreme cases, which rarely included challenges to restrictions on First Amendment rights, would Frankfurter step in as a judicial censor.[27]

Justice Hugo Black, who sat at Frankfurter's left elbow on the bench, advocated a judicial role in First Amendment cases that was light-years away from that of his testy colleague. A constitutional literalist, Black sat in the conference room as a judicial policeman, ready to flag down errant officials. The command of the First Amendment that legislators pass "no law" that restricted the freedoms of religion, press, speech, and assembly was, in Black's mind, a constitutional stop sign. "No law means no law," he was fond of repeating. This brand of judicial activism made Black a special target for Frankfurter's scorn.[28]

Although Chief Justice Stone generally remained aloof as Black and Frankfurter battled over First Amendment cases, his colleagues were loosely grouped under the contrasting doctrinal banners waved by the two justices. Three members of the Court often voted with Frankfurter in cases that raised issues of legislative and executive powers: Owen Roberts, a former corporate lawyer; Stanley Reed, a legal conservative who had loyally defended New Deal statutes before the Court as Solicitor General but who shared Frankfurter's views on judicial restraint; and Robert Jackson, a former Attorney General under Roosevelt. To Frankfurter's annoyance, the austerity of his judicial vision and the intervention of political factors produced occasional defections among this group, but these three members of the Court normally looked to him for leadership in the conference room.[29]

Hugo Black headed a more cohesive bloc within the Court. William O. Douglas, who had zealously policed the financial community as head of the Securities and Exchange Commission, and Frank Murphy, who had served as governor of Michigan and as Attorney General under Roosevelt before his Court appointment, voted consistently with Black and shared his activist judicial philosophy. Frankfurter did not hide his contempt for this trio, whom he collectively derided as "the Axis." Several of his 1943 diary entries reveal his disdain for Black and Douglas and his fears that their constitutional plague might infect the Court. A month before the Hirabayashi case was argued, Frankfurter worried that "Black with his vehemence and vitality and lack of savoir faire and ruthlessness and unflagging industry will before long absolutely control the Court." Himself a master of flattery who showered Roosevelt with sycophantic praise, Frankfurter reviled Douglas as "the most systematic exploiter of flattery I have ever encountered in my life." Frankfurter also suspected that Wiley Rutledge, a former law school dean who took his seat as the Court's newest member on February 15, 1943, might become a convert to Black's judicial theology. When Stanley Reed told him on March 6, just three weeks after Rutledge joined the Court, that their new colleague "seemed to vote wrong on all the important issues," Frankfurter expressed concern that Rutledge "will join the Axis" and provide Black with a solid four votes in cases that divided the two judicial blocs.[30]

A quartet of cases on the Court's docket in 1943 illustrated the doctrinal chasm that separated the two factions. All four cases involved challenges by members of the Jehovah's Witnesses sect to state and local laws that restricted the First Amendment rights of this evangelical group. Over the dissents of Frankfurter and his three acolytes—Reed, Roberts, and Jackson—the Court struck down in the first three of these cases laws designed to erect barriers between the Witnesses and the subjects of their street-corner and door-to-door preaching.[31]

The fourth case, in which Jackson deserted Frankfurter to write the Court's majority opinion, stung Frankfurter into a frenzy of denunciation. In striking down in the *Barnette* case a West Virginia law requiring schoolchildren, on pain of expulsion, to salute and pledge allegiance to the American flag, the Court abruptly overruled an opinion written three years earlier by Frankfurter in the *Gobitis* case, which involved a similar flag-salute challenge. The fact that the two laws were virtually identical rubbed in the affront. Frankfurter attributed this humiliation to Black and Douglas, whose concurring opinion in *Barnette* explained their shift of votes on the two cases and second thoughts about Frankfurter's earlier opinion. In his *Barnette* dissent, issued the week before the Court's opinion in the Hirabayashi case, Frankfurter made a point of berating the apostates. The flag-salute law which had been held in his *Gobitis* opinion "to lie within permissible areas of legislation," Frankfurter acidly noted, "is now outlawed by the deciding shift of opinion of two Justices."[32]

On the heels of this rebuff to his conviction that "one's own opinion about the wisdom or evil of a law should be excluded altogether when one is doing one's duty on the bench," Frankfurter took it upon himself to squelch any potential dissent in the Hirabayashi case. Chief Justice Stone hoped on his part to heal the wounds opened by the Jehovah's Witnesses cases. Perhaps as his own contribution to the healing process, Black joined Frankfurter and Stone as an ally in the Hirabayashi case. One factor behind this unlikely alliance was Black's service in World War I as an Army artillery officer. Although all this service was stateside, Black was proud of his military record and became a lifelong member of the American Legion. Victor Brudney, who got to know Black well as law clerk to Justice Rutledge in 1943, later described him as a "jingo" who backed the war effort without question. In addition, Black had been a down-the-line New Dealer during his earlier Senate service and shared with Frankfurter a devotion to the President who had appointed both men to the Supreme Court. Finally, the Japanese American cases raised none of the First Amendment issues over which Black and Frankfurter had clashed in the Jehovah's Witnesses cases.[33]

Black's statement at the outset of the May 17 conference forecast the outcome of the Hirabayashi case. "I want it done on narrowest possible points," he announced, according to the sketchy conference notes made by Douglas. Along with Murphy's even briefer notes, these two sources constitute the only existing record of the closed-door conference. Douglas recorded Stone's quick agreement that the Court should confine its decision to the curfew violation alone. Stone offered two reasons for avoiding the evacuation issue. First, he stated, the concurrent sentences on the curfew and evacuation counts made a decision on the latter unnecessary; as noted earlier, precedent supported this position but did not demand it. Stone's second point was that Hirabayashi's "failure to report" for evacuation "did not necessarily mean he would be sent to camp." General DeWitt's exclusion orders provided "many exceptions" for those ordered to report, Stone told the conference.[34]

The Chief Justice was in error on this question. Hirabayashi fit within none of the narrow exemptions to the exclusion order, a fact evident from the record before the Court. Had he reported for evacuation as ordered, Hirabayashi would inevitably have been shipped to the Puyallup Assembly Center to join his parents, brothers, and sister. None of his colleagues challenged Stone's erroneous assertion. The justices were obviously straining to evade the evacuation issue in the Hirabayashi case, and Stone's first reason for doing so satisfied them. Significantly, Stone's comments at the conference hinted at his doubts that evacuation could meet constitutional standards. According to Douglas, the Chief Justice admitted that there "may be difference between curfew of this kind and going to concentration camp." Since the record did not reveal that Hirabayashi had asked Judge Black to impose concurrent sentences as a way to escape further jail time, the Court remained unaware of the irony that Hirabayashi had himself knocked down the first hurdle to the final affirmance of his conviction.[35]

Douglas also recorded other doubts expressed by Stone in his conference comments. First noting a "grave question as to delegation," the point stressed at oral argument by Harold Evans, Stone answered this question in the negative. In passing Public Law 503, he said, Congress had approved Roosevelt's decision to authorize the Army to exclude from the West Coast "any or all persons" designated by DeWitt, and had therefore "contemplated doing what was done." Stone finessed the after-the-fact implications of his statement with a rhetorical question: "does order have relation to espionage and sabotage—if it does problem of delegation drops out." The glaring absence of standards set out in Public Law 503 to confine DeWitt's orders within constitutional limits passed at the Supreme Court conference without any recorded comment.[36]

The issue that most bothered the Chief Justice was the "discrimination" imposed on Japanese Americans by DeWitt's orders. "It is jarring to me that U.S. citizens were subjected to this treatment," Stone confessed at the conference. He had particular reason to be sensitive to the constitutional implications of racial and national discrimination in the Hirabayashi case. Five years earlier, in the famous Footnote Four to his opinion in the *Carolene Products* case, Stone had proclaimed that legislation directed at particular racial or national groups, and other "discrete and insular minorities" who had suffered histories of prejudice, should be subjected to "more exacting judicial scrutiny" than laws that affected the business community or other groups with unhindered access to the political process. In terms of judicial review, legislation in the latter category needed only a "reasonable" basis in fact, whereas laws that discriminated against minority groups placed on the government the burden of demonstrating a "compelling state interest" that justified the unequal treatment.[37]

Despite his evident qualms about the discrimination against Japanese Americans, Stone told the conference (according to Douglas's abbreviated notes) that the constitutionality of DeWitt's orders "all depends . . . if there was reasonable basis as of time action was taken." Admitting that "no one doubts that many Japs are loyal," Stone found in the Pearl Harbor attack the "earmarks of treachery" that he attributed by implication to Japanese Americans. "In view of our whole history of relationship with them," Stone said of the group singled out for internment, there was "grave danger that these people would create damage." Justice Murphy's conference notes indicate that Stanley Reed and Owen Roberts both expressed doubts about the application of the curfew order to "a certain type of citizen" to the exclusion of others. Murphy's notes did not record a direct response by Stone to the question posed by

Reed and Roberts. Douglas, however, reported that Stone told the conference that it was possible to "draw line between Japs and Italians."[38]

Although Stone defended DeWitt's orders against the delegation and discrimination challenges, his arguments on these issues omitted an essential ingredient of constitutional analysis: that of locating in the Constitution itself the sources of legislative and executive authority for the challenged military orders and their statutory support. In his conference presentation, Stone raised the constitutional umbrella of the government's "war powers" for protection. These powers, he said, were "not limited to the conduct of hostilities" but included "all sorts of defensive activities" as well. The Chief Justice did not expand on the nature of the possible "defensive" measures covered by the war powers doctrine. Neither the Constitution nor Supreme Court precedent, in fact, put any flesh on this doctrinal skeleton. Stone himself had canvassed the potential sources of the government's wartime powers a year earlier, in a 1942 opinion that upheld the convictions by military tribunal of eight German saboteurs who had landed by submarine on Long Island and the Florida coast. The saboteurs had been quickly captured and convicted; the military tribunal sentenced six of them to death and imposed life sentences on the other two. Their appeal to the Supreme Court in the *Quirin* case, which delayed but did not prevent the executions, argued that they had been denied due process protections that a civilian court would have been required to provide.[39]

Writing for a unanimous Court in October 1942, three months after a hasty hearing and decision, Stone dissected the Constitution in search of the elusive war powers. He began with a truism: "Congress and the President, like the courts, possess no power not derived from the Constitution." Stone then turned to his text and pointed to thirteen separate provisions in Articles I and II, which respectively specify the powers of Congress and the President. In terms of the Japanese American cases, four of these provisions shed some light on Stone's later opinion. Congress is empowered to "provide for the common Defense" and to "make all Laws which shall be necessary and proper" in executing this national purpose, and is the body authorized to "declare War" on other nations. The President is granted "executive Power" and is charged with the duty to "take care that the Laws be faithfully executed." Finally, the Constitution adds to the President's civilian powers the post of Commander-in-Chief of the armed forces.[40]

"The Constitution thus invests the President as Commander in Chief with the power to wage war which Congress has declared, and to carry into effect all laws passed by Congress for the conduct of war," Stone concluded in his *Quirin* opinion. The punishment of enemy saboteurs under existing provisions of federal law may well have fit under Stone's war powers umbrella. During the Hirabayashi conference, however, the Chief Justice could only point to an unspecified "grave damage" that Japanese American citizens, many of them concededly loyal, might inflict through espionage and sabotage, evidence of which was totally lacking in the record before the Court. He nonetheless concluded, in the conference remarks recorded by Douglas, that DeWitt's curfew orders were "not beyond war powers." Stone's final remark before he ended discussion and put the Hirabayashi case to his colleagues for a vote revealed, despite his agreement with Black's initial admonition that the Court avoid the evacuation issue, his nagging concern that if Hirabayashi "had been in [a] concentration camp," a much "graver question" would confront the Court.[41]

Significantly, the conference produced none of the verbal fireworks that had exploded during recent sessions. Disarmed by Black's opening comment, Frankfurter apparently sat in silence through the meeting. By tradition, voting proceeded in reverse order of seniority, with the Chief Justice voting last. Stone looked first to Wiley Rutledge, and the junior justice voted to affirm Hirabayashi's convictions. One by one, his colleagues echoed Rutledge's vote. Frank Murphy, however, broke the string of votes to affirm and reserved his vote; he thus retained his right at a later time to cast a vote on either side. Unanimity in the Hirabayashi case thus hinged on Murphy's final vote.[42]

Chief Justice Stone's final decision at the May 17 conference was to assign to himself the task of writing the Court's opinion in the Hirabayashi case. He recorded no reason for exercising this prerogative of his position; most likely, as in the *Quirin* case, Stone wished to place the imprimatur of his office on a case that raised basic constitutional issues during wartime, and hoped as well to head off potential conflicts that an assignment to a member of one of the Court's antagonistic factions might produce. Bennett Boskey, a 1940 Harvard Law School graduate who served as Stone's law clerk during this term, later confirmed this assessment. "Stone felt that certain types of cases of great national importance were cases that would be a good and proper thing for the Chief Justice to write the opinion," he said. Stone might also have felt, in view of Murphy's reservation of his vote, that his prestige as Chief Justice and skills as a mediator might succeed in forging the unanimity that he obviously desired.[43]

With Boskey's help, Stone worked hard over the two weeks that followed the conference to draft an opinion that would satisfy his colleagues. He knew that members of the Court were entitled, up to the minute that an opinion was formally announced, to change their votes and to issue concurring or dissenting opinions. With this fact in mind, Stone and Boskey labored to produce a draft opinion that "put things on as narrow a ground as possible," as Boskey later said. The first draft, sent to the Court's basement print shop on May 30, ran to fifteen printed pages. The first seven recited in unexceptional manner the chronology of the Hirabayashi case and of Executive Order 9066, Public Law 503, and DeWitt's curfew and evacuation orders.[44]

Stone's draft moved into uncharted constitutional waters on page 8, in its discussion of the ephemeral war powers of the government and the role of the courts in reviewing the exercise of these powers. Stone began with a phrase from a speech made by his predecessor, Charles Evans Hughes. "The war power of the national government is 'the power to wage war successfully,' " Stone wrote in quoting Hughes. The war power, Stone added in his own interpretation of this truism, "is not restricted to the winning of victories in the field and the repulse of enemy forces. It embraces every phase of the national defense, including the protection of war materials and the members of the armed forces from injury and from the evils which attend the rise and progress of war." With a citation to his own opinion in the *Quirin* case, Stone added that in reviewing "the choice of means" by which the legislative and executive branches of the government exercise the war powers granted to them by the Constitution, "it is not for any court to sit in review of the wisdom of their action or substitute its judgment for theirs."[45]

Having thus limited the Court's reviewing role to that of deference to legislative and executive judgment, Stone adopted the test of "reasonableness" that he had seemingly rejected five years earlier in Footnote Four to the *Carolene Products* case. The only question that faced the Court, he wrote in addressing DeWitt's discrimination against Japanese American citizens, was "whether in light of all the facts and circumstances there was any substantial basis for the conclusion . . . that the curfew was a protective measure necessary to meet the threat of sabotage and espionage which would substantially affect the war effort." In answering this question, Stone swallowed whole the "racial characteristics" arguments made in the briefs submitted by the Justice Department and the three West Coast states and repeated by Solicitor General Fahy in his oral argument before the Supreme Court. Citing allegations that Japanese Americans posed a fifth-column danger, their concentration around West Coast defense facilities, their supposed adherence to Shintoism, the education of some 10,000 American-born Kibei in Japan, and the system of dual citizenship maintained under Japanese law, Stone concluded that "the nature and extent of the racial attachments of our Japanese inhabitants to the Japanese enemy were consequently matters of grave concern" to General DeWitt.[46]

Perhaps in light of the constitutional collision between the minimal standard of judicial review set out in his *Hirabayashi* draft and the "more exacting judicial scrutiny" he had promised in the *Carolene Products* case, Stone felt compelled to proclaim his devotion to the principles of racial equality. "Distinctions between citizens solely because of their ancestry," he wrote, "are by their very nature odious to a free people whose institutions are founded upon the doctrine of equality." Only those measures necessary "for the successful prosecution of the war," Stone explained, could displace this doctrine and justify military orders "which place citizens of one ancestry in a different category from others." In reaching this conclusion, Stone referred four times on one page to the "facts and circumstances" which, he claimed, "show that one racial group more than another" constituted "a greater source of danger" to the Army's wartime efforts.[47]

Stone's draft opinion sparked flares of protest among four of his colleagues. The first was easily extinguished. Stone's careless discussion of the delegation question troubled Stanley Reed, the Court's most cautious member. Reed was particularly sensitive to delegation issues, since as Solicitor General in the 1930s he had twice been burned by the Supreme Court in opinions that rejected crucial New Deal statutes on this ground. In his *Hirabayashi* draft, Stone had written that in passing Public Law 503, Congress had both reached back to ratify Executive Order 9066 and reached forward to authorize DeWitt's curfew orders. "The question then is not one of the congressional power to delegate," Stone asserted, "for Congress has itself approved the orders."[48]

Reed objected to Stone's formulation. "It seems to me that the contrary is true;" he wrote the Chief Justice on May 29, "that the question is of the congressional power to delegate and that Congress has not approved the order under which this man was convicted." Reed suggested that the opinion merely state that Public Law 503 "is a sufficient delegation of the power to issue curfew" orders and that Stone avoid any implication that "Congress has approved the curfew orders." Stone willingly conceded on this technical but important point. The delegation question, he wrote in later drafts and in the final opinion, was that of "whether, acting together, Congress and the Executive could leave it to the designated military commander to appraise the relevant conditions" and to act accordingly. His sole objective met, Reed signed on with a letter of praise to Stone: "It seems to me that you have stated a very difficult situation in a way that will preserve rights in different cases and at the same time enable the military forces to function. It is a thankless job but you have done it well."[49]

Justice Douglas raised more serious objections to Stone's first draft and proved more tenacious than Reed in pressing them. He sprinkled his copy of the draft with question marks in the margins and wrote to Stone on May 31 with "some suggestions on your first circulation. They are aimed at the most part to eliminate any suggestion of racial discrimination." The only member of the Court from the West Coast, Douglas had lived from the age of five in Washington state and spent his summers at a remote cabin in Goose Prairie. Douglas was throughout his thirty-six-year career on the Court a consistent supporter of racial equality and sympathized during World War II with the Japanese Americans evacuated from his home state, some of whom he had grown up and gone to school with.[50]

In his letter to Stone, Douglas objected particularly to a sentence in the draft opinion asserting that, because of prejudice against them, Japanese Americans "have maintained here a racial solidarity which has tended to prevent their assimilation as an integral part of the white population . . . and has encouraged their attachment to Japan and Japanese institutions." Douglas responded that " 'racial solidarity' and lack of 'assimilation' do not show lack of loyalty as I see it. They may of course give rise to conditions which may breed disloyalty. But that is quite a different matter." Douglas also felt strongly that the opinion should put the government on notice that, in supporting the curfew orders as necessary but temporary measures, the Court questioned the necessity of evacuation and internment. "Is not the justification for dealing with Jap citizens as a group," he asked Stone, "the fact that the exigencies of war and the necessities of quick action in defending the nation against invasion do not necessarily permit enough time to sort out the sheep from the goats? Is it not necessary to provide an opportunity at some stage (although not necessarily in lieu of obedience to the military order) for an individual member of the group to show that he has been improperly classified?"[51]

Stone apparently did not respond to this letter from Douglas, who promptly drafted a four-page concurring opinion which he circulated on June 3. Whether Douglas felt slighted by Stone's silence and wrote his opinion as a rebuke is unclear, but his move (in which Justice Rutledge initially joined) had a shock effect on his colleagues. It was an almost schizophrenic opinion, displaying simultaneously two sides of Douglas's complex personality. He began with a saber-rattling speech that matched the jingoism of the Hearst press: "We are engaged in a war for survival against enemies who have placed a premium on barbarity and ruthlessness. Self-preservation comes first. The United States wages war to win. And the war power in its command over the people and resources of the nation is ample for that purpose." Douglas then outdid Frankfurter in judicial deference to military judgment. "The decisions necessary for victory are largely military ones. . . . [C]ourts cannot sit in judgment on the military necessities which underlie those decisions." Douglas professed his belief that General DeWitt had acted in "good faith" in his conclusion that "among citizens of Japanese ancestry there were those who would give aid and comfort to the Japanese invader and act as a fifth column before and during an invasion."[52]

The first protest against this abdication to military authority came, not from a member of the Court, but from Douglas's law clerk. Vern Countryman, a Montana native and a 1942 graduate of the University of Washington Law School, had lived in Seattle during the evacuation. He had several Japanese American classmates in law school "and one day they weren't there anymore," he recalled. "I knew them very well and I thought the whole thing was ridiculous." Countryman later attributed Douglas's position to the influence of General DeWitt. "Douglas encountered DeWitt on the West Coast the previous summer and he filled him with horrible stories about Japanese submarines lurking off the coast. He really thought we had a hell of an emergency, and DeWitt sold him a bill of goods. I argued with him about paying so much attention to the military but I didn't get anywhere."[53]

In the second half of his concurrence, Douglas displayed his contrasting passion for individual rights and procedural fairness. He expanded in this section on the points made in his letter to Chief Justice Stone. "I think it is important to emphasize that we are dealing here with a problem of loyalty not assimilation," Douglas wrote. "Loyalty is a matter of mind and heart not of race. That indeed is the history of America." Douglas then boldly raised the evacuation issue his colleagues had voted to duck and went even further in questioning the internment program. In noting that "guilt is personal under our constitutional system," Douglas held out the prospect that Japanese Americans could test the legality of DeWitt's exclusion orders and their subsequent detention. He pointed out that a conscientious objector to military service, after his induction, "may obtain through *habeas corpus* a hearing on the legality of his classification by the draft board." If a person detained solely "on account of ancestry" could adequately "demonstrate his loyalty to the United States," Douglas suggested, "the reason for the continued application of the order to him would cease." He concluded by urging that the Court "make certain that we leave no inference that American citizens could be denied for the duration of the war all opportunity to show that they were improperly classified as actual or potential fifth columnists and therefore were unlawfully detained."[54]

There is no doubt that Douglas sincerely believed the views expressed in his draft concurrence, both the patriotism of the first section and the hostility to internment in the second. But the process by which the Court reaches agreement in contentious cases, between the initial conference vote and the announcement of opinions, often resembles a judicial poker game. Douglas may have intended his draft as a bargaining chip, intended to bluff Stone into making concessions in the Hirabayashi opinion. If so, he miscalculated the reactions of other players in this high-stakes game. Felix Frankfurter was outraged by the draft opinion and immediately launched a lobbying campaign designed to persuade Stone to call Douglas's bluff. Frankfurter had already indicated his down-the-line support for Stone's own first draft: "I go with you cheerfully all the way," he had written the Chief Justice.[55]

Philip Elman, a recent Harvard Law School graduate who served as Frankfurter's law clerk in 1943, later explained a possible source of the justice's heated reaction to the implication made by Douglas that the War Department was unlawfully holding Japanese Americans in detention. "Frankfurter was not only very close and devoted to Roosevelt, but he was even more devoted to Henry Stimson. There was also Jack McCloy, a close friend who owed his job to Frankfurter. I don't think he regarded McCloy as a litigant" in the Japanese American cases, Elman said. Under his judicial robe, Frankfurter wore a symbolic uniform during the war. "He saw himself as a member of the President's war team," Elman added. "He went to war on December 8, 1941, literally." Within the week that preceded his outburst against Douglas, Frankfurter had met with both McCloy and Stimson to hash over War Department policies and problems; there is no evidence that the three friends discussed the Japanese American cases, but Frankfurter's intimate involvement in War Department business hardly made him a neutral in Douglas's attack on the Army's internment program.[56]

As soon as Frankfurter read his copy of Douglas's draft opinion, he rushed to Black's chambers and enlisted the leader of "the Axis" in the crusade to stiffen Chief Justice Stone's spine. In a letter to Stone on June 4, the day after Douglas circulated his draft, Frankfurter reported the "two-hour talk I had with Brother Black who put my anxiety about this business vividly when he told me that he had been arguing against

Douglas' invitation to bring 'a thousand *habeas corpus* suits in the district courts.' " According to Frankfurter, Black said that "so far as he was concerned, if he were the Commanding General he would not allow [the Japanese Americans] to go back even if the Court should establish their loyalty." Frankfurter added his own view that it would be "deplorable beyond words to hold out hopes . . . that there may be modes of relief for those now in the internment camps." He urged Stone to "overcome your natural hesitation and send for Brother Douglas and talk him out of his opinion by making him see the dangers that he is inviting."[57]

After dispatching this letter to Stone, Frankfurter sent a memorandum to him later that day, suggesting language in the Court's opinion designed to close the door that Douglas left open for the Japanese Americans. Frankfurter proposed the addition of this statement: "We need not now attempt to define the ultimate boundaries of the war power nor do we intimate any view concerning any issue not now before us. We decide only . . . that the curfew order as applied, and at the time it was applied, was within the boundaries of the war power." Within hours, Stone circulated to the Court a memorandum that went even further in closing the gates of the internment camps: "We need not now attempt to define the ultimate boundaries of the war power. Nor do we have any occasion to decide whether circumstances and conditions which may have arisen since petitioner's disobedience of the curfew order, which are not before us, would afford a basis for judicial inquiry as to petitioner's loyalty or as to any other fact having a bearing on the danger of espionage and sabotage. Whether or to what extent such issues could be adjudicated in the courts, and whether the courts could provide a procedure for determining the loyalty of individual members of the group of citizens of Japanese ancestry, are questions which are likewise not before us in this case. We intimate no views concerning them. We decided only that the curfew order as applied, and at the time it was applied, was within the boundaries of the war power."[58]

In going even beyond the language suggested by Frankfurter, Stone's memorandum raised the stakes in what had become a game of mutual bluff. The pressure on Douglas increased at the Court's conference on June 5. At this meeting, Frankfurter wrote in his diary, Black repeated his statements that "he did not think that the courts could review anything that the military does," that "he would not allow a thousand habeas corpuses to be brought," and that "if he were the commanding General, he would not let the evacuated Japanese come back even if the Court directed that to be done." Justice Jackson then added his opinion that Douglas's draft "was a 'hoax' in that it promised something that could not be fulfilled." After these strong words, Chief Justice Stone moved to reduce the tension around the table by voicing "the eager hope that all who have ideas as far as expression or omission should let him know them and he would do his best to meet the variant suggestions."[59]

Douglas reacted in two ways to this application of peer pressure. He first sent a note to Justice Rutledge, whose name was still on the draft of Douglas's concurrence, asking that Rutledge "turn over in your mind this week end the question whether I should stick with my concurring opinion in the Jap case if the C. J. takes out all the stuff in his opinion on assimilation and mistreatment." The following Monday, on June 7, Douglas made a final appeal to Stone on the "racial characteristics" issue, asking that the Chief Justice eliminate from his draft opinion four paragraphs that cast doubt on the loyalty of Japanese Americans. Douglas then matched this request with a veiled threat to change his concurrence to a dissent, should Stone fail to meet his demands on the internment issue: "The nub of the matter is that I could not go along in an affirmance of the judgment below except on the assumptions (a) that the group treatment was temporary; (b) that the individual must have an opportunity to be reclassified as a loyal citizen." In view of Stone's determination that the Hirabayashi case did not raise either the evacuation or internment issues, Douglas acknowledged the probable futility of his threat: "That may be too great a gap for us to bridge."[60]

Conscious that both Frankfurter and Black were adamant on the issue, Stone stood pat and called Douglas's bluff. "I am anxious to go as far as I reasonably can to meet the views of my associates," he wrote to Douglas on June 9, "but it seems to me that if I accepted your suggestions very little of the structure of my opinion would be left, and that I should lose most of my adherents." Stone told Douglas that he intended "to stand by the substance of my opinion" and suggested that Douglas "express your views in your concurring opinion as you have already done." By the time Douglas received this letter, Rutledge had abandoned the joint concurrence and had decided to write his own, more moderate, concurring opinion. Forced to play his cards alone, Douglas tossed in his hand. Subsequent drafts of his concurrence softened the suggestion that habeas corpus offered an escape from internment and omitted entirely the hint that Douglas would vote to support such suits.[61]

In the published version of his concurring opinion, Douglas stated his views in circumspect fashion. The remedy of habeas corpus as a challenge to internment "is one of the large and important issues reserved by the present decision," he wrote. Referring to the leave regulations of the War Relocation Authority, he admitted that "an administrative procedure has been established to relieve against unwarranted applications'' of DeWitt's exclusion orders. Douglas refused, however, to surrender unconditionally on the issue. If it ''were plain that no machinery was available whereby the individual could demonstrate his loyalty as a citizen in order to be reclassified'' and thus be released from internment, he wrote, ''questions of a more serious character would be presented.'' This partial retreat satisfied Stone, who promptly excised from his opinion all the language in his June 4 memorandum except the two sentences drafted by Frankfurter. With Douglas out of the game, the Court closed ranks against the Japanese Americans on the internment issue.[62]

Chief Justice Stone faced a more serious challenge to his campaign for unanimity in the Hirabayashi case from Justice Murphy, who had reserved his vote on the case at the Court's initial conference on May 17. According to Felix Frankfurter, admittedly a biased participant in the internal debate over the Japanese American cases, Murphy shared his scorn for the draft opinion that Douglas had initially circulated. ''The most shocking thing that has ever been written by a member of this Court,'' Frankfurter recorded Murphy as telling him before the subsequent conference on June 5. Calling the Douglas draft ''a regular soapbox speech,'' Murphy reported to Frankfurter that Douglas considered the section of Stone's opinion discussing the war powers issue ''partly addressed to the American Legion.'' ''Well, if the Chief's was addressed to the American Legion,'' Murphy said to Frankfurter, ''Bill's was addressed to the mob.''[63]

If Frankfurter concluded from these comments that Murphy disagreed with the substance of Douglas's opinion, he quickly learned better. In fact, aside from his quarrel with the bombastic tone of the draft opinion, Murphy's criticism was that Douglas had conceded too much to Stone on the war powers issue and too little on the ''racial characteristics'' question. Of all the Court's members, Murphy was perhaps the most sensitive to racial issues and the most likely to dissent in the Hirabayashi case. He had dealt sympathetically with racial and ethnic minorities during his career in politics and public service. As mayor of Detroit and governor of Michigan during the 1930s, he won the votes of blacks and Polish Catholics alike and welded these and other minorities into a potent New Deal coalition. During his short term as Attorney General, Murphy created the Civil Liberties Unit in the Department of Justice, and in a 1939 speech pledged that his office would ''protect civil liberties for . . . the people of all racial extractions in our midst." He had also lived in Asia as Governor-General and Commissioner of the Philippines, and had brought back from that experience "a devotion to the Philippines as a new nation," according to John Pickering, his law clerk in the 1943 term.[64]

Another factor that affected Murphy's attitude in the Hirabayashi case was his identification, as a member of the Irish and Catholic minorities, with the Japanese Americans as a group subject to prejudice and hostility. Murphy "had a terrible streak of religious fervor in him," Pickering recalled, "and felt very strongly about religious freedom and race." In a case decided by the Supreme Court on the same day as the *Hirabayashi* opinion, Murphy expressed some of these views in his majority opinion in the *Schneiderman* case. A longtime official of the Communist Party, Schneiderman was a naturalized American citizen who had been stripped of his citizenship for his political activities and beliefs. Murphy wrote for the Court in restoring Schneiderman's citizenship, over a dissent by Chief Justice Stone in which Frankfurter and Roberts joined. Murphy expressed his belief in America as a melting pot in writing that "we are a heterogeneous people. In some of our larger cities a majority of the schoolchildren are the offspring of parents only one generation, if that far, removed from the steerage of the immigrant ship. . . ."[65]

Just as Douglas had done, Murphy marked his questions about Stone's draft opinion in the Hirabayashi case in the margins of his copy. Next to Stone's claim that the existence of Japanese-language schools gave evidence of "attachments to Japan" among the Japanese Americans, Murphy noted that this statement could apply with equal logic to "Catholic and other church schools." He voiced his concern with the racial issue at the Court's conference on June 5, which led Frankfurter to record in his diary that "we are all agreed" on the case "with the possible exception of Brother Murphy who still has his worries about drawing the line on the score of what he calls 'ancestry.' "[66]

Frankfurter's own worry that Murphy might follow his doubts into dissent led to an exchange of hastily scribbled notes during the conference. At the time, Murphy was writing an opinion in a set of cases that upheld Indian tribal rights, and Frankfurter "good humoredly chided him" about the disparity between these and the Japanese American cases. "Are you writing Indian cases on the assumption that rights depend on ancestry?" Frankfurter asked in his first note. "If so—I cannot give my imprimatur to such racial discrimination!" Murphy let the sarcasm pass in his reply: "Felix, I would protect rights on the basis of ancestry—But I would never deny them." Later that day, after Murphy announced that he intended to dissent in the Hirabayashi case, Frankfurter switched from sarcasm to sermon in an appeal for unanimity: "Please, Frank—with your eagerness for the austere functions of the Court and your desire to do all that is humanly possible to maintain and enhance the *corporate* reputation of the Court, why don't you take the initiative with the Chief in getting him to take out everything that either offends you or that you would want to express more irenically." Murphy ignored this plea for judicial pacifism from the Court's war hawk and went ahead with the drafting of his dissent.[67]

Three of his colleagues felt the lash of Murphy's displeasure in the first draft of his Hirabayashi dissent. Chief Justice Stone's assertion, based on the alleged "facts and circumstances" of the religious and cultural traits of the Japanese American population, that the Court could not "reject as unfounded the judgment of the military authorities . . . that there were disloyal members of that population" who "could not readily be isolated and separately dealt with, and constituted a menace to the national defense and safety," prompted a scathing rebuttal from Murphy: "If there were substantial evidence that citizens of Japanese ancestry were generally disloyal . . . the curfew order and other restrictions imposed on them might be defended. . . . But such evidence is lacking. On the other hand, there is good reason to believe that the action of the military authorities was based primarily if not solely on a widespread belief that persons of Japanese descent had not been and could not be assimilated and that by and large they gave primary allegiance [to] the Empire of Japan. It does not appear that any serious effort was made to segregate aliens, or isolate disloyal elements, or apprehend those who fomented and encouraged the spread of Japanese ideas and propaganda, such as members of the Society of the Black Dragon. Instead of this, by a gigantic round-up no less than 70,000 American citizens are placed under a special ban and deprived of their liberty because of a particular racial inheritance. . . . This is so utterly inconsistent with our ideals and traditions, and in my judgment so contrary to constitutional sanctions, that I cannot lend my assent."[68]

Murphy next took a swipe at Douglas, whose draft concurrence he considered fainthearted and an invitation to military absolutism. In the "soap-box speech" Murphy had denounced to Frankfurter, Douglas had compared the military orders applied to the Japanese Americans with the military draft: "A nation which can require the individual to give up his freedom and lay down his life . . . certainly can demand these lesser sacrifices from its other citizens." Murphy denounced this language as simplistic. "We are told that the restrictions on personal liberty imposed by this statute," he answered Douglas, "are less severe than those established in pursuance of the draft law and previously upheld by this Court in Selective Draft Cases. . . . But the latter make no discrimination between citizens on the basis of ancestry, in contravention of due process and the fifth amendment." Murphy also criticized his colleague's flag-waving claim that a country that "wages war to win" cannot "sit in judgment" on the decisions of its generals. "Undoubtedly we must wage war to win, and do it with all our might," replied Murphy. "But the might of America lies in something else, something that is unique. It will avail us little to win the war on the battlefield and lose it at home. We do not win the war, on the contrary we lose it, if we destroy the Constitution and the best traditions of our country."[69]

Murphy finally used his draft dissent in the Hirabayashi case to settle a score with Frankfurter. In his dissent in *Barnette*, the Jehovah's Witnesses flag-salute case then before the Court, Frankfurter had made a point of his Jewish heritage in justifying his position of judicial deference to laws that restricted the rights of a religious minority. "One who belongs to the most vilified and persecuted minority in history is not likely to be insensible to the freedoms guaranteed by our Constitution," Frankfurter began. "But as judges we are neither Jew nor Gentile, neither Catholic nor agnostic. We owe equal attachment to the Constitution and are equally bound by our judicial obligations whether we derive our citizenship from the earliest or the latest immigrants to these shores." Murphy considered this language both sanctimonious and hypocritical, and he appealed personally to Frankfurter (as did other members of the Court) to remove it from the *Barnette* dissent, to no avail. Murphy's subtle but pointed response to this rebuff came in the draft of his Hirabayashi dissent. DeWitt's curfew order, he wrote, "bears a melancholy resemblance to the treatment accorded to members of the Jewish race in Germany and other parts of Europe. We cannot close our eyes to the fact that for centuries the old world has been torn by racial and religious wars, has been put on the rack and has suffered the worst kind of anguish, due to inequality and discrimination. There was one law for one and a different law for another." Murphy left unstated but clear the implication that judges faced an inescapable duty to strike down laws based on any form of racial or religious discrimination, and should not hide in the bunker of judicial restraint.[70]

As the day for final decision approached, Murphy developed second thoughts about his isolated position as the only dissenter in the Hirabayashi case. Justice Stanley Reed applied the first gentle push. "Murphy had a considerable rapport with Justice Reed, their chambers were next to each other, and Reed had been making various suggestions about the

Schneiderman case'' on which Murphy was writing the Court's opinion, John Pickering recalled. The first draft of Murphy's dissent in Hirabayashi had conceded that if ''substantial evidence'' existed that Japanese Americans were ''generally disloyal,'' or had ''otherwise by their behavior furnished reasonable ground'' for dealing with them as a group, the curfew order ''might be defended and upheld against legal attack in the light of the conditions and the military situation which then prevailed.'' Reed found this argument ''appealing'' but not totally convincing. ''If you admit this you give your case away,'' he wrote Murphy. ''Military protection only needs reasonable grounds, which this record has. You cannot wait for an invasion to see if loyalty triumphs.'' Murphy bowed to this criticism. ''Whether the record provides reasonable grounds, whether the evidence shows 'general disloyalty,' is a question of opinion,'' he informed Pickering on June 8. ''I assumed it did not.'' Nonetheless, he instructed Pickering to strike the offending sentences from the draft.[71]

The final push from Frankfurter was less gentle. ''Of course I shan't try to dissuade you from filing a dissent,'' he wrote Murphy on June 10 in attempting just that task, ''not because I do not think it highly unwise but because I think you are immovable.'' He asked Murphy, however, to consider whether ''it is conducive to the things you care about, including the great reputation of this Court, to suggest that everybody is out of step except Johnny, and more particularly that the Chief Justice and seven other Justices of this Court are behaving like the enemy and thereby playing into the hands of the enemy? Compassion is, I believe, a virtue enjoined by Christ. Well, tolerance is a long, long way from compassion—and can't you write your views with such expressed tolerance that you won't make people think that when eight others disagree with you, you think their view means that they want to destroy the liberties of the United States and 'lose the war' at home?''[72]

Reed's appeal to precedent more likely affected Murphy's decision to withdraw his dissent than Frankfurter's appeal to patriotism. In any event, Murphy took a pencil to the printed version of his dissent. He first changed ''Mr. Justice Murphy, dissenting,'' to ''concurring.'' Next to go was the language that had denied to the military ''unlimited authority'' over civilians ''outside the actual theatre of military operations,'' and his conclusion that the curfew order ''is discriminatory and therefore fails to comply with the requirement of due process of law contained in the Fifth Amendment.'' In its place, Murphy wrote that, in light of ''the risk of sabotage and espionage, the military authorities should not be required to conform to standards of regulatory action appropriate to normal times.'' In response to Reed's criticism, Murphy conceded that "the military authorities could have reasonably concluded" that individual determinations of the loyalty of Japanese Americans "could not be made without delay that might have had tragic consequences." His final concession to unanimity was agreement that General DeWitt "made an allowable judgment at the time the curfew restriction was imposed."[73]

Murphy made little attempt to hide his true feelings behind the cosmetic changes in his concurrence. Six of the eight paragraphs of the published version, in fact, read like the dissent they were intended to be. The result of the curfew, he wrote, "is the creation in this country of two classes of citizens for the purposes of a critical and perilous hour—to sanction discrimination between groups of United States citizens on the basis of ancestry. In my opinion this goes to the very brink of constitutional power." Finally allied with his colleagues, Murphy stepped back from the constitutional cliff over which his initial dissent had thrown DeWitt's orders.[74]

For the sacrifice of his individual doubts to the Court's collective certitude, Murphy received a battlefield commendation from the Court's symbolic Provost Marshal General, Felix Frankfurter: "Frank—I congratulate you on the wisdom of having been able to reach a concurrence." John Pickering later said that Murphy "expressed to me unhappiness that he had not persisted in a dissent. If he'd gotten any adherents to that circulated dissent I don't think he would have changed." It seems clear that Justice Douglas, despite the implicit threat made to Chief Justice Stone that he might dissent, had no real intention of doing so. Justice Rutledge, however, came close to adding a second vote to Murphy's initial dissent.[75]

After removing his name from Douglas's concurrence, Rutledge drafted one of his own. "I have strong sympathy with Mr. Justice Murphy's views," he wrote. "Judged by peacetime standards, the statute involves a delegation of concentrated, unconfined power over civilian citizens and the order a racial discrimination only war's highest emergency could sustain." He labeled DeWitt's curfew order "something which approaches the ultimate stain on democratic institutions constitutionally established." Seemingly on the brink of joining Murphy's dissent, Rutledge retreated and finally filed a more moderate one-paragraph concurrence. He took exception in his published concurrence to Stone's suggestion that "the courts have no power to review any action a military officer may 'in his discretion' find it necessary to take" in situations that required "some degree of military control short of suspending habeas corpus." Speaking of General DeWitt, Rutledge wrote that there may be "bounds beyond which he cannot go . . . . But in this case the question need not be faced and I merely add my reservation without indicating an opinion concerning it.'' Rutledge later admitted his doubts in a note to Stone: ''I have had more anguish over this case than any I have decided, save possibly one death case in the Ct. of Appeals. I am now clear to go with you,'' he added, hinting that he had given serious thought to joining Murphy's dissent.[76]

The last spark of dissent from his colleagues finally extinguished, Chief Justice Stone put the finishing touches on his *Hirabayashi* opinion. Stone made one change from his first draft that seemed minor; he removed a paragraph that cited the number of Japanese-language schools on the West Coast and that identified as a ''significant feature of the Japanese training of youth'' inculcation in the tenets of the Shinto religion. In excising this paragraph and the footnote that identified its source as the ''Report on Japanese Activities'' of the House Committee on Un-American Activities, Stone obscured his reliance on the amicus brief of the West Coast states, drafted on DeWitt's orders by Captain Herbert Wenig, in which this material appeared. The ''racial characteristics'' argument in Stone's opinion in fact relied heavily on this brief, but Stone might have had second thoughts about identifying the Court with this hard-line source.[77]

Stone made a second change to meet the criticism of Justice Reed that Public Law 503, as the statutory basis for DeWitt's orders, ''has not sufficient standards to meet the requirements of proper delegation.'' In the initial draft of his *Hirabayashi* opinion, Stone had written that the Court's ''investigation here does not go beyond the inquiry whether . . . the challenged orders and statute afford a reasonable basis for the action taken in imposing the curfew.'' His answer to this central question was that ''Congress and the military authorities acting under its direction have constitutional authority to appraise the danger in the light of facts of public notoriety.'' Implicit in Reed's letter to Stone was the suggestion that reliance on ''facts'' about the Japanese Americans on the basis of ''judicial notice'' failed to establish an adequate link between congressional intent and DeWitt's orders.[78]

In responding to Reed's suggestion that he make this link explicit, Stone added three pages to his published opinion. This new material skated with heavy strides over very thin ice, both in factual and constitutional terms. Stone conceded that Public Law 503 ''does not in terms establish a particular standard to which the orders of the military commander are to conform, or require findings to be made as a prerequisite to any order.'' The lifeline that Stone threw across this ice was a rope that tied together Executive Order 9066, Public Law 503, and DeWitt's military orders as ''parts of a single program'' that established as the standard given to DeWitt "the necessity of protecting military resources . . . against espionage and sabotage." According to long-standing Supreme Court precedent, standards set out by Congress for executive action required some finding in fact as a basis for their implementation. "Here the findings of danger from espionage and sabotage," Stone wrote, "and of the necessity of the curfew order to protect against them, have been duly made."[79]

Stone did not, and could not have from the record before the Court, specify with any precision what "findings" General DeWitt had made with respect to the dangers presented to military security by Japanese Americans. This deficiency, however, did not faze the Chief Justice. "The military commander's appraisal of facts in the light of the authorized standard, and the inferences which he drew from those facts, involved the exercise of his informed judgment," Stone wrote in his published opinion. "But as we have seen, those facts, and the inferences which could be rationally drawn from them, support the judgment of the military commander, that the danger of espionage and sabotage to our military resources was imminent, and that the curfew order was an appropriate measure to meet it."[80]

Stone wrote his *Hirabayashi* opinion without knowledge of the Ringle report, the withholding of which Edward Ennis had denounced as a "suppression of evidence." Nor did he know that DeWitt's own intelligence staff had disclaimed any involvement by Japanese Americans in espionage or sabotage in the period after Pearl Harbor. Whether knowledge of this material would have affected the outcome of the case is a matter of speculation. Stone made it clear, however, that the "rational basis" standard of judicial review employed in the Court's analysis left DeWitt with virtually unlimited discretion in his assessment of the situation on the West Coast. In view of the war powers possessed jointly by Congress and the executive branch, Stone concluded, "it is not for any court to sit in review of the wisdom of their action or substitute its judgment for theirs." All that was left for Stone to do was to dispose of the due process issue raised by the singling out of Japanese American citizens in DeWitt's orders, a task made easy by reliance on the "racial characteristics" data presented under the judicial notice doctrine.[81]

Stone employed a minimal standard of judicial review to cut a clear path from Executive Order 9066 to DeWitt's orders. The withdrawal of Justice Murphy's dissent cleared the last obstacle from this path, the *Milligan* case. Lawyers on both sides had devoted dozens of pages of their briefs and hours of argument before the Court of Appeals and the Supreme Court to this significant precedent, and Murphy had scribbled a note to himself during the Supreme Court argument: "Ex parte Milligan . . . governs this case.'' His draft dissent stressed its importance as a barrier to military control over civilians. ''Having elected to proceed without resort to martial law, the government was necessarily subject to the Constitutional limitations which govern the exercise of the war power,'' Murphy had written, including in those limitations the due process protection against racial discrimination. Murphy's removal of this language from his published concurrence allowed Stone to dismiss the troubling precedent in a single sentence: ''The exercise of [the war power] here involves no question of martial law or trial by military tribunal.'' Put in these narrow terms, Stone's conclusion was correct. But the holding implicit in *Milligan*, that military restrictions on the rights of citizens could be imposed only through martial law, escaped his analysis. The Chief Justice simply drove a constitutional bulldozer over this central issue.[82]

During the month that began with the Court's conference on May 17, five members of the Court—Roberts, Reed, Douglas, Rutledge, and Murphy—had voiced serious doubts about the legality of DeWitt's orders and their constitutional basis. Compromise, cajolery, and their own concerns that the Court should maintain unity in wartime finally persuaded this potential majority for reversal to make Stone's opinion unanimous. The Chief Justice had labored through four printed drafts of his *Hirabayashi* opinion to meet the objections of the doubters and to blunt the sharp edges of the three concurring opinions. With characteristic flattery, Frankfurter placed his benediction on Stone's final product: ''You have labored with great forbearance and with concentration to produce something worthy of the Torah.''[83]

Stone announced the *Hirabayashi* and *Yasui* opinions on June 21, 1943, at the Court's last session of the year. As decisions in criminal cases, their outcome directly affected only the defendants. Fred Korematsu, whose case had been returned to the Court of Appeals on June 1, had been granted leave by the WRA to work in Salt Lake City and remained on his job while he waited for a further ruling. Federal marshals took Minoru Yasui from the Minadoka Relocation Center in Idaho back to Portland, where Judge Fee resentenced him to the nine months he had already served in jail and returned him to the internment camp.[84]

Gordon Hirabayashi became the only defendant forced back to prison by the Supreme Court. His subsequent experiences resembled the plot of a Keystone Kops film. After serving two months of his ninety-day sentence, Hirabayashi had been released on bail to await the outcome of his appeal and was working with the American Friends Service Committee in Spokane, Washington. "A couple of FBI agents came to pick me up while I was mowing the lawn," he recalled. "They took me down to the office of the federal attorney, who told me that I'd have to serve the rest of my sentence in the Spokane county jail. 'I can't send you to the federal road camp at Fort Lewis because that's in the restricted area,' he said, 'and the only other road camp we have is at Tucson, and we don't have any money to send you there. So you'll have to serve it here.' I didn't want to go back to jail, so I said 'What if I go on my own to Tucson?' That was okay with him, and so I went on my own. It was against my principles to pay my way to prison, so I hitchhiked. I stopped off in Idaho to visit with my parents for a few days, and saw other friends along the way. It took me about two weeks from the time I left Spokane, and when I got to Tucson the federal marshal didn't have any papers on me and wanted to send me back. 'Someday you're going to find those papers and I'm going to have to interrupt what I'm doing and come back,' I said, 'so you might as well find them and get this over with.' I went out to a movie, and when I came back they had found the papers at the bottom of a file. So they took me about thirty miles up to the camp, and I did my sentence there. The funny thing was that the camp was also in a restricted area, but they let me stay there anyway."[85]

The Supreme Court's opinions came at a time of heated debate over the treatment of Japanese Americans in the internment camps and second thoughts about the necessity for their continued detention. Press reactions to the decisions reflected the geographical and political split over these issues. The Washington *Post* expressed liberal opinion on the East Coast in a June 25 editorial entitled "Stigma by Ancestry." Observing that "the Supreme Court has performed a duty for which it obviously had little relish," the *Post* cited the three concurring opinions in the *Hirabayashi* case as evidence that "some of the justices entertain grave misgivings" about the evacuation and detention issues the Court had avoided. The *Post* urged the Court not to evade its duty to "pass upon the constitutionality of our continuing discrimination against American citizens because of their racial heritage. The outright deprivation of civil right which we have visited upon these helpless, and, for the most part, no doubt, innocent, people may leave an ugly blot upon the pages of our history."[86]

On the West Coast, in contrast, the Los Angeles *Times* hailed the *Hirabayashi* opinion as "heartening news for the Pacific Slope, where opinion has held with similar unanimity that the presence of any Japs here is dangerous in wartime." The *Times* welcomed the Court as an ally in the campaign for continued internment: "Agitation for the return of Japs to the Pacific Coast—which has gained recruits in high circles in Washington—gets its devastating answer from the clear analysis of the situation by Justice Stone and the unanimous opinion of the Supreme Court." Public officials on the West Coast voiced similar sentiments. Representative J. Leroy Johnson, a California Republican, promptly proposed to Congress the postwar deportation of all Japanese aliens and "disloyal" citizens. "This is a way to get rid of a group that may make future trouble," he explained. And California governor Earl Warren told the press that "nothing more destructive to our defense could happen than to release the potential fifth columnists." Warren predicted that the return of Japanese Americans to the West Coast would result in widespread sabotage and "a second Pearl Harbor in California."[87]

With the Korematsu case back in the Court of Appeals in San Francisco, and with the Endo case now ready for decision by Judge Roche, it seemed certain that the Supreme Court would soon confront the issues of evacuation and detention. While the Court took a respite from the cases during its summer recess, the lawyers on the two sides resumed their battles without a break. In this second round of conflict, divided loyalties and charges of misconduct led to such bloody skirmishes within the two legal camps that an entire term of the Supreme Court passed before its members confronted the challenge posed by the *Post* editorialist. In the meantime, the Japanese Americans whose fate rested on the outcome of the Korematsu and Endo cases endured their second full year of internment.

10

"No Longer Any Military Necessity"

LESS THAN THREE months passed between the time the Court of Appeals in San Francisco sent the trio of criminal cases to the Supreme Court in March 1943 and the decisions that were handed down in June. With the scene of the legal struggle over the remaining Korematsu and Endo cases shifted back to the West Coast, lawyers on both sides of these cases anticipated that lower court judges—with the *Hirabayashi* opinion as precedent—would rule promptly on the evacuation and detention issues left to them for decision. Regardless of the rulings by the West Coast courts, the lawyers expected to return to the Supreme Court within several months for "another bite at the apple," as ACLU staff counsel Clifford Forster predicted on June 22. Government lawyers also agreed that the second round of cases "will reach the Supreme Court . . . during the Term opening this fall," WRA Solicitor Philip Glick wrote in July.[1]

The Korematsu and Endo cases were, in fact, ready for decision by the Supreme Court before its summer recess in June 1944. But the Court did not actually decide the two cases until the following December, eighteen months after the rulings in the Hirabayashi and Yasui cases. Judicial foot-dragging was not the culprit in this delay. What neither Forster nor Glick took into account, in their first flush of optimism, was that legal and partisan politics would combine to hold up presentation of the Korematsu and Endo cases to the Supreme Court.

This chapter will examine the factors that kept the majority of Japanese Americans behind barbed wire during this eighteen-month period. The following chapter will recount the behind-the-scenes battles among government lawyers that led, during this same period, to bitter charges by Justice Department lawyers that their War Department colleagues were foisting "lies" on the Supreme Court in the Korematsu case. These two topics overlap in time; their separate treatment is justified, however, by the active involvement of lawyers for the Japanese Americans in the first and their ignorance of the events that took place in the second. In conjunction, however, these two related chapters illustrate the significance of the comment by Edward Ennis of the Justice Department, in a September 1944 conversation with Clifford Forster, that "there were many confidential matters" which could not be shared by the two lawyers. Behind this comment lay a legal scandal of unprecendented scope and consequence.[2]

The Supreme Court set the scene for this chapter with its *Hirabayashi* opinion. In ducking the evacuation issue in that case, the Court had all but guaranteed that the Korematsu case would return from the Court of Appeals for an ultimate ruling on the legality of evacuation. The detention issue raised in the side-tracked Endo case additionally faced the Supreme Court with an even more troubling legal question.

The first impetus for judicial action in these cases came from ACLU lawyers. Clifford Forster wrote to Saburo Kido on June 22, 1943, that "we must now press to get the Korematsu case up to the Supreme Court, and by all means it is imperative that the Endo case be rushed up in time for the Supreme Court to decide the case in October." Over the next six months, however, the ACLU national office displayed no further interest in the Korematsu case and moved to abandon the Endo case as a challenge to the detention of Japanese Americans. The explanation for this abrupt shift of sentiment rests in the relations of the Union's national office with two sets of lawyers. Over the past year, Forster and ACLU director Roger Baldwin had lost confidence in the legal skills of Wayne Collins and James Purcell, who respectively represented Fred Korematsu and Mitsuye Endo. At the same time, Edward Ennis and John Burling of the Justice Department came to constitute an unofficial board of legal strategy in the cases along with Baldwin and Forster. This crossing of legal lines produced a complete reversal of the strategy initially proposed by Forster. In their subsequent effort to find replacements for the Korematsu and Endo cases, Baldwin and Forster became, in effect, agents of the Justice Department.[3]

The ACLU's role in the Endo case illustrates the pitfalls of legal politics. Of the two pending cases, the habeas corpus petition filed by Purcell offered the best chance for an early judicial decision. It also promised (assuming a favorable decision by the Supreme Court) practical benefits to the Japanese Americans. A decision that detention was unlawful would force open the gates of the internment camps, whereas the evacuation program at issue in the Korematsu case had long since been completed. At the least, a favorable decision would require the release of those Japanese Americans certified by the WRA as "loyal" and willing to remain away from the West Coast. It was possible, in addition, that a sweeping decision against detention might strike down the WRA's restrictive leave regulations and the Army's refusal to permit the return of Japanese Americans to the "restricted zones" on the West Coast. In either event, the stakes in the Endo case were high.

The fact that Forster addressed his letter to Kido rather than Purcell reveals the problem that faced the ACLU. Purcell had brought the Endo case without support from the ACLU. Over the year since its filing, Purcell's objections to what he considered "meddling" by the ACLU had turned into active hostility toward the Union. Forster was thus forced to approach Kido, who maintained good relations on both sides of this schism, as a middleman. "I urge you to press him," Forster wrote about Purcell, "to get the district court to make a ruling so that we can get the case certified to the Supreme Court."[4]

Purcell replied promptly to this secondhand request. "I communicated with the Judge," he wrote to Forster, "informing him that I desire that the Endo case be ruled on." Judge Michael Roche, before whom the petition had been pending for close to a year, had stretched the rules while he waited for guidance from the Supreme Court. The *Hirabayashi* opinion eliminated his last excuse for inaction. Two weeks later, on July 2, Judge Roche issued a terse, two-sentence order. He first dismissed the habeas corpus petition on the ground that it did not present a valid claim of unlawful detention and then ruled that Endo had failed to exhaust her administrative remedies as a precondition to release from the Tule Lake Relocation Center in northern California.[5]

As a matter of law, Roche's ruling was clearly erroneous. Mitsuye Endo had completed an application for leave clearance under the existing WRA regulations on February 19, 1943, the only procedure required for those who wished to leave the relocation centers. The WRA had not acted on her application at the time Judge Roche issued his ruling, but this failure to complete the processing of the request for leave clearance had no legal bearing on the status of her habeas corpus petition. WRA officials moved quickly to grant the application and delivered a notice of leave clearance to Endo on August 23. This move shifted the administrative initiative back to Endo and placed her in a legal Catch-22. The next step under WRA rules was submission of an application for indefinite leave, which required that Endo agree to remain away from the "restricted zone" on the West Coast. However, such an agreement would jeopardize the possible success of a suit against California cials, seeking restoration to the state job from which she had been dismissed for being "unavailable" for work. Endo could hardly agree to leave the West Coast, as a prerequisite to release from Tule Lake, and still affirm her willingness to resume her job in Sacramento.[6]

The moves that followed Judge Roche's ruling turned administrative confusion into legal chaos. Attorney General Biddle led off with a warning to WRA Director Dillon Myer. The concurring opinions in the *Hirabayashi* case, Biddle wrote in late July, made it difficult to predict whether the WRA's detention program "would command the assent of a majority of the Court if the issue were placed squarely before it." Biddle hinted that WRA officials could "avoid the dangers indicated by the opinions" if they eliminated the regulations that required applicants for leave to remain under WRA jurisdiction after their release. This suggestion, however, ignored the fact that the Army's exclusion orders stood in the way of Mitsuye Endo and other Japanese Americans who demanded the right to return to their West Coast homes and jobs.[7]

Biddle's suggestion fell on deaf ears. Convinced that Executive Order 9066 "authorizes detention of all evacuees, as a step in effectuating the leave program," WRA Solicitor Philip Glick relied on a theory of "precautionary detention" as an answer to the Justice Department claim that detention lacked statutory sanction. Glick rested his novel theory on the assumption that the WRA possessed the power to hold Japanese Americans behind barbed wire in order to protect them against hostility in areas where their presence might be resented. Admitting that the WRA's statutory power "does not authorize precautionary detention *per se,*" Glick nonetheless asserted that "our right to detain the potentially dangerous evacuees until the others have been relocated" carried with it an implied power to place restrictions on the right of concededly loyal Japanese Americans to leave the internment camps "in order to protect the effectiveness of the relocation program."[8]

Glick's effort to put the "precautionary detention" theory into practice created further complications in the Endo case. Glick and Myer decided in mid-1943 to convert the Tule Lake Relocation Center in which Endo was held into a "segregation" camp for "potentially dangerous evacuees." They transferred into the Tule Lake camp more than 17,000 Japanese Americans, including those who had requested repatriation to Japan, those who had answered no to Questions 27 or 28 of the WRA loyalty questionnaire administered in the preceding four months, and members of the Kibei group educated in Japan. To make room for the "disloyals" sent from other camps to Tule Lake, Mitsuye Endo was transferred on September 22, 1943, to the Central Utah Relocation Center in Topaz, which placed her outside the jurisdiction of the Court of

Appeals in San Francisco. James Purcell had filed an appeal from Judge Roche's order in this court on August 26. Endo's involuntary transfer thus raised the question of whether her case had been "mooted" and would require that she file a separate habeas corpus petition with the federal district court in Salt Lake City.[9]

In authorizing Endo's transfer from Tule Lake to Topaz, Glick did not intend to deprive her of the right to appeal the order of Judge Roche. He did hope, however, that she would abandon her challenge to the WRA's legal power to require her agreement to remain away from Sacramento in exchange for her release. Glick even made a trip to Topaz to make this plea in person. "Miss Endo, you're clearly a person who has been loyal to the United States all the time," he recalled telling her. "You've never said or done anything to raise the slightest question about you. The FBI report on you gives you complete clearance. All you need do is ask for the right to leave the center and you can go. Any leave we grant you will expressly exclude return to the restricted area, but we'll help you relocate anywhere else in the United States."[10]

Glick's efforts at persuasion were predictably unavailing. In a follow-up letter to Clifford Forster, he conceded that "Miss Endo has a perfectly clear loyalty record, and . . . we are ready to permit her to leave the center at any time." Glick added that "I do not see how the question of exhaustion of administrative remedy can be reached" in light of this decision. What Glick did not know was that the ACLU's national board, deciding that Judge Roche had ruled correctly in the Endo case, had agreed "not to encourage test cases where administrative remedies are not exhausted unless detention is unduly prolonged." Forster earlier had gone to Washington along with Roger Baldwin to consult with John Burling of the Justice Department about the Endo case. "As you know," Forster advised Ernest Besig on October 1, "we have never thought the Endo case was too strong." According to Forster's report, Burling "said that if the appeal were dropped in the Endo case she could be released at once, as that was the only reason she was still being detained." Forster than urged that Besig "see Purcell and suggest that this be done."[11]

On his part, Besig had mixed feelings about this request from New York. He already suspected that Purcell might not press the Endo case with proper diligence. "Jim Purcell is working in the mayoralty election, so he may be neglecting his law practice," Besig had reported to Forster in September. He resented even more, however, Forster's request that he urge Purcell to abandon the case. "I talked to Purcell about your letter," Besig replied on October 13 with obvious relish, "and, to be frank, he said, 'You can tell your New York office to go to hell!' " Besig had little doubt that Forster had enlisted the Justice Department in this campaign. On a visit to San Francisco in October, Edward Ennis contacted Purcell through A. J. Zirpoli, the federal attorney who represented the government in the Endo case. "When Zirpoli told him why Ennis wanted to see him," Besig wrote Forster with equal relish, "Purcell turned it down as a waste of time."[12]

While the Endo case languished on the Court of Appeals docket, the Korematsu case moved past it on the road to the Supreme Court. The decision in the case by the Court of Appeals caught the lawyers on both sides by surprise. In a unanimous opinion issued on December 2, 1943, six months after the Supreme Court had sent that case back to San Francisco, all seven members of the appellate panel upheld Korematsu's conviction on the basis of the Supreme Court's *Hirabayashi* opinion. Noting that the Supreme Court "did not expressly pass upon the validity of the evacuation order" at issue in the Korematsu case, the judges pointed to the holding in *Hirabayashi* that "the government of the United States, in prosecuting a war, has power to do all that is necessary to the successful prosecution of a war," even at the expense of the due process rights of citizens. Chief Justice Stone's sweeping interpretation of the war powers doctrine, the Court of Appeals concluded, "so clearly sustains the validity of the proclamation for evacuation . . . that it is not necessary to labor the point."[13]

The surprising aspect of the Court of Appeals opinion was not its outcome—despite the Supreme Court's explicit reservation of the evacuation issue in *Hirabayashi*, its treatment of the war powers question almost invited this outcome—but its issuance without further argument by the lawyers involved. The only argument before the Court of Appeals had taken place in February 1943 on the government's motion to dismiss the Korematsu case. Judicial rules did not require that the court hear additional argument. Nonetheless, the questions left undecided by the Supreme Court in *Hirabayashi* were sufficiently broad in scope that a second round of argument seemed warranted to Judge Denman. In a lengthy concurring opinion that rivaled his earlier dissent to certification in the Hirabayashi case in hostility to General DeWitt, Denman suggested that the due process questions passed over by his colleagues had been "resolved in favor of an uncontrolled military autocracy" without adequate argument.[14]

The Court of Appeals opinion placed on Wayne Collins, as the losing lawyer, responsibility for taking the Korematsu case back to the

Supreme Court. The Court's rules required that Collins file a petition for certiorari within thirty days. Collins was then unable to draft a petition, however, because of an injury to his neck and arm. "He hasn't been able to do much work," Ernest Besig reported to Osmond Fraenkel on December 21, "so some other move has to be made in the Korematsu case." As a move to buy time, Collins filed with the Court of Appeals a motion for a rehearing in the case. Such motions were rarely granted, and the court rejected it on January 7, 1944. But his delaying tactic gave Collins an additional month in which to draft a certiorari petition.[15]

Whether the Supreme Court would vote to hear the Korematsu case and decide the evacuation issue, or rest on the Court of Appeals opinion as a proper application of *Hirabayashi* to this question, created doubt among the lawyers on both sides. Osmond Fraenkel anticipated a denial of certiorari "in view of the closeness of the issues to those already decided." Justice Department lawyers expressed less certainty but shared with ACLU lawyers in New York a desire to keep Collins away from the Supreme Court. In a memorandum to Solicitor General Fahy, Edward Ennis blasted Collins as "egregiously ill-equipped professionally to assert his client's rights adequately." Ennis based his acerbic attitude partly on his low estimation of the argument made by Collins in February 1943, when the two men faced the Court of Appeals in the Korematsu case. He also faulted Collins for failing in his certiorari petition to make the point that DeWitt's evacuation order would lead directly to Korematsu's detention. A strong argument on this point, Ennis felt, might persuade the Supreme Court to reverse the Court of Appeals in the case.[16]

Ennis could hardly prevent Collins from filing a certiorari petition in the Supreme Court, although he could possibly convince Fahy to file a brief urging that the Court reject the petition. Ennis much preferred that the detention issue reach the Court in the Endo case, assuming that the Court of Appeals decided the case in time for it to reach the Supreme Court before the end of its term in May or June of 1944. As a vehicle for a judicial determination that detention of Japanese Americans was unlawful, however, the Endo case presented several complications. One resulted from Endo's transfer from Tule Lake in California to the internment camp in Topaz, Utah, which removed her from the jurisdiction of the Court of Appeals in San Francisco. As a result, Solicitor General Fahy believed that the Endo case had been mooted, the legal term for a case that no longer presented a justiciable issue. Under a strict application of this judicial doctrine, James Purcell would be forced to file a brand-new habeas corpus petition with the federal court in Salt Lake City. If Fahy adhered to this position, the Endo case could not possibly reach the Supreme Court before its summer recess in 1944.[17]

Endo's refusal to complete an application for indefinite leave presented a second complication. Either the Court of Appeals or the Supreme Court might seize on this issue as a means of evading the detention issue by ruling that Endo had not exhausted the administrative remedies offered by the WRA regulations. Finally, Ennis had learned that Purcell intended to relinquish his right to argue the Endo case before the Supreme Court to Wayne Collins, a prospect that he contemplated with dread. Confronted with this trio of problems, Ennis arranged a strategy session with ACLU director Roger Baldwin on January 24, 1944. Ennis first raised his complaint that Collins had mishandled the Korematsu case. In a report to Clifford Forster, Baldwin noted that Ennis "pointed out that the main point on which the Supreme Court might differentiate" the Korematsu and Hirabayashi cases "is that to report for evacuation was equivalent to reporting for detention." Korematsu's conviction "could hardly be sustained" by the Supreme Court if this issue were pressed, Ennis added. He also told Baldwin that Collins had made a "mistake" in submitting the rehearing motion to the Court of Appeals, since this tactic offered the court a chance to "correct its opinion so as to make an appeal to the Supreme Court more difficult."[18]

Ennis then turned the discussion to the Endo case. It raised "questions of the utmost importance," he told Baldwin, urging that the ACLU file an amicus brief with the Court of Appeals. The brief filed by Purcell "misses all of the main points," Ennis complained. The major omission in Purcell's brief, Ennis felt, was the argument that the WRA action in transferring Endo from California to Utah did *not* in fact remove jurisdiction over the case from the Court of Appeals in San Francisco, since she had not initiated this move. An ACLU brief that raised this point was essential in light of Fahy's wavering on the mootness issue.[19]

In reaching agreement on a joint strategy in the pending cases, both Ennis and Baldwin executed an about-face from their earlier positions that the Endo case should be dropped or derailed. The prospect that the Supreme Court might review the Korematsu case without reaching the detention issue, and the uncertain fate of the Endo case in the Court of Appeals, led to the adoption of two related tactics. Baldwin took the initiative in both efforts. His first move was to enlist Charles Horsky as a volunteer lawyer in the Endo case, with the formal invitation offered by Al Wirin. Horsky and Ennis were close friends and had worked together in the Solicitor General's office before the war. A Montana native and a Harvard Law School graduate, Horsky had gone on to a partnership in the prestigious Washington law firm of Covington, Burling, Rublee and Shorb. "Horsky was ready-made for us," Baldwin later said, "a liberal in a conservative law firm, known to the Supreme Court judges and higher officials for his engaging personality and legal ability." Assigned the task of preparing the amicus brief suggested by Ennis, Horsky quickly became a central figure in plotting tactics with ACLU and Justice Department lawyers. Baldwin also hoped that Collins might be persuaded to relinquish Supreme Court argument in the cases to Horsky, or at least to share his time as Frank Walters had done with Harold Evans in the Hirabayashi case.[20]

Baldwin's second tactic was borrowed from the Hirabayashi and Yasui cases. In a move designed to assure that the Endo case would reach the Supreme Court before its summer recess, he asked Ernest Besig to urge that Purcell petition the Court of Appeals for certification of the case. Purcell agreed and requested that Besig prepare the necessary forms. The plan soon encountered an unexpected snag, however. "I discovered from Al Zirpoli," Besig reported to Baldwin on February 1, that he "had no information about the Department's willingness to have the question certified." Besig archly suggested that before the next such request from New York, "the necessary preliminary work be done in advance in order to save our time and money." A week later, Purcell learned from Besig that "the Government had changed its mind. Since the Department of Justice is now opposed to certification, such a step is impossible in the Endo case."[21]

Ennis had not changed his mind, but Solicitor General Fahy and Attorney General Biddle had made it necessary to call off the certification move while they refereed a dispute between Ennis and Philip Glick. In fact, Ennis had precipitated the conflict in a January 19 telephone conversation with WRA lawyer Maurice Silverman, who served as Acting Solicitor while Glick visited the West Coast. Anticipating at the time that the Court of Appeals would hear arguments in the Endo case, Ennis was then drafting the Justice Department's brief. "He will not sign a brief that takes the position that detention after leave clearance is valid," Silverman wired Glick after this conversation. WRA lawyers had sent Ennis their own draft, which argued for the legality of detention. Ennis held out the option that a brief defending detention "might be possible if you would sign it," Silverman informed his superior. Glick knew perfectly well that a Justice Department brief submitted without the signatures of its lawyers would be perceived by the Court of Appeals judges as a white flag from the government.[22]

Ennis expanded on his objections in a January 20 letter to Glick. Where "the authority to detain is as doubtful as it is in this case," he wrote, the Justice Department had an obligation to "be completely frank with the courts'' and confess ''the doubts that we feel'' on the detention issue. The ''doubts'' expressed by Ennis were actually a conviction that neither Executive Order 9066 nor Public Law 503 authorized detention as a step subsequent to evacuation. Executive Order 9102, through which President Roosevelt established the War Relocation Authority, authorized WRA control of the ''relocation, maintenance, and supervision'' of Japanese Americans as part of the evacuation program. Since Roosevelt had set up the WRA before Congress passed the broad enforcement statute, Glick considered this fact a sufficient statutory basis for the detention program. Ennis disagreed, but admitted to Glick that ''a serious constitutional question such as this . . . is a point of policy for the decision of the Solicitor General'' and offered to hold up filing of the Endo brief until Glick had a chance to take an appeal to Fahy.[23]

With Glick still on the West Coast, Ennis made his own case to Fahy in a lengthy memorandum on January 21, confessing his hope that the government would lose the Endo case. ''As a matter of constitutional government and proper race relations,'' Ennis argued, ''a decision that this detention was unlawful would be the first step on the road back'' to acceptance of Japanese Americans on the West Coast. ''This case should be used realistically as a vehicle to aid that arduous journey,'' he added. Admitting that the Justice Department ''may not be free to confess error in this case'' and to express ''its belief that this detention is unconstitutional,'' he proposed instead that the government simply outline ''the legal considerations to the court'' without taking an affirmative position. A judicial decision against detention, Ennis further argued, might blunt the strength of West Coast groups opposed to the return of Japanese Americans, some of which had ''pledged to murder them if they return even after the war.'' Ennis informed Fahy that he should expect to hear from Glick, ''who feels that the Government should argue directly for detention,'' but he advised the Solicitor General to reject the WRA position.[24]

Even before Glick's return to Washington, Ennis discovered that Fahy and Biddle had decided to avoid a judicial test of the detention issue. Fahy's legal caution (and perhaps a desire not to risk his Supreme Court batting average) prevailed. Their strategy was to moot the case by persuading the WRA to withdraw the regulation that required a formal application for indefinite leave after leave clearance had been granted, as it had to Mitsuye Endo in August 1943. The effect of this ploy would be to remove the only barrier to her release from the Utah camp. The exclusion orders still in effect would prohibit Endo from returning to California, but an effort to secure that right would require a new and separate suit. Ennis argued against mooting the case at a

January 26 meeting with Fahy and Biddle. He lost this battle and duly informed Glick that his superiors "are not convinced that a Supreme Court decision should be sought now" through the certification route.[25]

The high-level decision to oppose certification made it increasingly likely that the Korematsu case alone would reach the Supreme Court before adjournment in June. Ennis badly wanted the Court to consider the evacuation and detention issues together, hoping that the legal weakness of the latter would undermine judicial support for the former. In a last-ditch effort to keep the Endo case alive, he enlisted Glick as an ally in the certification campaign. "Although normally the case would not reach the Supreme Court this Term," he wrote Glick on January 28, "we must not eliminate the possibilities of its expedition by certified questions as in the *Hirabayashi* case." Fahy's suggestion that the WRA change its regulations "merely in order to avoid a decision in the case," Ennis argued, might "give unfortunate encouragement to improper types of anti-Japanese American sentiment." If Glick agreed, Ennis wrote, he would arrange a meeting with Biddle "to settle the matter whether we shall file the brief and litigate the question or seek to terminate it."[26]

With this encouragement, Glick moved quickly to rescue the Endo case. He first prompted Dillon Myer to call the Attorney General on February 1 to arrange the meeting Ennis had suggested, and Biddle agreed to a conference in his office on February 3. Glick then drafted a letter for Myer, advising Biddle of the position the WRA officials intended to present. The backdrop of the argument that the Endo case be expedited through certification to the Supreme Court included ferocious attacks on the WRA by the press and politicians, spurred by a recent riot at the Tule Lake segregation center and charges that WRA officials permitted pro-Japanese groups to parade under the Rising Sun flag. The political heat produced by these attacks later prompted President Roosevelt to place the WRA under the protective wing of the Interior Department on February 16, 1944. Fahy's proposal to end detention through administrative action, Glick argued, "would create a considerable outcry in the newspapers and in Congress" and fuel the charges of the WRA's "enemies who have repeatedly charged that the Authority ignores the national interest in time of war in order to protect and pamper the evacuees." Should the Supreme Court hold detention invalid, "the very fact of the Court's decision would serve to provide public justification for such a change in the program." Glick hoped for a decision upholding detention but urged on Biddle that "we should be willing to have a court test of the validity of our action'' regardless of the outcome.[27]

The meeting in Biddle's office ended in compromise. Glick and Myer addressed their appeal to a skeptical Fahy. ''We urged him not to drop the Endo case,'' Glick recalled. ''We told him that her lawyer wouldn't permit her to terminate this case, and that she wanted to go ahead. I predicted that the Supreme Court would say that detention pending sorting is clearly constitutional; if the war power didn't allow that, what would the war power allow? Our only difficulty was that Fahy wanted to follow the course that a lawyer would normally follow. But he agreed with Dillon and me after this discussion that he would take the case to the Supreme Court.'' Fahy balked, however, at certification as a shortcut to the Supreme Court and insisted that the case proceed through argument before the Court of Appeals.[28]

The compromise hammered out at the February 3 conference included a further concession to the WRA officials. Fahy instructed Ennis, who was responsible for writing the brief due in the Court of Appeals on February 29, to adopt the ''precautionary detention'' theory pushed by the WRA as a justification for detention. Based on the argument that protection of Japanese Americans against ''acts of violence and disorder'' provided sanction for their detention at least until public hostility to their release subsided, this theory struck Ennis as legally untenable. He followed Fahy's instructions and inserted into the draft brief material provided by the WRA on public hostility toward Japanese Americans. Ennis went no further, however, than to characterize this data as providing a ''not wholly unreasonable basis'' for detention. He additionally refused to acknowledge that detention had any constitutional support, limiting the government's position to the factual foundation prepared by WRA lawyers.[29]

Temporary allies at the meeting in Biddle's office, Ennis and Glick ended their truce within a week. In a lengthy letter to Ennis on February 9, Glick listed nineteen objections to the draft brief. After conceding that Ennis had ''gone a long way toward taking a definite position'' in support of the ''precautionary detention'' theory, Glick complained that Ennis had pulled away the constitutional prop on which the theory rested. He objected particularly to Ennis's concession that ''the constitutionality of detention in this case is doubtful, and that the Government does not urge that the detention is valid but merely presents the relevant considerations of law and fact involved.'' In place of this hands-off attitude, Glick recommended ''substituting a sentence stating that it is the Government's position that authority has been granted by the President and Congress to detain such persons as the appellant and that such detention is constitutional." Glick vented his frustration by suggesting that the draft brief "will open the Government to the charge of throwing the case" but pulled his punch by assuring Ennis that "of course we know that you intend no such thing."[30]

Against this background of internal dissension, developments in both the Korematsu and Endo cases made another shift in strategy necessary. Wayne Collins filed a petition for certiorari in the Korematsu case with the Supreme Court on February 8. After months of silence, War Department lawyers rejoined the legal battle with a request that the Justice Department cooperate in a judicial test of General DeWitt's evacuation orders. In a February 25 letter to Attorney General Biddle, John J. McCloy pointed out that "while the question of the legality of evacuation was specifically reserved in the Supreme Court's decision in the Hirabayashi case, the principles which were enunciated as a basis for the decision may well compel a decision in favor of the government in the Korematsu case." Adding that the Court of Appeals had extended the Supreme Court's approval of DeWitt's curfew orders to evacuation, McCloy told Biddle that "I would not like to see any action taken by the government which might be considered as casting doubt" on the constitutional connection between the two cases.[31]

Speaking for Biddle in a response to McCloy's letter, Solicitor General Fahy displayed his usual caution. The position of the Justice Department, he told McCloy, was that the Court of Appeals had correctly interpreted the *Hirabayashi* opinion "as controlling on the question of the validity of evacuation." He added that the Justice Department's answer to Collins's certiorari petition stated that "the validity of subsequent detention is not properly in issue" in the Korematsu case. Only if the Court desired to review the detention issue would Fahy support a hearing. However, Collins had ignored this point in the brief that accompanied his petition, and Fahy had no intention of filling in this gap.[32]

Depite Fahy's hint that it let the Court of Appeals opinion stand, the Supreme Court announced on March 27 that it would hear the Korematsu case and scheduled argument for the two-week period that began on April 17. Since the Court of Appeals had put the Endo case on its calendar for May 16, after the last argument session in the Supreme Court, there seemed no chance that the two cases could be argued together in Washington. Ennis and Baldwin resigned themselves to this prospect. To their surprise, James Purcell and Judge Denman joined in a frantic effort to certify the Endo case to the Supreme Court in time for argument with Korematsu. Denman, who believed that General DeWitt's evacuation orders were part of a "single program" that led inexorably to "deportation and imprisonment in a relocation stockade," took an unusual judicial initiative. "He called me and said he thought the case raised issues of national importance," Purcell recalled, "and asked if I would object to certification. I told him I would be delighted." On April 14 Purcell filed a motion asking the Court of Appeals to certify the case, and Denman promptly informed Frank Hennessey, the U.S. attorney in San Francisco, that he would hear arguments on the motion on April 24.[33]

This unexpected development produced a flurry of action on both sides. John Burling, acting for Edward Ennis, immediately urged Fahy to remain neutral on the issue. Reminding him that "we have not taken a definite position in our brief" on detention, Burling wrote that "I do not see how we could very well oppose the motion to certify." Fahy remained skeptical about certification. "I think the Circuit Court should decide this case," he replied to Burling on April 17. "It is pretty late to certify the question to the Supreme Court and have it properly presented at this Term."[34]

Fahy learned the next day, however, that Judge Denman had already drafted the questions he intended to present to the Supreme Court and had decided to dispense with the scheduled hearing. Denman called A. J. Zirpoli, the assistant U.S. attorney who was handling the Endo case, into his chambers on April 18 and showed him the questions. Zirpoli promptly called Burling in Washington and alerted him that "Denman was seeking to coerce the Government into agreeing" with Purcell's certification motion. "Zirpoli stated that Denman had asked him to send a telegram to the Department" requesting that it cooperate, Burling reported to Ennis, "which Zirpoli refused to do on the ground that it would have been insulting." Zirpoli also told Burling that Denman's questions "were unfavorable to the Government." After a quick consultation with Fahy, Burling called Zirpoli back and instructed him "not to take an adamant position not to certify but to indicate the feeling that the Solicitor General was opposed to it." He suggested that Zirpoli inform Denman that the Supreme Court had scheduled its last oral argument for May 3 and that since lawyers on both sides would need at least two weeks to prepare and print their briefs, "it would be impossible to get the case argued this term." Zirpoli agreed that this fact should dissuade Denman "since Denman's anxiety to get the case certified was based on his belief that it could be rushed to the Supreme Court this Term."[35]

Denman was determined, however, to proceed with his plan despite the Justice Department's opposition. He issued the certificate on April 22 and rushed it to the Supreme Court, where it was filed in the Clerk's office three days later. The four questions that accompanied the certificate were, as Zirpoli had reported, worded in a manner hostile to the government. Denman phrased the first and most important question in these terms: "Has the War Relocation Authority the power to hold in its custody . . . an American citizen, now more than twenty months after such citizen has been evacuated from her residence in California, without any right in such citizen to seek a release from such custody in a hearing by the Authority with the substantial elements of due process for the determination of facts warranting her further detention, because such citizen is of Japanese ancestry?" Denman's additional questions cast doubt on the power of WRA officials to require that Endo comply with WRA leave regulartions after a determination that she "is loyal to the United States."[36]

Belated as it was, certification of the Endo case fit into the strategy fashioned three months earlier by Edward Ennis and Roger Baldwin, which anticipated the simultaneous argument of the Korematsu and Endo cases before the Supreme Court. The obvious weakness of the Endo case on constitutional and statutory grounds, they reasoned, might lead the Court to strike down evacuation as well as detention. Judge Denman's abrupt action, however, threw this strategy into disarray in giving Solicitor General Fahy a chance to convince the Supreme Court that both cases should be deferred until the fall of 1944. An additional complication was that James Purcell, who was tied up with other cases in San Francisco, had authorized Wayne Collins to argue the Endo case on his behalf. Expecting to argue the Korematsu case during the week of April 24, Collins took a train to Washington on the 19th. In anticipation of Denman's certification move, Collins brought with him a letter from Purcell designating him to argue the Endo case as well.[37]

Rodger Baldwin had already tried to displace Collins from the Korematsu case. He suggested to Ernest Besig on March 28, the day after the Supreme Court voted to hear the case, that Osmond Fraenkel was "quite keen" to present the argument. Besig replied directly to Fraenkel that Collins had rejected the offer, "much as he appreciates your kind offer to supplement what he has to say." Baldwin tried a month later to keep Collins away from the Supreme Court in the Endo case. He wrote Besig on April 24 that Charles Horsky had volunteered to brief and argue the case, and he asked Besig to see whether Purcell would accept Horsky as a replacement for Collins. Reminding Baldwin that the ACLU national board had earlier withheld support for the case, Besig added that Purcell's earlier reaction to this lack of confidence "may help you in appreciating his present response to your offer."[38]

With Collins now camped out in Washington, Ennis moved to defer Supreme Court action on the Endo case. He had learned from Horsky that Collins would ask the Court to put off argument in the Korematsu case if the two cases were not heard together. On April 26, the day after Denman's certificate reached the Court, Ennis suggested to Fahy that "the only proper course seems to be to send the [Endo] case back at once" to the Court of Appeals for argument and decision, adding that "an extra burden is cast upon the Government to protect the rights of these individuals because of serious inadequacy of their counsel." Fahy complied with this request, and the Supreme Court acted first with an announcement on May 2 that the Korematsu case "will not be argued this term." Rather than return the Endo case to San Francisco, however, the Court accepted Denman's certificate and ordered on May 8 that both cases be argued at the beginning of the next term in October 1944.[39]

The Court's action meant that Mitsuye Endo would remain behind barbed wire until the decision in her case. On the other hand, Ennis and Baldwin now had time to reshape their strategy. At Baldwin's suggestion, Horsky met with Ennis and Burling to discuss the Korematsu case. His Justice Department friends stressed that a Supreme Court reversal of Korematsu's conviction "depends upon a demonstration that the case involves more than evacuation," Horsky reported. "Jack thinks that if it is properly argued, the Court will be forced to pass on the detention issue but it is still a point which was not raised at any time in the proceedings below." The three lawyers agreed that only by linking evacuation with detention could the Court be persuaded that its *Hirabayashi* opinion was not controlling.[40]

Baldwin got a similar lecture when he met with Ennis and Burling on May 31. He reported to Osmond Fraenkel that "they insist we file a brief amicus curiae in the Korematsu case. It need be practically only on one point—that evacuation meant detention." Horsky later said about these strategy sessions that "Ennis was going to the limit of propriety. Eddie was pressing the boundaries of what a government lawyer could properly do in a case, although he felt very strongly about it." Horsky added, however, that "detention was an obvious point to make, and would have been made whether he suggested it or not." With four months available for the task, Horsky set to work on the ACLU brief.[41]

Pressure from West Coast politicians, especially California Governor Culbert Olson and Attorney General Earl Warren, had influenced General DeWitt to press for the evacuation and internment of Japanese Americans in 1942. Similar pressures from the West Coast congressional delegation affected President Roosevelt's decision to authorize these programs through Executive Order 9066. Two years later, Roosevelt's concern for partisan advantage in the 1944 congressional elections persuaded the President to reject the recommendations of DeWitt's successors that "military necessity" no longer required internment or the continued exclusion of Japanese Americans from their West Coast homes. The lawyers who drafted the Korematsu and Endo briefs over the summer and fall of 1944 remained unaware of the behind-the-scenes debate over the politics of detention. The background of this debate, and the series of remarkable White House meetings at which Roosevelt turned down proposals to end internment and exclusion, illustrate in its most naked form the dominance of politics over law when the two collide.

During the period that DeWitt headed the Western Defense Command, there was no question that Japanese Americans would remain behind barbed wire. "There isn't such a thing as a loyal Japanese," he stated flatly in January 1943 to General Allen Gullion, rejecting a WRA proposal that camp residents cleared for "loyalty" be released to work in war plants. As the tide of war turned in the Pacific and public hostility toward Japanese Americans eased, however, DeWitt's hard-line policies finally exhausted the patience of War Department officials who viewed him as a hindrance to the eventual end of internment. On September 17, 1943, DeWitt was transferred (and in effect cashiered) from the Presidio in San Francisco to the Army and Navy Staff College in Washington. He was succeeded by General Delos C. Emmons, a West Point graduate and longtime commander of the Army Air Force. Emmons came to California from Hawaii, where he had replaced General Short as Army commander ten days after Pearl Harbor. The fact that Emmons had resisted pressures for the mass internment of Japanese in Hawaii, who made up more than a third of the population and had been castigated as "saboteurs" by Navy Secretary Frank Knox and by the Roberts Commission report on the Pearl Harbor attack, made his choice to succeed DeWitt significant and signaled a shift in attitude toward West Coast internment.[42]

Shortly after Emmons arrived at the Presidio, WRA Director Dillon Myer met with Assistant Secretary of War McCloy to urge a review of the internment and exclusion programs. After their Pentagon meeting on October 5, 1943, Myer wrote McCloy to suggest "the return of evacuees to the West Coast" after the War Department decided that "the military necessity for total exclusion from this area no longer exists." Myer pointed out that the WRA had nearly completed its program of loyalty screening and the segregation of "disloyal" Japanese Americans in the Tule Lake internment camp. In a reference to the Endo case,

Myer added that he doubted "whether continued detention and continued exclusion from the evacuated areas, under present military conditions, would be sustained by the courts." Myer asked McCloy that "you and General Emmons" work with WRA officials "for the purpose of reviewing the whole problem."[43]

A month after he met with Myer, McCloy raised the issue with Emmons and sent him a copy of Myer's letter. "I suppose that we might as well face the fact that before the end of the war," McCloy added in a letter of his own, "the day will come when we cannot in honesty say that exclusion of all Japanese is still essential." McCloy warned the new commander, however, that West Coast politics dictated a policy of caution. "I do not know how you feel about this West Coast problem," he wrote Emmons on November 5. "I do know that your handling of the Japanese population in Hawaii has elicited favorable comment from many sources. The situation in California is not the same. You have no doubt become aware of the existence of active and powerful minority groups in California whose main interest in the war seems to take the form of a desire for permanent exclusion of all Japanese" from the West Coast. "This means that considerations other than of mere military necessity enter into any proposal for removal of the present restrictions" on the return of Japanese Americans. McCloy also hinted that Emmons should adopt an arms-length policy toward the WRA. "The War Relocation Authority has somewhat the view that the Army, having accomplished their evacuation," he wrote of the Japanese Americans, "has a responsibility in accomplishing their safe return. It is certainly not up to the Army to do any crusading," McCloy concluded.[44]

In his reply to McCloy, Emmons displayed an equal sensitivity to political factors. "This Tule Lake situation has aroused a tremendous amount of anti-Japanese feelings on the West Coast," he remarked about reactions to the recent riot at the segregation camp. Spurred by "the wildest kind of stories" in the press, Emmons told McCloy, "the politicians are riding along at full speed." He suggested that the War Department "let this feeling subside before any considerable number of Japanese are returned to the Coast." Given the WRA's control of the camps, Emmons added, it should be up to Myer "to obtain the support of Governor Warren and other Western States governors on a sound plan for relocating Japanese" in the West Coast states. "I am quite sure that if we ram down their throats any plan" designed by the War Department, Emmons told McCloy, "such political opposition would be aroused as to completely nullify even a perfectly sound plan."[45]

Confronted with opposition from McCloy and Emmons, Myer abandoned his efforts to change War Department policy. Two members of Roosevelt's cabinet, however, soon took up the WRA's crusade for a liberal release-and-return program. Attorney General Francis Biddle, a reluctant advocate of evacuation in 1942, expressed his repentance to Roosevelt on December 30, 1943. "The present practice of keeping loyal American citizens in concentration camps on the basis of race for longer than is absolutely necessary is dangerous and repugnant to the principles of our Government," he wrote the President. Concerned more with partisan politics than legal principle, Roosevelt ignored this appeal from Biddle.[46]

Interior Secretary Harold Ickes, the acerbic and outspoken "curmudgeon" to whose department Roosevelt transferred control of the WRA in February 1944, added his voice to Biddle's. Ickes peppered the President with letters asking that the internment and exclusion programs be ended, to which Roosevelt responded with vague assurances that he would keep Ickes' views in mind. Ickes delegated to Abe Fortas, his chief deputy as Interior Undersecretary, the task of working out with McCloy's office a change in policy. Fortas, a Yale Law School graduate with a decade of service in New Deal legal offices, proved to match McCloy in caution and political sensitivity. Captain John M. Hall, who met with Fortas in March as McCloy's legal advisor, reported that "Fortas was not immediately interested in any modification of the West Coast restrictions" and had urged that "any substantial resettlement is impossible until a thorough public relations job has been done." Fortas suggested to Hall a two-step program "to build up public confidence in the manner in which the Japanese are being handled." The first step involved completion of the WRA's loyalty screening process and the subsequent transfer to the Justice Department of control over the Tule Lake segregation camp. As a second step, Fortas recommended establishment of "an inter-departmental board . . . through which all persons of Japanese descent would have to clear before being released" from internment. Along with these programs, designed to persuade the public that no "disloyal" Japanese Americans would be released, Fortas suggested that General Emmons issue an "exhortation" that the West Coast public "be fair to the people" allowed back after the completion of segregation and screening.[47]

Secretary of War Henry L. Stimson brought the detention issue to a head at a White House cabinet meeting on May 26, 1944, two weeks after the Supreme Court deferred argument in the Korematsu and Endo cases until October. Stimson's role in raising the question with Roosevelt was ironic; as a Republican, he had laid down as a condition for assuming his post that he would remain free from considerations of partisan politics. Another irony was that Stimson persuaded Biddle, his deferential fellow cabinet member, to abandon the demand that Roosevelt act to end internment, while Ickes rejected Fortas's cautionary advice and became an advocate of the immediate release of all "loyal" Japanese Americans.[48]

Stimson prepared for the cabinet meeting by discussing with Biddle the political and legal factors involved in the release of Japanese Americans. "Biddle said that there was the likelihood of an adverse decision on our power to hold them . . . in a test case which would not be tried until next fall," Stimson recorded in his diary. He convinced Biddle, however, that the Supreme Court's probable rejection of detention in the Endo case should not dictate an earlier release through presidential action. At the meeting, Stimson told the cabinet that the War Department favored "freeing those who had been screened and found loyal" but cautioned that "careful timing and methods should be used." Stimson's diary entry contained no mention of political factors, citing as "the only military reason for not setting them free" the prospect that violence against Japanese Americans might provoke "reprisals in Japan against our own prisoners." Biddle's notes, however, recorded that Stimson had admitted that internment could be ended "without danger to defense considerations but doubted the wisdom of doing it at this time before the election." Roosevelt ended the discussion, according to Stimson, with a decision that "the evacuees should be distributed in small numbers over the United States rather than dumped on California." Such a policy, of course, would prevent Japanese Americans from returning to their hmmes.[49]

The only dissenter at the cabinet meeting was Interior Secretary Ickes, who argued for total and immediate release. He expanded on his objections in a letter to Roosevelt on June 2 urging "revocation of the orders excluding Japanese Americans from the West Coast." Ickes pointed out that Stimson "believes that there is no longer any military necessity" for exclusion, and he cited six reasons to support his argument. Two of these reasons were that the "psychology of Japanese Americans in the relocation centers becomes progressively worse" with continued detention, and that children in the camps "are becoming a hopelessly maladjusted generation, apprehensive of the outside world" and cut off from association with other Americans. Ickes based these arguments on reports from Abe Fortas, who had recently visited several internment camps and had been appalled by living conditions in these drab, crowded camps and dismayed by the resentment of their residents. Fortas had also explored the legal issues raised by internment, aided by John P. Frank, who joined his staff after serving as law clerk to Justice

Hugo Black. Ickes heeded Fortas and Frank in arguing that exclusion "is clearly unconstitutional in the present circumstances." His appeal to the President ended with a prediction that "the continued retention of these innocent people in the relocation centers would be a blot upon the history of this country."[50]

Roosevelt responded to Ickes' fervent letter on June 12. "The more I think of the problem of suddenly ending the orders excluding Japanese Americans from the West Coast," he wrote, "the more I think it would be a mistake to do anything drastic or sudden." Roosevelt suggested that Ickes explore two methods of handling what was to the White House a delicate political problem. He first proposed the return of a small number of families to West Coast areas where hostility had receded—"nothing sudden and not in too great quantities at any one time." The President also suggested that Japanese Americans be dispersed across the rest of the country—"one or two families to each county as a start." Roosevelt reminded Ickes of the need to placate public opinion. "As I said at Cabinet, I think the whole problem, for the sake of internal quiet, should be handled gradually," he concluded.[51]

Before Roosevelt sent this letter to Ickes, War Department officials had begun drafting a plan for the return of Japanese Americans to the West Coast. General Emmons, after a review of measures to protect defense facilities against sabotage, concluded that the "military necessity" for exclusion had ended and proposed to McCloy that a "subtantial number" of families be permitted to return to their homes. When Roosevelt called him to the White House on June 13, McCloy expected a discussion of the plan drawn up by Emmons. He was surprised to find himself in the middle of a political strategy session. When McCloy returned to his Pentagon office, he called Emmons to report on the meeting. "I just came from the President a little while ago," McCloy said; "he put thumbs down on this scheme." Roosevelt had repeated his instructions to Ickes that Japanese Americans be returned "very gradually" to the West Coast. "He was surrounded at the moment by his political advisors," McCloy added, "and they were harping hard that this would stir up the boys in California and California, I guess, is an important state." McCloy spoke at the same time to Colonel Joel Watson, who headed Emmons's legal staff, and added that Roosevelt had insisted no publicity be given to the return of Japanese Americans. "He doesn't want, in other words, to stir up the California situation," McCloy said.[52]

McCloy accepted Roosevelt's directive and passed it on to the Presidio in San Francisco. He received another surprise two weeks later. Emmons was reassigned at the end of June to the Army Air Force and was replaced as head of the Western Defense Command by General Charles H. Bonesteel, a third-generation West Point graduate who came from the command of Allied troops in Iceland. McCloy wrote to Bonesteel on June 27, informing him that Roosevelt had rejected the plan drafted by Emmons for a large-scale return of Japanese Americans to the West Coast. The limited plan approved by the President, McCloy wrote, required that Bonesteel revise Emmons's plan and keep it "secret" to avoid public disclosure.[53]

Bonesteel responded with an emphatic rejection of McCloy's request. "My study of the existing situation leads me to a belief," he wrote McCloy on July 3, "that the great improvement in the military situation on the West Coast indicates that there is no longer a military necessity for the mass exclusion of the Japanese from the West Coast as a whole." Over the next two months, Bonesteel pressed McCloy for permission to revoke the exclusion orders issued by General DeWitt in 1942. Conscious of the electoral concerns behind Roosevelt's directive, McCloy parried with Bonesteel until September, when the General proposed a move that created consternation in the War Department. He had reviewed the Endo case, Bonesteel informed McCloy, and found "that there is nothing in Miss Endo's record which warrants her continued exclusion" from the West Coast. "Under the circumstances," he stated, "I propose to issue a certificate of exemption in the usual form to Miss Endo unless you direct me to take other action."[54]

McCloy understood clearly the sweeping implications of Bonesteel's challenge. Endo's habeas corpus petition sought her release from detention and not a judicial determination that she could return to the West Coast. Exemption from DeWitt's exclusion orders, however, would obviously undermine the WRA's power to require that Endo comply with its leave regulations and would effectively moot the case less than a month before its scheduled argument in the Supreme Court. Bonesteel had discovered that he retained control, under DeWitt's delegation to the WRA of authority to issue leave permits, to act unilaterally and to supersede the WRA in exercising this function. An exemption order based on this retained authority, McCloy recognized, would wipe out both detention and exclusion. Confronted with this ploy, he appealed to Bonesteel to withhold any action. "An order broad enough to moot the case," he argued in a September 19 letter, would have "a very bad effect on the Supreme Court . . . and, as a result, might have a bad effect on the chances of winning the Korematsu case, which is to be argued the same day."[55]

In his reply to McCloy's letter, Bonesteel turned the argument around. Unless he took steps to moot the Endo case by issuing the exemption certificate, Bonesteel countered, the government might lose the Korematsu case as well. He pointed out to McCloy on September 28 that "detention of Miss Endo and others in the centers can only be justified as a necessary incident of the exlusion and evacuation of the Japanese. If this is true, the detention is not warranted if the exclusion is not justified." McCloy's claim that the two issues were separable, and the two cases thus unrelated in the legal questions they raised, did not impress Bonesteel. He had learned, he informed McCloy, "that our opponents intend to tie the Endo and Korematsu cases together very closely and that they intend to use material in the Endo case to assist in winning the Korematsu case." He enclosed with his letter "a statement which shows the strategy and procedure which the attorneys for the Endo and Korematsu interests intend to follow in presenting those cases to the Supreme Court." Bonesteel identified the source of the strategy document only as "first-hand information presented to one of my representatives," but it most likely came from the FBI, which maintained surveillance of Wayne Collins and had earlier offered documents taken from Collins's office to Justice Department lawyers.[56]

This pilfered document convinced Bonesteel that failure to moot the Endo case would "probably jeopardize the Korematsu case." He told McCloy that he saw no effective rebuttal to the argument that "there is no military justification for the continued detention of Miss Endo and that the action of the military authorities in her case is unwarranted and unreasonable." Bonesteel warned that if "the Supreme Court learns, as our opponents plan that it shall learn, that Miss Endo is being detained unreasonably and without proper basis it may result in the loss of the Korematsu case." The determined General applied a final prod to McCloy: "Failure to act will, in my opinion, leave the War Department and the Army open to criticism." Bonesteel left between the lines his opinion of who would deserve the resulting criticism.[57]

This confrontation between the Presidio and the Pentagon ended with the intervention of Solicitor General Fahy. On October 4, a week before Fahy was scheduled to argue the Korematsu and Endo cases before the Supreme Court, McCloy informed Bonesteel that Fahy considered it "very improbable" that the Court would rule on the exclusion issue in either case, and he added that issuance of the exemption certificate "will substantially weaken" the government's position before the Court. Bonesteel bowed to this pressure but in return threatened to issue an order to "drop mass exclusion" and allow the return of Japanese Americans to the West Coast. He wrote McCloy on October 25 that he had drafted a release-and-return plan and proposed a Pentagon conference "any time" after October 30 to work out the final details.[58]

McCloy's response to this proposal displayed once again the impact of politics on the internment issue. Discussions with "those who will have the ultimate decision" on the question, McCloy replied, revealed "a disposition not to crowd action too closely upon the heels of the election." Informing Bonesteel that "many of the considerations will have to be dealt with on high political rather than military levels," he suggested that "we shall have a greater opportunity for constructive plans at a date somewhat later than November 6th." The presidential and congressional elections, McCloy was well aware, would be held on November 7. Bonesteel dutifully remained on the West Coast, and on November 7 Roosevelt gained election to a fourth term and the Democrats picked up four House seats in California.[59]

Politics finally gave way to the legal process at the first cabinet meeting after the elections. Attorney General Biddle raised the issue and "advised the President I thought the Supreme Court, in the Japanese test cases, would turn down the government." He proposed that "it would be wiser for us to turn the Japs back now as the Army had suggested, it having been held up until after election." His electoral problems behind him, Roosevelt agreed and instructed Biddle and Stimson to prepare a plan that would transfer control of the Tule Lake segregation center to the Justice Department and authorize the release of all Japanese Americans certified as "loyal" by Biddle. Stimson assigned the task of reviewing General DeWitt's proclamations and exclusion orders to General Bonesteel. On December 13, 1944, Stimson reported to Roosevelt that the War Department had determined "that the continued mass exclusion from the West Coast of persons of Japanese ancestry is no longer a matter of military necessity." The likelihood of an "unfavorable court decision" in the Edno case, Stimson added, required that detention be ended promptly.[60]

His War Department superiors deprived General Bonesteel of the personal satisfaction of announcing the end of internment and exclusion. After less than six months in the Presidio, he was replaced on December 10 by General Henry C. Pratt. A week later, Pratt issued Public Proclamation No. 21, which rescinded all of DeWitt's evacuation and exclusion orders and restored to all Japanese Americans not subject to individual exclusion orders or interned at Tule Lake "their full rights to enter and remain in the military areas of the Western Defense Command." It is unclear whether or not Pentagon displeasure with his persistent advocacy of this policy lay behind Bonesteel's transfer. However, he drafted the proclamation issued by Pratt and did everything but put his signature on it.[61]

Six months passed between the cabinet meeting on May 26 at which

Stimson stated that the internment of Japanese Americans could be ended "without danger to defense considerations" and his admission to Roosevelt that their mass exclusion from the West Coast "is no longer a matter of military necessity." Roosevelt's desire for partisan advantage in the 1944 elections provides the only explanation for the delay in ending internment. Political pressure influenced the evacuation and internment debates in 1942, and political concerns held up the release of Japanese Americans almost three years later. Between these two episodes, they received a cruel and unnecessary civics lesson in the power of politics to dictate military and judicial decisions.

11

"The Printing Stopped at About Noon"

THE FINAL BATTLE within the ranks of government lawyers over the test cases began late in the afternoon of January 7, 1944. John Burling and Edward Ennis had just received from the War Relocation Authority a copy of the 618-page *Final Report* on the evacuation program submitted to the War Department by General DeWitt. After a hurried reading of the initial chapters, Burling placed a call to the Pentagon office of Captain John Hall. "It is the first we have seen of it, just a few minutes ago," Burling told McCloy's legal deputy. "We have glanced at it and have noticed that it has various references to the participation of this Department in the beginning of the program." Burling then came to the point of his call. Until the Justice Department had a chance to comment on the report, he and Ennis wanted the War Department to hold up its official publication and release to the press."[1]

"I think it is out now," Hall replied blandly. "I don't know whether it has been released, but it has certainly been published." Burling reacted to Hall's statement with incredulity. "You mean it was published," he responded, "without sending anybody in the Department of Justice a copy?" The two lawyers sparred for a few minutes over the past history of DeWitt's report. Burling reminded Hall that in April 1943, during the Justice Department's preparation of the Supreme Court brief in the Hirabayashi case, McCloy had assured Attorney General Biddle that "this report would not be released." Hall admitted his recollection of McCloy's agreement but explained that the Justice Department had not been consulted about the reversal in policy because the report "seemed pretty historical to me." Burling ended the conversation on a note of frustration: "Well, there is nothing I can do except go tell Ennis. He will probably want to speak to Biddle."[2]

Burling's implicit threat that the Attorney General might intercede to block the release of the *Final Report* hung in the air for the next two weeks. Justice Department lawyers made no move during this time to force compliance with their request for an opportunity to comment on the report, while Hall remained silent about plans for its public release. This impasse ended with a splash on January 20, when newspaper headlines across the country reported DeWitt's accusations against the Justice Department and his charges that Japanese Americans were guilty of widespread acts of espionage.

DEWITT RAPS BIDDLE FAILURE TO CHECK JAPS headlined the Los Angeles *Times*. "Reluctance of the Justice Department to enforce restrictions against Japanese aliens on the Pacific Coast and to carry out military requests for control over American citizens of Nipponese ancestry," the *Times* reported, "are disclosed in the War Department's final report on the Japanese evacuation program just made public." In an accompanying editorial, "DeWitt Shows Plenty of Reasons for Removing Japs," the *Times* cited the report's allegations of "Jap spying activity" along the West Coast. "The disclosures not only justify the original ouster of the Japanese population," the editorial concluded, "but show why they should not be permitted to return, at least while the war lasts."[3]

DeWitt's espionage charges dominated most of the press accounts of his report, which had been prepared under the direction of Colonel Karl Bendetsen, the architect and engineer of the evacuation program. The report linked Japanese Americans to submarine attacks on coastal shipping in the weeks that followed Pearl Harbor, citing "hundreds of reports nightly of signal lights visible from the coast, and of intercepts of unidentified radio transmissions" from the mainland to offshore submarines. "Japs Attacked All Ships Leaving Coast," the Washington *Post* headlined its article on the report. In its front-page coverage of DeWitt's charges, the San Francisco *Examiner* attributed the end of the submarine attacks to the evacuation program. "Signals from the shore aided the Japanese in attacks on the west coast early in the war," the *Examiner* reported, quoting DeWitt's statement that evacuation had "virtually eliminated" the reports of shore-to-ship signaling.[4]

Edward Ennis took the release of the *Final Report* as a personal affront. DeWitt's criticism of Justice Department insistence that standards of due process be followed in applying the alien enemy regulations that Ennis had drafted at the outset of the war stung his professional pride. In addition, his realization that the War Department had deliberately withheld the critical sections of the report during preparation of the Hirabayashi brief rankled Ennis. "Those War Department sons of bitches were double-crossing us at every point," he exclaimed in a later interview.[5]

The past record of what Ennis saw as War Department duplicity, however, concerned him less at the time than the potential impact of the *Final Report* on the pending Korematsu case. A month before Justice Department lawyers learned of the report's release in the Washington *Post*, the Court of Appeals in San Francisco had upheld the conviction of Fred Korematsu and a Supreme Court review of that decision seemed inevitable. It was clear to Ennis that the Justice Department would necessarily be required to deal with the *Final Report* in its Korematsu brief, as the official justification of the evacuation program. But he was appalled at the prospect of asking the Supreme Court to take judicial notice of a document that cast doubt on the Attorney General's commitment to the defense of the West Coast against sabotage and espionage. Ennis also harbored doubts about the veracity of DeWitt's allegations that Japanese Americans had engaged in espionage activities well after the Pearl Harbor attack.

As a first step in his effort to protect the Justice Department against possible embarrassment before the Supreme Court, Ennis asked Attorney General Biddle late in January 1944 to put the FBI to work on a dissection of the DeWitt report. Shortly after Biddle approved this request, Ennis and Burling secured his agreement to an additional suggestion that the Federal Communications Commission be asked to report on DeWitt's specific charges that Japanese Americans had maintained radio contact with Japanese submarines along the West Coast. What these two agencies reported to the Attorney General not only refuted DeWitt's espionage allegations, but precipitated an internal battle within the government that lasted for eight months and ended with a dramatic showdown between Justice and War Department lawyers.[6]

The first response to Biddle's requests to the FBI and FCC came in a "Personal and Confidential" memorandum from J. Edgar Hoover on February 7. The FBI had investigated claims in the *Final Report* that "there was a possible connection between the sinking of United States ships by Japanese submarines and alleged Japanese espionage activity on the West Coast," he informed Biddle. Summarizing the results of a thorough search of FBI records, Hoover wrote that "there is no information in the possession of this Bureau . . . which would indicate that the attacks made on ships or shores in the area immediately after Pearl Harbor have been associated with any espionage activity ashore or that there has been any illicit shore-to-ship signaling, either by radio or lights."[7]

Hoover phrased his cover letter to Biddle in cautious terms. In the lengthy memorandum he attached to this letter, however, Hoover more directly rejected the specific espionage allegations in the DeWitt report. DeWitt's claim that "substantially every ship leaving a West Coast port was attacked by an enemy submarine" in the weeks after Pearl Harbor, Hoover noted, could not be "associated with any espionage activity ashore." He pointed out to Biddle that "undoubtedly the Japanese Navy had made preparations for submarines to proceed to the West Coast immediately after Pearl Harbor and, quite naturally, if such preparations were made these attacks would follow."[8]

Hoover's memorandum next addressed DeWitt's allegation that "there were many evidences of the successful communication of information to the enemy" from the mainland, a charge linked in the *Final Report* to three instances of Japanese shelling and bombing of the West Coast in 1942. Only one of these attacks, the ineffective shelling of an oil refinery near Santa Barbara on February 23, 1942, occurred before the evacuation of Japanese Americans. The other two were the shelling of the Oregon coast near Fort Stevens on June 21, and the dropping of an incendiary bomb in a forest near Brookings, Oregon, on September 9. FBI investigations of each attack, Hoover reported, turned up "no evidence of shore-to-ship signaling and no evidence of a landing in the area." Hoover attributed the Japanese choice of targets in these attacks to the fact that "the Japanese had for years prior to the outbreak of the war collected information as to locations of military and naval installations, as well as data relative to the coast lines of the United States," a fact confirmed by the 1941 break-in of the Japanese consulate in Los Angeles and the subsequent arrest of Itaru Tachibana, who headed the Japanese espionage network on the West Coast.[9]

The Hoover memorandum satisfied Ennis that the DeWitt report contained "false and erroneous statements about shore-to-ship signaling in the period before evacuation." Ennis was more concerned by assertions in the *Final Report* of illicit radio transmissions to Japanese submarines, especially since DeWitt charged the Justice Department with having "impeded" the Army's search for clandestine transmitters. After an informal inquiry to the staff of the Federal Communications Commission, the civilian agency responsible for the monitoring of all radio operations, Ennis reported to Biddle on February 26 that the FCC was "disturbed by the false statements about illegal radio transmitters" made by DeWitt.[10]

Ennis drafted for the Attorney General a letter to the FCC chairman, James Lawrence Fly, requesting a report on FCC radio-monitoring operations on the West Coast between December 1941 and July 1942. The Justice Department request specifically asked whether the FCC "was engaged in endeavoring to identify radio signals reported to be from unlawful radio transmitters and whether it attempted to locate such transmitters." Asking that he "be advised of the extent of [*sic*] which the information above requested was transmitted to General DeWitt or his subordinates," Biddle noted the Justice Department's responsibility "for any statement of facts in support of evacuation in pending and future litigation on the constitutionality of various aspects of the evacuation program."[11]

By the time Fly sent his first reply to the questions posed to the FCC on February 26, the Supreme Court had voted to review the Korematsu case, and Justice Department lawyers were hard at work on the government's brief. Fly's initial report, dated April 1, and a follow-up memorandum sent to the Justice Department three days later, left Ennis and John Burling in a virtual state of shock. The FCC chairman provided documentation that DeWitt had been personally informed by the FCC staff, both before his evacuation recommendation and afterward, that *not one* of the reports of illicit radio transmissions had been verified. In his April 1 memorandum to Biddle, Fly reviewed in detail the FCC's monitoring operations and the reports from his staff of the Army's own operations. "The fact is that military personnel was entirely incapable of determining whether or not the many reports of illicit signaling were well-founded," he reported in summarizing his staff reports. "The basic trouble observed was the lack of training and experience of military personnel carrying on the monitoring and direction-finding work."[12]

Fly cited in his April 1 report a long list of training deficiencies and technical errors on the part of DeWitt's radio intelligence staff. The cumulative effect of these problems, most of them attributable to the inexperience of recently drafted operators and to out-of-date and poorly maintained equipment and technical instructions, was that the Army "repeatedly made wholly inaccurate reports of the existence of illicit stations along the West Coast." Fly ended his first report to Biddle with this conclusion: "In view of such inadequacies as these in the Army's handling of radio intelligence matters and the fact that the Commission's investigations of hundreds of reports, by the Army and others, of unlawful or unidentified radio signals showed that in each case there either was no radio transmission involved or that it was legitimate, the statements in the Report indicating the existence of illicit radio signaling along the West Coast cannot be regarded as well-founded."[13]

The most conclusive evidence of misrepresentation in the *Final Report* came in two memoranda submitted to Fly by George E. Sterling, who headed the FCC's Radio Intelligence Division. The first was a report of a meeting held in DeWitt's office at the Presidio on January 9, 1942, more than a month before DeWitt recommended the mass evacuation of Japanese Americans and more than a year before his *Final Report* cited "the interception of illicit radio transmissions" as a justification for the evacuation. Only four days before he invited Sterling to this meeting, DeWitt had clashed with James Rowe over the Justice Department's reluctance to authorize warrantless raids on the homes of Japanese Americans in the search for shortwave radio transmitters. In this atmosphere of apprehension, Sterling met with DeWitt and five members of his staff, including the head of Army intelligence and the Chief Signal Officer of the Western Defense Command.[14]

Sterling's account of this conference, prepared later that day, bristled with scorn and disparagement of DeWitt and his staff. He reported that DeWitt opened the meeting with "quite a discourse on the Japanese" and claims of "radio transmitters operated by enemy agents in California sending messages to ships at sea." He continued, "Since Gen'l DeWitt seemed concerned and, in fact, seemed to believe that the woods were full of Japs with transmitters, I proceeded to tell him and his staff" about the organization and procedures of the FCC's radio monitoring operations. "I explained how we determined the general area in which an unauthorized station was operating and how we closed in on it with mobile units and other specialized equipment, including the all-frequency response receiver. I know it virtually astounded the General's staff officers."[15]

Sterling confessed his astonishment at the inadequancies of the Army's operations. "Frankly, I have never seen an organization that was so hopeless to cope with radio intelligence requirements." The FCC official's list of Army deficiencies was extensive. "The personnel is unskilled and untrained. Most are privates who can read only ten words a minute. They know nothing about signal identification, wave propagation and other technical subjects, so essential to radio intelligence procedure. They take bearings with loop equipment on Japanese stations in Tokio . . . and report to their commanding officers that they have fixes on Jap agents operating transmitters on the West Coast. These officers, knowing no different, pass it on to the General and he takes their word for it. It's pathetic to say the least."[16]

One consequence of his meeting with Sterling was that DeWitt sent a formal request to the War Department on January 15, 1942, for "the immediate establishment of a joint Radio Intelligence Center for the purpose of coordinating and evaluating radio intercept . . . information now being collected by the Army, Navy, and FCC." In a memorandum to Fly on March 25, 1944, Sterling reported on the activities of this installation between December 1941 and July 1942. Assisted and observed by members of DeWitt's staff, the FCC operated sixteen monitoring stations on the West Coast as well as mobile units capable of pinpointing "the exact house and room in which a transmitter was located if necessary." Early in 1942, the FCC set up at DeWitt's request a system of roving coastal patrols equipped with mobile direction-finding units. "The particular purpose of these patrols was to ferret out any enemy transmission from the shore to ships at sea," Sterling noted. These units had investigated a total of 760 reports of suspicious radio signals in the period that ended on July 1, 1942. Of this number, 641 turned out not to be radio signals at all. The remaining 119 reports were traced to Army and Navy transmitters, licensed commercial stations, police equipment, stations located in Japan, and phonograph oscillators. "No cases involved signals which could not be identified," concluded Sterling. In a later interview, Sterling was emphatic in stating that "there wasn't a single illicit station and DeWitt knew it." He characterized DeWitt's staff as "completely incapable" of conducting radio intelligence work. When he received a copy of the *Final Report* from DeWitt, Sterling had underlined in red ink its claim about illicit transmission. "I was surprised that it had been left in the Report after the information we had furnished the General and his staff," he recalled.[17]

Fly summarized Sterling's reports in a memorandum to the Attorney General on April 4, 1944, in which he also answered Biddle's inquiry about "the extent to which General DeWitt or his subordinates were informed of the operations of the Commission's Radio Intelligence Division." The FCC chairman assured Biddle that DeWitt and his staff "were kept continuously informed of the Commission's work, both through occasional conferences and day-to-day liason." Fly concluded his report with this assurance: "There were no radio signals reported to the Commission which could not be identified, or which were unlawful. Like the Department of Justice, the Commission knows of no evidence of any illicit radio signaling in this area during the period in question."[18]

The bombshells of the FBI and FCC reports did not explode until the final battle over the Korematsu brief. Assuming that the Supreme Court would hear the case in May 1944, John Burling first alerted Solicitor General Fahy to the significance of the reports in an April 13 memorandum. The "unmistakable inference" of the *Final Report*, Burling wrote, was that "among the most important factors making evacuation necessary" were reports of "frequent signaling by unlawful radio transmitters from Japanese-Americans on shore to submarines at sea." Burling noted that the FBI had concluded that "no one was ever seen signaling from a house or elsewhere to Japanese ships off shore" and that the FCC had found that "there was no unlawful radio signaling going on." Burling did not mince words in his conclusion: "We are now therefore in possession of substantially incontrovertible evidence that the most important statements of fact advanced by General DeWitt to justify the evacuation and detention were incorrect, and furthermore that General DeWitt had cause to know, and in all probability did know, that they were incorrect at the time he embodied them in his final report to General Marshall."[19]

The decision by the Supreme Court to defer argument of the Korematsu and Endo cases until October provided Justice Department lawyers with a respite from the dilemma that faced them. The prospect of a confrontation with the War Department over the veracity of the *Final Report* seemed inevitable, and Burling and Ennis were relieved when they learned early in May that they would not face a showdown with only a few days available to reach agreement on the wording of the Supreme Court briefs. Burling in particular was concerned that the War Department might repeat the tactic it employed in the Hirabayashi case, when it executed an end-run around the Justice Department by placing an earlier version of the *Final Report* before the Supreme Court in the guise of an amicus brief prepared for the West Coast states by Captain Herbert Wenig. Burling's suspicions were confirmed, he reported to Ennis on April 25, when he learned from a "highly confidential informant in the War Department" that Attorney General Kenny of California intended to file an amicus brief in the Korematsu case and that "this brief may be prepared with the collaboration of the Western Defense Command."[20]

Burling's informant was correct in confirming that Wenig had resumed his dual role as an Army lawyer and assistant to Kenny. Expecting to conceal their surreptitious efforts from the Justice Department a second time, Army lawyers reached an agreement late in March with General Delos Emmons (who had succeeded DeWitt by that time) to "collaborate fully, but informally," with Kenny and his West Coast counterparts "in the preparation of a joint brief to be filed by them as amicus curiae" in the Korematsu case. Word of the FBI and FCC reports to the Justice Department, however, reached McCloy's office in the Pentagon and apparently forced a shift in War Department tactics. Colonel Harrison Gerhardt, McCloy's executive officer, warned the head of Army intelligence on May 1 that the Justice Department "does not believe" the espionage claims in the *Final Report*. Most likely as a consequence of this warning, the West Coast amicus brief carefully avoided any citation to the report and simply directed the Supreme Court to its *Hirabayashi* opinion for support of DeWitt's evacuation program.[21]

By the time that Burling completed a draft of the Korematsu brief in early September, he was determined to make a frontal attack on the *Final Report*. The sole concession in his brief to the "military necessity" claim advanced by the War Department was an admission that Army officials, in the period that preceded evacuation, had "ample ground to believe that imminent danger then existed of an attack by Japan upon the West Coast." Burling appended to this statement, which referred the Court to the earlier Hirabayashi brief for support, a footnote designed to alert the Court to the Justice Department's disavowal of the DeWitt report:

"The Final Report of General DeWitt is relied on in this brief for statistics and other details concerning the actual evacuation and the events that took place subsequent thereto. The recital of the circumstances justifying the evacuation as a matter of military necessity, however, is in several respects, particularly with reference to the use of illegal radio transmitters and to shore-to-ship signaling by persons of Japanese ancestry, in conflict with information in the possession of the Department of Justice. In view of the contrariety of the reports on this matter we do not ask the Court to take judicial notice of the recital of those facts contained in the Report."[22]

Burling's attempt to wave this red flag before the Supreme Court first encountered opposition from Solicitor General Fahy. Unwilling to disclose to the Court the existence of the FBI and FCC reports, Fahy amended the footnote to read simply that "the views of this Department" differed from those of the War Department on the contested issues. Although the change in wording seemed minor, it concealed the existence of the FBI and FCC reports that refuted DeWitt's espionage charges. Burling promptly appealed to Assistant Attorney General Herbert Wechsler in an effort to retain the footnote in its original form. A former Columbia Law School professor, Wechsler had replaced Fahy as director of the War Division over the summer and now shared supervision of the Korematsu brief with the Solicitor General. Burling reminded Wechsler in a September 11 memorandum that the FBI and FCC had identified "intentional falsehoods" in the *Final Report*. "In view of the fact that General DeWitt in his official report on the evacuation has sought to justify it by making important misstatements of fact," Burling wrote, "I think it is important that this Department correct the record insofar as possible and certainly we should not ask the Court to take judicial notice of these facts."[23]

Burling reviewed for Wechsler the record of conflict over DeWitt's report. Noting that the War Department had earlier claimed the document was "secret" but had leaked it to the West Coast attorney generals for use in their amicus briefs in the Hirabayashi case, Burling also claimed that Captain John Hall had made "untrue" statements in January 1944 about the report's publication. "In view of all these circumstances," Burling told Wechsler, "it seems to me that the present bowdlerization of the footnote is unfortunate. There is in fact a contrariety of information and we ought to say so." He predicted another conflict with McCloy: "I assume that the War Department will object to the footnote and I think we should resist any further tampering with it with all our forces."[24]

Edward Ennis and John McCloy had first clashed over the evacuation of Japanese Americans at the acrimonious meeting in Attorney General Biddle's living room on February 17, 1942. Although McCloy had won that initial battle, the respective duties of the two lawyers—McCloy's for the implementation of evacuation and Ennis's for its legal defense—almost guaranteed an eventual climax to their personal conflict. Their last confrontation over evacuation began on September 30, 1944. Ennis received a call that Saturday morning from Captain Adrian Fisher, who had recently replaced John Hall as McCloy's legal deputy. Fisher informed Ennis that McCloy had gone over the page proofs of the Korematsu brief and had instructed him to request that the footnote Burling had drafted be changed to remove the repudiation of the *Final Report*. Ennis told his caller that it was too late—the brief was at that moment on the printing presses.[25]

What happened during the forty-eight hours that followed Fisher's call to Ennis turned the long series of skirmishes between Ennis and McCloy into a last-ditch legal battle. According to Burling's account of these climactic two days, McCloy fired the first shot with a call to Solicitor General Fahy shortly before noon on September 30. McCloy made a personal appeal to Fahy for the removal of Burling's footnote. "Presumably at Mr. McCloy's request," Burling wrote, "the Solicitor General had the printing stopped at about noon."[26]

While the presses ground to a halt, Fahy instructed Ennis and Burling to negotiate a solution to the crisis with their War Department opponents. After more than two years of conflict with McCloy over the evacuation issue, the two Justice Department lawyers were in no mood to compromise. Searching through their files for records of the internal conflict, Ennis and Burling sat down after a lunchtime strategy session and drafted a memorandum to Wechsler cast in the form of a virtual indictment of the War Department. In arguing "most strongly" that Burling's footnote be retained without change in the Korematsu brief, they stated that the Justice Department "has an ethical obligation to the Court to refrain from citing" the *Final Report.* The memorandum cited the FBI and FCC reports to Biddle which, Ennis and Burling asserted, "establish clearly that the facts are not as General DeWitt states them in his report and also that General DeWitt knew them to be contrary to his report." DeWitt's claim that "he was forced to evacuate the entire population" of Japanese Americans, Wechsler was told, rested on false allegations that members of this group "were engaged in extensive radio signaling and in shore-to-ship signaling." Ennis and Burling were scathing in their denunciation of the *Final Report:* "The general tenor of the report is not only to the effect that there was a reason to be apprehensive, but also to the effect that overt acts of treason were being committed. Since this is not so it is highly unfair to this racial minority that these lies, put out in an official publication, go uncorrected."[27]

McCloy's move in persuading Fahy to stop the printing of the brief prompted Ennis and Burling to urge that Wechsler take the conflict directly to Attorney General Biddle. "Much more is involved than the wording of the footnote," they insisted. "The failure to deal adequately now with this Report cited to the Supreme Court either by the Government or other parties, will hopelessly undermine our administrative position in relation to this Japanese problem." The two lawyers still feared that the War Department would again smuggle the *Final Report* into the Supreme Court under cover of the amicus brief of the West Coast states. "We have proved unable to cope with the military authorities on their own ground in these matters," they told Wechsler. "If we fail to act forthrightly on our own ground in the courts, the whole historical record of this matter will be as the military choose to state it. The Attorney General should not be deprived of the present, and perhaps only, chance to set the record straight."[28]

Wechsler disregarded the request that he take the question to the

Attorney General; he perhaps did not want to disturb Biddle on a week-end and most likely assumed that his own skills at conciliation would produce a resolution of the internal crisis. Having served as Biddle's special assistant since 1940, Wechsler was secure in the confidence the Attorney General had in him. Wechsler's low-key demeanor—Biddle described him as "cheerfully patient" and praised "the sobriety of his measured judgment"—made him an effective buffer between his agitated subordinates and the cautious but hot-tempered Solicitor General. In contrast to Ennis and Burling, whose hostility to McCloy made the issue to them one of personal vindication as well as a question of professional integrity, Wechsler's lack of a private stake in the conflict disposed him toward an accommodation with the War Department. In a later interview, Wechsler defined his position on the disputed footnote as that of searching for "negotiated language in a situation that from the War Department's and the Solicitor General's point of view was a public relations problem."[29]

Wechsler did, however, send the Ennis-Burling memorandum to Solicitor General Fahy on the afternoon of September 30. The two lawyers had attached to it a complete record of the conflict over the DeWitt report, including the FBI and FCC reports to Biddle and a transcript of Burling's conversation with John Hall on January 7, 1944, which they claimed "clearly brings out the evasion and falsehood used in connection with the publication of the report" on the part of the War Department.[30]

Confronted with the outrage expressed by Ennis and Burling, and with the full record before him for the first time, Fahy decided to stand behind the original version of the Burling footnote. He was consequently in no mood to sympathize with the request brought to him by Adrian Fisher at six o'clock on Saturday afternoon. According to Fisher, McCloy had received a teletype from DeWitt's office urging that the War Deaprtment insist that the Supreme Court take judicial notice of the *Final Report*. McCloy accordingly dispatched Fisher to Fahy's office as his emissary. "I've never seen such an explosion in my life," Fisher later said. "He said 'No—we didn't know anything about the report, it's a terrible document, and you people didn't approve of its publication. I'm going to put a footnote in the brief expressly disavowing it and saying the Court should pay no attention to it.' "[31]

Burling's account of this confrontation, prepared two days later, differed from Fisher's recollections. "Captain Fisher took the position that he would not defend the accuracy of the report but that the Government would deal with sufficient honesty with the court if it would merely refrain from reciting the report without affirmatively flagging our criticism thereof." Fisher and Burling differed as well on the outcome of the September 30 meeting. Fahy's response, Fisher later said, was to say after his initial outburst that "I will not put in the express disavowal if you can give me the War Department's assurance that they will not try to have this document made part of the record." Presumably, Fahy was demanding that McCloy keep the *Final Report* out of the amicus brief of the West Coast states. Burling's account, based on a report from Herbert Wechsler, who attended the meeting, was that Fahy informed Fisher that "he would think about it over Sunday but that he was disposed to keep the footnote in some manner."[32]

Fahy was still committed on Monday, October 2, to a footnote that alerted the Supreme Court to the "contrariety of reports" about DeWitt's claims of radio transmissions and signaling by Japanese Americans. Encouraged by this show of support, Ennis and Burling decided to press for a further repudiation of DeWitt's criticisms of the Justice Department. The two lawyers agreed, according to Burling, "that an effort should be made to make clear that there were misstatements other than those pertaining to radio transmitting and signaling, particularly with respect to the activities of this Department." Ennis and Burling took the draft of their proposed footnote to Wechsler, only to discover that Wechsler had already sent Fahy's toned-down version to the Justice Department print shop with instructions to resume printing of the Korematsu brief.[33]

Urging that Fahy be given a chance to consider the more critical draft of the footnote, Ennis and Burling held out the threat that they would refuse to sign the brief. Prompted by desperation and frustration, this tactic confronted Wechsler with a serious dilemma. It was likely, he recognized, that a sharp-eyed member of the Supreme Court (or one of the law clerks) would notice the omission of Ennis's and Burling's names from the brief, since both lawyers had signed the government's brief on the Hirabayashi case, and surmise that there was dissension within the Justice Department over the Korematsu case. Confronted with rebellion on the part of his subordinates, Wechsler placed a call to Ralph F. Fuchs, the lawyer on Fahy's staff who had been delegated responsibility for the final drafting and printing of the Korematsu brief, and ordered a second halt of the printing presses.[34]

Ennis and Burling soon learned that their last-second tactic had failed. Wechsler promptly drafted an alternative to the footnote that Fahy had handed him earlier that morning. Designed to break the impasse with the War Department, this substitute eliminated any reference to the espionage allegations in the DeWitt report: "We have specifically recited in this brief the facts relating to the justification for the evacuation, of which we ask the Court to take judicial notice; and we rely upon the Final Report only to the extent that it relates to such facts."[35]

Wechsler's choice of wording was undoubtedly intended to distinguish between reliance on DeWitt's claims that the failure of the "voluntary migration" campaign justified forcible evacuation and endorsement of the disputed espionage allegations. As a matter of semantics, however, it was possible to interpret this version of the footnote as supporting the entirety of the *Final Report*. The "facts" cited in the brief on the evacuation question included the Court's finding in its *Hirabayashi* opinion that "[e]spionage by persons in sympathy with the Japanese Government" had aided the Pearl Harbor attack, and the assertion that "the opportunity for espionage and sabotage" on the West Coast justified evacuation. Even if read as Wechsler obviously expected, as a careful distinction between the two elements of the DeWitt report, his version would require a discriminating between-the-lines reading to discern any substantive criticism of the report.[36]

With his substitute draft and Burling's original version in hand, Wechsler presented both to Fahy. Pressed for time, and perhaps unwilling to exacerbate the dispute within the Justice Department, Fahy reacted with a display of indecision. The Solicitor General told Wechsler that either version was acceptable to him. Rather than deciding the issue himself, however, Fahy directed that Wechsler put the choice to Captain Fisher. According to Burling, Wechsler called the Pentagon shortly before noon; after reading to Fisher both versions of the footnote, Wechsler "asked him to select whichever was the least displeasing to the War Department." Sharing Fahy's reluctance to risk any further confrontation with McCloy, Wechsler made his preference clear. "I think we could drop out any specific reference to matters in controversy," he told Fisher, noting that his own watered-down version was "put in the gentlest conceivable way."[37]

Although Fisher needed no prompting, he was obviously unwilling to make a decision before consultation with McCloy and asked Wechsler for a half-hour in which to reply. Since Wechsler had a prior engagement, he instructed Burling to take the return call from the Pentagon. When Fisher called back at noon, he informed Burling that although "he desired to maintain his position of objecting to any footnote" that cast doubt on the DeWitt report, "within the choice given, he greatly prefered Mr. Wechsler's version" over Burling's. In a report to Ennis prepared later that afternoon, Burling summarized this final communication from the War Department: "Captain Fisher and I then discussed the matter and he stated that, as a personal matter, he was not much concerned whether the Supreme Court took judicial notice of the DeWitt report at all but that he was concerned with inter-departmental friction and wear and tear. He was well pleased with Mr. Wechsler's suggestion since it minimized the appearance of controversy between the Departments."[38]

By the chance of Wechsler's schedule, it fell to Burling to raise the flag of surrender in the battle with the War Department over the veracity of the DeWitt report. Burling recorded the outcome of the battle on a note of resignation: "I then informed Mr. Fuchs of Captain Fisher's choice and he and I agreed that the proof should be returned to the printer for final printing." Three days later, on October 5, a Justice Department messenger delivered the Korematsu brief to the Supreme Court clerk. In small type at the bottom of page 11, the footnote drafted by Herbert Wechsler provided the only hint of reservations about the War Department's justification of evacuation. Semantic ambiguity had replaced forthright repudiation. The final page of the brief, urging that the Supreme Court affirm Korematsu's conviction, included the names of Edward Ennis and John Burling. Institutional loyalty had prevailed over personal conscience.[39]

In addition to the unsuccessful effort by Ennis and Burling to repudiate the "lies" in the DeWitt report on the espionage issue, the Korematsu brief provoked a second conflict within the Justice Department. Although it lacked the last-minute showdown with the War Department that added drama to the footnote battle, the internal debate over the detention issue raised equally serious questions about the *Final Report* and the responsibility of the Justice Department to offer an accurate record to the Supreme Court. Complicated by the tangled chronology of DeWitt's evacuation orders, and compounded by the failure of Wayne Collins to press the issue as Korematsu's lawyer, the conflict over detention exposed again the dilemma faced by government lawyers forced to balance professional obligation and personal conviction.

John Burling confronted this dilemma in the Korematsu case with an admitted bias against the entire evacuation and internment program. "As you know, I never believed the evacuation itself necessary," he confessed to Solicitor General Fahy in April 1944. Burling had nonetheless defended evacuation in the Hirabayashi case, believing that "there were grounds of which we could and did ask the Court to take judicial notice, which indicated that it was within the allowable area of military judgment." On its face, the Korematsu case raised only the evacuation question the Court had ducked in the Hirabayashi case. Two factors, however, placed Burling in a bind when Ennis assigned him early in 1944 to draft the Korematsu brief. The first stemmed from the release of the DeWitt report late in January. After the FBI and FCC reports on DeWitt's espionage claims, the two Justice Department lawyers scrutinized the remainder of the *Final Report* closely and with suspicion. What Burling read about the link between evacuation and detention convinced him that DeWitt had misled the War Department on this issue as well.[40]

Two sentences in the *Final Report* led Burling to question the assumption that the Korematsu case did not properly raise the detention issue. In an unstated reference to the April 7, 1942, conference between federal and state officials in Salt Lake City, the report implied that the program of "voluntary migration" from the West Coast had been ended as a result of the opposition expressed at this meeting to any movement of Japanese Americans to the interior states. The *Final Report* put the Army's conclusion in these words: "Essentially, military necessity required only that the Japanese population be removed from the coastal area and dispersed in the interior, where the danger of action in concert during any attempted enemy raids along the coast, or in advance thereof as preparation for a full scale attack, would be eliminated. That the evacuation program necessarily and ultimately developed into one of complete Federal supervision, was due primarily to the fact that the interior states would not accept an uncontrolled Japanese migration."[41]

The obvious implication of this assertion was that the Army intended, at least until the time of the Salt Lake City conference, to permit Japanese Americans to leave the West Coast after a brief period of detention in the assembly centers. Burling was initially willing to defend this assembly center detention on two grounds: first, that it was a temporary phase of the "voluntary migration" program; and, second, that one of its purposes was to afford the Army an opportunity to screen the "disloyal" from the loyal Japanese Americans. After close examination both of the *Final Report* and the record of the Korematsu case, Burling concluded that neither ground was valid. He put his conclusions to Fahy in a memorandum dated April 13, 1944. "Contrary to the assumptions upon which we in this office have been going for some time," Burling wrote, "the original detention was not ordered as a mere temporary expedient, to be in effect for a few days while the persons were removed from California, nor was it in any sense hypothetical or speculative."[42]

Burling based his argument on a conversation with Philip Glick of the War Relocation Authority. Glick had told him, Burling reported to Edward Ennis, that WRA director Milton Eisenhower rather than DeWitt had been responsible for the decision to hold Japanese Americans in assembly centers and subsequently to transfer them, without any opportunity to leave on a voluntary basis, to relocation centers for a period of indefinite internment. "The first move of the liberals was reactionary," Burling quoted Glick. Noting that both DeWitt and Eisenhower claimed that "detention was the only alternative to having the hundred thousand evacuees wandering over the country," Burling quizzed Glick as to why "no effort was made to try out a scheme of providing voluntary assembly or relocation centers to provide shelter for people who did not find anywhere else to go." Replying that "he supposed Eisenhower's opinion on this subject was that there inevitably would be a few reckless people who would go out even though they had no place to go and that these people might stir up violence," Glick added that "once you get around to the theory that you must do something to avoid violence, then detention is a logical consequence."[43]

Burling had no stomach for the "preventive detention" theory that Glick offered as a justification for internment. In his April 13 memorandum to Fahy, Burling admitted that there had been "considerable social commotion when the Japanese started to go eastward" during the period that preceded DeWitt's "freeze order" of March 27, 1942. On the other hand, he stressed, the government "took substantially no steps to reassure the public or to indicate that the spy scares were exaggerated. A really fair attempt at a system of voluntary migration was never attempted." More important to Burling was the difficulty of making a defense of detention to the Supreme Court under the judicial notice doctrine. Referring Fahy to the assertion in the *Final Report* that the detention decision followed the expressions of public hostility voiced at the Salt Lake City conference, Burling noted that "we could only defend detention on the ground that evacuation was necessary and that evacuation could not be carried out without detention."[44]

Aware that Fahy was a stickler for factual accuracy, Burling argued that the allegedly necessary connection between evacuation and detention "is not a matter of law, but is a matter of fact, and almost the only available confirmation of the alleged fact is General DeWitt's statement." The Justice Department "can support detention only if it informs the Court, on the strength of its own reputation for veracity," that DeWitt's claim was factually true. "We, however, believe it is not so," Burling wrote to Fahy; "we know that General DeWitt has made false statements in his evacuation report, and we therefore should not take the position in court" that the *Final Report* constituted an adequate defense of detention. In a subsequent memorandum to Fahy, Burling noted the problem of presenting DeWitt's claim to the Supreme Court:

"The number of Japanese-Americans who would have migrated to the interior, had voluntary camps been provided, is not a fact susceptible of judicial notice, nor is the extent to which civil disorder might have occurred. The validity of detention, therefore, depends upon facts of which the Court cannot readily take notice."[45]

In Burling's opinion, detention was the central issue in the Korematsu case. The sequence of the military orders that applied to Korematsu made it clear that he could not have escaped detention in the Tanforan Assembly Center. Before the "freeze order" that took effect on March 29, 1942, Korematsu was under no legal compulsion either to move from or remain in San Leandro. After that date he had no choice but to remain, subject to further order. Civilian Exclusion Order No. 34, issued on May 3, required that he report for evacuation to Tanforan on the following day, and additionally made it a crime to remain in San Leandro after May 9. In effect, the only legal choice open to Korematsu on May 9 was to report for detention; moving from and remaining in San Leandro were equally proscribed by DeWitt's orders and equally subjected Korematsu to criminal prosecution.[46]

His reading of the record convinced Burling that a challenge to detention was the only alternative to the legal Hobson's choice that Korematsu had confronted. However, he knew that Fahy was unlikely to approve a brief conceding that detention was at issue in the case. Two points of legal doctrine, both related to the particular facts of the Korematsu case, provided Fahy with reasons to sidestep the detention question. The first rested on the judicial doctrine that a defendant who failed to raise a possible defense at trial lacked "standing" to raise the issue on appeal. Korematsu had been charged solely with violating the provision of DeWitt's order that made it a crime to "remain in" San Leandro after May 9, 1942. Neither at the district court trial nor before the Court of Appeals had Wayne Collins attacked the provision that required Korematsu to report for "transfer to" the Tanforan Assembly Center. It was obvious that the government could have included the latter charge in its prosecution of Korematsu. Since it had not, Collins most likely never considered it necessary to raise the detention issue.[47]

Closely related to this point was the "separability" doctrine. Under this judge-made doctrine, a defendant charged with violation of a statute or administrative regulation imposing separate duties on him or her could not attack the legality of a provision not included in the initial charge. Application of this doctrine to the Korematsu case was based on the assumption that the requirements that Korematsu not "remain in" San Leandro after May 9 and that he "report to" the designated civilian control station for transfer to Tanforan were separable aspects of the evacuation program. In legal logic, the separability of these two provisions of DeWitt's order precluded an attack on the detention that would have followed reporting for evacuation. Implicit in this doctrine was the idea that separate duties involved separate remedies for relief from the penalties their violation imposed. In theory, had the government charged Korematsu with failing to report for evacuation, he could have raised additional defenses. And, if Korematsu had reported for evacuation as ordered and subsequently been detained in Tanforan, the remedy of habeas corpus would have been available to him as a challenge to detention.[48]

Burling recognized that invocation of the standing and separability doctrines rested on an argument that the provisions of DeWitt's order did in fact impose separate duties on Korematsu. Given the purpose of the order—that of herding Japanese Americans into Tanforan, with indefinite detention in store—Burling considered this argument an evasion of the issue. Hoping at least to alert the Supreme Court to the legal flaws in the argument that Korematsu could not challenge the detention that faced him, Burling confronted Fahy's determination that the Justice Department was obligated to defend detention. In drafting the Korematsu brief, he took the tack of appealing to Fahy's innate legal caution. Conceding that Collins's failure to raise the issue at trial permitted the government to argue that Korematsu "was without standing to raise any question of detention" before the Supreme Court, Burling urged that Fahy limit the brief to this narrow contention.[49]

In his first memorandum to Fahy on the issue, Burling outlined four possible approaches. He put his own preference in these words: "We could argue that detention is not raised, first, because of various formal procedural considerations, and, second, that the record does not present a basis for determining the grave constitutional questions involved. . . . We could then go on, in urging the Court not to decide these questions in the absence of a fuller record, to explain what the considerations pertaining to detention are as a basis for the argument that the questions cannot be decided in the absence of more facts." If Fahy approved this approach, Burling obviously hoped for a remand to a lower court which might reverse Korematsu's conviction after a hearing that would expose the direct link between evacuation and detention.[50]

Burling's second alternative stepped back from the suggestion that the Court remand the case: "We could argue that detention was not raised and say that if the Court should decide to consider detention, we would not care to take a position." However, the Justice Department would "give the arguments for detention in full" and additionally would "advert to the opposing considerations." The third alternative adopted a hands-off attitude: "We could urge that no question of detention is raised on the present record and merely stop at that point. This clearly would have the advantage of suggesting to the Court that we had doubts as to detention, but would have the greater disadvantage of not giving to the Court our analysis of the legal problems involved."[51]

Burling placed at the end of his strategy outline the approach he considered the least preferable: "After arguing that detention was not raised, we could make an argument that if the Court should permit petitioner to raise it, then it was valid. As I have said, I regard this last alternative as highly undesirable." Noting that his initial draft of the Korematsu brief was "cast in the form of the first alternative above," Burling assured Fahy that he was willing to "rewrite it in the form of alternatives 2 or 3." Reminding the Solicitor General of "the great public and historic importance of not putting this Department in the position of defending the detention of 70,000 American citizens not charged with crime and selected on the basis of race," Burling urged that Fahy "determine personally which alternative you wish pursued."[52]

To his surprise, Burling encountered no opposition from the War Department on the approach to detention he had urged on Fahy. Despite the Pentagon's agreement, Burling still feared that Fahy was wavering on the question. Requesting on April 17 "an opportunity to speak to you before a decision affirmatively is made to support detention," Burling noted to Fahy that the draft of the Korematsu brief avoided "taking the position that American citizens may be detained because they are the objects of race prejudice." Fahy did not respond to the request for a meeting, although the initial deadline for completion of the brief was rapidly approaching. Burling vented his frustration in a memorandum he sent to Ennis on April 21; in a parody of Glick's "preventive detention" theory, he proposed sending to Felix Frankfurter the following addition to the Supreme Court brief:

"The members of this Court must be keenly aware that they are at the present time in danger of mob violence at the hands of Southern legislators. Thus they would be the first to admit that they could be detained by a General seeking to protect them from lynching. Similarly, it will not be denied that persons of the Negro Race could have been concentrated during the Detroit Race Riot last Spring, or that in areas where the Ku Klux Klan threatened violent measures, persons of the Catholic and Jewish faiths could be interned. From this it would seem to follow ineluctably that it was within the due process clause to place persons of Japanese ancestry in protective custody."[53]

Burling lost his battle on the detention issue. As he had feared, Fahy adopted the position that the Justice Department would urge on procedural grounds that the Supreme Court not consider the question, but that the Court should uphold detention if it determined that Korematsu had properly raised the issue. More than half of the final brief filed in October 1944—32 of 59 pages—dealt with these two contentions.

The brief submitted to the Supreme Court began with a concession that, had Korematsu obeyed DeWitt's exclusion order, he "would have found himself for a period of time, the length of which was then not ascertainable, in a place of detention." It did not follow, the brief then argued, "that this detention, which did not become actual, is an issue in the present case." As Burling had suggested before he changed his mind, the brief cited both the standing and separability doctrines to support this contention. Korematsu had been "solely charged with remaining where he had no lawful right to be." His defense at trial "was no broader than this charge and no evidence was introduced by the Government to meet wider issues." The brief further noted that if Korematsu had been charged with failure to report for evacuation, "he could have defended the disobedience charged against him; if he had been detained instead, habeas corpus would have been available to test the validity of his detention."[54]

Although the brief's argument on the standing issue rested on longstanding precedent, application of the doctrine was subject to judicial discretion. The concession that detention would have followed obedience to the exclusion order made reliance on this doctrine a risky proposition. With precedent on the separability issue much less settled, the brief retreated to an argument that rested more on rhetoric than logic. Korematsu "should not now be permitted to seek indirectly to nullify the vital military measure of exclusion . . . because of the claimed invalidity of accompanying features of the exclusion program," the brief suggested. "The exclusion was a measure taken under the urgency of military necessity, based upon a threat of invasion, at a critical point in the war." It would be "scarcely consistent with the national security or welfare," the Court was urged, to allow Korematsu to attack DeWitt's order "not because of its own invalidity but because of the alleged unconstitutionality of the means adopted to effectuate it, when violation of these means is not charged."[55]

Clearly apparent between the lines of the Justice Department's argument on the separability issue was an admission that it stood on shaky precedential scaffolding. The doctrine required, as the Supreme Court had held in one of the five cases cited in the brief, that each element in the challenged statute or regulation have the "capacity to stand alone." In none of these five cases had the defendants been "subjected to actual disadvantage" by the statutory or regulatory provisions claimed to be inseparable from those at issue, the Korematsu brief conceded. On the other hand, Korematsu "was confronted with alternative courses of action which involved either a violation of some feature of the exclusion program or submission to evacuation accompanied by detention." The brief tried to wriggle out of this logical dilemma with circular reasoning. Returning to the standing doctrine, the Justice Department claimed that since Korematsu had been charged solely with remaining in San Leandro, "the alternative he adopted" as a challenge to the exclusion order precluded any collateral attack on detention.[56]

Fahy and Burling obviously shared an awareness that the Supreme Court might yield to a determined assault on the standing and separability arguments. They differed, however, on the fall-back position that detention was defensible in the Korematsu case. The final brief demonstrated that Fahy had prevailed in the internal debate on this question. Burling had argued in April 1944 that the defense of detention in the *Final Report* was factually erroneous, and that the "preventive detention" rationale was not supported by facts of which the Court could properly take judicial notice. Despite Burling's objections, however, the brief that Fahy approved relied almost entirely on DeWitt's claims on detention.

The final brief asserted that detention had replaced "self-arranged migration" for two reasons: first, "to alleviate tension and prevent incidents involving violence between Japanese migrants and others"; and second, "to insure an orderly, supervised, and thoroughly controlled evacuation with adequate provision for the protection of the persons of evacuees as well as their property." Presented as if the only choices open to DeWitt in implementing the evacuation program were those of an "uncontrolled mass evacuation" and forcible detention, the brief disregarded Burling's argument that Japanese Americans should have been offered the alternative of temporary refuge in assembly centers on a voluntary basis. In defending the decision to impose detention on the entire group, the brief asked the Supreme Court to take judicial notice of DeWitt's claims: "The belief of the military authorities in the danger of violence has not been shown to have been unreasonable. The existence of that belief is undisputed. The Final Report of General DeWitt states that 'widespread hostility' had developed 'in almost every state and every community. It was literally unsafe for Japanese migrants' . . ."[57]

The "facts" offered the Court in support of DeWitt's conclusion lacked any specificity: "The report refers to 'one example among many' of actual threats against evacuees. These are said to have numbered 'several thousand.' " In fact, these quotations from the *Final Report* were twisted out of context and misrepresented its actual claims. The "one example" cited in the report was that of "an aged Issei couple" named Hayakawa who moved to Santa Fe, New Mexico, before the "freeze order" of March 1942: "The racial prejudice against the Hayakawas was so severe that the family petitioned Wartime Civil Control Administration requesting that they be permitted to join the evacuees assembled at Tanforan. The Hayakawa case is cited as . . . illustrative of the intensity of public feeling. Multiply this by several thousand and it will become apparent why it was necessary for the Army to abandon voluntary migration." Obviously, the *Final Report* stated neither that "actual threats" had been made against this one family nor that any of the "several thousand" additional cases involved threats of violence. There was in fact no evidence that the Army had compiled such reports. In this regard, the brief's characterization of these claims as "factors of common knowledge" clearly abused the doctrine of judicial notice.[58]

Perhaps aware of this deficiency, Justice Department lawyers shifted to Korematsu the "heavy burden" of countering the claims of the *Final Report*. The brief's inversion of the normal burden of proof on this issue exposed a gap in legal logic. As noted earlier, the Supreme Court brief stated that "no evidence was introduced by the Government to meet wider issues" than those raised by the single charge against Korematsu. The suggestion that Wayne Collins should nonetheless have attempted at the trial level a factual refutation of the *Final Report,* well before it was written or published, bordered on the bizarre. The alternative proposition, that Collins was required to assume this task before the Supreme Court, contradicted the brief's argument on the standing issue. Without making clear to the Court which position it adopted, the Justice Department concluded that Collins had failed a test with no correct answer. "Petitioner has not borne the burden which rested upon him," the brief asserted. "The indications of hostility to the evacuees, which lay at the basis of the decision to impose detention . . . have not been negatived."[59]

The seeming inconsistency of the arguments on standing and the burden of proof on detention illustrates the inherent risk of argument in the alternative—that of internal contradiction. Another element of the Korematsu brief displayed a similar consequence of Fahy's decision to disregard Burling's cautionary advice. A defense of detention required the showing of a link between legislative intent and executive implementation. Such a showing in the Hirabayashi case had rested on congressional approval of Executive Order 9066 as a basis for DeWitt's curfew orders. It was obvious to Burling that detention lacked any similar legislative sanction. Unlike the curfew, "detention was not contemplated by the President or by Congress but was decided upon by the West Coast authorities and based upon an extraordinary twisting of Executive Order 9066," he had argued to Fahy in April 1944.[60]

Since the stated purpose of Roosevelt's order was the prevention of espionage and sabotage, the validity of detention consequently depended on a showing that it was a necessary means by which to effectuate this defensible end. However, the argument in the Korematsu brief that the provisions of DeWitt's exclusion order were "separable" and thus able to "stand alone" in the face of legal attack implied a separation of purpose behind exclusion and detention. Admission that exclusion and detention shared an identical purpose would logically erase this distinction and undermine the separability argument. Stretching the doctrine of judicial notice once again, the final brief suggested that the alternative to detention "might well have been to shift the locale of the danger of espionage and sabotage without eliminating it." The claim that Japanese Americans located hundreds of miles from the West Coast might pose a "maximum" danger to military security and provide a potential aid to a Japanese invasion of the West Coast had more than a touch of absurdity. "This danger is not referred to in official reports upon the evacuation as it was actually conducted," the brief conceded. "That it should have received consideration in the light of other factors relied upon seems evident, however." The Court was left to surmise what these factors might be.[61]

In bridging the chasm between the separability argument and the purported congressional intent to approve DeWitt's detention decision, the Korematsu brief threw a rope tied to President Roosevelt: "The detention in Assembly Centers . . . was a means of accomplishing the evacuation and of mitigating the harmful consequences of the exclusion which was ordered for the purpose of preventing espionage and sabotage on the West Coast. Hence the detention was a collateral measure closely related to the exclusion and, as such, came within the purpose as well as the literal terms of Executive Order No. 9066." Regardless of any purported unstated intent, the "literal terms" of Roosevelt's initial order certainly contained no authorization of detention. Even by implication, the assertion of a link between intention and implementation in the detention argument left the separability argument dangling.[62]

At the conclusion of their argument that detention involved "a valid exercise of the war power," the Justice Department lawyers who signed the Korematsu brief acknowledged the limitations of reliance on the *Final Report* as a document deserving of judicial notice by the Supreme Court: "In essence, the military judgment that was required in determining upon a program for the evacuation was one with regard to tendencies and probabilities as evidenced by attitudes, opinions, and slight experience, rather than a conclusion based upon objectively ascertainable facts.'' Whether the Court would read these words as understandable caution or as a confession of error awaited final decision of the Korematsu case.[63]

John Burling and Edward Ennis signed the Korematsu brief as an expression of institutional loyalty. The intervention of John McCloy had ended their battle to repudiate in explicit terms the espionage allegations in the DeWitt report, and Solicitor General Fahy had rejected Burling's objections on the detention question. Convinced that the evacuation and internment of Japanese Americans violated moral standards and constitutional demands, the two Justice Department lawyers had stretched the limits of professional obligation in meeting with Roger Baldwin and Charles Horsky to help shape the legal strategy of the American Civil Liberties Union in the Korematsu case. Based on their belief that Wayne Collins lacked the legal competence necessary for an effective challenge to Korematsu's conviction, Burling and Ennis recognized that the ACLU brief in the case held the only prospect of an argument able to move the Supreme Court from unanimous affirmance in the Hirabayashi case to reversal in Korematsu.

The ninety-eight-page brief that Collins submitted to the Supreme Court did little to alter the conclusion about his competence. Collins substituted excoriation of General DeWitt for a reasoned challenge to the legality of DeWitt's evacuation orders and additionally ignored the detention issue. Claiming that DeWitt had instituted ''a veritable reign of terror'' over Japanese Americans, Collins equated him with Mussolini and Hitler in the ''barbarianism'' with which citizens had been ''driven from their homes like cattle'' and imprisoned in ''concentration camps.''[64]

Employing once again the ''shotgun'' approach that Ernest Besig had earlier deplored as a waste of legal ammunition, Collins leveled a total of twelve constitutional charges against DeWitt's exclusion order. In addition to the delegation and due process arguments at the core of Korematsu's challenge, Collins added claims that the order constituted a ''bill of attainder'' directed personally at Korematsu, that it inflicted ''cruel and unusual punishment'' in violation of the Eighth Amendment, that it violated the proscription against ''slavery and involuntary servitude'' of the Thirteenth Amendment, and that it imposed ''a corruption of blood" on Korematsu "upon the theory of the constructive treason of his remote ancestors" in violation of Article III of the Constitution.[65]

Although Collins cited a number of prior Supreme Court cases in support of his more substantive legal points, his brief was short on analysis and long on vituperation, accusing DeWitt of harboring a "messianic delusion" and of "toying with the notion of a military dictatorship" over Japanese Americans. Collins ended his brief with an unusual and impolitic challenge to the Supreme Court: "General DeWitt let Terror out to plague these citizens but closed the lid on the Pandora box and left Hope to smother. It is your duty to raise the lid and revive Hope for these, our people, who have suffered at the hands of one of our servants. Do this speedily as the law commands you. History will not forget your opinion herein."[66]

Weighed against the government's brief, Collins's effort could only be considered a disaster. Its rhetorical excesses aside, the most glaring deficiency in the brief was the failure to join issue on the detention question. Recognition of this omission had led Ennis and Burling to urge that the ACLU file an amicus brief designed to force the Supreme Court to confront the issue directly. The two Justice Department lawyers could not, by policy, turn over to the ACLU the reports from the FBI and FCC that refuted the espionage allegations in the DeWitt report, documents that would have destroyed the government's defense of evacuation as a matter of "military necessity." An attack on detention, however, did not depend on the availability of records protected by confidentiality. The public record of DeWitt's orders, along with analysis of the legal doctrine that dealt with Korematsu's standing to challenge detention, made possible an effective attack on the reasoning and conclusions of the Justice Department brief.

Enlisted by Roger Baldwin to draft the ACLU brief, Charles Horsky needed little prompting from his Justice Department friends to launch an assault on the brief that Ennis and Burling had signed. Horsky phrased the central question in the twenty-seven-page ACLU brief in these words: "The issue in this case is the validity of military detention under armed guard of civilian citizens of Japanese ancestry." Dismissing with scorn the government's attempt "to persuade this Court that the issue before it is solely one of the validity of the evacuation" of Japanese Americans from the West Coast, Horsky exploited to the full the government's admission that Korematsu "had but two choices" in his response to DeWitt's exclusion order—"to violate the Order and mandatory Instructions, or to submit to internment for an indefinite period of time."[67]

Horsky built his argument that the Supreme Court could not evade the detention question in the Korematsu case on the wording of De-

Witt's exclusion order. Confined by the earlier "freeze order" to Military Area No. 1, Korematsu had been subsequently "forbidden to leave" the area designated in Civilian Exclusion Order No. 34 and "forbidden to remain" within it. The only alternative to criminal prosecution was to report for transfer under armed guard to the Tanforan Assembly Center. Legally trapped in a corral whose only gate literally opened into a converted race track, Korematsu faced either internment or jail. "By any rational principle," Horsky argued, "he must now be able to question the validity of that imprisonment, and to go free of the stigma of criminal conviction if that imprisonment was illegal or unconstitutional."[68]

Having argued that Korematsu had standing to challenge detention, Horsky dismissed as "simply nonsense" the government's separability claim. The Justice Department brief conceded that Korematsu "was confronted with alternative courses of action which involved either a violation of some feature of the exclusion program or submission to evacuation accompanied by detention." It nonetheless argued that detention was a separable phase of the evacuation program that Korematsu could only challenge, after transfer to Tanforan, through a habeas corpus proceeding. This logic struck Horsky as absurd. "The Government's brief admits that internment was the only way to avoid a violation of the Order," he wrote. "Unless words have lost their ordinary meaning, nothing could have been more *inseparable* than immediate internment."[69]

Since there was no guarantee that the Supreme Court would reach the detention question in the Korematsu case, despite Horsky's argument that it constituted the central issue, the ACLU brief confronted the evacuation question with a direct and pointed assault on the "military necessity" claim. Blasting the *Final Report* as a "wholly untrustworthy" document, the ACLU brief pointedly contrasted DeWitt's espionage allegations with the expurgated footnote on this issue in the Justice Department brief: "This singular repudiation of General DeWitt's testimony on the military necessities, which obviously could be required only by the existence of reliable conflicting information from other sources, is made even more remarkable by comparison of the Government's brief and Chapter II of the DeWitt Report." DeWitt's claim that "illegal radio signals which could not be located" had provided a basis for his evacuation recommendation, Horsky wrote, was "wholly inconsistent" with the technology of radio intelligence. "It is well known," he added, "that radio detection equipment is unbelievably accurate; a 'fix' can be obtained which will locate a radio transmitter not only in a specific house, but in a specific room."[70]

The striking parallel in the phrasing of this sentence in the ACLU brief and the reports submitted by the FCC to Attorney General Biddle suggests that Horsky had been shown the suppressed FBI and FCC reports by Edward Ennis and John Burling. During his drafting of the ACLU brief, Horsky had met for strategy sessions with his Justice Department friends and had most likely discussed with them the dispute over DeWitt's report and the internal battle over Burling's original footnote in the Korematsu brief. Four decades later, Horsky professed not to remember the details of these discussions. "It's possible that I might have heard about the disagreements within the Department before the brief was filed," he said, "but I don't think so."[71]

There seems little doubt, however, that Horsky left these strategy sessions with valuable information. Horsky obviously could not quote directly in the ACLU brief from the suppressed documents that provided a "repudiation" of the *Final Report*. He did what he could, however, to plant the seeds of suspicion that crucial evidence had been withheld from the Supreme Court.

In shaping ACLU strategy in the Korematsu case, Roger Baldwin adopted the tactic of a double-barreled attack on DeWitt and the *Final Report*. The amicus brief that Horsky drafted aimed its fire at the "military necessity" justification of evacuation and devoted just a few sentences to the argument that "not military security but race prejudice" had led DeWitt to recommend evacuation. The ACLU brief in the Hirabayashi case had argued that racism lay behind the internment of Japanese Americans, but it had rested largely on published accounts of racial hostility on the part of nativist groups for evidence of this pressure. DeWitt's statement in June 1943 that "a Jap's a Jap," and his reference in the *Final Report* to Japanese Americans as members of an "enemy race," convinced Baldwin that the ACLU should directly charge DeWitt with racism. Baldwin decided against making this argument in the ACLU's own brief, preferring that it focus exclusively on the points raised by Horsky. He therefore delegated the task of preparing a separate brief to Al Wirin, who served both as ACLU counsel in Los Angeles and as counsel to the Japanese American Citizens League. Wirin in turn recruited Morris Opler, the anthropologist on the War Relocation Authority staff who had written the amicus brief for the JACL in the Hirabayashi case the previous year. Opler was "willing to do it, on the side," Wirin informed Baldwin in April 1944.[72]

The brief that Opler prepared over the next six months offered a sharp contrast to Horsky's lawyerly brief. Opler cited only two Supreme Court opinions in his two-hundred-page brief. Substituting more than three hundred academic works and newspaper articles for legal analysis, the JACL brief combined scholarship and journalism in its attack on the *Final Report.* Both in form and substance, Opler's brief bore a remarkable similarity to *An American Dilemma,* the massive study of racism toward blacks written by the Swedish sociologist, Gunnar Myrdal, and published earlier in 1944. Incorporated a decade later in the briefs submitted by the NAACP to the Supreme Court in the school segregation cases, this seminal study was cited approvingly by the Court in *Brown* v. *Board of Education.* Opler wrote his brief in the Korematsu case with Myrdal's study as a model.[73]

In his dissection of the *Final Report,* Opler directed his scorn at DeWitt's claim that Japanese Americans constituted "a large, unassimilated, tightly knit racial group, bound to an enemy nation by strong ties of race, culture, custom and religion." Those who made this argument, he wrote, "always confuse the concept of 'intermingling,' with the concept of 'assimilation.' " Drawing on Myrdal's study, Opler compared the experience of Japanese Americans with that of blacks in Harlem. "In all important aspects of behavior they conform closely to common American standards," he wrote of blacks. "Yet they dwell by themselves in a special section of the city. In the same way, because of property restrictions, persons of Japanese ancestry often lived together in certain sections of West Coast cities. But this is no more reason than it is in the case of the Negro to assume that they were not there conforming to genuine American habits of thought and action."[74]

Opler's brief quoted at length from newspaper accounts of hostility toward Japanese Americans, linking those who sought to "eliminate their competitors" out of economic greed to DeWitt's evacuation recommendation. Opler concluded with a direct assault on DeWitt: "We contend that General DeWitt accepted the views of racists instead of the principles of democracy because he is himself a confessed racist. This is no discovery of ours and it requires no extended argument on our part to prove this. General DeWitt has gone to unusual lengths to make perfectly clear his unalterable hostility, *on racial grounds,* to all persons of Japanese ancestry, regardless of citizenship and regardless of evidences of loyalty."[75]

Between them, the ACLU and JACL briefs questioned virtually every assertion in the *Final Report.* Horsky's attack on the factual veracity of DeWitt's espionage claims was matched by Opler's argument that racist motivations had led to evacuation. Although Roger Baldwin did not put it in explicit terms, the combination of the two amicus briefs reflected a strategy of placing DeWitt on trial before the Supreme Court. Arguments based on constitutional objections to evacuation had failed to sway the Court in the Hirabayashi case. The decision of John Burling and Edward Ennis to point ACLU lawyers in the direction of the factual flaws in the *Final Report,* and DeWitt's own expressions of racism, made possible in the Korematsu case an approach that was less defensive. The concurring opinion of Justice Murphy in the Hirabayashi case hinted that a more aggressive approach might now have a chance of success. With DeWitt as a defendant, the Court might look at Korematsu as a victim of military error and racism.

The Supreme Court scheduled argument in the Korematsu and Endo cases for the same time in October 1944. While the lawyers on both sides struggled with the detention issue in their Korematsu briefs, they approached the task of briefing the Endo case almost as an afterthought. This disparity in effort is less puzzling that it seems in retrospect. Fahy's decision to defend detention in the former case saddled Justice Department lawyers with the burden of argument in the alternative, and with a record that was riddled with conflicting demands on Korematsu. In contrast, detention was not only the sole issue in the Endo case but one on which even Fahy was virtually willing to concede defeat.

The demands of the adversary system required that the Justice Department make some show of opposition to the argument that Mitsuye Endo had been unlawfully detained. The obvious difficulty was that none of the executive or legislative measures that purported to authorize the evacuation of Japanese Americans made any reference to detention. Confronted with this dilemma, the government's brief pointed wildly around the legal landscape in search of authority and precedent. It first suggested to the Supreme Court that congressional appropriations of funds to the War Relocation Authority, enabling the WRA to administer its relocation centers, implied support for the detention program. The brief additionally noted that the Court had sustained the temporary detention of jurors and material witnesses in criminal cases and also cited cases of domestic "insurrection" for precedent.[76]

Admitting by implication that none of the American cases could be stretched to cover the "indefinite" detention of a concededly loyal citizen, the government's brief looked abroad for support. In the Emergency Powers Act of 1939, the Court was told, England had authorized the detention without trial of citizens "whose detention appears . . . to be in the interests of public safety or the defence of the realm." The Endo brief conceded that the detention issue "is not ruled by any of these precedents, although all of them suggest considerations which bear upon it." These considerations included "the inherent difficulty of relocating a large number of individuals of all ages and capabilities who have been uprooted from their homes, their occupations, and their accustomed surroundings."[77]

The government's argument that Mitsuye Endo could not challenge her detention unless she complied with the WRA's leave regulation had a half-hearted flavor. Holding her in detention "pending such application is not so unreasonable or so unrelated to the causes which gave rise to it as it transcend the war power," the brief suggested. The Justice Department pointedly failed to argue that Endo's detention was constitutionally valid. The Supreme Court was simply asked to decide the question of whether detention "can be sustained as a valid exercise of the war power or must be stricken down as a denial of due process to the persons affected." The footnote that followed this question gave the Supreme Court a ready-made answer. Quoting a recent statement by former Supreme Court justice James F. Byrnes to a congressional committee, the Endo brief all but conceded the issue:

"The detention or internment of citizens of the United States against whom no charges of disloyalty or subversiveness have been made, or can be made, for longer than the minimum period necessary to screen the loyal from the disloyal, and to provide the necessary guidance for relocation, is beyond the power of the War Relocation Authority. In the first place, neither the Congress nor the President has directed the War Relocation Authority to carry out such detention or internment. Secondly, lawyers will readily agree that an attempt to authorize such confinement would be very hard to reconcile with the constitutional rights of citizens."[78]

Handed this concession on a silver platter, Endo's lawyers needed only to signal their agreement to the Supreme Court. Wayne Collins, to whom James Purcell had delegated the brief in the Endo case, found this simple task beyond his abilities. Passing up the invitation to "readily agree" with Fahy's offer of surrender, Collins expended seventy-three pages in a fervid attack on the "despotic power" allegedly claimed by President Roosevelt and the "monstrous doctrine" that Roosevelt could delegate to General DeWitt the power to deprive Mitsuye Endo of her liberty. "To find a parallel in modern times we are bound to look in the concentration camps of Germany" and follow "the example of the Madman of Berchtesgaden," Collins wrote in an impolitic effort to link Roosevelt and Hitler.[79]

Collins found himself equally incapable of restraining his hatred of DeWitt. In a second amicus brief submitted on behalf of the Northern California ACLU, he blasted detention as a "vicious program" that "betrays a wanton willingness to ignore the constitutional rights and liberties" of Japanese Americans. Obsessed with DeWitt's statement that "a Jap's a Jap," Collins lashed out with the claim that "the General cannot be an American either but necessarily must be of the foreign nationality that attached to his own ancestors." Shocked by the intemperance and irrelevance of this *ad hominem* attack, Roger Baldwin complained to Ernest Besig. Baldwin reminded Besig that the ACLU national board had not authorized the Northern California branch to file a separate amicus brief and complained that Collins had written and signed two briefs in the case. "Our lawyers are shocked by the extraordinary, not to say unethical, procedure of an attorney of record also preparing and signing an amicus brief," Baldwin wrote. "The impropriety is too obvious to merit comment." The "embarrassment" that Baldwin later attributed to the lack of authorization, it seems clear, stemmed rather from Collins's rhetorical excesses.[80]

Although the vituperation that Collins directed at Roosevelt and DeWitt obscured his substantive points, his two briefs did in fact make the point that Endo had been detained without executive or legislative sanction. Baldwin felt compelled, however, to disregard the earlier decision of the ACLU board to remain aloof from the Endo case. The board reluctantly approved Baldwin's suggestion that ACLU general counsel Osmond Fraenkel prepare another amicus brief. Focusing directly on the facts of the case, Fraenkel's brief argued that "no power has been granted by the Congress or can constitutionally be granted to any agency of government to detain citizens indefinitely without the formulation against them of any charges whatever."[81]

Filling a gap left by Collins in both of his briefs, Fraenkel disputed the government's claims that the temporary detention of jurors and witnesses, the domestic "insurrection" cases, and the British wartime legislation added up to adequate precedent for Endo's detention. "These various references at the most might justify the continued detention of American citizens of Japanese ancestry who have been found to be disloyal and therefore dangerous," he argued. "That is not the case here, as petitioner has been expressly admitted in the [Justice Department] brief to be loyal and not dangerous." Fraenkel was himself moved to emotion—expressed with somewhat greater restraint than by Collins—in his response to the government's contention that detention was necessary to protect Japanese Americans against public hostility and possible violence. "This is the outrageous doctrine of 'protective custody' invented by the Nazis in their persecution of the Jews," he wrote. "It has no place in American life."[82]

The Supreme Court met for argument of the Korematsu and Endo cases on October 11, 1944. Stacked on the curved bench before each of its members were nine briefs which added up to more than a thousand pages. Confronted with this mountain of paper, it was understandable that the Court looked for guidance in deciding the cases to the oral arguments of the four lawyers who faced the justices. The question on the mind of every spectator in the courtroom was the same: With military victory over Germany and Japan almost assured, would the Court's unanimity in the Hirabayashi and Yasui cases yield to second thoughts about the necessity for the evacuation and detention of Japanese Americans?

12

"The Court Has Blown Up"

THE CHATTER of spectators that echoed from the marble walls of the Supreme Court chamber ceased abruptly at noon on Wednesday, October 11, 1944. Led by Chief Justice Stone, the black-robed justices took their seats behind the bench on the third day of the Court's new term. The composition of the Court remained unchanged from the time, seventeen months earlier, when it had heard arguments in the first round of the Japanese American test cases. Of the four lawyers who argued the Hirabayashi and Yasui cases, only Solicitor General Fahy was again present, now representing the government in the Korematsu and Endo cases. After pressure from Roger Baldwin, Wayne Collins had grudgingly agreed to share his time in the Korematsu case with Washington lawyer Charles Horsky. James Purcell, who had stubbornly resisted Baldwin's efforts to replace him with a more experienced advocate, was scheduled to face the Court alone as Fahy's opponent in the Endo case.

Easing formality with a friendly smile, the Chief Justice opened the Court's session with a traditional ceremony. Saburo Kido and Herbert Wenig stood among the eight lawyers who repeated after Stone the oath required for admission to the Supreme Court bar. The presence of Kido and Wenig added a note of irony to the proceedings that followed. Although both had sworn to uphold the Constitution, the two lawyers were on opposite sides of the constitutional issues before the Court that day. They had both practiced law in San Francisco before the Japanese attack on Pearl Harbor, but Kido had been forced into exile in Salt Lake City because of his Japanese ancestry while Wenig had donned an Army uniform as a military lawyer. Equals before the Supreme Court bench, the two lawyers returned to their courtroom seats unequal as citizens.

Neither of the Japanese American litigants was present to hear the arguments in their cases. Fred Korematsu was at work that afternoon in a Detroit machine shop. Despite his release on "indefinite leave" from the Central Utah Relocation Center eight months earlier, Korematsu remained in the technical custody of the War Relocation Authority. As a condition of the sentence imposed on him in 1942, he was additionally required to report monthly to a federal probation officer. Mitsuye Endo was at work that day in an office behind the barbed wire fence that surrounded the Utah camp. Unwilling to sign the WRA forms that had allowed Korematsu to be released from internment, Endo had chosen to remain in confinement rather than abandon her claim of the right to return to her home and job in Sacramento.[1]

The Supreme Court did not provide for the recording and transcription of oral arguments until 1955. Before that time, lawyers who wanted a record of their remarks were required to bring a stenographer with them. Solicitor General Fahy had hired a private court-reporting firm to record his arguments in the Korematsu and Endo cases, but the Justice Department now claims to have lost the transcript of the Korematsu argument. All that remains of the record are the sketchy, hand-written notes of Colonel Archibald King, who attended the session as an observer for the Judge Advocate General. In the absence of a full transcript, these "verbatim" notes form the basis of this account of the Korematsu arguments.[2]

Wayne Collins and Charles Horsky had met for the first time just three or four days before the Supreme Court session. In mapping their approach to the Korematsu argument, the two lawyers faced each other both as allies and adversaries. Collins resented the ACLU pressure that forced him to share his time before the Court with Horsky; the fact that Horsky had earlier served in the Solicitor General's office could hardly have eased the hostility that Collins felt toward government lawyers. On his part, Horsky had been told by his Justice Department friends that Collins was inclined to respond to judicial interrogation with invective. The prospect of an unseemly exchange between Collins and an abrasive questioner from the bench did not appeal to Horsky. Their relationship was further complicated by the fact that the separate briefs the two lawyers had signed took conflicting positions on the constitutionality of Executive Order 9066.

The Supreme Court had made it easier for Collins and Horsky to frame their strategy. Both lawyers recognized that it would be fruitless to launch a second assault on the delegation and war powers issues raised by Frank Walters and Harold Evans in the Hirabayashi case. The Court's opinion in that case had effectively foreclosed any further argument on those questions. In ducking the evacuation issue, however, the Court had left open to challenge the factual question of whether the "findings" of General DeWitt "would support orders differing from the curfew order" at issue in the Hirabayashi case. The Court had also left open the question of the link between evacuation and detention, holding that it was "unnecessary to consider" Fahy's earlier argument that reporting for evacuation "did not necessarily involve confinement in a relocation center." This factual question presented Collins and Horsky with a tempting target, since an affirmative answer would open the way to the claim that the detention of "loyal" citizens was unconstitutional. The Justice Department's brief in the Endo case, which virtually conceded that detention could not withstand a constitutional challenge, dictated an effort to convince the Court that evacuation and detention were inseparable.[3]

Collins and Horsky ended their strategy sessions with agreement on a two-pronged argument in the Korematsu case. Collins would first hammer at General DeWitt's exclusion orders on the ground that they lacked a factual basis in "military necessity." Horsky would follow with an argument that the exclusion orders led inescapably to detention and exploit the Justice Department's concession that Korematsu was a "loyal" citizen. This strategy rested on an assumption that the Supreme Court would strike down detention in the Endo case. Horsky had little doubt on that score, but he harbored a real doubt that Collins would open the Korematsu argument with a creditable showing.

According to Colonel King, Collins began his argument as planned, asserting that there had been "no military necessity for exclusion" at the time of the order requiring Korematsu to report for evacuation. Chief Justice Stone obviously understood that Collins intended to put General DeWitt on trial, a tactic that was evident in the brief that Collins had filed with the Court. Stone moved quickly to narrow the issue to the formal charge against Korematsu, that he was forbidden to "remain in" San Leandro after May 9, 1942. "Congress must have contemplated resting on 'entering and remaining' as those words are used in the statute," Stone remarked. Colonel King failed to record the replies Collins made to this or other questions from the bench, but it is unlikely that he passed up the chance to note that the only place Korematsu could "remain in" after May 9 was the Assembly Center from which he would concededly have been shipped to a Relocation Center.[4]

From the sequence of questions posed to Collins, it is clear that he doggedly continued to insist that Korematsu's convinction on the narrow charge brought against him could not stand if DeWitt lacked the "military necessity" on which the exclusion orders were predicated. That

Collins refused to budge from this stand is evident from the questions thrown at him by Justice Frankfurter: "Does your argument come to this: that there is no rational basis for [the] exclusion order? Do you think that we can say that there were no other facts that General DeWitt knew, which we do not? Did he say that he had no other facts?" It seems apparent from the disbelieving tone of Frankfurter's argumentative questions that Collins had preceded them with an attack on DeWitt's veracity and motivations.[5]

The only note of judicial skepticism about DeWitt's justification of exclusion came in a final question to Collins from Justice Jackson: "On what standard are we to say that he did not have any other facts?" Jackson presumably referred to the "facts" presented in the *Final Report* in support of the "military necessity" claim. According to Colonel King, Collins pointed Jackson to the admission in the Justice Department's brief that DeWitt had based his "military judgment" that mass evacuation was essential on "tendencies and probabilities as evidenced by attitudes, opinions, and slight experience, rather than a conclusion based upon objectively ascertainable facts." Jackson's question hinted that he might require something more of DeWitt.[6]

Collins left Charles Horsky with only thirteen minutes in which to forge a verbal link between evacuation and detention. Experienced and comfortable before the bench, Horsky knew that time mattered less than persuasion. "As a tactical matter," he recalled, "I decided to pay attention to one member of the Court I thought would be least likely to be favorable, Mr. Justice Roberts, and I would argue the point until I saw him nod his head and then I would go on to the next point." Horsky had picked his weather vane on the bench with a particular purpose in mind. Widely considered the Court's most conservative member, Roberts was a "strict constructionist" who frowned on executive action that went beyond the limits of statutory sanction. Horsky's argument rested on the claim that Congress had not authorized the detention of Japanese Americans. If Roberts nodded when Horsky made this point, the senior member of the Court might well influence his colleagues in the conference room.[7]

Colonel King did not record any questions from Roberts to Horsky. However, Chief Justice Stone provided an opening for the detention argument. "Is [the] question of confinement as distinct from exclusion present in this case," Stone inquired. Horsky pointed him to the concession in the Government's brief that Korematsu, "had he obeyed all of the provisions of the order and the accompanying Instructions, would have found himself for a period of time, the length of which was not then ascertainable, in a place of detention." However brief the period of detention, Horsky continued, it would have been unlawful, since Public Law 503 had not authorized the detention of Japanese Americans. Stone had given Horsky the chance he wanted to build a bridge between the Korematsu and Endo cases. It remained to be seen whether Roberts would cross the bridge and lead at least four of his colleagues with him.[8]

Before he relinquished the podium to Solicitor General Fahy, Horsky fired a parting shot at General DeWitt and the veracity of the *Final Report*. King's notes record only that Horsky called the Court's attention to the "extraordinary footnote" in the Government's brief. Horsky referred, of course, to the "bowdlerized" version of the footnote originally drafted by John Burling, which had repudiated in explicit terms the espionage allegations in the *Final Report*. Revised by Herbert Wechsler to put in "the gentlest conceivable way" the Justice Department's objections to these allegations, the footnote left to implication what Burling had stated bluntly. Without a transcript of the arguments, it is impossible to know whether Horsky informed the Court of the existence of the FBI and FCC reports on which Burling based his footnote, although Horsky had met with Burling and Edward Ennis before the argument to discuss the Korematsu case and to plan strategy.[9]

In any event, Horsky had learned from Al Wirin some of the facts from the public record that undermined the *Final Report*. Morris Opler, the War Relocation Authority official who prepared the brief that Wirin filed for the Japanese American Citizens League, had pieced together from newspaper reports a remarkably detailed indictment of the *Final Report*. "I pressed those arguments about the DeWitt Report before the Court and in effect almost accused Fahy of misleading the Court," Horsky recalled. "The reason I did it was that he didn't repudiate it in any way, shape, or form." In directing his outrage at the soft-spoken but hot-tempered Solicitor General, Horsky paid a price. "What I said about Fahy, in characterizing his reliance on that report, so irritated him that we were not on speaking terms for about a decade."[10]

It is unlikely that the Solicitor General allowed the Court to detect his irritation at Horsky. Before the bench, Fahy rarely displayed emotion or strayed from the outlines he prepared with meticulous care from the records and briefs of the cases he argued. The twenty-page outline Fahy took with him to the podium rested on the claim that detention was not an issue in the Korematsu case. He was prepared to defend detention, but only as a fall-back position in case he was pressed on the issue.

Colonel King's notes of the session indicate that Fahy did not get far into his outline before he was forced to present his defense.

As he had during argument of the Hirabayashi case, Justice Frankfurter led off with a question more suited to a law-school classroom. Frankfurter expressed some skepticism about the reach of that case as a precedent: "Is it conceivable that we should hold that a 24-hour curfew would be valid?" Fahy admitted that a round-the-clock curfew would not be reasonable. "What difference is there between detention in their homes and elsewhere," Frankfurter then asked about the restraints imposed on Japanese Americans. King did not record Fahy's response to this question, but the Solicitor General most likely retreated to the argument in his outline that detention was not an issue in the case since Korematsu "was never detained in an Assembly Center." Always the narrow legal craftsman, Fahy had included in his outline a reminder to the Court that the general principle favoring "judicial reluctance to reach constitutional issues unless required weighs against reaching them here."[11]

Fahy's appeal to judicial restraint failed to close off questioning on the detention issue. His outline included an argument that the prospect of "violence between the Japanese migrants" and those hostile to their resettlement in the Rocky Mountain states justified not only evacuation but internment as well. This was the "preventive detention" argument that WRA lawyers had pressed on their reluctant Justice Department colleagues. Fahy had no qualms about defending the temporary detention of Japanese Americans in assembly centers, but he knew that internment rested on constitutional quicksand. With the Endo case also before the Court, however, he was forced to explain why those held in assembly centers could not escape their subsequent internment. Preventive detention, however lacking in precedential support, offered the only remotely plausible legal ground on which Fahy could stand.[12]

At least three members of the Court intimated that this argument smacked of an open-ended invitation to the military. "Can you suggest any ground which would justify this Court in holding that temporary detention in assembly centers would not justify their permanent detention if the hostility to them should continue indefinitely," Justice Jackson asked about the detained citizens. Colonel King did not record Fahy's answer, but the sequence of questions suggests that he retreated once again to the claim that detention was not an issue in the Korematsu case. "Assuming all that you say," Justice Rutledge then inquired, "should not the order have given some assurance of the temporary character of the detention?" Fahy refused to begin an exercise in line-drawing, undoubtedly aware that it would be difficult to defend as a temporary expedient an internment program that had lasted for more than two years. "That is holding those in charge of the program to too strict a rule," he replied in suggesting that the Court had no business second-guessing General DeWitt.[13]

The outline of Fahy's oral argument contained one astounding section. Among his extensive quotations from the *Final Report* were DeWitt's claims that reports of "signal lights visible from the coast" and "intercepts of unidentified radio transmissions" had prompted the evacuation program. In light of Fahy's knowledge of the FBI and FCC reports that refuted these espionage allegations, their inclusion in the outline seems inexplicable. Fahy prepared this outline on October 10, only the day before his argument to the Supreme Court. The previous week, after a bitter debate within the Justice Department over this issue, he had signed and submitted to the Court a brief that claimed to rely on the *Final Report* "only to the extent" that it dealt with the mechanics of evacuation and internment. Colonel King did not record whether Fahy read or cited these excerpts during his argument. If not, he seemed clearly prepared to do so. If he did, the Solicitor General knowingly misled the Court on a crucial issue in the Korematsu case.[14]

Fahy concluded his argument on October 12, since the previous day's session had adjourned before his time expired. James Purcell then replaced him at the podium to argue the Endo case. His task was eased by the virtual concession in the government's brief that detention of a concededly loyal citizen had no statutory support. The tangled procedural history of the case, however, presented the Court with several puzzling questions. Mitsuye Endo had been transferred by the War Relocation Authority out of the jurisdiction of the circuit court that had certified the case to the Supreme Court. In addition, the willingness of the WRA to approve her release from internment made the case arguably moot, since she was technically free to leave at any time.

After his admission to the Supreme Court bar on October 9, Purcell sat in the courtroom for three days and observed the proceedings while he waited for his turn at the podium. He was relaxed and confident when he began to outline the background of the case. Justice Frankfurter, a stickler for procedural regularity, cut Purcell off with an opening question: "How did you get here?" (Legend has it that one hapless lawyer answered Frankfurter by explaining that he took a train from Texas to Washington and a trolley from Union Station to the Supreme Court.) Purcell knew that Frankfurter wanted a road map of the Endo case from its filing to certification. "Since it was complicated," Purcell later recalled, "I went into it in detail." For more than ten minutes, he took the Court through a step-by-step account of the tortuous course of the Endo case. "When I finished and asked Frankfurter if he would like more, Justice Murphy almost fell off the bench laughing." Turning from procedural issues to the substantive questions before the Court, Purcell stressed that Congress had given no hint in Public Law 503 that evacuation could entail any subsequent detention of the Japanese Americans. Granting for purposes of argument the government's right to detain them long enough to sift the disloyal from the loyal, Purcell flatly denied any right to hold Mitsuye Endo once she had been cleared as loyal.[15]

When he followed Purcell to the podium, Solicitor General Fahy assured the Court he would "raise no questions which would interfere with disposition of the case on the merits" and waived any procedural claims. The transcript of Fahy's argument has been located and shows that his defense of detention was half-hearted at best. Conceding that Congress had not granted any authority in Public Law 503 for the detention of Japanese Americans, Fahy retreated to the "preventive detention" argument under a white flag of statutory surrender. The requirement that Endo complete the WRA's leave regulation forms and agree to remain away from the West Coast, he told the Court, "contemplated that she would go to a community where the likelihood of untoward incidents could be avoided." The WRA had the "best interests" of Mitsuye Endo at heart, Fahy added, in refusing her permission to leave unless she agreed not to relocate in towns where "the situation is explosive and there would be repercussions."[16]

Justice Roberts expressed doubt that Endo could be detained until she accepted this condition. The Solicitor General had declined the request of Justice Rutledge, during argument of the Korematsu case, that he place a time limit on "temporary detention" in the assembly centers. Drawing such a line in the Endo case, Roberts challenged Fahy to defend it. "So the tutelage of this woman might extend for 25 years," he suggested, if the WRA considered it "to her best advantage." Fahy did not dodge this question, but responded with a simple no. Rather than drawing a line closer to the detention camp, Roberts bore down on this concession: "Why not? She might be a danger to the community for 25 years, as a result of the original evacuation." Fahy turned the question aside and restated his defense of the WRA. "A great deal has been accomplished under this program for the resettlement of these people," he assured Roberts, who refused to remove the verbal hook on which Fahy squirmed. "So a little violation of the Constitution might be winked at," Roberts shot back, "but not a violation for 25 years?" Fahy had no facility in courtroom fencing. "I think not, your Honor," he replied quietly. "I think no violation of the Constitution should be winked at."[17]

Chief Justice Stone added to the growing tension in the courtroom. "To put the case crassly," he told Fahy, "the war has done a great deal of injury to all of us. Can the Government take charge of me and order my affairs in order to remedy an evil, if I do not care to be remedied?" Fahy again replied in his quiet voice: "No, your Honor; I think not." Justice Roberts had initiated the hostile questioning that Fahy endured with outward equanimity. Perhaps aware from these clipped answers of Fahy's inner discomfort, Roberts quickly deflated the tension between him and the bench. "The Chief Justice was never evacuated," Roberts remarked from his seat at Stone's right. However weak as a quip, this interjection released a welcome burst of laughter in the courtroom.[18]

In a more relaxed atmosphere, Stone resumed his effort to extract from the Solicitor General a solid constitutional defense of detention. Fahy's argument that the WRA was "doing good" in its relocation program did not satisfy the Chief Justice. "But there is no constitutional power in the National Government to do good," Stone objected. "It must be related to some other power." Conscious that he stood on shaky ground, Fahy tiptoed back to his evacuation argument. "I am relating it to the original war power which gave rise to the situation," he explained. Stone remained skeptical. "The war power is a power for the prosecution of war, a power to do things required by the war," he reminded Fahy. "It is not a power to repair injuries which the war has produced." The exchange of a dozen questions and answers on this issue ended in an impasse between Stone and Fahy. "The question is whether the Government has the power to do something which may be very desirable, merely because it is doing good," concluded Stone on a note of resignation. Fahy seemed equally weary of this inconclusive debate. "I believe that the fact that it is doing good does not render its action unconstitutional," he replied.[19]

The nine members of the Supreme Court met to discuss and decide the Korematsu and Endo cases on October 16, 1944, a crisp Monday morning in Washington. Events outside the conference room could hardly have failed to affect the deliberations within. Both in the Pacific and Europe, the tides of war had shifted dramatically in the fifteen months since the Court had decided the Hirabayashi and Yasui cases. Fresh from bloody but decisive victories in the Mariana Islands, American troops were poised to return General Douglas MacArthur to the Philippines. Allied troops in Europe flowed through their beachhead in Normandy in pursuit of the retreating Germans, while Soviet soldiers battled their way toward Berlin.

Even while the Court met, Nisei troops of the 442nd Regimental Combat Team were engaged in bitter house-to-house combat in the French town of Bruyères. Already veterans of the Italian campaign, these members of the Army's "most decorated unit" received more than 18,000 decorations for valor by the war's end. Newspapers across the country reported the exploits of the Nisei soldiers and reminded the public that many of them had volunteered for service from internment camps. The press also reported that more than 30,000 Japanese Americans had been released from internment without incident. Like the rest of the public, members of the Court read the newspapers. In addition, the Washington gossip mill and close relations with high-placed officials made it likely that some of the Justices—Felix Frankfurter undoubtedly among them—knew of the Cabinet debate over the ending of internment.[20]

From his seat at the head of the conference table, Chief Justice Stone opened discussion of the Korematsu case. Two members of the Court, William O. Douglas and Frank Murphy, recorded the comments of their colleagues in scribbled and sketchy notes. Between them, these incomplete accounts indicate that Stone dominated the discussion and pressed for the most narrow construction of the case, as he had the year before in the Hirabayashi case. Douglas's notes show as well that Stone presented the facts of the case on the basis of a fundamental misconception. Stating the question before the Court, the Chief Justice put forward two choices: "Are we confined to [the] exclusion order or was it so tied in with relocation orders that it must be considered" in terms of detention? Stone's statement of the question obviously assumed that the exclusion order violated by Korematsu had been followed by a separate order providing for his transfer from an assembly to a relocation center. The Court "cannot say as a matter of fact that one who goes to assembly center will go into relocation center," Stone asserted, since "we cannot say such an order would ever be made."[21]

Stone was mistaken on this crucial point. The government's brief conceded that Japanese Americans "transported under military control" to assembly centers under the exclusion orders "were temporarily detained pending their transfer to Relocation Centers." As worded, the exclusion orders themselves necessarily led to detention for some period of time in the relocation centers. Stone's misreading of the record prompted his conclusion that, even though Korematsu "probably would" have been shipped to a relocation center had he obeyed the exclusion order, "we must read [the] order as if it said he should go to assembly center & stay there subject to further orders." Although the record made clear that General DeWitt had intended the exclusion orders as authorization for detention in relocation centers, Stone either ignored or remained ignorant of this fact.[22]

According to Douglas, the Chief Justice expressed confidence that his reading of the record "ends the case." Before he concluded, however, Stone addressed the "larger question" raised during oral argument by Charles Horsky. Adopting an even-handed pose in his role as discussion leader, Stone admitted that there had been "no suggestion of confinement" of Japanese Americans before congressional enactment of Public Law 503. Then, noting that "Congress appropriated funds for relocation centers" within weeks of its earlier action, he found it a "large order to say that Congress & the President never intended to confine people." Concluding that both the legislative and executive branches of government had contemplated the detention of Japanese Americans, Stone nonetheless argued that Korematsu had moved "too early to attack the confinement phase of the case on constitutional grounds." Oblivious of his capture in a logical trap, Stone urged his colleagues to "treat this merely as an exclusion order" and to disregard the dilemma in which the order had placed Korematsu.[23]

Stone's disparagement of the "ingenious argument" made by Horsky did not go unchallenged when the Chief Justice opened the floor for debate among his colleagues. Justice Owen Roberts, the target of Horsky's verbal seduction the week before, spoke next as the senior associate justice in accordance with tradition. Stressing that DeWitt's exclusion order did not give Korematsu a choice between leaving San Leandro or remaining there, Roberts concluded that his "only choice was to go to prison" as an alternative to detention. "That is so violative of constitutional rights of citizens," Douglas recorded of this statement, "that Roberts thinks he was wrongfully convicted."[24]

This statement represented a belated confession of error on Roberts's part. The question of whether Congress had intended to invest General DeWitt with the power to detain Japanese Americans had been equally at issue the year before in the Hirabayashi case. At Stone's urging, the Court had ducked the issue by confining its ruling to the curfew question. With detention now before the Court, despite the protestations of Solicitor General Fahy, Roberts felt compelled to put his objections on the record. Stone's admission to the conference that Congress had dealt with detention in an "off hand manner" undoubtedly offended Roberts, who long insisted on statutory precision as a precondition of enforceability.[25]

As the discussion proceeded in descending order of seniority, Roberts stood alone in opposition to the Chief Justice. The next three members of the Court who spoke—Hugo Black, Stanley Reed, and Felix Frankfurter—sided with Stone on the detention issue. However, the balance swung away from Stone with the defections of Douglas and Murphy. The conference notes of these two men did not record their own comments, but Stone must have counted them with Roberts on his mental scorecard. Murphy had initially dissented in the Hirabayashi case, and the grudging tone of Douglas's concurring opinion almost guaranteed that he would vote to reverse Korematsu's conviction.[26]

With the outcome of the case still in doubt, Stone was obviously distressed by the defection of Robert Jackson. More willing than Roberts to overlook statutory imprecision and to concede that Congress had contemplated the detention of Japanese Americans, Jackson reflected another echo of the Hirabayashi case in his comments to the conference. Stone had convinced his colleagues the year before that DeWitt had a "reasonable basis" for the decision to impose the curfew. The Court's inquiry into the facts on which this decision rested had been perfunctory at best. Perhaps out of deference to the Chief Justice, Jackson had remained silent during that discussion. Fifteen months later, he looked down the table and leveled a direct challenge at Stone. DeWitt's exclusion order was not "something we have got to accept without any inquiry into reasonableness," Jackson said firmly. No compelling reason had been shown, he added, for Korematsu's exclusion from the West Coast on the ground of "Japanese ancestry" alone. Murphy's conference notes, the only record of this confrontation, do not reveal that Jackson questioned the veracity of DeWitt's espionage allegations. However, Murphy did record Jackson's implicit criticism of Stone as an apologist for the military and for his acceptance of racial discrimination. "They say the courts have got to become a part of it," he said with an edge of sarcasm. Jackson refused to step beyond the Court's approval of the curfew as an exercise of military authority. "I stop with Hirabayashi," he concluded, "and no further."[27]

Obviously stung by this pointed rebuke, Stone responded with an appeal to the wartime unity of the branches of government. "You are saying that Congress [and the] President acting together," he replied, "are unable to protect us against military espionage and sabotage." Conscious that the score of probable votes was tied, and that only one member of the Court had not yet spoken, Stone made his final comment on the Korematsu case in words more suited to a halftime, locker-room pep talk: "If you can do it for curfew you can do it for exclusion."[28]

Wiley Rutledge, the target of Stone's appeal, had earlier expressed to him the "anguish" that preceded his vote in the Hirabayashi case. Unwilling to relive that painful experience, Rutledge looked around the conference table and spoke with words of resignation. "I had to swallow Hirabayashi," he confessed. "I didn't like it. At that time I knew if I went along with that order I had to go along with detention for [a] reasonably necessary time. Nothing but necessity would justify it because of Hirabayashi and so I vote to affirm."[29]

Stone could hardly have welcomed these remarks as a vote of confidence in his *Hirabayashi* opinion. The fragile unanimity he had forged in that case was now shattered beyond repair, and it is unlikely that the Chief Justice felt any satisfaction as he cast the final and deciding vote to uphold Korematsu's conviction. Even at the conclusion of the 5-to-4 vote in the conference room, Stone knew that members of the Court were free to change their votes before the opinion was announced from the bench. Perhaps with the fear in mind that Rutledge might have second thoughts about his reluctant vote, Stone assigned the task of writing the opinion to Hugo Black. Among those with whom Rutledge cast his vote, he looked to Black for support and guidance on the issues that divided the "Axis" from its opponents. Black thus faced the delicate task of writing an opinion that would satisfy both Rutledge and Frankfurter, whose divergent views on the Court's role as a constitutional censor were hard to reconcile.[30]

It seems ironic in retrospect that the Supreme Court debated the detention issue with such acrimony in the Korematsu case and divided over its outcome so closely. Detention was an issue in that case only as a matter of legal debate. In contrast, it posed an immediate and urgent question in the Endo case. Its resolution by the Court would affect not only Mitsuye Endo but some 70,000 other Japanese Americans still confined in relocation centers.

The cloud of tension within the conference room lifted as soon as Chief Justice Stone opened discussion of the Endo case. Douglas and Murphy both hinted in their conference notes that Stone had one eye on the clock, eager for a decision by the noon opening of the Monday session. Stone left no doubt he would vote to grant the writ of habeas corpus and to order Endo's release from internment. Presenting the case to the conference, he put the central question simply: "Can a loyal citizen be held in a relocation center under restraint with the privilege of release a condition?" The "whole basis" of the exclusion order Endo had obeyed and then challenged, Stone added, rested on the "presence of disloyal people among the mass of Jap citizens." Noting that Solicitor General Fahy had conceded Endo's loyalty at oral argument, the Chief Justice answered his own rhetorical question: "Once loyalty is shown the basis for the military decision disappears. This woman is entitled to summary release."[31]

Within a matter of minutes, Stone had reformed the Court's divided ranks. Fahy's argument, presented at length but with an obvious lack of conviction, that the WRA's leave regulations had been designed with the "best interests" of the Japanese Americans in mind, had failed to convince a single member of the Court. The only question that remained for discussion at the end of Stone's brisk presentation—that of Endo's transfer from the jurisdiction of the district court in which her petition had been filed—was quickly brushed aside in the rush to reach a decision.

Despite his eagerness to end the detention of "loyal" citizens, the Chief Justice hesitated to bend the rules of jurisdiction. "Can we release her," he asked his colleagues. "What is the authority of the Court in a case like this?" Solicitor General Fahy had offered during his oral argument to waive the mootness issue. Fahy even took the unusual step of submitting to the Court a letter from Abe Fortas of the Interior Department, promising to comply with any court order in the Endo case. Stone had no doubt that Fortas and the WRA officials under his supervision would obey such an order. He had qualms, however, about the wisdom of setting a precedent that might raise the problem of enforcement in a future case. Searching for an alternative, Stone suggested to the conference that "we could issue our own writ."[32]

Felix Frankfurter, who had taught federal procedure and jurisdiction at Harvard Law School, finally came to Stone's rescue. Thumbing through his copy of the Supreme Court's rules of procedure, Frankfurter pointed his colleagues to Rule 45(1): "Pending review of a decision refusing a writ of habeas corpus, the custody of the prisoner shall not be disturbed." Endo's transfer from California to Utah constituted a violation of this rule and required that WRA officials comply with any district court order that she be returned to California for a hearing. With this academic flourish, Frankfurter lifted the last barrier to Endo's release. Stone promptly polled the Court, which voted without dissent to return the case to the district court with instructions to grant the writ of habeas corpus. This decision required only that the lower court hold a hearing to determine whether Endo's detention was lawful. As a practical matter, the Supreme Court made a further hearing superfluous by ruling that the WRA had no statutory authority to detain Endo or other Japanese Americans whose loyalty had been certified.[33]

The Court followed tradition in confining its ruling to the narrowest issue that could provide the relief sought. Stone and his colleagues left undecided the broader constitutional questions of due process and equal protection: Did Congress have power in the first place to authorize detention, and did its application to Japanese Americans alone constitute an unlawful form of racial discrimination? There is no indication in the notes of Douglas and Murphy that any member of the Court raised these issues at the conference, or announced an intention to challenge the narrow ruling in a concurring opinion. Roberts and Murphy did later file separate opinions which in effect charged their colleagues with constitutional cowardice. Whether or not Stone knew at the time of these forthcoming broadsides, his assignment of the Endo opinion to Douglas seemed calculated to blunt their effect.

The Chief Justice had labored hard that Monday morning to achieve the outcomes of the Korematsu and Endo cases. Convinced that the Court must not compromise the exercise of the military's wartime powers over the civilian population, he was equally determined to affirm the primacy of Congress in setting limits on military authority. Stone displayed his prowess as an advocate in bending the Court to his will on these issues. In assigning the two opinions to Black and Douglas, he clearly had an eye on the potential critics of the Court's narrow rulings. Legal scholars, the press, and those among the public who questioned internment would find it hard to challenge the Court's most noted defenders of civil rights and liberties. Stone may not have foreseen, however, that the most savage and unsparing attacks on Black and Douglas would come from their own colleagues.

Hugo Black must have felt some trepidation as he began work on the Korematsu opinion. He knew that four dissenters lay in wait, eager to exploit any weakness in his first circulation of a draft opinion. He also recognized that the shift of a single vote from the precarious majority would reverse the outcome of the case. The opinion had to satisfy both Wiley Rutledge, whose reluctant vote in the conference barely concealed his suspicion of the "military necessity" argument, and Felix Frankfurter, who tolerated no criticism of military authority. Finally, Black wrote with the Chief Justice figuratively looking over his shoulder, since Stone had cut a narrow constitutional path in the Hirabayashi case from which Black could not wander far.

The facts of the Korematsu case, however, forced Black to venture into unmapped territory and to confront the question of detention. Black's first effort at the opinion revealed his caution as an explorer. In five pages, he struggled to defend the legality of the exclusion order Korematsu had violated. Black admitted at the outset that Korematsu had been caught between the dictates of DeWitt's initial "freeze order" and the subsequent exclusion order. "As a result of these orders," he wrote, "the petitioner was prohibited on the one hand from voluntarily leaving the area to go to other parts of the country; on the other hand he was commanded to submit himself for detention at an assembly center." Having accurately located the central question in the case, Black then lost his compass. "The argument is that we must treat the two orders as one and inseparable," he went on, with the intent of separating them.[34]

Black's draft opinion did not, however, further discuss the impact of the "freeze order" in creating the legal dilemma that Korematsu had confronted. The opinion revealed that Black had been misled by Stone's erroneous statement of the case to the conference. The Chief Justice had said nothing about the "freeze order" and its role in paving the road to the assembly centers, but had mistakenly asserted that Korematsu was subject to separate orders that directed him first to an assembly center and then to a relocation center. Building on this misconception, Black's first draft assumed that these were the "two orders" at issue. With the argument that "exclusion and detention under guard are separate situations," Black contradicted his admission that the exclusion order led directly to detention. Having separated exclusion and detention in his mind, he found it "certainly conceivable that one might be legally justifiable while another was not."[35]

In pursuing this point, Black strayed into the relocation centers and the issues raised in the Endo case. "For instance," he wrote, "detention of a person in a large group might be temporarily justifiable until separation of the loyal from the disloyal could be accomplished, while detention and restrictions thereafter were not." Since the stated purpose of holding Japanese Americans in assembly centers was simply to facilitate their evacuation from the West Coast to the interior states, and purportedly had nothing to do with "loyalty" sifting, this digression evaded the question of whether detention in assembly centers was "legally justifiable." Black completed his circle around the detention question by returning to the *Hirabayashi* case for the proposition that "the different orders involved in the program may pose different questions, and are not to be considered as in all respects legally identical." Stone's opinion in *Hirabayashi*, of course, had carefully avoided any ruling on the legality of detention. Perhaps abashed by his own evasion, Black finally retreated to the narrow wording of the charge against Korematsu:

"In this case the conviction was for remaining in a prohibited area, and we shall not here pass upon the legality of an internment the petitioner might have, but had not suffered."[36]

Before he sent his first draft to the Court's print shop to be set in type and circulated to his colleagues, Black had second thoughts about its failure to deal with two of the issues stressed by Wayne Collins during his oral argument. Collins had vehemently denounced the entire evacuation program as a product of General DeWitt's racial prejudice against Japanese Americans. Obviously reluctant to meet these charges head on, Black nonetheless felt compelled to deflect them. In the first printed version of his opinion, he answered that if the exclusion order "sprang—as it has been argued that it does—from racial prejudice, a wholly different issue would be posed" in the case. Black read the record before the Court, however, in such a way as to "find no such purpose behind the orders or the Act of Congress." Collins had made the additional point that DeWitt's orders lacked any basis in "military necessity" at the time of the exclusion order to which Korematsu had been subject. Without elaboration, Black denied that "all danger of Japanese invasion of the West Coast had disappeared, and that there was no longer any military necessity for taking precaution against espionage and sabotage in case of attack."[37]

Black may have brushed aside these arguments because he considered them irrelevant and unworthy of extended rebuttal. More likely, however, he dealt with them so briefly in order to avoid offering clear targets to the dissenters. At this stage of the opinion-writing process, Black seemingly preferred to force the dissenters to shoot first, with his own ammunition held in reserve. The first printed draft of the opinion, in consequence, was little more than a carbon copy of Stone's opinion in the *Hirabayashi* case. More than constitutional caution lay behind this tactic: Black not only forced those who aimed at his opinion to fire on the Chief Justice as well, but also required that they explain their desertion from the ranks.

The printed draft of Black's opinion reached the desks of his colleagues on November 8, 1944. The previous day, Franklin Roosevelt had swamped Thomas Dewey by a margin of 333 electoral votes in gaining an unprecedented fourth term in the White House; Black operated with the margin of a single vote. Judicial politics thus dictated that he do everything possible to placate those in the majority. Conflicting demands on the author of a majority opinion, one that he strengthen a particular argument and another that he soften it, have occasionally led to such fratricide that the original majority has disintegrated. Given the vehemence of the dissenters, Black was fortunate in escaping this fate.

Two members of the majority, Stanley Reed and Wiley Rutledge, approved the draft without comment. Felix Frankfurter and Chief Justice Stone, however, expressed reservations that compelled Black to revise his opinion on major points.

Frankfurter concealed his objections behind a pose of indifference. "I am ready to join in your opinion without the change of a word," he said in preface and then suggested that Black change several words and thus alter a key sentence. The "one small matter of phrasing" at issue dealt with the role of the Supreme Court in reviewing acts of the other branches of government. Black had addressed the question in these terms: "Congress having placed on the civil courts a duty to enforce military orders has manifested its purpose to assure those constitutional safeguards which courts are charged to protect." Frankfurter had a fundamental quarrel with the implication of these seemingly innocuous words. Judicial deference to legislative and executive powers formed the core of his view of the Court's function, and he feared that Black had inadvertently armed the dissenters with a powerful weapon by opening General DeWitt's orders to judicial scrutiny of their motivation and factual basis.[38]

Frankfurter had appointed himself as Black's scout among the dissenters, and passed on the news that Robert Jackson considered the military orders unconstitutional and intended to turn this sentence against Black. "I should feel happier," Frankfurter wrote to Black on November 9, if the opinion made it clear that Congress had intended nothing more than "making disobedience of a military order a criminal offense." What Frankfurter left unstated was his hope that Black would remove from the opinion any suggestion that the Court should exercise its peacetime role as a constitutional watchdog. "I am content with whatever you do," he assured Black, who promptly struck the offending sentence from the opinion. Frankfurter was not content, however, to remain silent when Jackson later revived the judicial-review issue in a biting dissent. The subsequent duel between Jackson and Frankfurter will be recounted shortly; the point here is that Black removed himself from the line of fire at Frankfurter's urging.[39]

In commenting on the draft opinion, Chief Justice Stone assured Black that he had dealt with the case in "exactly the right way." But, like Frankfurter, he followed this flattery with a fundamental critique of the opinion. Stone attempted first to rescue Black from the consequences of his foray into the relocation centers. Although the printed draft claimed that "the alleged illegality of the prospective internment was not directly in issue" in the case, Black nonetheless had implied that Korematsu would have been sent to a relocation center had he reported as ordered to the assembly center. Stone had disputed at the Court's conference that the two forms of detention were linked, and was chagrined to find the link acknowledged in Black's opinion. He pointed out that at the time Korematsu "refused to go to the assembly center no one had been sent to a relocation center" and that "many who were sent and who are now being sent to the assembly centers are not sent to relocation centers."[40]

These statements were highly misleading. In the first place, the transfer to relocation centers of those who reported to assembly centers had been planned well before issuance of the exclusion order that applied to Korematsu. Second, only a very few of the Japanese Americans—those who were elderly, ill, or institutionalized—were not transferred to relocation centers. Disregarding these facts, Stone suggested that Black revise his opinion to state that "it does not follow, as a matter of fact or of law," that Korematsu's detention in an assembly center "will result in his detention in a relocation center." The Chief Justice added to this proposed revision, however, a second suggestion that obviously produced in Black second thoughts about the whole question of detention.[41]

Stone had quickly spotted in the draft opinion Black's reluctance to deal with the constitutionality of assembly center detention, and reminded him that "we do have to determine whether the temporary segregation in an assembly center" was lawful. Compliance with the exclusion order left Korematsu with no choice other than detention in the assembly center. Acknowledging this fact, Stone suggested that Japanese Americans "could lawfully be assembled at a point within a military area and detained there preparatory to some other lawful disposition of them—either (a) exclusion, (b) transfer to another military area, (c) release under limited control or surveillance after investigation of their loyalty." Each of these grounds for detention rested, of course, on the "military necessity" and "disloyalty" claims that Wayne Collins and Charles Horsky had vigorously disputed. Notwithstanding these countering arguments, Stone proposed that "what is done at an assembly center is a mere incident to the authority to control these people" extended to the War Department by President Roosevelt. It seemed clear to him, the Chief Justice concluded, that "detention at the assembly centers . . . has the same constitutional sanction as the curfew order in *Hirabayashi*."[42]

It is unlikely that Black failed to appreciate the irony in Stone's assurance that a defense of detention was "implicit" in the draft opinion. Black had, in fact, deliberately evaded the question in his effort to confine the Court's holding to the narrow wording of the charge against

Korematsu. Having decided to go no further, Black did not welcome Stone's suggestion that the nonexistent defense of detention "has to be spelled out to some extent in order to show the reader why you reach the result you do." Black remained silent for more than three weeks after this advice reached him on November 9. Battered by the dissenters and backed into a corner by Stone's later threat to answer them himself, Black finally forged a compromise that both addressed and evaded the detention issue.[43]

Beginning on November 29 the Court's messenger delivered to Black a daily succession of dissenting opinions, each of which exploited a separate weakness in his printed draft. The first came from Owen Roberts, who amplified his comment at the conference that Korematsu's "only choice was to go to prison" as an alternative to detention. Starting with the declaration of war against Japan on December 8, 1941, Roberts set out a detailed chronology of the evacuation and internment program that concluded with the filing of charges against Korematsu on June 12, 1942. He singled out from the blizzard of edicts issued during this six-month period the "freeze order" of March 27 and the exclusion order of May 3. Caught in the vise of these two orders, Roberts argued, Korematsu had no lawful choice: "The two conflicting orders, one which commanded him to stay and the other which commanded him to go, were nothing but a cleverly devised trap to accomplish the real purpose of the military authority, which was to lock him up in a concentration camp."[44]

Roberts had no doubt that "exclusion was but a part of an over-all plan for forcible detention" of the Japanese Americans. Given the "stark realities" of this plan, he had nothing but scorn for Black's "suggestion that it is lawful to compel an American citizen to submit to illegal imprisonment on the assumption that he might, after going to the Assembly Center, apply for discharge by suing out a writ of habeas corpus" as Mitsuye Endo had done. Black's claim that Korematsu could only challenge the exclusion order "from within prison walls," Roberts wrote, constituted "a new doctrine of constitutional law" and an evasion of the facts of the case. His reading of the record convinced Roberts that Korematsu had been convicted "solely because of his ancestry, without evidence or inquiry concerning his loyalty and good disposition towards the United States."[45]

Aside from his equation of internment with the concentration camps of Nazi Germany, Roberts confined his critique of Black's opinion to the limits of statutory interpretation. He conceded that a "temporary" period of detention, to last no longer than the duration of the "emergency" that confronted the Army after the Pearl Harbor attack, might have been justified. Had the exclusion order subjected Korematsu to such a limited form of detention, Roberts agreed that "the *Hirabayashi* case would be authority for sustaining it." Stressing that his concession dealt with a "hypothetical case" and not the one before the Court, Roberts added in a footnote that he would not "preclude judicial inquiry and determination whether an emergency ever existed and whether, if so, it remained" at the time of the exclusion order in question.[46]

The dissent that Robert Jackson sent to his colleagues on November 30 raised the question of judicial review with a vengeance. Jackson addressed most of his fifteen-page assault on Black's opinion to the issue buried by Roberts in a footnote. Agreeing with Roberts that the military orders "were so drawn that the only way Korematsu could avoid violation was to give himself up to the military authority," Jackson then returned to the question he had posed to Frank Walters during argument of the Hirabayashi case, when he asked whether application of the orders to Japanese Americans alone constituted a "bill of attainder" in violation of the Constitution. Despite his agreement with Walters on this issue, Jackson had deferred to Chief Justice Stone in joining the Court's unanimous opinion. With unanimity shattered in the Korematsu case, Jackson now voiced his earlier objection to "an attempt to make an otherwise innocent act a crime merely because this prisoner is the son of parents as to whom he had no choice, and belongs to a race from which there is no way to resign."[47]

Jackson did not differ with Roberts in concluding from these facts that the exclusion order applied to Korematsu failed to meet constitutional standards. The two dissenters parted company, however, at the threshold of the judicial-review issue at which Roberts had hesitated. In contrast to the hint by Roberts that a properly limited exclusion order might meet the test of judicial scrutiny, Jackson refused to put the Court at the service of the War Department. "I can see no path of duty," he wrote, "but to hold that a civil court cannot be required to enforce a military order so unconventional in character as to raise doubts of its constitutionality." It was clear to Jackson that courts "must abide by the Constitution, or they cease to be courts and become instruments of policy. To hold otherwide is to subordinate the courts to local military power."[48]

Returning in his draft dissent to the eras of Andrew Jackson and Abraham Lincoln, Jackson noted at length the "frequency of clashes in our history between the military and the judicial power" and found in these disputes "the Achilles heel of our constitutional system." But to concede that military power was "wholly removed from judicial examination" might well lead to an absolutism that "would approximate Lenin's definition of a dictatorship." Pointing to Black's opinion, Jackson darkly suggested that "we may as well say that any military order will be constitutional and have done with it."[49]

Despite this note of bitter resignation, Jackson roused himself for an attack on General DeWitt and the credibility of his *Final Report,* which he labeled "a self-serving statement by one interested in vindicating his own fairness." Noting that the lengthy brief of the Japanese American Citizens League "points out omissions and defects in the DeWitt report which if credited leave it far from a convincing document," Jackson inserted in his draft opinion a two-page footnote that included excerpts from the JACL brief taking issue with the espionage allegations of the *Final Report.*[50]

In contrast to the straightforward approach of Roberts' dissent, a curious kind of judicial schizophrenia pervaded Jackson's draft opinion. The bulk of his opinion was devoted to the unconstitutionality of DeWitt's orders on the ground of racial discrimination. Jackson made clear as well his skepticism about the "military necessity" claims behind the orders. However, he concluded this demolition job with a caveat. "My duties as a justice as I see them," Jackson wrote, "do not require me to make a military judgment as to whether General DeWitt's evacuation and detention program was a reasonable military necessity or an hysterical and prejudiced exercise of a little brief authority." Enforcement of military orders which had "no place in law under the Constitution" was, in consequence, "nothing that Congress may require courts vested only with judicial power under that Constitution to apply." Implicit in Jackson's opinion were two opposing contentions: one that DeWitt's orders were unreasonable and thus not "law" in the constitutional sense; the other that the Court had no business in judging their reasonableness.[51]

Whatever its lack of consistency, this slashing attack on Black's draft of the majority opinion threw the Court into turmoil. Justice Murphy, still at work on his equally outraged dissent, quickly penned a note to his law clerk, Eugene Gressman: "Read this and perish! The Court had blown up on the Jap case—just as I expected it would."[52]

The Court had indeed blown up over the Korematsu case. But as the dust settled during the week that began on December 1, Black emerged from the explosion with a strengthened majority, the product of a hasty effort to patch the weak spots in his draft opinion. Engineered by Chief Justice Stone, this repair job was complicated by additional assaults on the opinion from Douglas and Murphy and by the distraction of a continuing feud between Frankfurter and Jackson. The revised draft that Black circulated to his colleagues on December 8 showed the seams of this judicial carpentry. If Black did not convincingly answer the dissenters, he at least persuaded one to join the majority.

Black might well have despaired on December 1 of an end to the Court's divisions over his opinion. Not only did he receive on that Friday a draft of Douglas's dissent to add to those of Roberts and Jackson, but the Court's messenger also delivered a letter from Stone (in which the Chief Justice enclosed a concurring opinion) and two separate drafts of a concurrence by Frankfurter. With the dissents of Roberts and Jackson already on his desk, and with Murphy's on its way from the printer, Black confronted the unenviable task of revising his opinion to meet the objections of all but two of his colleagues—only Reed and Rutledge had remained silent.

Critics often charged that William O. Douglas wrote sloppy opinions, designed more to reach a desired result than to explain his reasoning. It seems fair to conclude that Douglas never wrote a sloppier or less reasoned opinion than the draft of his dissent in the Korematsu case. Douglas appeared more eager, in fact, to defend General DeWitt and the internment program than to defend his conclusion that Korematsu had been unlawfully convicted. DeWitt's evacuation program, the dissent began, "had every earmark of good faith" as a measure designed to prevent espionage and sabotage. Douglas went on to argue that assembly centers "were conceived as the device for compelling evacuation and making it more orderly and efficient." Conceding that Public Law 503 "does not mention any authority to detain," he found such authority by implication. "The power to detain stems from the power to exclude," Douglas asserted. If DeWitt had the power to order Korematsu's exclusion from San Leandro, "the right to do it by force if necessary must be implied. And any forcible measures must necessarily entail some degree of detention or restraint whatever method of removal is employed."[53]

Korematsu's detention in an assembly center did not bother Douglas, as it did Owen Roberts. What did bother him was that, between the issuance of the exclusion order on May 3, 1942, and Korematsu's arrest on May 30, assembly center detention "had become merely the first stage in the trip to a Relocation Center." Douglas noted that DeWitt had announced on May 19 the eventual transfer of Japanese Americans then held in assembly centers to relocation centers. This sequence of events seemed critical to Douglas: Korematsu's arrest between May 3 and 19 would have been lawful, while his only choice after May 19 "was to go to jail or submit to indefinite detention in a Relocation Center." Since this latter form of detention was more than "an incident to exclusion," Douglas found it unlawful. Although Korematsu "could not lawfully refuse to be evacuated," the dissent concluded, "he could lawfully resist the indefinite detention which was in store for him if he submitted."[54]

Hinging the case on the date of Korematsu's arrest must have struck Douglas as an evasion of the detention issue. He admitted as much in conceding that DeWitt had contemplated before May 19 the establishment of relocation centers. Douglas also faced the conflict between this dissent and the statement in his opinion in the Endo case—already in print—that "initial detention in Relocation Centers was authorized" under Public Law 503. If not incompatible, the two opinions were at least incongruent.[55]

Without attributing ulterior motives to Douglas, it seems possible that his dissent was intended to extract a concession from Black. He suggested as much in a letter to Black on December 6, 1944. When he drafted his dissent, Douglas wrote, he read the charge against Korematsu as if the crime alleged had been "committed after the Relocation Centers had been put into full operation." Other members of the Court, however, argued that Korematsu's violation of the exclusion order occurred the day it was issued, rather than the day of his arrest. "I see no purpose in holding out on a mere point of construction" of the formal charge, Douglas assured Black. "Therefore, I would be willing to waive my difficulties and join in the opinion of the Court provided one addition was made. As you know, I think evacuation and detention in an Assembly Center were inseparable. You do not think so." The "accommodation" that Douglas proposed took the form of a paragraph drawn from his dissent, acknowledging the lawfulness of assembly center detention as a consequence of the evacuation. Aware of Black's reluctance to reach this issue, Douglas tactfully suggested that the opinion attribute his view to a "minority" of the Court.[56]

While Black mulled over this proposal, he also faced pressure from Stone, who sent him on December 1 a two-page concurring opinion which the Chief Justice called "a brief statement of what I think is the minimum that should be said in this case." Stone was concerned about the impact of the argument in Roberts' dissent that Korematsu's obedience of the exclusion order would have led to his "illegal imprisonment" in a relocation center. Again displaying his ignorance of the record, Stone urged that Black add to his opinion the statement that Korematsu "has not been convicted of violating a relocation order and in fact has never been subjected to such an order." The point made by Roberts, who correctly read the record, was that Japanese Americans who reported to assembly centers were later shipped to relocation centers without the issuance by DeWitt of any intervening order. Stone nonetheless asked Black to assert that the Court would only "decide the serious constitutional issue which petitioner seeks to raise here when a relocation order is in fact applied or is certain to be applied to him, and we are advised of its terms."[57]

Although he obviously hoped to include Douglas in the majority and to placate the Chief Justice, Black deferred his response to their proposals while he worked on further revisions of the majority opinion. Of more immediate concern to Black were the imputations of the dissenters that he condoned a program based on racism. Seven years had passed since critics of his appointment to the Supreme Court had raised the touchy issue of Black's earlier membership in the Ku Klux Klan, which he had joined as a young Alabama lawyer and politician. Black had repudiated his Klan membership and certainly gave no hint, either in the Senate or on the Court, of lingering racial prejudice. But he remained sensitive about the issue. The charge in Roberts' dissent that Japanese Americans had been herded into "concentration camps" stung him, as did the denunciations in Murphy's dissent.

Murphy had reluctantly withdrawn his original dissent in the Hirabayashi case at Frankfurter's urging, but had lashed out in his concurrence at the Court's approval of a program "based upon the accident of race or ancestry." The curfew upheld by the Court "goes to the very brink of constitutional power," Murphy had written. The exclusion of Japanese Americans at issue in the Korematsu case, he wrote at the outset of his second dissent, "goes over 'the very brink of constitutional power' and falls into he ugly abyss of racism."[58]

Murphy's dissent read much like the one Jackson had earlier circulated. Both men conceded DeWitt's power to adopt "all reasonable means" in combating the dangers of espionage and sabotage on the West Coast. Neither found any substantial evidence in the record of the Korematsu case, or in the *Final Report* as part of that record, that DeWitt's exclusion orders met this test of reasonableness. Murphy and Jackson parted company, however, on the question of the Court's role in reviewing this evidence. The fact of racial discrimination alone convinced Jackson of the unconstitutionality of the orders, which he said "do not pretend to rest on evidence" and were thus "not susceptible of intelligent judicial appraisal." Murphy agreed that the orders constituted "an obvious racial discrimination" and deprived Japanese Americans of their constitutional rights. Unlike his fellow dissenter, Murphy assumed the task of deciding if the orders "have some reasonable relation to the removal of the dangers of invasion, sabotage and espionage." Murphy might well have adopted this pose simply to knock down a straw man; he nonetheless assured his colleagues that "we must not erect too high or too meticulous standards" in judging DeWitt's orders.[59]

Much like the prosecutor he once was, Murphy placed DeWitt on a figurative witness stand and posed the rhetorical question of whether DeWitt believed that "*all* persons of Japanese ancestry may have a dangerous tendency to commit sabotage and espionage and to aid our Japanese enemy in other ways." DeWitt's testimony came from the *Final Report.* Starting with his claims that Japanese Americans belonged to an "enemy race" and were disloyal as a group, Murphy added a string of citations to the "disloyalty" claims in the *Final Report:* adherence to Shinto, dual citizenship, Japanese-language schools, and a half-dozen others. To each of these claims, Murphy appended in footnotes a countering source of evidence, largely drawn from the JACL brief written by Morris Opler. Summing up, he concluded that each of DeWitt's allegations "has been substantially discredited by independent studies made by experts in these matters." Murphy then pointed beyond DeWitt at the real culprits in the case; his major witness on this point was Austin Anson of the Salinas Vegetable Grower-Shipper Association. "We're charged with wanting to get rid of the Japs for selfish reasons," Anson had said. "We do. It's a question of whether the white man lives on the Pacific Coast or the brown men."[60]

Murphy then moved to the "military necessity" issue and addressed DeWitt's charges that Japanese Americans "were responsible for three minor isolated shellings and bombings of the Pacific Coast area, as well as for unidentified radio transmissions and night signalling." Nothing in the record supported these allegations, Murphy answered, nor was there any evidence that the FBI and military intelligence agencies "did not have the espionage and sabotage situation well in hand" after Pearl Harbor. The opinion ended on a note of accusation: "I dissent, therefore, from this legalization of racism."[61]

Black's response to the accusations of the dissenters was defensive. He quickly drafted a two-page addition to the majority opinion, with Roberts' use of the loaded term "concentration camp" its primary target. "Our task would be simple, our duty clear," Black wrote, "were this a case involving the imprisonment of a loyal citizen in a concentration camp because of racial prejudice." It first seemed appropriate to Black that he admit "that the course of American life and thought has been increasingly polluted by the warped psychology of race hatred." However, he argued that racism was less a product of domestic turmoil than "a reflection of the witch's brew that has lately been served up abroad." Black had second thoughts about blaming America's enemies for its racial problems and scratched these last two sentences from his revisions. But he retained a sentence designed as a rebuke to Roberts: "Regardless of the true nature of the assembly and relocation centers—and we deem it unjustifiable to call them concentration camps with all the ugly connotations that term implies—we are dealing specifically with nothing but an exclusion order."[62]

Narrowing the issue in this way hardly answered the dissenters, and Black's recognition of this fact led him to a flat denial. "Korematsu was not excluded from the Military Area because of hostility to him or his race," Black asserted. "He *was* excluded because we are at war with the Japanese Empire" and because "evidence of disloyalty on the part of some" of the Japanese Americans had raised fears of espionage and sabotage. Aware from the dissents of Jackson and Murphy that the *Final Report* offered no proof of this claim, Black reached beyond the record of the Korematsu case. "That there were members of this group who retained loyalties to Japan has been confirmed by investigations made subsequent to the exclusion," he wrote. "Approximately five thousand American citizens of Japanese ancestry refused to swear allegiance to the United States and to renounce allegiance to the Japanese Emperor, and several thousand evacuees requested repatriation to Japan."[63]

Black's reliance on this purported evidence of widespread disloyalty reflected a judicial grasping at straws. The "investigations" to which he referred were in fact the results of the Selective Service questionnaires administered by the War Relocation Authority to all adult internees. Confronted with a demand that they renounce an allegiance to Japan they never had, several thousand American citizens in the internment camps had refused to comply. WRA officials themselves considered this questionnaire—drafted by the War Department—misleading and coercive. Black also lumped together the small number of American citizens who had requested repatriation with the much larger group of aliens. More to the point, Black's reference to events that occurred long after completion of internment undercut his disavowal of any intention "to decide momentous questions not contained within the framework of the pleadings or the evidence in this case." This statement, part of

Black's compromise with Stone and Douglas on the touchy question of detention, hardly squared with his use of "evidence" that grew out of the detention program.[64]

Having devoted much of the preceding week to the task of drafting his rebuttal to the dissenters, Black put off his final negotiations with Douglas and Stone until he circulated a revised version of the majority opinion on December 8, 1944. This version again dodged the detention issue. Since Korematsu had been convicted of remaining in San Leandro and not of failing to report to an assembly center, Black wrote, "we cannot in this case determine the validity of those separate provisions" of the exclusion order. Douglas remained adamant on this issue and approached his reluctant colleague later that day with another offer to abandon his dissent in return for a bargain on detention. The two men quickly struck a deal. "At the request of Justice Douglas," Black informed the Court that afternoon, his opinion now included a paragraph that began with this sentence: "Some of the members of the Court are of the view that evacuation and detention in an Assembly Center were inseparable." Unwilling to assert his agreement with this statement, Black in turn extracted a concession from Douglas, a concluding sentence that underlined Black's position that detention was not at issue in the Korematsu case: "But whatever view is taken, it results in holding that the order under which petitioner was convicted was valid."[65]

In striking his bargain with Douglas, Black won over a dissenter at the price of exposing the cracks among the new majority, which now stood at 6-to-3. Chief Justice Stone, however, demanded a further concession. "Your latest edition of the opinion," he wrote to Black on December 9, "gives me some difficulties." The crux of Korematsu's objection to the exclusion order "involved his being subject to a relocation order, and your opinion does not show why that is not true." Black's revised opinion had, in fact, dropped any reference to a separate relocation order; it seems apparent that Black had returned to the record and discovered that such an order was a figment of Stone's imagination. The Chief Justice nonetheless suggested that Black could have no "possible objection" to a denial that Korematsu's obedience of the exclusion order "would result in his detention under a relocation order." If Black made this assertion, Stone assured him, "I can join you with a clear conscience."[66]

Black had taken pains in the opinion circulated on December 8 to correct Stone's error and to note that the exclusion order alone was at issue in the case. Undoubtedly eager to avoid further haggling over the opinion, Black made one last compromise. Adopting the language of Stone's concurrence, he wrote in the final version that "we cannot say either as a matter of fact or law" that Korematsu's detention in an assembly center "would have resulted in his detention in a relocation center." However shaky as a statement of fact, this sentence made no mention of a separate relocation order. But another sentence did so. "It will be time enough to decide the serious constitutional issues which petitioner seeks to raise," Black added, "when an assembly or relocation order is applied or is certain to be applied to him, and we have its terms before us." This addition to the opinion assuaged the Chief Justice at the cost of consistency. Having conceded to Douglas that exclusion and detention were "inseparable" parts of the internment program, the dential that detention was at issue before the Court widened the cracks among the majority to a chasm.[67]

Before he returned the revised opinion to the Court's printer for the last time, Black changed his mind about a paragraph he had earlier drafted and then crossed out. Perhaps in response to Murphy's dissent, he had insisted that there was "a factual foundation of record" in the Korematsu case to support the mass evacuation of Japanese Americans. "We conclude that the government's action was predicated not on racial prejudice, but upon the compelling urgencies of national defense." The Court was not, however, insensitive to issues of racial discrimination. "All laws directed primarily at racial or ethnic groups are immediately suspect," Black wrote. "But that is not to say that they are all unconstitutional." What cleared DeWitt's actions from judicial suspicion was that the potential dangers of sabotage and espionage "demanded a solution in terms of the Japanese-American group."[68]

Why Black eliminated this paragraph from the opinion he circulated on December 8 is unclear. The most likely reason is that it called attention to the standard of judicial review that Stone had proposed in his *Carolene Products* opinion, that the Court apply a test of strict scrutiny to legislation affecting racial minorities. Even without citation to Stone's earlier opinion, a reference to his test in the Korematsu case might prove embarrassing. Under fire from the dissenters, however, Black retrieved his earlier draft and revised the paragraph for his final opinion. The published version read that "legal restrictions which curtail the rights of a single racial group are immediately suspect" and must be subjected to "the most rigid scrutiny" by the Court. Black then carved out a wartime exception to Stone's test: "Pressing public necessity may sometimes justify the existence of such restrictions; racial antagonism never can."[69]

Properly applied, the strict scrutiny test required that the government demonstrate both a "compelling" need for the racial restrictions and the absence of a "less restrictive alternative" to them. Black did not directly address either of these elements of the test in his published opinion. The odd placement of this paragraph in the opinion—stuck in the middle of the chronology of the case—suggests that Black inserted it at the last minute, more as window dressing than as a plank in the opinion's foundation. Seven pages later, in his last paragraph, Black discovered the requisite need for mass evacuation in General DeWitt's fears of a Japanese invasion of the West Coast and the "evidence of disloyalty" among the Japanese Americans. By implication, he dismissed the issue of alternatives with the assertion that "the need for action was great, and time was short." Black ended his opinion on a plaintive note of judicial deference to the military: "We cannot—by availing ourselves of the calm perspective of hindsight—now say that at that time these actions were unjustified."[70]

The apologetic tone of Black's opinion left one member of the Court unsatisfied. Well before he received the final draft, Felix Frankfurter had concluded that the opinion was insufficiently firm on the question of judicial restraint. As a hard-liner on this issue, deference to military judgment mattered less to Frankfurter than capitulation to congressional action. Eager to put his views on the record, Frankfurter dashed off a one-paragraph concurring opinion on December 1. "I find nothing in the Constitution which denies to Congress the power to enforce a military order by making its violation an offense triable in the civil courts," he told his colleagues.[71]

Unlike Douglas and Stone, whose bargains with Black were designed to forge a consensus on the Korematsu case, Frankfurter's real quarrel was not with Black. The first draft of Black's opinion left no room for compromise on the issue that most concerned Frankfurter. Resigned to Black's equivocation on judicial review, he lashed out instead at Robert Jackson for suggesting that DeWitt's orders were beyond the pale of congressional power. Frankfurter took violent exception to this position, and to a sentence in the first draft of Jackson's dissenting opinion. "Our forefathers were practical men," Jackson had written of his colleague's heroes, "and they had no delusions about war being a lawless business." Frankfurter wasted no time in responding to this sacrilege. Harry Mansfield, his law clerk at the time, recalled that Frankfurter enlisted Mansfield's wife, who was then working on a graduate degree in history, in tracking down the wartime records of each member of the Constitutional Convention. Her research, extracted from sources scattered throughout the Library of Congress, enabled Frankfurter to respond that Jackson had made a statement "not reasonably to be attributed to the hard-headed Framers, of whom a majority had had actual participation in war."[72]

For reasons he kept to himself, Jackson pared his dissent from fifteen pages to five, eliminating both the sentence to which Frankfurter objected and the historical context in which it rested. Unwilling to holster his rhetorical guns, Frankfurter retained his rebuttal to Jackson in the final version of his concurring opinion, which also included the claim that DeWitt's exclusion orders could not "be stigmatized as lawless because like action in times of peace would be lawless." Hugo Black, who had stretched his conscience to its limits in revising the Korematsu opinion to satisfy Douglas and Stone, could hardly have welcomed Frankfurter's unsolicited concurrence. Unable to disarm his vociferous colleague, Black could only sidestep the duel betweeen Frankfurter and Jackson. Defending the honor of his congressional allies, Frankfurter ended his opinion with a bow to their endorsement of DeWitt's orders: "That is their business, not ours."[73]

William O. Douglas waited impatiently while Black tinkered with the Korematsu opinion. Quick and facile with his pen, Douglas had sent his colleagues a lengthy opinion in the Endo case on November 8, the same day they received the first version of Black's opinion. None of the Supreme Court's rules required that opinions in the two cases be released together. Political factors, however, held up announcement of the Endo opinion for several weeks. The Court's response to these outside pressures, which will be discussed shortly, provides a telling insight into the linkage of law and politics.

Judging the significance of an opinion on the basis of its length is often misleading. Douglas wrote twenty-four pages to Black's eight, but devoted most of this space to a recitation of the military orders and leave regulations imposed on Japanese Americans by General DeWitt and the War Relocation Authority. The last four pages of the opinion discussed the question of the lower court's jurisdiction in the case, a point made superfluous by Solicitor General Fahy's concession on the issue during his oral argument. The Court was not required to accept Fahy's assurance that the WRA would in fact return Mitsuye Endo from Utah to California for further proceedings in her case. In citing fifteen prior cases on this issue, however, Douglas hinted at his reluctance to confront the constitutional question raised by Endo's detention.

Fourteen pages into his opinion, Douglas finally reached the central issue, only to leave it unanswered. "We are of the view that Mitsuye Endo should be given her liberty," he stated for a unanimous Court. Douglas then matched Black in his determination to evade the question of detention. "In reaching that conclusion," he continued, "we do not come to the underlying constitutional issues which have been argued. For we conclude that, whatever power the War Relocation Authority may have to detain other classes of citizens, it has no authority to subject citizens who are concededly loyal to its leave procedures."[74]

The impact of this holding, which would require the WRA to release not only Mitsuye Endo but every Japanese American who had been cleared for loyalty and wished to leave the relocation centers, masked the narrow ground on which it rested. All that Douglas accomplished, and all that the Court intended, was to strike down the WRA's requirement that Endo and others in her situation complete the leave forms as a condition for release. The half-hearted defense of these regulations by Solicitor General Fahy in his oral argument made this outcome almost inevitable. Douglas only stated the obvious when he wrote that the WRA's "authority to detain a citizen or to grant him a conditional release as protection against espionage or sabotage is exhausted at least when his loyalty is conceded." By definition, a loyal citizen would not aid the enemy and posed no danger to military facilities.[75]

Douglas adopted the pose of statutory censor in reaching his goal of releasing Endo from detention. "Neither the Act nor the orders use the language of detention," he wrote in referring to Public Law 503 and DeWitt's exclusion orders. Given this literal approach, of course, the Court's opinions in the Hirabayashi and Korematsu cases would equally fail the test imposed by Douglas. Justice Roberts, to whom this approach was natural, based his dissent in the Korematsu case on such a stringent reading of Public Law 503. Douglas made his point, however, as a camouflage for his real purpose, which soon became evident. "We do not mean to imply," he explained on the Court's behalf, "that detention in connection with no phase of the evacuation program would be lawful. The fact that the Act and the orders are silent on detention does not of course mean that any power to detain is lacking." The silence of the President and Congress meant only that "any such authority which exists must be implied." What could not be found in the language of Public Law 503 was easily discovered in the broad "war power" invested by the Constitution in the executive and legislative branches. Chief Justive Stone had said as much in the Hirabayashi case, Douglas wrote approvingly.[76]

Despite his disclaimer, Douglas felt obliged to raise the constitutional issues that James Purcell had argued to the Court, if only to dismiss them as outweighed by "the exigencies of war." Due process protections of the Fifth Amendment; safeguards provided to criminal defendants in the Sixth Amendment; and the privilege of habeas corpus all demonstrated that "the Constitution is as specific in its enumeration of many of the civil rights of the individual as it is in its enumeration of the powers of his government." He noted these provisions "not to stir the constitutional issues which have been argued at the bar," Douglas wrote, but to indicate the Court's approach to presidential and congressional action "that touches the sensitive area of rights specifically guaranteed by the Constitution." Having stirred these issues to a boil, Douglas cooled the pot with an assurance that all three branches of the federal government "are sensitive to and respectful of the liberties of the citizen." Detention of the Japanese Americans, he concluded, met constitutional standards so long as such detention was "narrowly confined to the precise purpose of the evacuation program."[77]

Every member of the Court agreed with the outcome of the Endo case. Two of his colleagues, however, rejected the reasoning of the opinion and needled Douglas in separate concurrences. Justice Murphy considered the endorsement of detention, for whatever purpose, as "another example of the unconstitutional resort to racism inherent in the entire evacuation program." He also pointed out the Court's evasion of the question of Endo's right to return to California, from which she remained excluded. Citing cases that included as a privilege of citizenship "the right to pass freely from state to state," Murphy wrote that "her exclusion from a place where she would otherwise have a right to go is a position I cannot sanction."[78]

On his part, Justice Roberts complained that "the court endeavors to avoid constitutional issues which are necessarily involved" in the detention question. Douglas hid his head in the sand and ignored "patent facts" in suggesting that DeWitt "exceeded the authority granted by executive order in this case," Roberts charged. Given congressional appropriation of funds to the War Relocation Authority, the argument that Congress had not authorized detention struck him as an evasion of the issue. Roberts knew that the courts were obligated to read statutes in their full context of congressional action and executive implementation. "Such a basis of decision will render easy the evasion of law and the violation of constitutional rights," he wrote of Douglas's effort to single out the WRA's leave regulations from the entire detention program. Roberts concluded that "the court is squarely faced with a serious constitutional question"—did Endo's detention violate "the guarantee of due process of law"? "There can be but one answer to that question. An admittedly loyal citizen has been deprived of her liberty for a period of years. Under the Constitution she should be free to come and go as she pleases."[79]

Whether or not these barbed critiques pricked his conscience, Douglas felt no need to respond to Murphy and Roberts, at least on paper. As his later negotiations with Black demonstrated, Douglas had narrowly crafted the Endo opinion to form a close fit with the Korematsu opinion. Complaints that he evaded constitutional issues were less bothersome to Douglas than possible objections that his opinion might undercut Black's equally cautious effort. What did bother Douglas, however, was the intrusion of outside pressure into the timing of the announcement by the Court of the Endo opinion.

Douglas got wind of these pressures sometime between the first circulation of his opinion on November 8, and November 28, when he expressed his impatience to Chief Justice Stone. "I think an opinion in this case should be announced on December 4," Douglas urged, "unless prior to that time Mitsuye Endo either has been released or has been promised her immediate and unqualified release." Without indicating the source of his information, Douglas complained that "the matter is at a standstill because officers of the government have indicated that some change in detention plans are under consideration." Conceding that official requests to defer release of his opinion reflected "important administrative considerations," Douglas noted that Endo "has not asked that action of this Court be stayed." The Court should "act promptly and not lend our aid in compounding the wrong by keeping her in unlawful confinement through our inaction any longer than necessary to reach a decision" about ending the detention of Japanese Americans, he concluded this appeal to the Chief Justice.[80]

Stone ignored the letter from Douglas and held up release of the Endo opinion for another three weeks. What Douglas never learned was that Stone had enlisted in the high-level campaign to protect President Roosevelt from the political consequences of the decision to end the internment program. Directed from the White House and coordinated in the Pentagon by John McCloy, this effort had succeeded over the past six months in holding off the demands of Interior Secretary Ickes and General Bonesteel that Japanese Americans be allowed to leave the internment camps and return to their West Coast homes.

Although the decision to open the camp gates had been made soon after the November elections, public announcement of this move was complicated by the Endo case. White House officials, and perhaps Roosevelt himself, undoubtedly hoped to blunt criticism of their lengthy delay in making this decision by announcing it from an executive-branch office. Waiting until after the Supreme Court issued an opinion that declared the detention of "loyal" citizens to be unlawful might strike the press and the public as capitulation to the judiciary. McCloy maintained almost daily contact with Justice Frankfurter, and these two friends constituted the most direct link between the Court and the War Department. Despite his assurance to members of the California congressional delegation, made public during the week of December 11, that "no immediate easing of restrictions was in prospect," McCloy had been engaged for weeks in behind-the-scenes negotiations with Justice and Interior Department officials and with the White House over the internment issue.[81]

Members of the Supreme Court have consistently proclaimed a firm policy against the discussion of pending cases with anyone outside the Court. Breaches of the secrecy injunction are certainly rare, and there is no documentary record of such a breach in the Endo case. Secondhand evidence that Frankfurter leaked word of the timing of the Endo decision to McCloy comes from Roger Daniels, a historian who has written extensively about the internment. Daniels has recently asserted, citing an unnamed source who worked in McCloy's office at the time, that "McCloy was told by Frankfurter of the date the Supreme Court would issue the Endo opinion." Despite the hearsay quality of this evidence, it seems clear that the War Department was privy to the Court's timetable in the Korematsu and Endo cases.[82]

The Court announced its opinions in both cases on December 18, 1944, a Monday. One day earlier, in an unusual Sunday statement, the War Department issued a press release in the name of General Henry Pratt, who then headed the Western Defense Command. "Those persons of Japanese ancestry whose records have stood the test of Army scrutiny during the past two years," Pratt informed the press, would be released from internment after January 2, 1945, and would be "permitted the same freedom of movement throughout the United States as other loyal citizens and law-abiding aliens." In revoking the mass exclusion orders issued in 1942 by General DeWitt, his successor freed Mitsuye Endo and some fifty thousand other Japanese Americans cleared for loyalty to return to their West Coast homes. Pratt's order included a major exception: those "about whom information is available indicating a pro-Japanese attitude will continue to be excluded on an individual basis." This restriction left close to twenty thousand internees, most of them held in the Tule Lake "segregation center" in northern California, behind barbed wire for presumed disloyalty. Over the next several months, military officials served individual exclusion orders on some five thousand Tule Lake residents, raising in the process a new round of legal challenges to "disloyalty" as a ground for continued detention.[83]

Pratt's announcement met with decidedly mixed reactions on the West Coat. Three years after Pearl Harbor, combat still raged in the Pacific and hostility toward the Japanese Americans remained strong. Press reports of the new policy played up the potential for vigilante action: OUTBREAK OF VIOLENCE SEEN BY NIPS' RETURN headlined the

Los Angeles *Times*. Public officials did their best, however, to generate an atmosphere of law and order. California governor Earl Warren, an original advocate of mass evacuation, now proclaimed his belief that "all Americans will join in protecting constitutional rights . . . and will maintain an attitude that will discourage friction and prevent civil disorder." Trading on his good relations with state and local law-enforcement officials, Warren extracted pledges of protection for the Japanese Americans and prosecution of those who might harass or attack them. After a telephone conference with Warren, the governors of Oregon and Washington issued similar appeals. In the end, the scare headlines proved to be overblown: the return of Japanese Americans to the West Coast prompted only a scattering of violence.[84]

Coming as it did on the heels of the War Department move, release by the Supreme Court of the Korematsu and Endo opinions brought a muted response from the press, both in news coverage and editorial comment. Not surprisingly, those papers that commented on the decisions lined up as they had on the Hirabayashi case. The Washington *Post* displayed its sentiments in an editorial entitled "Legalization of Racism." Endorsing the outcome of the Endo case, the *Post* denounced Black's opinion in the Korematsu case and wondered when the Court "will ever be able to assert the rights of citizens against a plea of military necessity." In contrast, the Los Angeles *Times* deplored the revocation of DeWitt's orders and took Douglas to task in an editorial headed "We Shan't Pretend to Like It." The lack of any "magic method" by which the loyalty of Japanese Americans could be "infallibly" determined, argued the *Times,* required that detention be continued until the war's end. Despite their divergent positions, however, both papers expressed puzzlement about the Court's reasoning in the two cases. "Laymen may be pardoned if they find these verdicts contradictory," the *Post* told its readers, while the *Times* found it strange that Black and Douglas could speak for the Court "in practically the same breath" and yet reach opposing outcomes.[85]

It is unlikely that many newspaper readers thought much about the question implicit in this editorial head-scratching. The public's gaze was riveted on news from the front lines in Europe and the Pacific, as the war came to a climax in both theaters of combat. Those who wrote and read these editorials, however, failed to perceive that Black and Douglas had in fact spoken with the same breath. The apparent conflict between the two opinions masked the congruence of their holdings: Subject only to explicit congressional approval, the Supreme Court had made clear, military officials faced no constitutional barriers to the wartime detention of American citizens singled out on a racial basis.

13

"Watergate Hadn't Happened Yet"

THIS BOOK OPENED with an account of the initial responses of two government officials—Edward J. Ennis and John J. McCloy—to the shocking news of the Japanese attack on Pearl Harbor on December 7, 1941. It ends with an account of the appearances of these two lawyers before a congressional commission in November 1981, almost forty years later.

Placing the spotlight on Ennis and McCloy in the opening and closing chapters of this book seems appropriate for three reasons. First, they took opposing positions in the internal debate between their respective departments—Justice and War—that culminated in President Roosevelt's decision in February 1942 to authorize the evacuation of Japanese Americans from the West Coast. Second, they bore the major share of responsibility within their departments for the conduct of the internment cases decided by the Supreme Court in 1943 and 1944. Finally, their testimony before the Commission on Wartime Relocation and Internment of Civilians in 1981—testimony that differed in tone and substance—offers a unique opportunity to listen to the retrospective evaluations by these key officials of their wartime actions.

Ennis and McCloy were not, of course, the only participants in the evacuation debate and the internment cases. Some forty lawyers took part, over a period of three years, in the legal battles that preceded and followed Roosevelt's signing of Executive Order 9066, and twenty judges ruled on the cases that challenged the internment orders. In putting these events into perspective, this concluding chapter will draw on the reflections of those lawyers and judges who later discussed their wartime actions. Among these participants, however, Ennis and McCloy uniquely personify the internment battles. Opposed at the time, they remain opposed after four decades of legal, social, and political upheaval. Their commission testimony provides both the drama of confession and the sparks of confrontation.

The background of forces that led to their appearances before the blue-ribbon commission reveals much about the lingering impact of the internment, both on Japanese Americans themselves and on a nation finally willing to face its responsibility for this wartime program. The first official effort to make amends for the injustice of internment came in 1948 with congressional enactment of the Japanese-American Evacuation Claims Act. Limited to compensation for property losses which could be proved by records, an impossible task for most potential claimants, this law doled out $37 million in response to claims that totaled $148 million; the Federal Reserve Bank had estimated that Japanese Americans lost $400 million in property. Losses of earnings and profits from businesses and farms sold in 1942 under distress conditions, and compensation for deprivations of constitutional rights, were not covered by the 1948 law.[1]

Thirty years passed before the "redress and reparations" movement, led largely by younger Japanese Americans whose parents and grandparents still bore the psychological scars of internment, gained enough political backing to persuade Congress to establish the Commission on Wartime Relocation and Internment of Civilians in 1980. Divisions within the Japanese American community lay behind the adoption of the commission approach. The militant wing of the redress movement had prevailed on Seattle congressman Mike Lowry to introduce in 1979 a bill providing for $25,000 payments directly to those who had been interned or to their heirs. Convinced that the Lowry bill stood no chance of passage, leaders of the Japanese American Citizens League—with Washington lobbyist Mike Masaoka at their helm—campaigned for the commission alternative, hoping that the backing of a prestigious panel would add strength to the redress effort.

Attracted to the JACL's more modest proposal, congressional leaders shunted the Lowry bill to a legislative siding and pushed through a bill that established a nine-member commission chaired by Joan Z. Bernstein, a Washington lawyer and former Carter administration official. Her fellow panelists included former Supreme Court justice Arthur Goldberg and two former Massachusetts congressmen, Senator Edward Brooke and Representative Robert Drinan. The only Japanese American member was Philadelphia judge William Marutani, who had been interned as a teenager.*

*The commission also included Dan Lungren, vice-chair and a California Republican representative; Arthur Flemming, chair of the U.S. Civil Rights Commission; Ishmael

Congress directed the commission to "review the facts and circumstances" that had led to Executive Order 9066 and to the "detention in internment camps of American citizens," including both Japanese Americans and Alaskan Aleuts; 900 of the latter had been evacuated from the Aleutian and Pribilof Islands and interned during the war. Charged with the additional task of recommending "appropriate remedies" to Congress, the commissioners held a series of hearings across the country between July and December 1981. Most of the 750 witnesses who testified at these sessions were Japanese Americans who related in emotional, often tearful, words their memories of internment and the psychic wounds they still endured. For many of these witnesses, this was the first time they had spoken openly of their experiences.[2]

Edward Ennis appeared before the commission on the afternoon of November 2, 1981. White-haired and ruddy at 73, he assured the panel that "my personal connection with these matters some 40 years ago is so close and intimate that I would not miss the opportunity to appear before you." Ennis wore two hats at the hearing: one as the wartime director of the Alien Enemy Control Unit of the Justice Department; the other as spokesperson for the American Civil Liberties Union. After leaving the Justice Department in 1946, he had set up a small law firm in Manhattan that specialized in immigration law and had immediately joined the ACLU's national board. Ennis served as ACLU general counsel from 1955 to 1969 and had chaired the board between 1969 and 1977.

Ennis first submitted to the commission a statement of the ACLU's forthright position: "It is the view of the ACLU that the mass evacuation and subsequent detention of the entire Japanese-American population from the West Coast in 1942 was the greatest deprivation of civil liberties by government in this country since slavery." The ACLU statement added that any "monetary redress" recommended to Congress "should be substantial in view of the serious and sustained violation of civil liberties suffered by the evacuees."[3]

The irony of the contrast between his ACLU and Justice Department roles did not escape Ennis. Referring to the internment cases, he admitted that he had "argued the cases in the lower courts, and wrote the briefs for the Solicitor General for the Supreme Court of the United States. I think I should confess that." Returning to his early debates with Attorney General Biddle over the legality of mass evacuation, En-

Gromoff, a Russian Orthodox priest from Alaska; and Hugh Mitchell, former Washington Senator.

nis professed resignation over the eventual judicial resolution of the issue: "As it turned out, what the Supreme Court says determines what is constitutional or unconstitutional. The Attorney General was right, and I was wrong."[4]

Although none of the commissioners addressed it directly, the question of the government lawyer's dual responsibility—as the advocate for his federal client and as defender of the Constitution—underlay many of the questions posed to Ennis. Pressed by Judge Marutani to pass judgment on his War Department counterparts, Ennis took a firm position but diplomatically refrained from mentioning names. "I believe what happened," he replied, "was that these distinguished men, perfectly honest and able men, somehow conceived their job to be lawyers for a client, and they went to the President with what the military commander on the West Coast asked them to do and presented that. They did not exercise the independent civilian authority they should have exercised."[5]

Ennis passed up the chance before the commission to settle old scores with his War Department adversaries. A week before his public testimony, during an interview with me in his New York office, he had expressed himself in similar but more pointed terms. "I told them it was a lot of God-damned nonsense," he said of his disputes with Stimson and McCloy over the internment issue. "These guys just acted as attorneys for the military authorities and gave them whatever they asked for without any independent determination of its propriety, which I thought as the high officers of the military they were required to exercise."[6]

But once the internment decision had been made and ratified by Roosevelt, Ennis had defended it as a government lawyer. Asked by Senator Brooke to reflect on his wartime actions from the perspective of the present, he stressed the demands of duty: "I can't see myself now as I did then opposing the programs and then going in and defending them. But as an attorney at the Department of Justice that was my responsibility." Ennis had made this point to me a week earlier: "I guess my position was that a government attorney's responsibility was to state what his position was and then to do the job that his superiors determined."[7]

In his interview with me, Ennis offered an explanation of why he and John Burling (who died in 1959) had swallowed their doubts and continued to work on the internment cases. He raised, in discussing this question, the option of resignation as an alternative to internal opposition. "I'm still wondering why Burling and I didn't just throw up our hands and quit. Why didn't we throw the whole thing up? I really believe we didn't throw it up because we didn't want to put it in the hands of Justice Department lawyers who were gung-ho for the Army's position. I think we felt that we'd just stay with it and do the best that we could, which wasn't a hell of a lot." Ennis also confessed to the commission, without prompting, that "when I look back on it now I don't know why I didn't resign."[8]

Ennis had in fact talked of resigning after the showdown with McCloy in Attorney General Biddle's living room on February 17, 1942, after Biddle abandoned his opposition to evacuation. There seems little doubt that his resignation at that point would not have affected Roosevelt's decision to sign the executive order approved at this meeting. It seems more likely, however, that had Ennis and Burling resigned in October 1944, in protest at Solicitor General Fahy's capitulation to McCloy over the disputed footnote in the Korematsu brief, such a dramatic step might well have changed the outcome of that crucial case.

Confronted in October 1973 with a presidential demand that he fire Watergate Special Prosecutor Archibald Cox, Elliot Richardson had resigned as Attorney General. When he discussed with me his wartime conflict between the demands of conscience and duty, Edward Ennis offered a final reason for the choices he made: "Watergate hadn't happened yet."[9]

John J. McCloy sat down at the witness table before the commission on the morning of November 3, 1981. Bald and stocky at 86, he combined an impressive dignity with a suggestion of bulldog pugnacity. The atmosphere inside the crowded Senate hearing room that morning was charged with tension. Many of those in the audience behind McCloy had themselves been interned, and others were the children and grandchildren of Japanese Americans who had been herded into internment camps by Army troops.

Intentional or not, the commission's scheduling of witnesses had separated Ennis and McCloy by a day and thus prevented a direct confrontation between the wartime adversaries. But with Ennis's confessional testimony fresh in the minds of the commissioners and many in the audience, the prospect of sharp questioning of the former War Department official added a sense of anticipation to the proceedings. McCloy's introduction to the panel as "one of the most distinguished Americans" of his time—an encomium bestowed by commissioner Arthur Goldberg—suggested instead that he would receive the deference due "the chairman of the American establishment," the title bestowed on McCloy by Richard Rovere as long ago as 1962.[10]

McCloy had indeed earned this title in the years that followed his departure from the War Department in 1945. Adding his name and clout to the powerful New York law firm of Milbank, Tweed, Hadley, and McCloy, he shuttled between private and public roles—often combining both—over the next three decades. From 1947 to 1949 he served as president of the World Bank, moving from this post to that of American high commissioner in occupied West Germany, a position he held for three years as an advocate of German rearmament and industrial revival. In addition to chairing the boards of both the Chase Manhattan Bank and the Ford Foundation, Mcloy headed for thirteen years—1961 to 1974—the President's General Advisory Committee on Arms Control and Disarmament. More than two dozen colleges and universities, both American and foreign, have conferred honorary degrees on McCloy. This record of positions and plaudits lends support to his designation by historian Alan Brinkley as "the most influential private citizen in America."[11]

The deference shown McCloy by the commissioners was not shown by those in the audience. "I cannot forget," he later complained to Edward Brooke, "the quite unrestrained hissing which took place during my examination whenever I spoke favorably of any government action." McCloy endured several eruptions of hissing during the four hours he spent at the witness table. First insisting that the forced removal of Japanese Americans from the West Coast "was a relocation program and not an internment," he prompted one round of hissing in urging the commission to agree with him that "the whole operation was as benignly conducted as wartime conditions permitted." Another followed his claim, phrased in Orwellian terms, that "on the whole the deconcentration of the Japanese population and its redistribution throughout the country resulted in their finding a healthier and more advantageous environment" than that of the hostile West Coast states.[12]

Questioned by Brooke about the factual justification for internment, McCloy remembered "seeing reports of pretty well authenticated pieces of espionage." He placed more stress, however, on "the need for the protection of the Japanese population from possible local disorders, demonstrations and reprisals." Combining these factors in the internment equation, McCloy suggested that the commission would "be well advised to conclude that President Roosevelt's wartime action . . . was taken and carried out in accordance with the best interests of the country, considering the conditions, exigencies and considerations which then faced the nation."[13]

One commissioner refused to defer to the unrepentent witness. "I'm wondering whether or not the best interest of the country was served by uprooting 120,000 people and destroying their lifetime work," inquired

Judge Marutani when his turn at questioning began. McCloy's response that Japanese Americans had not been "adversely affected" by their internment prompted Marutani to lean forward and raise his voice: "What other Americans, Mr. McCloy, fought for their country while their parents, brothers and sisters were incarcerated?" The two lawyers were now shouting at each other. He had visited the internment camps, McCloy shot back, and assured Marutani that their residents were "not distressed" by the conditions they had endured. His composure shaken by this heated exchange, McCloy reminded Marutani of the "surprise attack" that had initiated the war and concluded that internment had been adopted "in the way of retribution for the attack that was made on Pearl Harbor."[14]

Stunned by this admission, Marutani asked the stenographer to read it back. McCloy quickly sought to retract his statement: "I don't think I like the word retribution." But the term—and its implications—remained on the record.[15]

At the time of this commission hearing, its staff had not been provided by the Justice Department with the records that detailed McCloy's involvement in the internal battles over the government's briefs in the Supreme Court cases that challenged the wartime orders. Commission counsel Angus Macbeth, however, raised the issue in an oblique fashion when he referred McCloy to the testimony given the previous day by Edward Ennis. Dismissing his wartime adversary's objections to the constitutionality of the internment program as "really irrelevant 40 years after the attack" on Pearl Harbor, McCloy offered his assessment of Ennis: "He sees a civil liberties problem under every bedstead, but we couldn't follow his sensitivities in that regard." The Supreme Court had settled these constitutional questions, McCloy concluded with a stamp of finality.[16]

Unbending in his defense of internment, McCloy urged the commissioners to avoid any recommendations to Congress that might restrict the powers of future administrations to adopt similar measures. "I don't mean to be alarmist," he prefaced this advice, "but within 90 miles right now of our shore" was a Cuban government hostile to the United States. Posing the prospect of armed conflict between the two countries, McCloy reminded the panel of the large numbers of Cubans who live in Florida—failing to note that most are avowed opponents of the Castro regime and that all are protected by the Constitution. His question to the commission was both rhetorical and suggestive: "Wouldn't you think seriously about moving those people out if there was a raid there?"[17]

The passage of four decades has not shaken McCloy's conviction that "men of real statesmanship and integrity" had acted reasonably in ordering the wartime internment of Japanese Americans. His involvement in this episode raised no conflict of conscience and duty. McCloy stood firm in his final judgment: "There is, I submit, nothing whatever for which the country should atone."[18]

Edward Ennis and John McCloy have placed their retrospective views of the internment program on the public record. What of the other officials and lawyers who played significant roles in this episode, from the initial evacuation decision through the final Supreme Court decisions? How did they later assess their own actions in responding to wartime pressures? And how did they judge the actions of others, both allies and adversaries? Can we draw from their reflections and recollections any lasting lessons about the process of justice at war?

Pieced together from a wide range of sources—memoirs, letters, interviews, and public testimony—this account of what participants later said and wrote about themselves and others is necessarily incomplete. Some, most notably President Roosevelt and General DeWitt, left no record of their thoughts on these questions. The comments of others are brief and unrevealing. What emerges from the available record, however, is revealing about the nature of certitude and doubt. Clustered along the spectrum of subsequent positions on internment are three groups. Colonel Karl Bendetsen and Justice Hugo Black represent the true believers whose convictions at the time about the validity of the internment program remained unshaken and, if anything, became more adamant in later years. In the middle, and the largest in number, are those who subordinated their personal doubts to the demands of duty and who later found justification for their wartime actions in the outcome of the Supreme Court test cases. Three government lawyers—Charles Fahy, Herbert Wechsler, and Philip Glick—represent this group. ACLU director Roger Baldwin and Justice William O. Douglas exemplify the third group, those who later expressed regret that they had failed to take a position of public opposition to the internment program.

Karl Bendetsen resigned his Army commission in 1946 and returned to law practice in his native state of Washington. Two years later, he moved back to the Pentagon as a civilian official and repeated his earlier rise through the ranks. Beginning as counsel and special assistant to the Secretary of Defense, Bendetsen played a central role in the reorganization of the armed services before he left the Pentagon in 1952 as Undersecretary of the Army. Turning to the business world, he wound up as chairman of the Champion Corporation, a multinational enterprise that he helped to expand from a domestic base in the lumbering and papermaking industries.

Called before the Commission on Wartime Relocation in November 1981, Bendetsen retained at 74 both his military bearing and attitude. As the architect and engineer of the internment program, he displayed not the slightest hint of doubt about the correctness of his wartime actions. The ancestral origins of the Japanese Americans remained in his mind as the primary justification for their forced removal from the West Coast. Given the "very real prospect" in the months after Pearl Harbor of Japanese forces landing on the coast, he told the commission, "you couldn't expect all the Japanese persons to resist them and remain loyal to the United States." Later in his testimony, Bendetsen repeated his belief that Japanese Americans "would have a very difficult time" resisting the impulse to assist the invading Japanese troops. Pressed by Senator Brooke to explain the basis for his assertions, Bendetsen offered a succinct answer: "Human nature."[19]

Aggressive in his defense of internment, Bendetsen became defensive when the questioning turned to his role in preparing the *Final Report* of General DeWitt. Commission counsel Angus Macbeth grilled Bendetsen about the authorship of Chapter 2, which contained the espionage allegations that led to the showdown between Justice and War Department lawyers over their veracity. "I really don't remember," he first responded to MacBeth's inquiry about the source of these allegations. He then recalled that the "source of the material was the Office of Naval Intelligence and the FBI." Bendetsen added that the contents of Chapter 2 "were not my observations or conclusions, because I really had no time to turn my attention to it."[20]

Although MacBeth had earlier alluded to "attacks" on the *Final Report* "by the Justice Department in 1944," he dropped this line of inquiry after Bendetsen's assurance that any review of Chapter 2 "really was no part of my role." Two aspects of this exchange, however, deserve reference to the record. Bendetsen's claim that the ONI and FBI had provided the material used in Chapter 2 hardly squares with the consistent denials by these intelligence agencies that Japanese Americans were disloyal as a group or had committed any acts of espionage. And in April 1943, Bendetsen had reported to the Pentagon at McCloy's orders to work with Captain John Hall in revising this chapter and had reported to DeWitt on the progress of these revisions. One reason that Macbeth accepted Bendetsen's account was that the commission had not received at the time of his appearance the ONI, FBI, and FCC reports that refuted the disloyalty and espionage claims of Chapter 2. Considering the crucial nature of these reports, it seems puzzling that the commission made no further effort to secure from Bendetsen any clarification of his testimony.[21]

The ranks of true believers include two members of the Supreme Court. Hugo Black, whose judicial legacy rests on his First Amendment opinions, never disowned his opinion in the Korematsu case. "I would do precisely the same thing today," he insisted several years before his death in 1971. "I would probably issue the same order were I president. We had a situation where we were at war." Black's comments illustrate the power and persistence of racial stereotypes. "People were rightly fearful of the Japanese," he explained, because "they all look alike to a person not a Jap." In a significant amendment to his wartime opinion, Black shifted to a defense of internment based on the discredited "preventive detention" argument. Had Japanese forces "attacked our shores," he said, "you'd have a large number fighting with the Japanese troops. And a lot of innocent Japanese-Americans would have been shot in the panic. Under these circumstances I saw nothing wrong in moving them away from the danger area."[22]

Another member of the Court rested his later defense of the internment cases on entirely different grounds. Stanley Reed—the only justice who did not write an opinion in these cases—provided evidence in his subsequent comments that his votes had been influenced by Dewitt's espionage allegations. Judicial support for the internment of Japanese Americans, he said in his oral history memoir, had been based on DeWitt's claims "that a number of them had cooperated with the Japanese" in espionage activities. "Now, maybe it was hysteria," he admitted. "But the record shows that there were authenticated cases of such treasonable actions." There is no way of knowing whether Reed's position, particularly in the Korematsu case, might have been changed by knowledge that Justice Department lawyers had branded as "lies" the espionage charges presented to the Court in General DeWitt's report. Reed's comment that Japanese Americans "were easily identifiable" among the West Coast population, placing him at odds with Black on this issue, suggests that the debunking of DeWitt's charges might have shifted his vote on the Korematsu case. Based on his reading of the wartime record, however, the Court's silent member stood firmly on his votes in the conference room.[23]

Charles Fahy suffered no pangs of conscience in later years. After his appointment by President Truman to the federal court of appeals for the District of Columbia, the former Solicitor General gained repute as a judicial liberal. Civil rights lawyers found an ally on the bench, and Fahy often voted against the government in the "loyalty" cases that came before him during the McCarthy era. The seeming anomaly of his roles—wartime advocate for the military and judicial defender of civil rights and liberties—is easily resolved. The lawyer has a duty to his client; the judge to his position as independent arbiter of the law. In arguing the Japanese American cases to the Supreme Court, Fahy identified his clients as President Roosevelt and Secretary of War Stimson. "I considered it to be my unequivocal obligation," he later said, "to seek to sustain their action with all the ability I could muster. This was my duty as I saw it."[24]

Fahy's only recorded comments on the wartime cases, given in an oral history memoir that remained closed until his death in 1981, revealed little of the internal disputes within the Justice Department and nothing of the battles with the War Department. Without referring to Edward Ennis and John Burling by name, he recalled "a strong sentiment in some quarters in the Department that the government was wrong in *Korematsu*." Fahy's recollection of his argument to the Supreme Court in that case displayed his own sentiment: "I described the situation as vividly as I could, including the close call at Midway and the thin heroic line which turned back the enemy, without which we might have had to defend much farther East, perhaps even in California."[25]

Fahy's conception of his function as a government lawyer was simple: personal doubts about the wisdom of the policies he defended were irrelevant, and he left to the Supreme Court the judgment of their legality. "I thought the evacuation unnecessary and unwise," he confessed to Francis Biddle in a 1962 letter, "but did think it would be upheld as constitutional if the military decided it was necessary." Edward Ennis remained skeptical about the depth of Fahy's doubts: "I don't think he had them. I think the Army was his client and he was putting forth the best arguments he could for them." Whichever of these later evaluations is more accurate, Fahy certainly stood before the Supreme Court bench as an effective advocate for the actions of Roosevelt and Stimson.[26]

Herbert Wechsler participated in the Japanese American cases as director of the Justice Department's War Division. Returning after the war to the faculty of Columbia Law School, he became well known as the expositor of the position that the Supreme Court should defer to legislative judgments and apply "neutral principles" in its task of constitutional interpretation. In looking back on his involvement in the wartime cases, Wechsler applied his judicial formula to his lawyer's role. Speaking to a 1957 conference on "Problems of Public and Private

Conscience,'' he discussed the dilemma he had faced in supervising the preparation of the Supreme Court brief in the Korematsu case. Defending the internment of Japanese Americans ''in what in any fair estimate should be called 'concentration camps,' '' he confessed, had been a distressing task.[27]

Wechsler recalled his dilemma in these terms: ''Should I have declined to assume the preparation of a brief in support of the constitutionality of what the President of the United States had ordered on the recommendation of his distinguished Secretary of War? I might have done that. In fact, however, I did not.'' The brief he signed ''presented the strongest arguments that I felt could be made in support of the validity of the action taken by the President and . . . the Supreme Court sustained its validity.'' More open than Fahy in his opposition to internment, Wechsler nonetheless resolved his personal doubts with a similar deference to the Supreme Court. It had not been ''my responsibility to determine whether the evacuation was constitutional or not constitutional,'' he said. It had been the Court's duty to decide that question. The only way to avoid ''what might otherwise prove to be insoluble dilemmas of choice,'' Wechsler concluded, ''is to recognize a separation of functions'' between lawyers and judges.[28]

In a later interview with me, Wechsler was more candid in his recollections but equally firm in defending his wartime position. Aligning himself with Ennis and Burling, he stated that ''we'd been deeply disturbed by the unnecessary evacuation and by the self-deception of the top brass of the War Department like McCloy and Stimson, who'd been led by the nose by second-rate people like Colonel Bendetsen.'' Forced by his official role to frame a defense of the evacuation, Wechsler had put aside his personal feelings and performed his duty as a lawyer. ''I think it came out all right,'' he told me. ''That's the way I've lived with it all these years.''[29]

Philip Glick followed John McCloy at the witness table before the Commission on Wartime Relocation. The two men offered a contrast both in stature and demeanor. Wispy and brightly alert at 75, the former WRA solicitor was eager to share his wartime recollections. Glick had remained in government legal posts for several years after closing up the WRA in 1946, including service with the Federal Housing Authority and the State Department. After another two decades in private law practice, he was then in semi-retirement. Glick had no desire to justify the original decision to evacuate and then to intern the Japanese Americans; what he defended was the WRA's performance of ''a very difficult task, to make the relocation centers as habitable, as endurable, even as comfortable as we possibly could.''[30]

When commission counsel Macbeth turned the questioning to the WRA's role in the legal defense of detention, Glick explained his conception of the government lawyer's function. Once the President "had determined that the evacuation was necessary and valid, and that WRA was now to function as a defender and assister of the evacuees," he said, "its lawyers should enforce the decision of the President until the courts had an opportunity to pass upon the constitutionality" of the detention program. Noting that the Supreme Court had evaded the constitutional issues raised in the Endo case, Glick added that "I'm confident that had the Supreme Court chosen to pass on constitutionality . . . they would have held that the United States had the power to detain pending sorting" of the Japanese Americans by loyalty.[31]

Shortly before his commission appearance, Glick discussed these issues with me and offered his account of the Endo case. "I felt that the evacuees, in their own interest, ought to be challenging the constitutionality of the detention within the relocation centers, even detention pending sorting. After looking over the various cases, we decided that Mitsuye Endo was a good case." Against his personal sympathy for Endo's legal challenge, Glick balanced his professional duty. "My staff and I had a number of discussions of this problem, just what do we do. And we decided—it didn't take a great deal of soul-searching—we are the government's lawyers. We are the President's lawyers. If this was to be challenged, the government had a right to look to the lawyers who were working for it to defend the government. We owed it to the President and to the American people to defend what we believed to be constitutionally defensible." Both at the time and since, Glick professed satisfaction with the Court's holding that an initial period of detention of American citizens, charged with no crime but suspected of disloyalty, could be lawful.[32]

Those participants in the Japanese American cases who later repented their wartime positions make up a small but chastened group. Francis Biddle, who as Attorney General had based his objection to evacuation on pragmatic rather than constitutional grounds, wrote in his 1962 memoir that "I thought at the time that the program was ill-advised, unnecessary, and unnecessarily cruel, taking Japanese who were not suspect . . . from their homes and from their businesses to sit idly in the lonely misery of barracks while the war was being fought in the world beyond." In allocating the blame for the evacuation decision, Biddle assumed an equal share with Secretary of War Stimson: "If Stimson had stood firm, had insisted, as apparently he suspected, that this wholesale evacuation was needless, the President would have followed his advice. And if, instead of dealing exclusively with McCloy and Bendetsen, I had urged the Secretary to resist the pressure of his subordinates, the result might have been different. But I was new to the Cabinet, and disinclined to insist on my view to an elder statesman whose wisdom and integrity I greatly respected.''[33]

In a later interview conducted in 1968, Biddle more pointedly identified John McCloy as the primary culprit in the evacuation decision. ''McCloy, I think more than anyone believed in this. I never excuse him for doing this.'' James Rowe, the Attorney General's wartime assistant, later expressed his view that Biddle's professed deference to Stimson constituted a self-serving excuse. ''We should have gone and fought in the White House,'' Rowe told me in an interview. He recalled the showdown with McCloy and General Gullion in Biddle's living room with exasperation. ''When Biddle quit on me so suddenly, I knew something had happened, but I didn't know what it was.'' What had happened, Rowe later discovered, was that Biddle had taken his orders from Roosevelt without putting up an argument.[34]

ACLU director Roger Baldwin also blamed his failure to take a stronger stand against the wartime treatment of Japanese Americans on those to whom he was responsible for policy guidance. Reminded by an interviewer that Dwight Macdonald—the political essayist and literary critic—had earlier called his reaction to the internment ''feeble and confused,'' Baldwin became defensive. ''That wasn't my fault,'' he responded. ''I take no responsibility for that. That was because our West Coast branches wouldn't go along with us.'' This was itself a feeble response, since what the San Francisco ACLU branch had refused to go along with was the national board's decision to bar any constitutional challenge to Roosevelt's executive order, a policy Baldwin had initially opposed. When his interviewer noted Baldwin's reluctant submission to the board on this issue, he confessed that ''I'm ashamed of it now.''[35]

Ernest Besig, who had defied the ACLU board's edict as director of the dissident San Francisco branch, dismissed Baldwin's confession as weak and self-serving. ''There were many friends of Roger's who were part of the administration under the Roosevelt regime,'' he later told me. ''Roger used to go the rounds in Washington and meet with all these guys, and he was more of a government representative than he was an ACLU representative for a while.'' Baldwin was matched as an object of Besig's scorn with Edward Ennis. Their joint action in forcing Wayne Collins into a subordinate role in the Korematsu case left Besig with a lingering sense of outrage. ''The damage he did to the Japanese," he said of Ennis, "is something that will never be erased from his record. There's something lacking in Ed that just didn't give him the courage to stand up. Roger subsequently admitted he was wrong and so did Ennis. But neither of these guys had the guts to stand up at the time."[36]

Besig's caustic words reflect his conviction that the informal collaboration between Baldwin and Ennis weakened the argument of the Korematsu case. Coming to Baldwin's defense, Clifford Forster later denied any intention to "sell out" the interests of the ACLU's client. In dealing with the government during those "critical times," he explained to me, "we needed its support on other matters" and the ACLU might "have suffered by our taking a violent anti-government position" on the internment issue. The former ACLU staff counsel, now a New York lawyer whose clients include many entertainment figures, suggested that "a juridical relationship between the government and the attorneys for the 'other side' " in the wartime cases had actually been to the ACLU's benefit. "Had the ACLU or Roger Baldwin and myself taken an unfriendly, adversary position," Forster claimed, the government's enforcement of the military orders imposed on Japanese Americans "might have been even worse than they were."[37]

Ennis also found a defender in James Rowe, his ally in the initial battles with the War Department over the evacuation decision. "If there is a hero in this whole story," he told the congressional commission, "his name is Edward Ennis." Rowe admitted that the opponents of evacuation "could have done a hell of a lot better job, and we didn't do it. The press was after us, Congress was after us, the mail was after us, and we were sort of reacting to all this." Rowe also confessed to me that he and Ennis had not waged an "intelligent fight" against their War Department adversaries. "We could have gone to the President, we could have delayed the process, but we did not." In assessing those who bested the Justice Department, Rowe took issue with Biddle, who pointed to McCloy as the culprit. "I think Bendetsen, who was very bright and energetic, was the real villain," he told me. "McCloy was distracted and distraught with a large number of problems and was essentially motivated, I think, to try to protect his boss, Henry Stimson, who was indeed a great man." Rowe's personal combat with Bendetsen over the first seven weeks of 1942, it seems likely, colored his own assignment of blame.[38]

Recantation of his wartime votes in the three criminal cases came late for William O. Douglas. Thirty years later he looked to Charles Fahy's arguments to the Supreme Court for justification. "We were advised on oral argument," Douglas wrote in a 1974 opinion that cited the Korematsu case as precedent, "that if the Japanese landed troops on our West Coast nothing could stop them west of the Rockies." The Court had been impressed, he added, by Fahy's claim that "the enclaves of Americans of Japanese ancestry should be moved inland, lest the invaders by donning civilian clothes would wreak even more serious havoc on our Western ports." Six years later, in the memoir of his four decades of Supreme Court service, Douglas scoffed at Fahy's wildly improbable scenario: "It was not much of an argument, but it swayed a majority of the Court, including myself."[39]

Douglas suffered a lapse of memory in his confession of error. "I wrote a concurring opinion, which I never published, agreeing to the evacuation but not to evacuation *via* the concentration camps," he wrote in his memoir. The opinion to which Douglas referred was in fact his *dissent* in the Korematsu case, which he had withdrawn after striking a deal with Hugo Black over the wording of the majority opinion. Douglas may have been reluctant to expose his switch of votes, or he may simply have failed to check the record; his book was completed after he had suffered a major heart attack. In either event, the former justice was finally willing to confess that "I have always regretted that I bowed to my elders and withdrew my opinion" in the Korematsu case. Douglas ignored his recent defense of General DeWitt in writing his last testament. "The evacuation case," he admitted, "was ever on my conscience."[40]

In its February 1983 report to Congress, the Commission on Wartime Relocation condemned the internment of Japanese Americans as a "grave injustice" and as the produce of decisions "conceived in haste and executed in an atmosphere of fear and anger at Japan." The commission's members agreed without dissent that "Executive Order 9066 was not justified by military necessity" but had been prompted instead by "race prejudice, war hysteria and a failure of political leadership."[41]

The commissioners placed the burden of responsibility for the internment program on officials at the highest levels of government. General John L. DeWitt, the ranking military officer on the West Coast, believed that "ethnicity determined loyalty" and "relied heavily on civilian politicians rather than informed military judgments" in recommending the evacuation of Japanese Americans to his War Department superiors. Secretary of War Henry L. Stimson, who sent this recommendation to the White House with his imprimatur, "failed to insist on a clear military justification for the measures General DeWitt wished to undertake." The trail of responsibility ended in the Oval Office. "President Roosevelt, without raising the question to the level of Cabinet discussion or requiring any careful or thorough review of the situation," concluded the commissioners, "agreed with Secretary Stimson that the exclusion should be carried out."[42]

The commissioners focused their investigation on the decisions that led to internment and on the impact of internment on the Japanese Americans. In contrast, the primary focus of this book has been on the legal challenges to the military orders that followed Roosevelt's approval of Executive Order 9066. But the high-level decisions that led to internment provide an essential background to the cases that reached the Supreme Court and deserve some comment here in addition to the commission's findings. In particular, it seems evident that the three officials singled out for condemnation by the commission evaded the legal questions raised by Executive Order 9066.

General DeWitt stood alone among those who played leading roles in the internment decision in lacking any formal legal training. However, there is no doubt that he understood the legal implications of his efforts to restrict the liberties of Japanese Americans. Three weeks after the Peal Harbor attack, he reminded General Gullion—the Army's chief law-enforcement officer—that "an American citizen, after all, is an American citizen." Under pressure from Gullion and Colonel Karl Bendetsen, DeWitt soon buckled in his resolve and proved the aptness of Attorney General Biddle's later comment that he was "a little too much influenced by his last visitor." DeWitt's initial response to Gullion displayed at least a trace of concern about his oath to defend the Constitution and some understanding that it protected American citizens regardless of their race or ancestry. His ingrained racism, however, led in the end to DeWitt's capitulation to the Army's hard-line lawyers and the lobbying of fearful California politicians.[43]

Of the three factors cited by the commission as determinants of the internment decision, racism and wartime hysteria influenced DeWitt's "final recommendation" to the War Department. Political leadership of the department rested with Stimson, an experienced lawyer whose reputation for integrity suggested an immunity to these pressures. Stimson in fact confided to his diary that mass evacuation would "tear a tremendous hole in our constitutional system." Why, then, did he place his prestige behind Executive Order 9066? One reason—as the commission noted—was that he failed to look critically at the espionage claims that DeWitt peddled through Gullion. Stimson was obviously preoccupied with the immense problems of the global conflict and had delegated the responsibility for the Japanese American situation to John McCloy. But even McCloy acknowledged Stimson's "tremendous influence" on the evacuation decision.[44]

Stimson was the one man who could personally have blocked the evacuation and internment programs. The fact that he approved DeWitt's recommendation, despite his constitutional qualms, stemmed from more than preoccupation. His own susceptibility to racial stereotypes helped to tip the balance. Stimson's diary provides evidence of his attitudes: the "racial characteristics" of Japanese Americans, he wrote, made it impossible to "understand or trust" them. During the evacuation debate in 1942, he also defended the Army's segregation of black soldiers to his skeptical friend, Archibald MacLeish. Professing that "all my instincts were in favor of justice to the Negro," he nonetheless denounced the "foolish leaders of the colored race" who failed to understand "the basic impossibility of social equality" in a society that forced the races apart by law. Although Stimson wrote in his 1947 memoir that he "fully appreciated" the feelings of Japanese Americans that their "forced evacuation was a personal injustice," he did not disavow his wartime decision to approve their internment. Always loyal to his hero, McCloy wrote in April 1983 that "to associate ignorant prejudice with Mr. Stimson" was an "affront" to his memory. Stimson's prejudice toward the Japanese Americans was certainly less virulent than DeWitt's unvarnished racism, but wartime pressures rubbed thin his veneer of tolerance.[45]

Franklin D. Roosevelt made the final decision to force the Japanese Americans from their homes in signing Executive Order 9066. If Stimson could have rejected DeWitt's evacuation proposal, Roosevelt could equally have refused to approve the order Stimson sent to the White House. Like the Secretary of War, the President was preoccupied with problems of global strategy in early 1942. The country had never been in such peril, and Roosevelt shouldered an awesome burden of wartime responsibility. In this atmosphere of anxiety, the rights of an isolated racial minority had little claim on his sympathies. Even McCloy admitted in his commission testimony that Roosevelt "carried some of the prejudices" toward Japanese Americans that had infected the West Coast.[46]

The question of responsibility remains: Did Roosevelt simply defer to Stimson and sign Executive Order 9066 without paying much attention to its constitutional implications, or did he act after a full review of these legal questions? The former view imputes a measure of negligence to the President, while the latter suggests a conscious decision to read the Constitution broadly as a wartime charter. Roosevelt died in 1945 without leaving any record of his thoughts and deliberations, and the testimony of participants in the evacuation debate is at odds. James Rowe, who had ready access to the White House and who guided the order to Roosevelt's desk, told the congressional commission that "I don't think he spent much time" on the issue. "It's a terrible thing to say," Rowe said, "but it was a minor problem with the President." In contrast, McCloy recalled that Stimson "was likely to dwell on the constitutional aspect of this" in his discussions with Roosevelt, and remembered several talks with Stimson "about the President's attitude" on the legal problems raised by the evacuation proposal.[47]

This conflict of testimony leaves unresolved the question of how closely and conscientiously Roosevelt considered the evacuation issue before he signed Executive Order 9066. Whether Rowe or McCloy more accurately portrayed the President's attention to the issue, there is little doubt that he joined Stimson in suppressing any constitutional qualms he may have harbored. Attorney General Biddle, the only high-ranking official to put the case against evacuation to Roosevelt, later recalled that "he made it very clear to me from the beginning that this was a decision for the Army." And, as late as October 1944, Roosevelt expressed no second thoughts about the constitutionality of internment. Solicitor General Fahy later said that he met with the President before arguing the Endo and Korematsu cases to the Supreme Court. "He had an intelligent grasp of the situation," Fahy remembered in his oral history memoir, "but made no suggestions as to their presentation." Finally, Roosevelt's decision to hold up the release of Japanese Americans from the internment camps—to gain a partisan advantage in the 1944 elections—provides a final count in the indictment of his political leadership.[48]

This historical record examined by the congressional commission amply supports its conclusion that the wartime internment of 120,000 Americans of Japanese ancestry resulted from racism, war hysteria, and the failure of leadership at the highest levels of government. Similarly, the historical record of the Japanese American wartime cases examined in this book supports the conclusion that their outcome reflected the failure of the legal system.

Just as the highest-ranking officials of the government share the responsibility for internment, the responsibility for its legal sanction lies with the lawyers and judges who joined to produce what Justice Robert Jackson aptly labeled, in his *Korematsu* dissent, "a loaded weapon ready for the hand of any authority that can bring forward a plausible claim of an urgent need." Four decades after their decision by the Supreme Court, these cases remain on the books, still aimed at the members of any racial or national minority held hostage to the acts of their country of origin. However difficult it may be to imagine that these opinions will be fired in a future courtroom battle, the claim of "pressing public necessity" made in 1944 by Hugo Black is quite capable of revival and repetition.[49]

Can the Court's loaded weapon be disarmed? As early as 1945, Eugene V. Rostow of the Yale Law School faculty blasted the wartime opinions as a judicial "disaster" and urged that "the basic issues should be presented to the Supreme Court again, in an effort to obtain a reversal of these war-time cases." The major obstacle to such an effort is the judicial principle of finality, which normally bars any attempt to secure a later reversal of a case decided by the Court. Only when a subsequent case brings before the Court a set of facts and legal issues closely related to those presented in an earlier case can the justices overrule a discredited opinion. But the country has "not been so unfortunate that a repetition of the facts has occurred to give the Court that opportunity," the congressional commission noted in 1983.[50]

Despite the principle of finality, the judicial system offers one narrow avenue of relief to a criminal defendant who has exhausted his appeals and served his sentence. The "ancient writ" of *coram nobis*—which requires evidence that the original conviction was tainted by governmental misconduct—makes possible an effort to seek a later reversal of that conviction. The records uncovered in the research for this book have led to the current effort to vacate the convictions of Gordon Hirabayashi, Min Yasui, and Fred Korematsu. Whether this effort will succeed depends on the responses of government lawyers and federal judges to the *coram nobis* petitions now before the courts in which these men were tried in 1942. Their decisions will be based on the records and briefs filed in these historic cases.

This book has offered an historian's account of the Japanese American wartime cases. It seems appropriate to conclude it with an account of how I became involved in the *coram nobis* effort as a lawyer. As part of my research as an author I met individually with the three wartime criminal defendants; during these interviews I showed each of these men the Justice Department records I had found in their case files and asked for their reactions. Gordon Hirabayashi and Min Yasui—who had both agreed without hesitation to my interview requests—each told me they had hoped for years to find some basis for reopening their cases and asked if I would be willing to represent them. I told them I would be glad to volunteer my services.

I met last with Fred Korematsu. Before I approached him, several people told me that he had not spoken with anyone about his case for forty years and would most likely decline my request to talk with him. When I called him and explained that I was writing a book about the wartime cases, I added that I had found some records that he might find interesting. After some hesitation, he invited me to his home. Sitting in his living room in San Leandro, only blocks from the street on which he was arrested in 1942, Fred told me about his arrest and trial in quiet and halting words, obviously reluctant to relive those painful experiences. He then read slowly and carefully through the Justice Department records I had brought with me. What he then said explains *why* I am working on these cases. Fred finally looked up and ended four decades of silence with these words: "They did me a great wrong."

Sources

THIS BOOK is based on three types of sources: the documentary record of the evacuation and internment of Japanese Americans, and of the cases that challenged General DeWitt's military orders; published materials about these topics; and interviews with participants. The first of these sources has provided by far the most extensive and important material I have relied on, although the others have offered a valuable supplement to this record. Full citations to the sources I have used are included in the chapter notes that follow; in this Note I will list and briefly discuss the most important of these sources.

The case files of the Department of Justice are included in the records of the Alien Enemy Control Unit; they are presently located in the General Litigation Section of the Department's Criminal Division in Washington, D.C. The records of several of the federal agencies involved in both the internment program and these cases are in the National Archives in Washington. These include Record Group 107, Records of the Assistant Secretary of War; Record Group 338, Records of the Western Defense Command; Record Group 389, Records of the Provost Marshal General; and Record Group 210, Records of the War Relocation Authority.

The papers of Attorney General Francis Biddle and Solicitor General Charles Fahy are in the Franklin D. Roosevelt Library in Hyde Park, New York. Fahy's papers include several files of official records on the Japanese American cases, and Biddle's include his notes on cabinet meetings. The FDR Library also has, in the President's papers (divided between the President's Secretary's Files and Official Files), correspondence and records used in this study. The voluminous diaries of

Secretary of War Henry L. Stimson are in the Manuscript Division of the Sterling Library at Yale University in New Haven, Connecticut; I used the microfilmed copy in the Widener Library at Harvard University.

The Manuscript Division of the Library of Congress in Washington has the papers of the following members of the United States Supreme Court: Chief Justice Harlan Fiske Stone and Justices William O. Douglas, Felix Frankfurter, Wiley Rutledge, and Hugo Black. The papers of Justice Frank Murphy are in the library of the University of Michigan in Ann Arbor, and additional papers of Justice Frankfurter are in the Manuscript Division of the Harvard Law School Library in Cambridge, Massachusetts.

An invaluable source for this book is the records of the American Civil Liberties Union, which are in the Mudd Library at Princeton University in Princeton, New Jersey. Minutes of the ACLU national board and press releases issued by the ACLU are on microfilms at the Harvard Law School Library. The records of the Northern California Civil Liberties Union are in the California Historical Society in San Francisco. The University of Washington Library in Seattle has the papers of Frank Walters, who represented Gordon Hirabayashi, and of Anne R. Fisher, who made an unofficial transcript of Hirabayashi's trial.

Other important primary sources used in this book include the oral history memoirs of Roger Baldwin, Charles Fahy, and Justice Stanley Reed, located in the Columbia Oral History Collection of the Columbia University Library in New York City, and the testimony of witnesses at the hearings of the Commission on Wartime Relocation and Internment of Civilians. I have drawn in this book from the testimony of Edward J. Ennis, John J. McCloy, Karl R. Bendetsen, James H. Rowe, Jr., and Philip Glick. The citations to this testimony in the chapter notes are to the reporter's transcripts, located in the commission's files in Washington. The commission plans to publish the testimony of all the witnesses at its hearings, but those volumes are still in preparation.

Among the published sources used in this book, several deserve mention here. The formal report to Congress of the Commission on Wartime Relocation, *Personal Justice Denied,* was issued in February 1983. Based on more than 10,000 pages of government records collected by the commission's research staff, and on the testimony of some 750 witnesses at the commission's hearings, this 467-page document stands as the most authoritative and complete account of the internment program. Second in importance to this official report is the book by Jacobus tenBroek, Edward N. Barnhart, and Floyd W. Matson, *Prejudice, War and the Constitution,* first published in 1954. The three sections of this book, "Genesis," "Exodus," and "Leviticus," deal in turn with the historical background of the internment, its implementation, and its constitutional aspects. The final section, written by Professor tenBroek, offers the most extensive and perceptive critique of the doctrinal and factual shortcomings of the Supreme Court opinions in the wartime cases yet written.

Several accounts of the evacuation and internment decisions have been written, and they differ in their assignment of responsibility among those who participated in these decisions. In addition to the "Exodus" section of the book by tenBroek and his colleagues, these accounts include Morton Grodzins, *Americans Betrayed,* Roger Daniels, *Concentration Camps USA,* Michi Weglyn, *Years of Infamy,* and Stetson Conn, "Japanese Evacuation From the West Coast," a chapter in the Army's official history of World War II. General DeWitt, of course, offered his own account of the evacuation and internment decisions in his *Final Report,* written under the supervision of Colonel Bendetsen.

This book has made extensive use of the published opinions of the Supreme Court in the Japanese American cases, as well as those of the lower federal courts. These opinions are cited in the chapter notes; readers wishing to consult them can find the Supreme Court opinions in volumes 320 and 323 of *United States Reports,* the official record of the Court's decisions, and the lower court opinions in the *Federal Supplement* and the *Federal Reporter.* Trial records and the briefs submitted to the Supreme Court, both by parties to the cases and amicus groups, are in volumes 320 and 323 of Records and Briefs of the Supreme Court, another official publication.

In addition to the "Leviticus" section of tenBroek's book, two law review articles—both published in 1945—provide detailed and scathing criticism of the Supreme Court opinions in the wartime cases. Eugene V. Rostow's article in the *Yale Law Journal,* "The Japanese American Cases—A Disaster," and Nanette Dembitz's article in the *Columbia Law Review,* "Racial Discrimination and the Military Judgment: The Supreme Court's Korematsu and Endo Decisions," are essential reading on these cases. In the years since the publication of these two articles, not a single legal scholar or writer has attempted a substantive defense of the Supreme Court opinions.

Interviews with participants in the wartime cases were an essential part of the research for this book. Listed below in alphabetical order are those persons I interviewed, along with the places and dates of these interviews:

Arthur Barnett, Seattle, January 8, 1982
Ernest Besig, San Francisco, January 12, 1982
Bennett Boskey, Washington, D.C., December 21, 1981

Victor Brudney, Cambridge, Mass., June 9, 1982
Vern Countryman, Cambridge, Mass., June 9, 1982
Roger Daniels, Salt Lake City, March 10, 1983
Nanette Dembitz, New York City, December 14, 1981
Philip Elman, Washington, D.C., December 21, 1981
Edward Ennis, New York City, October 23, 1981
Mary Farquharson, Seattle, January 9, 1982
Adrian Fisher, Washington, D.C., January 27, 1982
Clifford Forster, New York City, October 23, 1981
Osmond Fraenkel, New York City, October 23, 1981
Philip Glick, Washington, D.C., October 16, 1981
John Hall, Boston, January 13, 1982
Gordon Hirabayashi, Edmonton, Alberta, Canada, January 7, 1982
Charles Horsky, Washington, D.C., December 22, 1981
Fred Korematsu, San Leandro, California, January 12, 1982
Harry Mansfield, Boston, December 7, 1981
Morris Opler (telephone interview), Norman, Oklahoma, June 18, 1982
John Pickering, Washington, D.C., December 21, 1981
James Purcell, San Francisco, January 11, 1982
Arnold Raum, Washington, D.C., October 16, 1981
James Rowe, Jr., Washington, D.C., October 14, 1981
George Sterling (telephone interview), Peaks Island, Maine, August 4, 1982
Herbert Wechsler, New York City, October 23, 1981
Minoru Yasui, Washington, D.C., October 16, 1981
Alfonso Zirpoli, San Francisco, January 11, 1982

Unless otherwise noted, all citations in the chapter notes to interviews with these persons are to my notes and transcripts of the interviews listed above. All were tape-recorded except for those with Daniels, Hall, Opler, Purcell, Raum, Sterling, and Zirpoli.

Notes

SOURCE ABBREVIATIONS

ACLU, PUL	American Civil Liberties Union Papers, Princeton University Library
COHC	Columbia Oral History Collection, Columbia University Library
DOJ	Records of the Department of Justice, Washington, D.C.
FDRL	Franklin D. Roosevelt Library, Hyde Park, New York
FRC	Federal Records Center, Suitland, Maryland
LC	Manuscript Division, Library of Congress, Washington, D.C.
MUL	University of Michigan Library, Ann Arbor, Michigan
NA	National Archives, Washington, D.C.
NCCLU, CHS	Northern California Civil Liberties Union Papers, California Historical Society, San Francisco
RG	Record Group

CHAPTER 1: "LET'S NOT GET RATTLED"

1. Gordon W. Prange, *At Dawn We Slept* (New York, 1981), pp. 485, 553–87.
2. Interview with Edward J. Ennis.
3. Ibid.
4. Testimony of John J. McCloy, Commission on Wartime Relocation and Internment of Civilians, November 3, 1981, p. 6.
5. John Higham, *Strangers in the Land: Patterns of American Nativism, 1860–1925* (New York, 1963).
6. Los Angeles *Times*, December 8, 1941, p. 2.
7. Ibid., December 10, 1941, p. 1.
8. Morton Grodzins, *Americans Betrayed* (Chicago, 1947), p. 65; Los Angeles

Times, January 28, 1942, quoted in ibid., p. 382. For a discussion of the shifting press attitude toward Japanese Americans, see Grodzins, *Americans Betrayed,* pp. 377–99.

9. 7 *Federal Register* 1407.

10. Roger Daniels, *The Politics of Prejudice* (Berkeley, Cal., 1962), p. 3.

11. Ibid., p. 20.

12. Ibid.

13. Ibid., p. 25.

14. Ibid., pp. 35–41.

15. Ibid., pp. 41–44.

16. Ibid., pp. 87–92.

17. *Ozawa* v. *United States,* 260 U.S. 178 (1922).

18. See Higham, *Strangers in the Land,* note 5, *supra.*

19. Daniels, *Politics of Prejudice,* p. 55; Grodzins, *Americans Betrayed,* p. 7.

20. Statistics from U.S. Department of War, *Final Report: Japanese Evacuation From the West Coast, 1942* (Washington, 1943), p. 84.

21. Interview with Edward J. Ennis.

22. William Preston, *Aliens and Dissenters* (Cambridge, Mass., 1963), pp. 21–22; Francis Biddle, *In Brief Authority* (New York, 1962), pp. 207–8.

23. Data on McCloy from *Current Biography,* 1947. See also Alan Brinkley, "Minister Without Portfolio," *Harper's,* February 1983, pp. 31–46.

24. For an account of this litigation, see Robert T. Swaine, *The Cravath Firm and Its Predecessors* (New York, 1946), pp. 207–9, 636–43.

25. Henry L. Stimson and McGeorge Bundy, *On Active Service in Peace and War* (New York, 1947), pp. 342–43.

26. Bruce A. Murphy, *The Brandeis-Frankfurter Connection* (New York, 1982), pp. 201–5.

27. Data on Biddle from *Current Biography,* 1941; Frankfurter quote in Peter H. Irons, *The New Deal Lawyers* (Princeton, N.J., 1982), p. 221.

28. Biddle, *In Brief Authority,* pp. 157–60.

29. Biddle quotes from ibid., pp. 191, 184–85; Rowe quote from interview with James H. Rowe, Jr.

30. Data on Stimson from *Current Biography,* 1940.

31. Murphy, *The Brandeis-Frankfurter Connection,* pp. 195–99.

32. Quotes from proclamation from 6 *Federal Register* 6321–6323; Los Angeles *Times,* December 8, 1941, p. 1; statistics from Jacobus tenBroek et al., *Prejudice, War and the Constitution* (Berkeley, Cal., 1954), p. 101.

33. Bob Kumamoto, "The Search for Spies: American Counterintelligence and the Japanese American Community 1931–1942," *Amerasia Journal,* Vol. 6, No. 2 (Fall 1979), pp. 47–49.

34. Ibid., pp. 49–50.

35. Memo, Roosevelt to Chief of (Naval) Operations, August 10, 1936, Box 216, Folder A 8-5, RG 80 (General Records of the Navy Department), NA.

36. Memo, Roosevelt to Cabinet officers, June 26, 1939, File ASW .021, Box 10, RG 107, NA; Memo, "Proposal for Coordination of FBI, ONI and MID," June 5, 1940, ibid.

37. Quotes from Kumamoto, "The Search for Spies," p. 53; see Memo, "Report on Coordination of the Three Intelligence Services," May 27, 1941, File ASW .021, Box 10, RG 107, NA.

38. McCloy to Miles, November 2, 1940, File ASW 00.24, Box 14, RG 107, NA.

39. Kumamoto, "The Search for Spies," p. 58; also see Commission on Wartime Relocation, *Personal Justice Denied* (Washington, D.C., 1983), p. 54.

40. Ken Ringle, "What Did You Do Before the War, Dad?," *The Washington Post Magazine,* December 6, 1981, p. 54.

41. On the Tachibana raid and arrest, see ibid.; Prange, *At Dawn We Slept,* pp. 149–50; Kumamoto, "The Search for Spies," pp. 55–56; interview with Kenneth D. Ringle, Jr.

42. Kumamoto, "The Search for Spies," p. 57; G-2 Periodic Report, February 7, 1942, Western Defense Command records, Box 28, Federal Records Center, Suitland, Md.

43. Grodzins, *Americans Betrayed,* p. 233.

44. Statistics from ibid.; see also Note, "Alien Enemies and Japanese-Americans: A Problem of Wartime Controls," 51 *Yale Law Journal* 1316, p. 1323 (1942).

CHAPTER 2: "AN AMERICAN CITIZEN IS AN AMERICAN CITIZEN"

1. Data on DeWitt from *Current Biography,* 1942 and 1943.

2. Roger Daniels, *Concentration Camps USA* (New York, 1970), p. 36.

3. Los Angeles Times, December 9, 1941, p. 8.

4. Daniels, *Concentration Camps USA,* pp. 36–37.

5. U.S. Department of War, *Final Report: Japanese Evacuation From the West Coast, 1942* (Washington, D.C., 1943), p. 8.

6. Stetson Conn et al., "Japanese Evacuation From the West Coast," *The United States Army in World War II: The Western Hemisphere: Guarding the United States and Its Outposts* (Washington, D.C., 1964), p. 117.

7. Memo, Hoover to Tolson, Tamm, and Ladd, December 17, 1941, FBI file 100-97-1-67, Records of the FBI.

8. Ibid.

9. Quotes from Jacobus tenBroek et al., *Prejudice, War and the Constitution* (Berkeley, Cal., 1954), p. 103.

10. Quotes from Memo, Hoover to Tolson, Tamm, and Ladd, December 26, 1941, FBI file 100-2-2543, Records of the FBI.

11. Ibid.

12. Transcript of telephone conversation, DeWitt and Gullion, December 26, 1941, File 311.3, Records of the Western Defense Command, Civil Affairs Division; quoted in Conn, "Japanese Evacuation," p. 118.

13. Ibid.

14. tenBroek, *Prejudice, War and the Constitution,* p. 102.

15. Data on Gullion from *Current Biography,* 1943.

16. Data on Bendetsen from *Current Biography,* 1952; data on Rowe from *Who's Who in America,* 1979, and interview with James H. Rowe, Jr.

17. Daniels, *Concentration Camps USA,* p. 45.

18. Transcript, "Conference in Office of General DeWitt," January 4, 1942, Box 7, RG 338, NA.

19. Ibid.

20. Ibid.

21. War Department, *Final Report,* pp. 23–24.

22. Ibid., p. 23.

23. Ibid., p. 24.

24. Transcript, "Conference in Office of General DeWitt," note 18, *supra.*

25. War Department, *Final Report,* pp. 19, 21.

26. Ibid., pp. 21–22, 19.

27. tenBroek, *Prejudice, War and the Constitution,* p. 105.

28. Data on "restricted zones" from Conn, "Japanese Evacuation," pp. 119–20.

29. Memo, Hoover to Tolson, Tamm, and Ladd, December 17, 1941, FBI file 100-97-1-67, Records of the FBI.

30. Transcript, "Conference in Office of General DeWitt," note 18, *supra.*

31. Morton Grodzins, *Americans Betrayed* (Chicago, 1947), p. 65.

32. tenBroek, *Prejudice, War and the Constitution,* p. 77.

33. Grodzins, *Americans Betrayed,* p. 65.

34. Daniels, *Concentration Camps USA,* p. 47.

35. Grodzins, *Americans Betrayed,* pp. 66–67.

36. Ibid., pp. 27, 66–67.

37. Los Angeles *Times,* January 25, 1942, p. 1; text of Roberts Commission report in *Congressional Record,* Vol. 88, Part 8, p. A261.

38. Allen quotes in Los Angeles *Times,* January 28, 1942, p. 1; McLemore quote in San Francisco *Examiner,* January 29, 1942.

39. Transcript of telephone conversation, DeWitt and Bendetsen, January 29, 1942, RG 389, NA.

40. Transcript of telephone conversation, DeWitt and Bendetsen, January 29, 1942, ibid.

41. Transcript of telephone conversation, DeWitt and Gullion, January 30, 1942, ibid.

42. Transcript of telephone conversation, Bendetsen and Rowe, January 29, 1942, ibid.

43. Transcript of telephone conversation, Bendetsen and DeWitt, January 30, 1942, ibid.

44. Ibid.

45. Ibid.

46. Transcript of telephone conversation, Gullion and General Mark Clark, February 4, 1942, ibid.

47. Ibid.

48. Transcript of telephone conversation, DeWitt, Gullion, and Bendetsen, February 1, 1942, ibid.

49. Transcript of telephone conversation, Gullion and Clark, February 4, 1942, ibid.

50. Transcript of telephone conversation, DeWitt, Gullion, and Bendetsen, February 1, 1942, ibid.

51. Entry for February 3, 1942, Henry L. Stimson Diaries, Sterling Library, Yale University.

52. Ibid.

53. Ibid.; transcript of telephone conversation, DeWitt and McCloy, February 3, 1942, RG 389, NA.

54. Ibid.

55. Ibid.

56. Ibid.

57. Ibid.

CHAPTER 3: "BE AS REASONABLE AS YOU CAN"

1. Memo, "Alien Enemies on the West Coast (and Other Subversive Persons)," Bendetsen to Gullion, February 4, 1942, RG 389, NA.

2. Ibid.

3. Ibid.

4. Ibid.

5. Ibid.

6. Transcript of telephone conversation, Gullion and Clark, February 4, 1942, ibid; on congressional committees, see Jacobus tenBroek et al., *Prejudice, War and the Constitution* (Berkeley, Cal., 1954), p. 205.

7. Gullion and Clark transcript, ibid.

8. Morton Grodzins, *Americans Betrayed* (Chicago, 1947), pp. 71–73.

9. Ibid., pp. 73–74.

10. Ibid., p. 74.

11. Quote from Lerch in Stetson Conn et al., "Japanese Evacuation From the West Coast," *The United States Army in World War II: The Western Hemisphere: Guarding the United States and Its Outposts* (Washington, D.C., 1964), 128; Gullion quotes in Memo, Gullion to McCloy, February 6, 1942, File ASW 014.311, RG 107, NA.

12. Memo, "Luncheon Conversation with the President," February 7, 1942, Box 3, Folder—Roosevelt, Franklin D. Correspondence, Francis Biddle Papers, FDRL.

13. The role of these three lawyers in wartime decisions is discussed in Bruce A. Murphy, *The Brandeis-Frankfurter Connection* (New York, 1982), Chapter 6.

14. Memo, "The Japanese Situation on the West Coast," File 146-13-7-2-0, Records of the Alien Enemy Control Unit, DOJ.

15. Ibid.

16. Ibid.

17. Letter, Rauh to Joan Z. Bernstein, May 21, 1982; copy sent by Rauh to author.

18. Interviews with James H. Rowe, Jr., and Edward Ennis.

19. Biddle to Stimson, February 9, 1942, File ASW 014.311, RG 107, NA.

20. Entry of February 10, 1942, Stimson Diaries, Yale University Library.

21. Memo, "Evacuation of Japanese from the West Coast," February 10, 1942, Records of the Assistant Chief of Staff, G-2, Western Defense Command, Federal Records Center, Suitland, Md.

22. Ibid.

23. Entry of February 11, 1942, Stimson Diaries, Yale University Library.

24. Conn, "Japanese Evacuation," p. 131–32.

25. Ibid.

26. Ibid., p. 132.

27. U.S. Department of War, *Final Report, Japanese Evacuation From the West Coast, 1942* (Washington, D.C., 1943), p. 34.

28. Ibid., pp. 33–34.

29. Ibid., pp. 36–37.

30. Ibid., p. 37.

31. Conn, "Japanese Evacuation," p. 134.

32. Washington *Post,* February 12, 1942.

33. Ibid.; Pegler quoted in tenBroek, *Prejudice, War and the Constitution,* p. 86.

34. Biddle, "Memorandum to the President," February 17, 1942, PSF Confidential File, Box 10, Folder—C. F. Hawaii, FDRL.

35. Roger Daniels, *Concentration Camps USA* (New York, 1971), pp. 65–67; entry of February 17, 1942, Stimson Diaries, Yale University Library.

36. Interview, James H. Rowe, Jr., October 15, 1942, Files of Japanese American Evacuation and Resettlement Study, Bancroft Library, University of California, Berkeley, Cal.

37. Ibid.

38. Stimson quotes from entry of February 18, 1942, Stimson Diaries, Yale University Library; Rowe quotes from interview with James H. Rowe, Jr.

39. 7 *Federal Register* 1407.

40. Interview with James H. Rowe, Jr.

41. War Department, *Final Report,* p. 28.

42. Memo, Biddle to Roosevelt, February 20, 1942, Official File 4805, FDRL.

43. Memorandum of Telephone Conversation, Gufler and Bendetsen, February 21, 1942, File 740.00115 Pacific/war/220, Records of the Department of State, NA.

44. Memo, Bendetsen to McCloy, February 22, 1942, Box 6, RG 107, NA.

45. tenBroek, *Prejudice, War and the Constitution,* p. 117.

46. War Department, *Final Report,* p. 44.

47. Ibid., p. 30.

48. tenBroek, *Prejudice, War and the Constitution,* p. 114.

49. Ibid.

50. *Congressional Record,* Vol. 90, Part 2, pp. 2729–730.

51. Ibid., pp. 2722–24.

52. Ibid., pp. 2722–26.

53. 56 *Statutes* 173.

54. tenBroek, *Prejudice, War and the Constitution,* p. 118.

55. War Department, *Final Report,* pp. 44–48.

56. Entry of February 27, 1942, Stimson Diaries, Yale University Library.

57. See Milton Eisenhower, *The President Is Calling* (New York, 1974).

58. War Department, *Final Report,* pp. 297–98.

59. Commission on Wartime Relocation and Internment of Civilians, *Personal Justice Denied* (Washington, D.C., 1983), pp. 109–12.

60. Ibid., p. 103.

61. tenBroek, *Prejudice, War and the Constitution,* p. 123.

62. Memo, "Report on Meeting, April 7 (1942), at Salt Lake City, with Governors, Attorneys General, and Other State and Federal Officials of 10 Western States," Box 8, RG 107, NA.

63. Ibid.

64. Ibid.

65. Ibid.

66. Stimson quotes from Memo, Stimson to Roosevelt, April 15, 1942, File ASW 014.311, RG 107, NA.

67. See Dillon Myer, *Uprooted Americans: The Japanese Americans and the War Relocation Authority During World War II* (Tucson, Ariz., 1970).

68. War Department, *Final Report,* pp. 278–92.

69. Yoshiko Uchida, *Desert Exile: The Uprooting of a Japanese Family* (Seattle, 1982), pp. 132–33.

70. Washington *Post,* December 12, 1982, p. A1.

71. Testimony of John J. McCloy before Commission on Wartime Relocation, November 3, 1981, pp. 15, 80.

CHAPTER 4: "AM I AN AMERICAN OR NOT?"

1. John T. Noonan, *Persons and Masks of the Law* (New York, 1976).
2. See Clayborne Carson, *In Struggle: SNCC and the Black Awakening of the Nineteen Sixties* (Cambridge, Mass., 1981).
3. On Kido's career in the JACL, see Bill Hosokawa, *JACL In Quest of Justice* (New York, 1982), *passim.*
4. On Masaoka's career in the JACL, see Bill Hosokawa, *Nisei, The Quiet Americans* (New York, 1969), pp. 203–5; and Hosokawa, *JACL In Quest of Justice, passim.*
5. Hosokawa, *JACL In Quest of Justice,* p. 129; Tanaka quote from Roger Daniels, *Concentration Camps USA* (New York, 1970), p. 41.
6. Memo, "Japanese Activities, Los Angeles," Hood to Hoover, January 20, 1942, Records of the FBI (copy in files of CWRIC).
7. Ibid.; Hosokawa, *JACL In Quest of Justice,* p. 205.
8. Testimony of Mike M. Masaoka before House of Representatives, Select Committee Investigating National Defense Migration, 77th Cong., 2d Sess., February 23, 1942, pp. 11136–42.
9. Ibid.
10. Minutes of JACL National Council meeting, March 8, 1942, Salt Lake City, Vol. 2570, ACLU, PUL.
11. Interview with Minoru Yasui.
12. Ibid.
13. Wayne Morse to Roger Baldwin, April 19, 1943, Vol. 2468, ACLU, PUL.
14. Interview with Minoru Yasui.
15. Ibid.
16. Ibid.
17. Ibid.
18. Ibid.
19. Ibid.
20. JACL *Bulletin,* April 7, 1941, copy in Seattle JACL Papers, University of Washington Archives.
21. Ibid.
22. Statement of Minoru Yasui, April 17, 1942, ibid.
23. JACL *Bulletin* and Yasui Statement, ibid.
24. Interview with Minoru Yasui.
25. Memo, Special Agent in Charge, Denver, to Director, FBI, May 26, 1944, File 100-164195-43, Records of the FBI.
26. JACL *Bulletin,* note 20, *supra,* and ibid.
27. Interview with Minoru Yasui.
28. Memo, Special Agent in Charge, Seattle, to Director, FBI, May 23, 1942, File 146-42-20, DOJ.
29. Ibid.
30. Ibid.
31. Ibid.
32. Interview with Gordon Hirabayashi.

33. Ibid.

34. Ibid.

35. Ibid.

36. Ibid.

37. FBI memo, note 28, *supra*.

38. Ibid.

39. Interview with Gordon Hirabayashi.

40. Ibid.

41. Memo, Special Agent in Charge, Seattle, to Director, FBI, June 6, 1942, File 146-42-20, DOJ.

42. Interview with Gordon Hirabayashi.

43. FBI memo, note 28, *supra*.

44. Memo, Special Agent O. T. Mansfield, San Francisco, June 4, 1942, File 146-42-7, DOJ.

45. Ibid.

46. Interview with Fred Korematsu.

47. FBI memo, note 44, *supra*.

48. Ibid.

49. Memo, Special Agent G. E. Goodwin, San Francisco, July 11, 1942, File 146-42-7, DOJ.

50. Ibid.

51. Ibid.

52. Ibid.

53. Ibid.

54. San Francisco *Examiner*, June 2, 1942; June 14, 1942.

55. Interview with Ernest Besig.

56. Ibid.

57. *Korematsu* v. *United States*, draft opinion, undated, Box 276, Hugo Black Papers, LC.

58. FBI memo, note 49, *supra*.

59. Ibid.; Hi Korematsu to Francis Biddle, February 20, 1942, File 146-13-7-2-0, DOJ; interview with Fred Korematsu.

60. Interview with Fred Korematsu; FBI memo, note 49, *supra*.

61. Ernest Besig to Howard J. Lewis, ACLU, August 31, 1942, Vol. 2397, ACLU, PUL.

62. Interview with Fred Korematsu.

63. Interview with James Purcell.

64. Hosokawa, *Nisei*, pp. 315–16.

65. Interview with James Purcell.

66. Form, "Charges, Information of Time and Manner of Answer," Wayne Miller, State Personnel Board, State of California, April 13, 1942, File A15.07, Japanese American Evacuation and Resettlement Study, University of California Library.

67. Ibid.

68. Interview with James Purcell.

69. Ibid.

70. Ibid.

71. Ibid.

CHAPTER 5: "WE DON'T INTEND TO TRIM OUR SAILS"

1. See Peggy Lamson, *Roger Baldwin* (Boston, 1976); see also "In Defense of Everybody," *New Yorker*, July 11 and 18, 1953.

2. Ibid.

3. Ibid.

4. Baldwin to Besig, January 20, 1942, Box 4, Folder 82, NCCLU Papers, CHS.

5. Ibid.

6. Baldwin to Taft, January 30, 1942, ibid.

7. ACLU news release, March 1, 1942, Reel 9, ACLU Microfilms.

8. Lamson, *Roger Baldwin*, pp. 223–29.

9. Roger Baldwin Memoir, Columbia Oral History Collection, pp. 130–36.

10. Ibid.

11. Ibid.

12. ACLU Board minutes, March 2, 1942; letter, ACLU to Roosevelt, March 20, 1942; Reel 9, ACLU Microfilms.

13. ACLU Board minutes, March 23 and 30, 1942, ibid.

14. Ibid.

15. Roger Baldwin Memoir, COHC, p. 136.

16. New York *Times*, February 5, 1978, p. 25; Roger Baldwin Memoir, COHC, p. 184.

17. Interview with Ernest Besig.

18. Ibid.; Roger Baldwin Memoir, COHC, p. 184.

19. Taft to Baldwin, March 23, 1942, Box 4, Folder 82, NCCLU, CHS; Besig to Baldwin, March 13, 1942, ibid.

20. Besig to Baldwin, March 20, 1942, ibid; Besig to Baldwin, April 4, 1942, ibid.

21. Data on Black from Harold Chase et al., *Biographical Dictionary of the Federal Judiciary* (Detroit, 1976); Joseph R. Conlin, *Bread and Roses Too: Studies of the Wobblies* (Westport, Conn., 1969), pp. 77–78.

22. *Ex Parte Ventura*, 44. F. Supp. 520, 521–523 (W. D. Wash., 1942).

23. Ibid.

24. Charles (Burdell) to Tom (Clark), April 27, 1942 (with attached brief), File 146-13-7-2-0, DOJ.

25. Forster to Besig, June 1, 1942, Vol. 2465, ACLU, PUL.

26. Wirin to Forster, June 20, 1942, Vol. 2398, ACLU, PUL; Wakayama statement in *Congressional Record*, Vol. 86, Part 16, p. 3748.

27. Forster to Wirin, June 29, 1942, Vol. 2398, ACLU, PUL.

28. Wirin to Baldwin, February 25, 1943, ibid.

29. Forster to Besig, June 22, 1942, Box 4, Folder 82, NCCLU, CHS; interview with Ernest Besig.

30. Farquharson to Baldwin, May 14, 1942, Vol. 2470, ACLU, PUL; Baldwin to Farquharson, ibid; ACLU Board minutes, Reel 9, ACLU Microfilms.

31. Farquharson to Baldwin, May 22, 1942, Vol. 2470, ACLU, PUL; Farquharson to Baldwin, June 11, 1942, ibid; William Preston, *Aliens and Dissenters: Federal Suppression of Radicals 1903–1933* (New York, 1963), pp. 196–97, 214–16.

32. Interview with Arthur Barnett.

33. Interview with Ernest Besig.

34. Baldwin to Besig, June 8, 1942, Vol. 2397, ACLU, PUL; Besig to Baldwin, ibid.

35. Ibid.

36. Besig to Baldwin, July 17, 1942, ibid.

37. New York *Times*, December 10, 1959, p. 39; interviews with Arnold Raum and Adrian Fisher.

38. Interview with Nanette Dembitz.

39. Peter H. Irons, *The New Deal Lawyers* (Princeton, N.J., 1982), pp. 234–36.

40. Data on Cramer from *Who Was Who in America,* Vol. 4.

41. Data on Wenig from various War Department records; see notes to Chapter 8.

42. Interviews with John Hall and Adrian Fisher.

43. Glick to Ferguson, July 2, 1942, Box 336, RG 210, NA.

44. Walk to Glick, July 24, 1942, Box 330, ibid.; Baldwin to Besig, August 5, 1942, Vol. 2394, ACLU, PUL.

45. Interview with Philip Glick.

46. Walk to Glick, July 24, 1942, Box 330, RG 210, NA; interview with Philip Glick.

47. Memo, Ennis to Rowe, April 10, 1942, File 146-42-012, Section 1, DOJ.

48. Colonel Joel F. Watson, "The Japanese Evacuation and Litigation Arising Therefrom," 22 *Oregon Law Review* 46, 47 (1942).

49. Memo, Glick to Eisenhower, April 15, 1942, Document 6-0076, RG 210, NA.

50. *Yick Wo* v. *Hopkins,* 118 U.S. 356 (1886).

51. Glick memo, note 49, *supra.*

52. Ibid.

53. Memo, Ferguson to Bates, April 22, 1942, File 34.100, RG 210, NA.

54. Ibid.

55. ACLU Board minutes, May 11, 1942, Reel 9, ACLU Microfilms.

56. ACLU Board minutes, May 18, 1942, ibid.

57. Memo, "To the Active Members of the Corporation," May 22, 1942, Vol. 2444, ACLU, PUL.

58. List, "Ballot on Removal of Civilians from Military Areas," June 16, 1942, ibid.

59. ACLU Board minutes, June 22, 1942, Reel 9, ACLU Microfilms.

60. Baldwin to Wirin, Farquharson, and Besig, June 24, 1942, Vol. 2397, ACLU, PUL.

61. Wirin to Baldwin, June 27, 1942, Vol. 2398, ibid.

62. Farquharson to Baldwin, June 29, 1942, Vol. 2740, ibid.

63. Besig to Baldwin, July 2, 1942, Vol. 2397, ibid.

64. ACLU Board minutes, July 20, 1942, Reel 9, ACLU Microfilms; Fraenkel to Forster, June 17, 1942, Vol. 2470, ACLU, PUL.

65. Frank to Besig, July 8, 1942, Vol. 2397, ACLU, PUL; Besig to Forster, July 10, 1942, ibid.; Lucille Milner to Frank, July 17, 1942, ibid.

66. ACLU Board minutes, July 20, 1942, Reel 9, ACLU Microfilms; Milner to Besig, July 22, 1942, Box 4, Folder 83, NCCLU, CHS.

67. Entry of October 12, 1942, "Extracts From Diaries of Osmond K. Fraenkel Relating to American Civil Liberties Union, Part I: 1933–1950," ACLU, PUL.

68. Ibid.

69. See Harry N. Scheiber, *Wilson Administration and Civil Liberties, 1917–1921* (Ithaca, N.Y., 1960).

70. Fraenkel diary entry of October 12, 1942, note 67, *supra.*

CHAPTER 6: "WE COULD HAVE YOU INDUCTED"

1. *Yasui* v. *United States,* 320 U.S. 115 (1943), Transcript of Trial, Records and Briefs of the Supreme Court [cited below as Yasui Trial Transcript], p. 93.

2. Ibid.

3. Memo, Glick to Eisenhower, April 15, 1942, Document 6-0076, RG 210, NA.

4. Donaugh to Walk, May 29, 1942, Box 337, RG 210, NA.

5. Walk to Donaugh, June 6, 1942, ibid.

6. Ibid.

7. Ibid.

8. Ibid.

9. Ibid.

10. Charles (Burdell) to Tom (Clark), April 27, 1942 (with attached brief), File 146-13-7-2-0, DOJ.

11. Yasui Trial Transcript, pp. 111–12, note 1, *supra.*

12. Ibid., p. 156.

13. Ibid., pp. 194–96.

14. Ibid., pp. 196–98.

15. Ibid., pp. 186, 200.

16. Ibid., p. 205.

17. Ibid.

18. Ibid., pp. 206–8.

19. Ibid., pp. 208–9.

20. Edwin Ferguson to Philip Glick, July 11, 1942, Box 336, RG 210, NA.

21. Walk to Glick, July 24, 1942, Box 330, RG 210, NA.

22. Interview with Philip Glick; "Legal and Constitutional Phases of the WRA Program," U.S. Department of the Interior (Washington, D.C., 1945).

23. Interview with James Purcell; Bill Hosokawa, *Nisei, The Quiet Americans* (New York, 1969), pp. 424–25.

24. Hosokawa, *Nisei,* p. 425.

25. Ferguson to Glick, July 27, 1942, Box 337, RG 210, NA.

26. *Ex Parte Milligan,* 71 U.S. 2, 127 (1866); see Clinton Rossiter, *The Supreme Court and the Commander in Chief* (Ithaca, N.Y., 1951).

27. Hosokawa, *Nisei,* p. 425; interview with James Purcell.

28. Ferguson to Glick, July 27, 1942, Box 337, RG 210, NA.

29. Ibid.; *Ex Parte Milligan,* 71 U.S. 2, 137-142 (1866).

30. Charles Fairman, "The Law of Martial Rule and the National Emergency," *Harvard Law Review* 55 (1942), 1287–1302.

31. Ibid.

32. Ferguson to Glick, note 28, *supra.*

33. Ibid.

34. Maurice Walk to Philip Glick, July 24, 1942, Box 330, RG 210, NA.

35. Interview with James Purcell.

36. Memo, Ennis to Fahy, December 22, 1942, File 146-42-26, DOJ.

37. Purcell to Forster, June 23, 1943, Vol. 2465, ACLU, PUL.

38. *Korematsu* v. *United States,* 323 U.S. 215 (1944), Records and Briefs of the Supreme Court, Record, pp. 2–11 (cited below as Korematsu Trial Record).

39. Interview with Ernest Besig; Korematsu Trial Record, ibid.

40. Korematsu Trial Record, p. 23.

41. Ibid.

42. Ibid., pp. 24–25.

43. Interviews with Fred Korematsu and Ernest Besig.

44. *United States* v. *Hirabayashi*, No. 45736 (W.D. Wash. 1942), Brief in Support of Amended Demurrer to Indictment, files of Arthur Barnett.

45. *United States* v. *Hirabayashi*, 46 F. Supp. 657, 659, 661 (W. D. Wash. 1942).

46. Ibid., p. 659.

47. Interview with Gordon Hirabayashi; *Hirabayashi* v. *United States*, 320 U.S. 81 (1943), Records and Briefs of the Supreme Court, Record, pp. 31–32 (cited below as Hirabayashi Trial Record).

48. Interview with Frank L. Walters, October 21, 1970, Frank Walters Papers, University of Washington Library.

49. Hirabayashi Trial Record, pp. 32–33; "Notes on Hirabayashi Trial," Anne R. Fisher Papers, University of Washington Library. This account of the Hirabayashi trial is based on these two sources; no official transcript of the trial is available. See also Anne R. Fisher, *Exile of a Race* (Seattle, 1965), pp. 104–7, which provides an account of the trial based on her shorthand notes.

50. Ibid.

51. Ibid.

52. Ibid.

53. Ibid.

54. Ibid.

55. Ibid.

56. Ibid.; interview with Gordon Hirabayashi.

57. Interview with Gordon Hirabayashi.

58. *United States* v. *Yasui*, 48 F. Supp. 40 (D. Ore. 1942).

59. Ibid., pp. 49, 50, 53.

60. Ibid., p. 54.

61. Ibid., p. 55.

62. Yasui statement, November 18, 1942, Box 337, RG210, NA.

63. Transcript of Hearing, December 23, 1942, File 146-42-7, D0J.

64. Ibid.

CHAPTER 7: "THESE CASES SHOULD BE DISMISSED"

1. Memo, Ennis to Fahy, December 26, 1942, File 146-42-20, DOJ; Ennis to Fahy, December 19, 1942, File 146-42-7, ibid.

2. Memo, Ennis to Fahy, January 2, 1943, File 146-42-20, DOJ.

3. Ibid.; *Ex Parte Zimmerman*, 132 F.2d 442 (9th Cir. 1942).

4. Memo, Ennis to Fahy, January 5, 1943, File 146-42-20, DOJ.

5. Interview with Philip Glick; Glick to Walk, December 16, 1942, Box 336, RG 210, NA.

6. Walk to Glick, December 19, 1942, ibid.

7. Ibid.

8. Ibid.

9. Memo, Ennis to Fahy, January 8, 1943, File 146-42-20, DOJ.

10. Ibid.

11. Joel F. Watson, "The Japanese Evacuation and Litigation Arising Therefrom," *Oregon Law Review*, 22 (1942), p. 51.

12. ACLU Board minutes, September 14, 1942, Reel 9, ACLU Microfilms.

13. Besig to Baldwin, September 15, 1942, Box 4, Folder 83, NCCLU, CHS; Parsons to Frank, September 21, 1942, Vol. 2397, ACLU, PUL.

14. Holmes to Parsons, November 25, 1942, Box 4, Folder 83, NCCLU, CHS.

15. Besig to Baldwin, October 16, 1942, Vol. 2397, ACLU, PUL; Besig to Baldwin, October 29, 1942, Box 4, Folder 83, NCCLU, CHS.

16. Besig to Baldwin, December 14, 1942, Vol. 2397, ACLU, PUL.

17. Interview with Ernest Besig; Cabot to Baldwin, September 16, 1942, Vol. 2444, ACLU, PUL.

18. ACLU Board minutes, December 21, 1942, Reel 9, ACLU Microfilms; Baldwin to Besig, December 22, 1942, Vol. 2397, ACLU, PUL.

19. ACLU Press Release, October 8, 1942, Reel 9, ACLU Microfilms.

20. ACLU Press Release, November 11, 1942, ibid.

21. ACLU Board minutes, October 19, 1942, ibid.

22. ACLU Board minutes, November 11, 1942, ibid.

23. Fraenkel to Konvitz, November 27, 1942, Vol. 2468, ACLU, PUL.

24. Baldwin to Besig, February 1, 1943, ibid.

25. Besig to Baldwin, February 4, 1943, ibid.

26. Baldwin to Besig, February 8, 1943, ibid.; ACLU Board minutes, February 9, 1943, Reel 10, ACLU Microfilms.

27. Forster to Besig, February 17, 1943, Vol. 2468, ACLU, PUL; Besig to Forster, February 20, 1943, ibid.

28. Evans to Baldwin, January 14, 1943, Vol. 2470, ACLU, PUC.

29. Forster to Wirin, February 13, 1943, ibid.; Wirin to Forster, February 29, 1943, Vol. 2463, ibid.

30. Data on Wilbur from *Who Was Who in America,* Vol. 3.

31. Data on Denman from *Who Was Who in America,* Vol. 4; San Francisco *Examiner,* March 10, 1959, p. 1.

32. Interview with Arnold Raum; Denman to Henry L. Stimson, July 30, 1942, File ASW 014.311, RG 107, NA; Memo, McCloy to Harry Hopkins, July 15, 1942, ibid.

33. Jacobus tenBroek et al., *Prejudice, War and the Constitution* (Berkeley, Cal., 1954), pp. 313–15.

34. Ibid., p. 315.

35. Besig to Forster, February 20, 1943, Vol. 2466, ACLU, PUL.

36. *Sterling* v. *Constantin,* 287 U.S. 378, 401 (1932).

37. Farquharson to Baldwin, March 11, 1943, Vol. 2470, ACLU, PUL.

38. San Francisco *Examiner,* February 20, 1943, p. 4.

39. Besig to Forster, February 20, 1943, Vol. 2466, ACLU, PUL; Farquharson to Baldwin, March 11, 1943, ibid.

40. Philip Glick to Maurice Walk, February 26, 1943, Box 337, RG 210, NA.

41. San Francisco *Examiner,* February 20, 1943, p. 4.

42. New York *Times,* February 21, 1943, p. 23.

43. Besig to Forster, February 20, 1943, Vol. 2466, ACLU, PUL; Glick to Walk, February 26, 1943, Box 337, RG 210, NA.

44. Kenny to Wirin, February 13, 1943, Box 2, Folder—February 1–14, 1943, Robert Kenny Papers, Bancroft Library, University of California, Berkeley.

45. Ibid.

46. Martin Popper, "The Guild Contributes to Victory," *Lawyers Guild Review,* March–April, 1943, p. 6.

47. Charles Gordon, "Status of Enemy Nationals in the United States," ibid., November 1942, p. 16.

48. Memo, Ennis to Charles Fahy, February 23, 1943, File 146-42-1, DOJ.

49. Forster to Besig, March 19, 1943, Box 4, Folder 84, NCCLU, CHS.

50. This certification procedure was provided by Title 28, United States Code, Section 346.

51. Interview with Edward Ennis.

52. *Hirabayashi* v. *United States,* 320 U.S. 81 (1943), Records and Briefs of the Supreme Court, Record, p. 36.

53. Ibid., pp. 36–37.

54. Ibid., pp. 38–39.

55. Denman's amended dissent to the Hirabayashi certification is in *Toyosaburo Korematsu* v. *United States,* 140 F.2d 289, 300–304 (9th Cir. 1943).

56. Ibid.

57. Joseph P. Lash, *From the Diaries of Felix Frankfurter* (New York, 1975), p. 227.

CHAPTER 8: "THE SUPPRESSION OF EVIDENCE"

1. Glick to Dillon Myer, April 7, 1943, Box 330, RG 210, NA.

2. Baldwin to Morris, March 1, 1943, Box 47, Folder 1127, NCCLU, CHS.

3. Farquharson to Baldwin, March 11, 1943, Vol. 2470, ACLU, PUL.

4. Barnett to Morris, March 19, 1943, ibid.; Barnett to Morris, April 9, 1943, ibid.

5. Cummings to Baldwin, April 22, 1943, ibid.; Davis to Baldwin, April 21, 1943, ibid.; Baldwin to Farquharson, April 20, 1943, ibid.

6. Barnett to Morris, April 9, 1943, ibid.; Barnett to Evans, April 22, 1943, ibid.

7. Farquharson to Baldwin, April 29, 1943, ibid.; Baldwin to Farquharson, April 30, 1943, ibid.

8. Barnett to Evans, April 30, 1943, ibid.

9. Wirin to Forster, March 29, 1943, ibid.

10. Walters to Wirin, April 7, 1943, ibid.; Wirin to Baldwin, April 17, 1943, Vol. 2468, ibid.

11. Forster to Wirin, April 21, 1943, Vol. 2468, ibid.

12. Interview with Osmond Fraenkel; *Toyosaburo Korematsu* v. *United States,* 140 F.2d 289, 303 (9th Cir. 1943); *Hirabayashi* v. *United States,* 320 U.S. 81 (1943), Records and Briefs of the Supreme Court, Brief for Appellant, pp. 9–11.

13. *Hirabayashi,* Brief for Appellant, ibid.

14. Ibid., pp. 14–15.

15. Ibid., p. 21.

16. Opler to author, March 6, 1983; Mike Masaoka to Opler, May 13, 1943; both in author's files.

17. Interview with Morris Opler; Michi Weglyn, *Years of Infamy* (New York, 1976), pp. 142–43.

18. *Hirabayashi* v. *United States,* note 12, *supra,* Brief Amicus Curiae for the Japanese American Citizens League, index and *passim.*

19. Ibid., p. 125.

20. *Hirabayashi* v. *United States,* 320 U.S. 81, 96 (1943).

21. Baldwin to Opler, May 13, 1943, attached to letter, Opler to author, March 6, 1983, files of author.

22. *Hirabayashi* v. *United States,* note 12, *supra,* Brief Amicus Curiae for the Northern California Civil Liberties Union, pp. 58–59, 106–8.

23. ACLU Board minutes, April 26 and May 10, 1943, Reel 10, ACLU Microfilms.

24. Interview with Edward Ennis.

25. Interview with Nanette Dembitz.

26. Ibid.; Draft of *Hirabayashi* brief, no date, Box 36, Folder 1, Fahy Papers, FDRL.

27. Interview with Nanette Dembitz; Biddle to Knox, May 18, 1943, File 146-42-012, Section 3, DOJ.

28. Draft of *Hirabayashi* brief, note 26, *supra; Hirabayashi* v. *United States,* note 12, *supra,* Brief for the United States, p. 21.

29. Interview with Arnold Raum.

30. Ibid.; Brief for the United States, note 28, *supra,* pp. 66–67, 63.

31. Speech by Mike Masaoka to Convention of Japanese American Citizens League, Los Angeles, California, August 10, 1982, notes of author.

32. Dewitt to Chief of Staff, United States Army, January 27, 1943, File ASW 014.311, RG 107, NA.

33. Ibid.

34. Bill Hosokawa, *Nisei* (New York, 1969), pp. 370–72.

35. Glick to Myer, April 7, 1943, Box 330, RG 210, NA.

36. Glick to Walk, April 8, 1943, ibid.; Cramer to McCloy, April 26, 1943, Box 9, RG 107, NA.

37. Interview with John Hall; Hosokawa, *Nisei,* pp. 364–65.

38. Hosokawa, *Nisei,* p. 365.

39. Ibid., p. 371.

40. *Hirabayashi* v. *United States,* Brief for the United States, note 12, *supra,* pp. 61–63.

41. Ennis to Fahy, April 30, 1943, File 146-42-20, DOJ; "The Japanese in America," *Harpers Magazine,* October 1942, p. 492.

42. Ennis to Fahy, ibid.

43. Ringle to Chief of Naval Operations, "Report on Japanese Question," January 26, 1942, File ASW 014.311, RG 107, NA.

44. Ibid.

45. Ennis to Fahy, note 41, *supra.*

46. Ibid.

47. Ibid.

48. Interview with Arnold Raum.

49. *Hirabayashi* v. *United States,* Brief for the United States, note 12, *supra,* pp. 62–64.

50. Ennis to Fahy, note 41, *supra; Hirabayashi* v. *United States,* Brief for the United States, note 12, *supra,* pp. 61–62.

51. Brief for the United States, ibid., p. 29.

52. Ennis to Herbert Wechsler, September 30, 1944, Box 37, Folder 3, Fahy Papers, FDRL.

53. Ennis to Fahy, April 19, 1943; ibid.; Ennis to Wechsler, September 30, 1944, ibid.

54. U.S. War Department, *Final Report, Japanese Evacuation From the West Coast, 1942* (Washington, D.C., 1943), cited below as *Final Report.*

55. DeWitt to McCloy, April 15, 1943, File 319.1, Section 1, RG 338, NA.

56. The initial version of the *Final Report* is in File 319.1, Section 1, RG 338, NA. It is cited below as *Final Report,* Initial Version.

57. Ibid., p. 9.

58. DeWitt to Chief of Staff, note 32, *supra.*

59. New York *Times,* February 21, 1943, p. 23.

60. Transcript of telephone conversation, Bendetsen and McCloy, April 19, 1943, File 319.1, Section 1, RG 338, NA.

61. Ibid.; Radiogram, Barnett to DeWitt, April 26, 1943, ibid.

62. Radiogram, DeWitt to Barnett, April 27, 1943, ibid.; transcript of telephone conversation, Bendetsen and McCloy, April 19, 1943, ibid.

63. Ibid.; transcript of telephone conversation, Bendetsen and Barnett, April 29, 1943, ibid.

64. Memo, Bendetsen to DeWitt, May 3, 1943, ibid.; radiogram, Bendetsen to Barnett, May (no date) 1943, ibid.

65. *Final Report,* p. 9.

66. Hall to Bendetsen, June 7, 1943, File 319.1, Section 1, RG 338, NA; *Final Report,* p. vii.

67. Memo, Smith to Bendetsen, June 29, 1943, File 319.1, Section 1, RG 338, NA.

68. *Hirabayashi* v. *United States,* Brief for the United States, note 12, *supra,* pp. 62–65.

69. Ennis to Wechsler, September 30, 1944, note 52, *supra.*

70. See Wenig, "The California Attorney General's Office, the Judge Advocate General Corps, and the Japanese-American Relocation," Regional Oral History Office, Bancroft Library, University of California, Berkeley.

71. Kenny to Watson, May 1, 1943, *Hirabayashi* case file, RG 153, FRC.

72. U.S. House of Representatives, Select Committee on National Defense Migration, Hearings, San Francisco, 1942, pp. 10980, 10975.

73. *Congressional Record,* Vol. 88, Part 3, p. 2059; U.S. House of Representatives, Special Committee on Un-American Activities, *Report on Japanese Activities,* 1942, pp. 1723, 1726.

74. Ibid., pp. 1723, 1726, 1914, and *passim.*

75. Ibid., pp. 1723–25.

76. *Congressional Record,* note 73, *supra,* p. 2059.

77. *Report on Japanese Activities,* note 73, *supra,* pp. 1724–25.

78. Ibid., pp. 1917–18; Hearings, Select Committee on National Defense Migration, note 72, *supra,* p. 10978; *Final Report,* p. 11; *Hirabayashi* v. *United States,* Briefs and Records of the Supreme Court, note 12, *supra,* Brief Amicus Curiae of the States of California, Oregon, and Washington, pp. 14–15.

79. *Report on Japanese Activities,* note 73, *supra,* pp. 1922–23.

80. *Final Report,* p. 15; Brief Amicus Curiae of the West Coast States, note 78, *supra,* p. 11.

81. *Hirabayashi* v. *United States,* 320 U.S. 81, 96–102 (1943).

82. Ennis to Wechsler, September 30, 1944, Box 37, Folder 3, Fahy Papers, FDRL.

83. See Chapter 11 for a discussion of this issue.

CHAPTER 9: "SOMETHING WORTHY OF THE TORAH"

1. John P. Frank, *The Marble Palace: The Supreme Court in American Life* (New York, 1961), pp. 89–90.

2. 11 *U.S. Law Week* 3340 (1943).

3. Interview with Frank L. Walters, October 21, 1970, Walters Papers, University of Washington Library.

4. Ibid.

5. An account of the oral arguments in the Hirabayashi, Yasui, and Korematsu cases, including verbatim reports of questions and answers, is in 11 *U.S. Law Week* 3344–47 (1943). No transcript of the complete arguments has been located, and the following account is based on this source.

6. Ibid., pp. 3345–46.

7. Ibid., p. 3346.

8. Ibid.

9. Ibid.

10. Ibid.

11. Ibid.

12. Ibid.

13. Ibid.

14. Frank, *The Marble Palace,* p. 91.

15. 11 *U.S. Law Week* 3346 (1943).

16. Ibid., pp. 3346–47.

17. Ibid., p. 3347.

18. Ibid.

19. Ibid.

20. Ibid.; Outline of Oral Argument, October 10, 1944, Korematsu folder, Box 56, Fahy Papers, FDRL.

21. 11 *U.S. Law Week* 3347 (1943).

22. Wirin to Besig, May 13, 1943, Box 4, Folder 84, NCCLU, CHS; ACLU Board Minutes, May 17, 1943, Reel 10, ACLU Microfilms.

23. Fahy to Evans, May 12, 1943, Box 37, Japanese Relocation Cases folder III, Fahy Papers, FDRL; Glick to Walk, May 15, 1943, Box 36, RG 210, NA.

24. *Korematsu* v. *United States,* 319 U.S. 432 (1943); *Yasui* v. *United States,* 320 U.S. 115, 117 (1943).

25. *Hirabayashi* v. *United States,* 320 U.S. 81 (1943).

26. For an account of the "Constitutional Revolution" of 1937 and Roosevelt's subsequent Court appointments, see Peter H. Irons, *The New Deal Lawyers* (Princeton, N.J., 1982).

27. For an account of Frankfurter's pre-Court career, see Michael Parrish, *Felix Frankfurter and His Times: The Reform Years* (New York, 1982); a perceptive account of his judicial career and philosophy is in the introductory essay in Joseph P. Lash, *From the Diaries of Felix Frankfurter* (New York, 1975), cited below as *Frankfurter Diaries*.

28. For an account of Black's career, see Gerald T. Dunne, *Hugo Black and the Judicial Revolution* (New York, 1977).

29. See the introductory essay by Lash in *Frankfurter Diaries,* note 27, *supra*.

30. Ibid., pp. 209, 227, 175, 205.

31. The first three Jehovah's Witnesses cases were *Murdoch* v. *Pennsylvania,* 319 U.S. 105 (1943); *Martin* v. *Struthers,* 319 U.S. 141 (1943); *Douglas* v. *Jeannette,* 319 U.S. 157 (1943).

32. *West Virginia* v. *Barnette,* 319 U.S. 624, 665 (1943); *Minersville School District* v. *Gobitis,* 310 U.S. 586 (1940). For a perceptive analysis of Frankfurter's role in these cases, see Richard Danzig, "How Questions Begot Answers in Felix Frankfurter's First Flag-Salute Opinion," 1977 *Supreme Court Review* 257.

33. *West Virginia* v. *Barnette,* 319 U.S. 624, 647 (1943); interview with Victor Brudney.

34. Black quote from Murphy, "Conference Notes on *Hirabayashi* v. *U.S.,* 5-16-43" [*sic;* should be 5-17], Box 132, Murphy Papers, University of Michigan Library; Stone quotes from Douglas, Conference Notes, untitled, May 17, 1943, Hirabayashi case folder (Cert., Conference, and Misc. Memos), Box 79, Douglas Papers, LC (cited below as Douglas Conference Notes).

35. Douglas Conference Notes, ibid.

36. Ibid.

37. Ibid.; *United States* v. *Carolene Products,* 304 U.S. 144, 152 n. 4 (1938).

38. Douglas Conference Notes, ibid.; Murphy Conference Notes, note 34, *supra.*

39. Douglas Conference Notes, ibid.; *Ex Parte Quirin,* 317 U.S. 1 (1942).

40. *Ex Parte Quirin,* ibid., pp. 25–26.

41. Ibid., p. 26; Douglas Conference Notes, note 34, *supra.*

42. Douglas Conference Notes, ibid.

43. Interview with Bennett Boskey.

44. Ibid.; Stone, draft of *Hirabayashi* opinion, May 30, 1943, Box 79, Hirabayashi and Yasui cases folder, Douglas Papers, LC.

45. Stone, *Hirabayashi* draft opinion, ibid., p. 8.

46. Ibid., pp. 9–13.

47. Ibid., pp. 13–14.

48. Ibid., p. 7.

49. Reed to Stone, May 29, 1943, Box 68, Hirabayashi folder, Stone Papers, LC; Reed to Stone, June 3, 1943, ibid.; *Hirabayashi* v. *United States,* 320 U.S. 81, 91–92 (1943).

50. Douglas to Stone, May 31, 1943, ibid.; for an account of Douglas's career, see James Simon, *Independent Journey: The Life of William O. Douglas* (New York, 1980).

51. *Hirabayashi* draft opinion, note 44, *supra,* p. 11; Douglas to Stone, May 31, 1943, Box 68, Hirabayashi folder, Stone Papers, LC.

52. Douglas, draft of concurring opinion in *Hirabayashi,* June 7, 1943, pp. 1–2, note 44, *supra.* There are several versions of Douglas's concurring opinion in this box; the first draft is marked "WOD's desk copy."

53. Interview with Vern Countryman.

54. Douglas, draft concurring opinion, pp. 3–4, note 52, *supra.*

55. Frankfurter, handwritten note on Stone's draft opinion, note 44, *supra.*

56. Interview with Philip Elman.

57. Frankfurter to Stone, June 4, 1943, Box 68, Stone Papers, LC.

58. Memo, Frankfurter to Stone, June 4, 1943, ibid.; Stone, "Memorandum for the Court," June 4, 1943, ibid.

59. *Frankfurter Diaries,* pp. 251–52.

60. Douglas to Rutledge, no date (probably June 4, 1943), Box 95, October Term 1942—Corr. Douglas folder, Rutledge Papers, LC; Douglas to Stone, June 7, 1943, Box 68, Stone Papers, LC.

61. Stone to Douglas, June 9, 1943, Box 68, Stone Papers, LC.

62. *Hirabayashi* v. *United States,* 320 U.S. 81, 108–9 (1943).

63. *Frankfurter,* p. 251.

64. Sidney Fine, "Mr. Justice Murphy and the Hirabayashi Case," *Pacific Historical Review* 33 (May 1964) 195, 201; interview with John Pickering.

65. Interview with John Pickering; *Schneiderman* v. *United States,* 320 U.S. 118, 120 (1943).

66. Marginal notes by Murphy on Stone's draft opinion, Box 132, Murphy Papers, UML; *Frankfurter Diaries*, pp. 251–52.

67. *Frankfurter Diaries*, p. 252; Frankfurter to Murphy, June 6, 1943 [this date should be June 5]; Murphy to Frankfurter, June 5, 1943; Frankfurter to Murphy, June 5, 1943; all from Box 132, Murphy Papers, UML.

68. *Hirabayashi* v. *United States*, 320 U.S. 81, 99 (1943); Murphy, draft of dissenting opinion in *Hirabayashi*, pp. 4–5, Box 132, Murphy Papers, UML.

69. Douglas, draft concurrence, note 52, *supra;* Murphy, draft dissent, Box 132, Murphy Papers, UML.

70. *West Virginia* v. *Barnette*, 319 U.S. 646, 647 (1943); Murphy, draft dissent, Box 132, Murphy Papers, UML.

71. Interview with John Pickering; Murphy, draft dissent, Box 132, Murphy Papers, UML; Murphy to Pickering, June 8, 1943, ibid.

72. Frankfurter to Murphy, June 10, 1943, ibid.

73. Murphy, draft dissent, Box 132, Murphy Papers, UML; *Hirabayashi* v. *United States*, 320 U.S. 81, 112–13 (1943).

74. Ibid., p. 111.

75. Frankfurter to Murphy, no date, Box 132, Murphy Papers, UML.

76. Rutledge, draft concurrence, Box 93, Hirabayashi folder, Rutledge Papers, LC; *Hirabayashi* v. *United States*, 320 U.S. 81, 114 (1943); Rutledge to Stone, August 12, 1943 [this date is wrong and should probably be June 12], Box 68, Hirabayashi folder, Stone Papers, LC.

77. Stone, draft opinion, Box 68, Hirabayashi folder, Stone Papers, LC.

78. Ibid.

79. *Hirabayashi* v. *United States*, 320 U.S. 81, 103 (1943).

80. Ibid., pp. 103–4.

81. Ibid., p. 93.

82. Murphy, draft dissent, Box 132, Murphy Papers, UML; *Hirabayashi* v. *United States*, 320 U.S. 81, 92 (1943).

83. Frankfurter, handwritten note to Stone on Stone's draft opinion, no date, Box 86, Hirabayashi folder, Stone Papers, LC.

84. Interviews with Fred Korematsu and Minoru Yasui.

85. Interview with Gordon Hirabayashi.

86. Washington *Post*, June 25, 1943.

87. Los Angeles *Times*, June 22, 1943.

CHAPTER 10: "NO LONGER ANY MILITARY NECESSITY"

1. Forster to Saburo Kido, June 22, 1943, Vol. 2470, ACLU, PUL; Glick to Dillon Myer, July 15, 1943, Box 336, RG 210, NA.

2. Forster to Al Wirin, September 1, 1943, Vol. 2588, ACLU, PUL.

3. Forster to Kido, June 22, 1943, note 1, *supra*.

4. Ibid.

5. Purcell to Forster, June 23, 1943, Vol. 2465, ACLU, PUL.

6. The chronology of Endo's WRA status is in Glick, "Memorandum for the Files," August 9, 1944, Box 332, RG 210, NA.

7. Biddle to Myer, July 28, 1943, Box 336, RG 210, NA.

8. Glick to Maurice Walk, September 6, 1943, ibid.

9. On the "segregation" move, see Jacobus tenBroek et al., *Prejudice, War and the Constitution* (Berkeley, Cal., 1954), pp. 160–64; on Endo's transfer, see Glick, note 6, *supra*.

10. Interview with Philip Glick.

11. Glick to Forster, October 23, 1943, Box 326, RG 210, NA; ACLU Board minutes, August 9, 1943, Reel 10, ACLU Microfilms; Forster to Besig, October 1, 1943, Vol. 2465, ACLU, PUL.

12. Besig to Forster, September 10, 1943, Vol. 2465, ACLU, PUL; Besig to Forster, October 13, 1943, Box 4, Folder 84, NCCLU, CHS.

13. *Korematsu* v. *United States,* 140 F.2d 289, 290 (9th Cir. 1943).

14. Ibid., p. 298.

15. Besig to Forster, Box 56, Folder 1386, NCCLU, CHS.

16. Baldwin to Besig, December 13, 1943, Vol. 2469, ACLU, PUL; Ennis to Fahy, April 26, 1944, Box 37, Folder 3, Fahy Papers, FDRL.

17. See Glick, "Memorandum for the Files," note 6, *supra*.

18. Baldwin to Forster, January 24, 1944, Box 4, Folder 85, NCCLU, CHS.

19. Ibid.

20. Roger Baldwin Memoir, Columbia Oral History Collection, p. 131; interview with Charles Horsky.

21. Besig to Baldwin, February 1, 1944, Box 4, Folder 85, NCCLU, CHS; Besig to Forster, February 7, 1944, Box 47, Folder 1127, ibid.

22. Silverman to Glick, January 19, 1944, Box 326, RG 210, NA.

23. Ennis to Glick, January 20, 1944, ibid.

24. Ennis to Fahy, January 21, 1944, Box 3, Fahy Papers, FDRL.

25. Ennis to Glick, January 28, 1944, Box 336, RG 210, NA.

26. Ibid.

27. Myer to Biddle, February 1, 1944, Box 37, Folder 3, Fahy Papers, FDRL.

28. Interview with Philip Glick.

29. Glick to Ennis, February 9, 1944, Box 336, RG 210, NA.

30. Ibid.

31. McCloy to Biddle, February 25, 1944, Box 9, RG 107, NA.

32. Fahy to McCloy, March 14, 1944, ibid.

33. *Korematsu* v. *United States,* 140 F.2d 289, 293 (9th Cir. 1943); Burling to Fahy, April 14, 1944, File 146-42-26, DOJ; interview with James Purcell.

34. Burling to Fahy, ibid.; Fahy to Burling, April 17, 1944, Box 37, Folder 3, Fahy Papers, FDRL.

35. Burling to Ennis, April 18, 1944, File 146-42-26, DOJ.

36. 13 *U.S. Law Week* 3021 (1944).

37. Besig to Harrop S. Freeman, April 20, 1944, Box 56, Folder 1386, NCCLU, CHS; interview with James Purcell.

38. Forster to Besig, March 28, 1944, Box 4, Folder 85, NCCLU, CHS; Besig to Fraenkel, March 29, 1944, ibid.; Besig to Baldwin, May 3, 1944, ibid.

39. Ennis to Fahy, April 26, 1944, Box 37, Folder 3, Fahy Papers, FDRL; 12 *U.S. Law Week* 3317 (1944).

40. Horsky to Baldwin, May 6, 1944, Vol. 2585, ACLU, PUL.

41. Forster to Fraenkel, May 31, 1944, Vol. 2588, ibid.; interview with Charles Horsky.

42. Transcript of telephone conversation, January 14, 1943, Box 7, RG 338, NA; on Emmons, see Roger Daniels, *Concentration Camps USA* (New York, 1975), pp. 72–73.

43. Myer to McCloy, October 16, 1943, Box 9, RG 107, NA.

44. McCloy to Emmons, November 5, 1943, ibid.

45. Emmons to McCloy, November 10, 1943, ibid.

46. Biddle to Roosevelt, December 30, 1943. OF 4849, FDRL.

47. Hall to McCloy, March 2, 1944, Box 13, RG 210, NA.

48. On Stimson's condition, see Bruce A. Murphy, *The Brandeis/Frankfurter Connection* (New York, 1982), p. 198.

49. Entry of May 26, 1944, Henry L. Stimson Diaries, Yale University Library; Biddle, cabinet meeting notes, May 26, 1944, Box 1, Folder—Cabinet Meetings, January 44-May 45, Biddle Papers, FDRL.

50. Ickes to Roosevelt, June 2, 1944, Box 9, RG 107, NA.

51. Roosevelt to Ickes, June 12, 1944, ibid.

52. Transcript of telephone conversation, McCloy, Emmons, and Watson, June 13, 1944, ibid.

53. McCloy to Bonesteel, June 27, 1944, ibid.

54. Bonesteel to McCloy, September 15, 1944, ibid.

55. McCloy to Bonesteel, September 19, 1944, ibid.

56. Bonesteel to McCloy, September 28, 1944, ibid.

57. Ibid.

58. McCloy to Bonesteel, October 4, 1944, ibid.; Bonesteel to McCloy, October 25, 1944, ibid.

59. McCloy to Bonesteel, October 31, 1944, ibid.

60. Biddle, memo, November 10, 1944, Box 1, Folder—Cabinet Meetings, Jan. 44–May 45, Biddle Papers, FDRL; Stimson to Roosevelt, December 13, 1944, File 146-42-26, DOJ.

61. Headquarters, Western Defense Command, Public Proclamation No. 21, December 17, 1944, File 146-42-26, DOJ.

CHAPTER 11: "THE PRINTING STOPPED ABOUT NOON"

1. Transcript of telephone conversation, Hall and Burling, January 7, 1944, Box 37, Folder 3, Fahy Papers, FDRL.

2. Ibid.

3. Los Angeles, *Times*, January 20, 1944, pp. 2 and 4.

4. Washington *Post*, January 20, 1944, p. 2; San Francisco *Examiner*, January 20, 1944, p. 1.

5. Interview with Edward Ennis.

6. Ibid.

7. Memo, Hoover to Biddle, February 7, 1944, Box 37, Folder 3, Fahy Papers, FDRL.

8. Ibid.

9. Ibid.

10. Ennis to Biddle, February 26, 1944, ibid.

11. Biddle to Fly, February 26, 1944, ibid.

12. Fly to Biddle, April 1, 1944, ibid.

13. Ibid.

14. Memo, Sterling to files, "Conference with General DeWitt," January 9, 1942, Files of the Radio Intelligence Division, RG 173, FRC.

15. Ibid.

16. Ibid.

17. Sterling, Memorandum to the Chief Engineer, March 25, 1944, ibid.; interview with George Sterling; Sterling to author, August 22, 1982.

18. Fly to Biddle, April 4, 1944, Box 37, Folder 3, Fahy Papers, FDRL.

19. Burling to Fahy, April 13, 1944, ibid.

20. Burling to Ennis, April 25, 1944, File 146-42-7, DOJ.

21. Memo, Judge Advocate General to Deputy Chief of Staff, March 31, 1944, Korematsu case file, RG 153, FRC; memo, Gerhardt to Assistant Chief of Staff, G-2, May 1, 1944, Box 9, RG 107, NA.

22. Burling to Wechsler, September 11, 1944, File 146-42-7, DOJ.

23. Ibid.

24. Ibid.

25. Burling to Ennis, October 2, 1944, ibid.

26. Ibid.

27. Ennis to Wechsler, September 30, 1944, Box 37, Folder 3, Fahy Papers, FDRL.

28. Ibid.

29. Francis Biddle, *In Brief Authority* (New York, 1962), p. 159; interview with Herbert Wechsler.

30. Ennis to Wechster, note 27, *supra*.

31. Interview with Adrian Fisher.

32. Burling to Ennis, note 25, *supra;* interview with Adrian Fisher.

33. Burling to Ennis, ibid.

34. Ibid.

35. Fisher to McCloy, October 2, 1944, Box 9, RG 107, NA.

36. *Korematsu* v. *United States,* 323 U.S. 214 (1944), Records and Briefs of the Supreme Court, Brief for the United States, pp. 21–22 (cited below as *Korematsu,* Government Brief).

37. Burling to Ennis, note 32, *supra;* transcript of telephone conversation, Wechsler and Fisher, October 2, 1944, Box 9, RG 107, NA.

38. Burling to Ennis, ibid.

39. Ibid.

40. Burling to Fahy, April 13, 1944, Box 37, Folder 3, Fahy Papers, FDRL.

41. U.S. Department of War, *Final Report, Japanese Evacuation From the West Coast, 1942* (Washington, D.C., 1943), pp. 43–44 (cited below as *Final Report*).

42. Burling to Fahy, note 40, *supra*.

43. Burling to Ennis, April 12, 1944, File 146-42-7, DOJ.

44. Burling to Fahy, note 40, *supra*.

45. Ibid.

46. For the details of these orders, see *Korematsu,* Government Brief, p. 29.

47. Ibid.

48. Ibid.

49. Burling to Fahy, note 40, *supra*.

50. Ibid.

51. Ibid.

52. Ibid.

53. Burling to Fahy, April 17, 1944, Box 37, Folder 3, Fahy Papers, FDRL; Burling to Thomas Cooley, April 21, 1944, File 146-42-7, DOJ. There is no record that this memo was sent to Frankfurter, and it has not been found in Frankfurter's papers.

54. *Korematsu,* Government Brief, pp. 28–30.

55. Ibid., p. 31.

56. Ibid., p. 32.

57. Ibid., pp. 43 and 52.

58. Ibid., p. 52; *Final Report,* p. 106.

59. *Korematsu,* Government Brief, pp. 52 and 29.

60. Burling to Fahy, note 53, *supra*.

61. *Korematsu*, Government Brief, p. 55.

62. Ibid., p. 46.

63. Ibid., p. 57.

64. *Korematsu* v. *United States*, 323 U.S. 214 (1943), Records and Briefs of the Supreme Court, Brief for Appellant, pp. 30 and 98 (cited below as *Korematsu*, Appellant's Brief).

65. Ibid., pp. 46–50.

66. Ibid., p. 98.

67. *Korematsu* v. *United States*, note 64, *supra*, Brief Amicus Curiae of the American Civil Liberties Union, pp. 2 and 10 (cited below as *Korematsu*, ACLU Brief).

68. Ibid., p. 11.

69. Ibid., p. 12; *Korematsu*, Government Brief, p. 32.

70. *Korematsu*, ACLU Brief, pp. 24 and 21.

71. Ibid., pp. 21–22.

72. Ibid., Wirin to Baldwin, April 24, 1944, Vol. 2587, ACLU, PUL.

73. Gunnar Myrdal et al., *An American Dilemma* (New York, 1944); *Brown* v. *Board of Education*, 347 U.S. 483 (1954).

74. *Korematsu* v. *United States*, note 64, *supra*, Brief Amicus Curiae of the Japanese American Citizens League, pp. 152–53.

75. Ibid., pp. 196–97.

76. *Ex Parte Endo*, 323 U.S. 283 (1944), Records and Briefs of the Supreme Court, Brief for the United States, p. 78.

77. Ibid., pp. 78–80.

78. Ibid., pp. 82, 79–80.

79. *Ex Parte Endo*, note 76, *supra*, Brief for Petitioner, pp. 12 and 36.

80. Ibid., Brief Amicus Curiae of the Northern California Civil Liberties Union, pp. 30, 32–35; Baldwin to Besig, November 3, 1944, Box 4, Folder 85, NCCLU, CHS; Baldwin to Besig, October 26, 1944, ibid.

81. *Ex Parte Endo*, note 76, *supra*, Brief Amicus Curiae of the American Civil Liberties Union, p. 3.

82. Ibid., pp. 6–7.

CHAPTER 12: "THE COURT HAS BLOWN UP"

1. Interviews with Fred Korematsu and James Purcell.

2. "Notes Taken by Col. King at Hearing Before Supreme Court 11 and 12 October 1944," Korematsu file, Records of the Judge Advocate General, RG 153, FRC (cited below as *Korematsu*, King Notes).

3. Interview with Charles Horsky.

4. *Korematsu*, King Notes.

5. Ibid.

6. Ibid.

7. Interview with Charles Horsky.

8. *Korematsu*, King Notes.

9. Ibid.; interview with Charles Horsky.

10. Interview with Charles Horsky.

11. *Korematsu*, King Notes; Fahy, "Outline of Oral Argument in Supreme Court," October 10, 1944, Box 56, Korematsu folder, Fahy Papers, FDRL (cited below as Fahy, *Korematsu* Outline).

12. Fahy, *Korematsu* Outline.

13. *Korematsu,* King Notes.

14. Fahy, *Korematsu* Outline.

15. Interview with James Purcell.

16. Fahy, Transcript of Oral Argument in *Endo* case, File 146-42-26, DOJ, pp. 18–19, 26.

17. Ibid., p. 21.

18. Ibid., pp. 21–22.

19. Ibid., pp. 23–24.

20. Bill Hosokawa, *Nisei* (New York, 1969), pp. 403–13.

21. Douglas, handwritten notes, ''Conference of 10–16–44,'' Box 98, *Korematsu* case folder, Douglas Papers, LC (cited below as Douglas, *Korematsu* Conference Notes).

22. Ibid.

23. Ibid.

24. Ibid.

25. Ibid.

26. Ibid.; Murphy, handwritten notes, ''No. 20, O.T. 1944,'' Box 133, Murphy Papers, MUL. (cited below as Murphy, *Korematsu* Conference Notes).

27. Ibid.

28. Ibid.

29. Ibid.

30. The vote on the Korematsu case is recorded on a tally sheet in Box 89, Korematsu case folder, Douglas Papers, LC.

31. Douglas, handwritten notes, ''Conference 10-16-44, No. 70—Endo v. Eisenhower,'' Box 101, Endo case folder, Douglas Papers, LC.

32. Ibid.

33. Murphy, handwritten notes, ''No. 70-Endo,'' Box 133, Murphy Papers, MUL.

34. Black, typewritten draft of *Korematsu* opinion, no date, Box 276, Korematsu case folder, Black Papers, LC.

35. Ibid.

36. Ibid.

37. Black, printed draft of *Korematsu* opinion, November 8, 1944, Box 133, Murphy Papers, MUL.

38. Frankfurter to Black, November 9, 1944, Box 169, Folder 3, Frankfurter Papers, Harvard Law School Library.

39. Ibid.

40. Stone to Black, November 9, 1944, Box 73, Folder—Correspondence—Black 42–44, Stone Papers, LC; Black, draft of *Korematsu* opinion, note 37, *supra;* Douglas, *Korematsu* Conference Notes, note 21, *supra*.

41. Stone to Black, ibid.

42. Ibid.

43. Ibid.

44. Roberts, printed draft of *Korematsu* opinion, November 29, 1944, Box 133, Murphy Papers, MUL, pp. 2–6.

45. Ibid., pp. 1, 6–7.

46. Ibid., pp. 5–6.

47. Jackson, printed draft of *Korematsu* opinion, November 30, 1944, Box 98, Korematsu case folder, Douglas Papers, LC, pp. 2–4.

48. Ibid., p. 13.

49. Ibid., pp. 7–14.

50. Ibid., pp. 9–11.

51. Ibid., p. 15.

52. Murphy to Gressman, no date, Box 133, Murphy Papers, MUL.

53. Douglas, printed draft of *Korematsu* opinion, December 1, 1944, Box 98, Korematsu case folder, Douglas Papers, LC, pp. 1–2.

54. Ibid., pp. 3–4.

55. *Ex Parte Endo,* 323 U.S. 283, 301 (1944).

56. Douglas to Black, December 6, 1944, Box 98, Korematsu case folder, Douglas Papers, LC.

57. Stone to Black, December 1, 1944, Box 71, Korematsu case folder, Stone Papers, LC; Stone, typewritten draft of *Korematsu* opinion, ibid.

58. Murphy, typewritten draft of *Korematsu* opinion, no date, Box 133, Murphy Papers, MUL.

59. Jackson, printed draft of *Korematsu* opinion, note 47, *supra,* p. 9; Murphy, typewritten draft of *Korematsu,* opinion, Box 133, Murphy papers, MUL, p. 2.

60. Murphy opinion, ibid., pp. 3–5.

61. Ibid., pp. 5–7.

62. Black, typewritten draft of addition to *Korematsu* opinion, no date, Box 276, Korematsu case folder, Black Papers, LC.

63. *Korematsu* v. *United States,* 323 U.S. 215, 223 and 219 (1944).

64. Ibid., p. 222.

65. Black, printed draft of *Korematsu* opinion, December 8, 1944, Box 133, Murphy Papers, MUL, p. 7; memo, Black to Members of the Conference, December 8, 1944, Box 116, Korematsu and Endo cases folder, Rutledge Papers, LC.

66. Stone to Black, December 9, 1944, Box 71, Korematsu case folder, Stone Papers, LC.

67. *Korematsu* v. *United States,* note 63, *supra,* pp. 221–22.

68. Black, typewritten draft of addition to *Korematsu* opinion, note 62, *supra.*

69. *Korematsu* v. *United States,* note 63, *supra,* p. 216.

70. Ibid., pp. 223–30.

71. Frankfurter, printed draft of *Korematsu* opinion, December 1, 1944, Box 116, Korematsu and Endo cases folder, Rutledge Papers, LC.

72. Jackson, printed draft of *Korematsu* opinion, note 47, *supra,* p. 8; interview with Harry Mansfield; *Korematsu* v. *United States,* note 63, *supra,* p. 225.

73. Ibid., pp. 224–25.

74. *Ex Parte Endo,* note 55, *supra,* p. 297.

75. Ibid., p. 302.

76. Ibid., pp. 300–301.

77. Ibid., pp. 299 and 302.

78. Ibid., pp. 307–8.

79. Ibid., pp. 308–10.

80. Douglas to Stone, December 8, 1944, Box 74, Folder—Correspondence-Douglas 1944, Stone Papers, LC.

81. Los Angeles *Times,* December 18, 1944, p. 1.

82. Interview with Roger Daniels.

83. Los Angeles *Times,* December 18, 1944, p. 1. Although the exclusion cases are beyond the scope of this book, they form an integral part of the legal battles over the internment of Japanese Americans. See *Ochikubo* v. *Bonesteel,* 60 F. Supp. 916 (S.D. Cal. 1945). This opinion failed to overturn the exclusion orders, but the government withdrew all individual exclusion orders in 1946.

84. Los Angeles *Times*, December 18, 1944, p. 9 and 1.

85. Washington *Post*, December 21, 1944, p. 18; Los Angeles *Times*, December 19, 1944, p. B-4.

CHAPTER 13: "WATERGATE HADN'T HAPPENED YET"

1. Commission on Wartime Relocation and Internment of Civilians, *Personal Justice Denied* (Washington, D.C., 1983), pp. 118–21.

2. Ibid., p. 1.

3. Testimony of Edward J. Ennis before Commission on Wartime Relocation, November 2, 1981, pp. 144–49; Statement of American Civil Liberties Union, September 8, 1981, Commission files.

4. Ennis testimony, ibid., pp. 150 and 145.

5. Ibid., p. 153.

6. Interview with Edward Ennis.

7. Ennis testimony, note 3, *supra*, p. 197; interview with Edward Ennis.

8. Interview with Edward Ennis; Ennis testimony, ibid., p. 150.

9. Interview with Edward Ennis.

10. Testimony of John J. McCloy before Commission on Wartime Relocation, November 3, 1981, p. 4; Alan Brinkley, "Minister without Portfolio," *Harpers*, February 1983, p. 31.

11. Brinkley, "Minister Without Portfolio," p. 31.

12. McCloy to Brooke, November 25, 1981, Commission files; McCloy testimony, note 10, *supra*, pp. 6 and 15.

13. Ibid., pp. 86, 9, 19.

14. Ibid., pp. 34–37.

15. Ibid.

16. Ibid., p. 60.

17. Ibid., p. 50.

18. McCloy to Brooke, note 12, *supra*.

19. Testimony of Karl Bendetsen before Commission on Wartime Relocation, November 2, 1981, pp. 38, 77–78.

20. Ibid., p. 43.

21. Ibid., pp. 42–43.

22. Gerald T. Dunne, *Hugo Black and the Judicial Revolution* (New York, 1977), p. 213.

23. Stanley Reed, oral history memoir, COHC, pp. 305–7.

24. Charles Fahy, oral history memoir, COHC, p. 178.

25. Ibid.

26. Fahy to Biddle, December 12, 1962, Box 3, Biddle file, Fahy Papers, LC; interview with Edward Ennis.

27. Herbert Wechster, "Some Issues for the Lawyer," in Robert M. MacIver, ed., *Integrity and Comprise: Problems of Public and Private Conscience*, (New York, 1957), p. 123.

28. Ibid., pp. 123–24.

29. Interview with Herbert Wechsler.

30. Testimony of Philip Glick before Commission on Wartime Relocation, November 3, 1981, p. 133.

31. Ibid., pp. 146–48.

32. Interview with Philip Glick.

33. Francis Biddle, *In Brief Authority* (New York, 1962), pp. 213 and 226.

34. Interview with Francis Biddle, May 22, 1968, Collection 2010, Box 397, Tape 302, Japanese American Research Project, University of California, Los Angeles; interview with James Rowe.

35. Peggy Lamson, *Roger Baldwin* (Boston, 1976), pp. 238–40.

36. Interview with Ernest Besig.

37. Forster to author, November 11, 1982, author's files.

38. Testimony of James Rowe before Commission on Wartime Relocation, November 2, 1981, pp. 50 and 72; interview with James Rowe; Rowe to author, December 2, 1982, author's files.

39. *Defunis* v. *Odegaard,* 416 U.S. 312, 339 (1974); William O. Douglas, *The Court Years* (New York, 1980), p. 279.

40. Ibid., p. 280.

41. Commission on Wartime Relocation, *Personal Justice Denied,* p. 18.

42. Ibid., pp. 8–9.

43. Biddle interview, note 34, *supra*.

44. McCloy testimony, note 10, *supra,* p. 10.

45. Entries of February 10 and January 24, 1942, Stimson Diaries, Yale University Library; Henry L. Stimson and McGeorge Bundy, *On Active Service in Peace and War* (New York, 1947), p. 406; John J. McCloy, "Repay U.S. Japanese?," New York *Times,* April 10, 1983, Op-Ed page.

46. McCloy testimony, note 10, *supra,* p. 32.

47. Rowe testimony, note 38, *supra,* p. 74; McCloy testimony, ibid., p. 68.

48. Biddle interview, note 34, *supra;* Fahy oral history memoir, COHC, p. 178.

49. *Korematsu* v. *United States,* 323 U.S. 215, 246 (1944).

50. Commission on Wartime Relocation, *Personal Justice Denied,* p. 239.

Index